W9-ADV-940

The Ultimate Traveler's Guide
to Battlefields, Monuments
and Museums

THE 25 ESSENTIAL

World War II Sites

European Theater

2ND EDITION

CHUCK THOMPSON

GREENLINE PUBLICATIONS • SAN FRANCISCO, CALIFORNIA

The 25 Essential World War II Sites: European Theater is the second book in the Greenline Historic Travel Series (GHTS), which debuted in 2002 with *The 25 Best World War II Sites: Pacific Theater.* The series also includes *The 25 Best Civil War Sites* and *Colonial America and the American Revolution: The 25 Best Sites.* GHTS is published by Greenline Publications, which aims to provide readers with unique and significant travel experiences through a willingness to explore new approaches to guidebooks, combined with meticulous research.

The 25 Essential World War II Sites: European Theater is an independent guide. We welcome your views on our selections. The information contained in this book was checked as rigorously as possible before going to press. The publisher accepts no responsibility for any changes that may have occurred since or for any other variance of fact from that recorded here in good faith.

ISBN: 978-0-9787719-0-4
Library of Congress Control Number: 2007933983
Distributed by Publishers Group West
Second Edition 2007
Copyright © 2004, 2007 by Chuck Thompson
Foreword copyright © 2007 by George McGovern
All rights reserved

Series Editor	Christina Henry de Tessan
First Edition Editor	Kristin M. Poss
Contributors to First Edition	Ross McCammon (Auschwitz-Birkenau "The War Years" and Norway chapter); Jordan Rane (Auxiliary Sites: Balkans, Finland, Greece/Crete, Malta, North Africa, St. Petersburg)
Copy Editors	Gail Nelson, Elizabeth Stroud
Second Edition Cover Design	Samantha Glorioso
Original Book Design	DeVa Communications
Maps	Joyce Leong
Photographs	Chuck Thompson (except where indicated)
Transcription	Crys O'Neil
Cover Photographs	Top photo: Duxford Imperial War Museum, by Chuck Thompson; bottom photo: Normandy American Cemetery and Memorial, courtesy of American Battle Monuments Commission

For information about bulk purchases of Greenline books (ten copies or more), email us at bookorders@asdmedia.com. Special bulk rates are available for charities, corporations, institutions, and online and mail-order catalogs.

To reach us or for updated information on all Greenline books, visit the Greenline Publications website at **greenlinepub.com**.

GREENLINE PUBLICATIONS
P.O. Box 590780
San Francisco, CA 94159-0780

Greenline Publications is an imprint of ASDavis Media Group, Inc.

FOREWORD BY SENATOR GEORGE McGOVERN

Oft times we read that a book is unique. Sometimes that is true, more often it is an exaggeration. There is no doubt that this book is unique; it is absolutely essential as a dramatic, carefully documented description of the military sites that marked the course of World War II in Europe. No other volume exists in my memory or knowledge that provides such a rich, informative survey of these important sites.

As a professor of history (Ph.D., Northwestern), longtime political leader, and pilot of a B-24 bomber in WWII, I intend to carry this book with me on all future European visits. Anyone who browses through the 250 carefully crafted pages and imaginatively selected pictures will be filled with admiration for the author and publisher of *The 25 Essential World War II Sites: European Theater.*

One peruses in these pages such heart-stirring battle scenes and important sites as the Abbey of Montecassino, Anzio beachhead, Auschwitz, Hitler's birthplace, Bastogne, Battle of Britain, Beer Hall Putsch, Dieppe, Dunkirk, Omaha Beach, Remagen Bridge, and a host of others. My navigator, Sam Adams, flying as a substitute one day in 1944 with another crew, was shot down and was listed as missing in action. Forty years later, while visiting the American military cemetery in Florence, I came across these words on one of the many white marble crosses: "Lt. Sam Adams, missing in action."

This book is a pure jewel and the sites it covers reveal a multitude of disclosures of every conceivable kind.

—George McGovern

N

Russia

ARAL
SEA

CASPIAN SEA

BLACK SEA

Cyprus

25 Essential Sites
(page number in parentheses)

Note: Auxiliary Sites (#25) not identified on map

CHRONOLOGY OF THE
EUROPEAN WAR

1939

September 1: Germany invades Poland

September 3: Britain and France declare war on Germany

September 17: USSR invades Poland from east

November 30: USSR invades Finland

1940

April 9: Germany invades Norway

May 10: Germany invades Netherlands, Belgium, Luxembourg, France; Winston Churchill becomes British prime minister

May 26-June 4: British and French troops evacuate continent from Dunkirk, France

June 10: Italy declares war on Britain and France

June 14: German troops enter Paris

June 22, 24: France surrenders to Germany, Italy

July 4: Italy attacks British troops in Sudan

July 10-October 30: Battle of Britain

July 21: USSR absorbs Latvia, Lithuania, Estonia

August 3: Italy invades British Somaliland

September 7: London Blitz begins

September 13: Italy invades Egypt

September 27: Germany, Italy, Japan sign Tripartite Pact

November 1: Italy bombs Athens, attacks Greece

November 19: Greek troops force Italian retreat

November 20, 23: Hungary, Romania join Axis

December 9: British launch successful counterattacks on Italians in North Africa

1941

February 12: General Erwin Rommel assumes command of German-Italian Afrika Corps in North Africa

March 1, 25: Bulgaria, Yugoslavia join Axis

March 5: British troops arrive in Greece

March 24: Afrika Korps attacks British in Libya

April 23: Greece surrenders to Germany

May 2: British enter Iraq to forestall Iraq-Germany partnership

May 20-June 1: Germany invades and takes Crete by airborne assault

June 22: Germany invades USSR along 2,000-mile front

August 25: Britain and USSR jointly invade Iran (Persia) to forestall Iran-Germany partnership

October 20: Moscow goes under German siege that will fail in December

December 7: Japan attacks Pearl Harbor

December 8: U.S. declares war on Japan

December 10: Germany, Italy honor Tripartite Pact, declare war on U.S.

1942

January: Germany intensifies existing aerial campaign against Malta

June 20: Afrika Korps takes Tobruk

August 19: Canadian raid on Dieppe, France, fails

August 23: Battle of Stalingrad begins

October 23-November 4: Battle of El Alamein forces Afrika Korps to retreat into Libya, Tunisia

November 8: American Operation Torch forces land in Algeria and Morocco

November 13: British capture Tobruk

1943

January 12-24: Franklin Roosevelt, Churchill, others decide war strategy at Casablanca Conference

January 31-February 2: Germans surrender at Stalingrad, ending war's largest battle

March 20: Biggest Battle of the Atlantic day ends with 21 Allied ships lost to U-boat wolf packs

May 13: Afrika Korps surrenders in Tunisia, ending Axis resistance in Africa

July 5-12: Germans launch and lose Battle of Kursk; from now until end of war, Red Army is on advance through eastern Europe

July 10-August 17: Allies invade and capture Sicily

July 25: Benito Mussolini deposed as Italian leader

September 3-9: Allied invasion of Italian mainland

September 8: Italy surrenders to Allies

September 10: Germans seize Rome, begin defense of Italy

November 28-December 1: First Big Three conference—Roosevelt, Churchill, Josef Stalin—at Tehran

1944

January-May: Four Battles of Montecassino

January 22: Allies land at Anzio, Italy

January 27: Soviet forces enter Leningrad, ending near–900-day siege

February 15: Allies bomb Abbey of Montecassino

February 20-25: "Big Week" Allied bomber campaign turns tide of air war against Germany

June 4: Rome liberated by Allies

June 6: Allied D-Day landings on Normandy

June 9: USSR launches second Finnish campaign of war

July 28: U.S. breaks into open country of Normandy

August 25: Paris liberated by Allies

September 11: Americans penetrate German border

September-December: U.S.-German battles in Hürtgen Forest

September 17-25: Allies launch and lose Operation Market-Garden in Netherlands

September 24: Soviet troops enter Czechoslovakia

October 11: Soviet troops penetrate German territory in East Prussia

October 14: Allies capture Athens

November 30: Canadians penetrate Germany from Netherlands

December 16: Germany attacks Allies in Belgium and Luxembourg in Battle of the Bulge

December 16-26: Bulge siege of Bastogne ends in U.S. victory

1945

January 17: USSR captures Warsaw

January 27: USSR liberates Auschwitz-Birkenau concentration camp

January 28: Battle of the Bulge ends in Allied victory

February 4-11: Yalta Conference—Roosevelt, Churchill, Stalin—sets foundation of post-war Europe

March 7: U.S. captures Remagen bridge; Allies begin racing through Germany.

April 12: Roosevelt dies; Harry Truman becomes U.S. president

April 22-27: Allies capture Bologna, Genoa, Verona in Italy

April 25: U.S. and Soviet forces meet at Elbe River; Battle of Berlin begins

April 28: Mussolini murdered by partisans

April 30: Adolf Hitler commits suicide

May 2: Berlin surrenders to USSR; German forces in Italy surrender

May 4: Britain accepts German surrender in northwest Germany, Holland, Denmark

May 7: U.S. accepts unconditional German surrender in Reims, France

May 8-9: USSR accepts unconditional German surrender in Berlin

July 17-August 2: Potsdam Conference sets boundaries in Europe, surrender terms for Japan

November-October 1946: War Crimes Trial at Nuremberg

ACKNOWLEDGEMENTS

Anyone who has been involved in an undertaking as ambitious as this one understands that the name on the cover of the book represents merely the intersection of the work, talent and generosity of innumerable participants. Though it's impossible to catalog each favor done, apologies are nevertheless extended to anyone inadvertently left off this list of individuals who made this book possible.

Because a two-minute conversation can sometimes be as valuable as a two-hour airplane ride, I've listed names below without note of relative importance. No matter how much expertise, time or other considerations were involved, all assistance received during the course of this project was necessary, valuable and, above all, greatly appreciated. I would be remiss, however, for not paying special attention to British veteran Mr. Bob Reynolds, who greatly assisted this project from planning travel to providing insight on the manuscript.

Thanks and gratitude are extended to those who made invaluable contributions in the following locations. Anzio: Amerigo Salvini. Amsterdam: Marieke van der Linden, Mark Ricci. Austria: Superhosts John Thompson and Susie Schnitzer. East Anglia: Philip Search. Bastogne: Henri Mignon. Belgium: Jacques Gilson, Liliane Opsomer, Rosemary van Peer, Marcel and Matilde Schmetz, Mr. and Mrs. Tillmanns at Envisal Historical Museum. Berlin: Marlit Friedland, Natascha Kompatzki, Katja Kunipatz, Kirsten Schmidt. Cassino: Michele Di Lonardo, Federico Lamberti. Dunkirk: Lucien Dayan. England: Hannah Collingbourne. France: Louise O'Brien. Kursk: Victorvich Karakulov, Colonel Vyucheslav Budenny, Viktoria Danioova, Zoya Babich. Germany: Richard Reindorf, Sandra Tharas. Italy: Enzo Colombo, Elena Bernardi. London: Anya at St. Paul's Cathedral, Beverly Booth, Terry Charman, Amalie Dence, Carolyn King, Julie Maine, Ruth Reinicke, Mark Ricci again, Chris Woodcock, Chris Wren. Lyon: Sandrine Eveillard, Mrs. Claude van Peers. Moscow and Russia: The indefatigable Oleg Alexandrov and the irrepressible Michelle Thompson, Elena at Central Armed Forces Museum. Munich: Karoline Graf. Netherlands: Albert Boon, Tom Kramer. Normandy: Nicolas Leloup. Norway: Harald Hansen, Mette Aavatsmark, Inger Dragland, William Hakvaag, Ulf Eirik Torgersen. Nuremberg: Ursula Kraft, Michael Schönemann. Paris: Marie-Solène Fleury. Poland: Tony Cisneros. Remagen: Kurt Kleeman. Rome: Carlo Begliuti, Emanuela Cresti, Angela Lopez, Ilenia Santarelli. The Royal Canadian Military Institute and Pat White. Volgograd: Vladimir Shmargoun, Ludmilla Tiulikhova. Washington, D.C./USA: Jennifer Lloyd, Thompson family, Denise Anern.

Special thanks are extended to everyone at Greenline Publications and those who contributed such great work and effort, including Samia Afra, Roger Migdow, Crys O'Neil, Tammy Richards-LeSure and Debra Valencia. Ross McCammon and Jordan Rane are two of the best writers around. This book would still be a pile of confused files without editor Kristin Poss sorting it all out in record time. Greenline publisher Alan Davis has been a dedicated force behind this project, which he believed from the start was not just interesting but important. For that he deserves thanks and gratitude from veterans and all those who walk in their footsteps.

My mother, family and friends have all indulged me in this and other projects in one way or another and deserve endless thanks.

Joyce Leong can do everything from make maps to walk miles on end—she did both for this project—but her greatest talent is making doing both seem fun.

Table of Contents

Eisenhower Statue, Normandy

INTRODUCTION

wilight was descending on Adolf Hitler's great stage. The venue was the vast Nazi Party Rally Grounds in Nuremberg, Germany, but the year wasn't 1938 or even 1945. It was 2004. Sixty-five years had passed since the German dictator's last appearance at this site, but the memories of what had taken place here still felt near. Lugging a frayed knapsack and digital camera, Jodi Stavely moved around the mammoth tribune with visible unease. As the day's final visitors to the infamous Rally Grounds, Stavely and I had self-consciously kept to ourselves, spending the final minutes of sunlight quietly looking over the vast field that once vibrated with swastikas and Nazi salutes so strong that the entire world shook. Faced with such a scene, you tend to keep your thoughts to yourself, allow others a certain distance. Even so, I knew what Stavely wanted before she asked.

"Excuse me," she introduced herself somewhat awkwardly. "I feel strange asking, but would you mind taking my picture?" Though she didn't say it, what she meant was: "I feel vaguely criminal just standing on the spot from which Adolf Hitler delivered his most vitriolic speeches, let alone having my picture taken here like some grinning tourist, but this is a historic site, and I'd like to record the moment, so if you'd temporarily suspend moral judgment, snap a photo and then forget that I ever made such an unseemly request, I'd be forever grateful."

We introduced ourselves—she was from Tasmania, on an extended trip through Europe—and I took the picture. I told her that I understood her reluctance to be photographed here. Fair or not, there's a suggestion of whimsy, at least a lack of reverence, in posing for snapshots in places noted for infamy and brutality. I explained my own reasons for being here. I'd spent most of 2003 and part of 2004 tracing the course of World War II in Europe, cataloging sites for inclusion in a book that might help others to do exactly what she was doing.

> **Along with food and drink, a look at local history is often the most accessible and immediate way of connecting with a foreign culture.**

Travel does something to the ordinary person's interest in history. Someone who might never bother with a book on the ancient Mayan or Roman civilizations is suddenly gripped by the unshakable need to see Tikal when visiting Guatemala or the Colosseum in Rome. Many trips abroad revolve around such excursions. This makes perfect sense. Along with food and drink, a look at local history is often the most accessible and immediate way of connecting with a foreign culture. In the case of the European War—the term loosely employed in this book to describe any fighting anywhere, including North Africa and the Mediterranean, against the militaries of Nazi Germany and Fascist Italy—such sites provide an entry point into American as well as European and world history. Most of the globe was consumed and then refashioned by World War II. This book seeks to guide travelers in Europe to those places of its greatest importance and interest.

Word count being the implacable foe of every writer and unbreakable ally of every editor, various factors came into play when deciding which locations to leave in and which to leave out when compiling this limited list of "25 Essential." Final rankings, admittedly subjective, were constructed around a set of only slightly flexible guidelines. Sites were judged on the basis of three equally weighted qualities. First, their historic significance (Dieppe, France, was the scene of a horrible battle, but what occurred there pales in importance next to Stalingrad). Second, the amount and quality of relics or points of interest remaining at a given site (most Americans have heard of Dunkirk, but there's more to see from the Battle of the Bulge across vastly under-appreciated Belgium). Third, excluding any association with the war, each site was considered purely on its merits as a travel destination, its services, natural beauty and general desirability (London, Paris and Rome were obvious winners here). At or near the top of all three categories, Normandy finished first in overall score. Regrettably, there has to be a spot at the bottom of any list. Farther down, destinations may be tougher to travel to, or have slightly less to look at, but every destination covered here is worth a visit. In the end, it's a matter of personal preference.

As a companion to *The 25 Best World War II Sites: Pacific Theater*, this book borrows many of its predecessor's conventions. These include an established rating system (opposite page), though with one notable change. Although I'd told Stavely I found nothing inappropriate about snapping her photo in Nuremberg, I admit to sharing some of her reservations about any treatment of Nazi Germany that might be interpreted as less than respectful to the memory of the millions who suffered during the war. The five-star rating system was devised simply as a tool to help travelers prioritize schedules. A battlefield where thousands died isn't necessarily a "good" place, but it's often an important one, a point reflected by the number of stars accompanying the description that appears in this book. Still, there's something unsettling about "rating" sites directly connected to the Holocaust, such as the vast remains of the concentration camp at Auschwitz-Birkenau. Though in some fashion the entire war can be connected to Adolf Hitler and the Nazi Party's persecution of European Jewry, those sites directly related to the Holocaust are not rated but simply described.

A peripheral note on the ratings: one can be sure that an infantry "mopping up" operation that might pass as a throwaway line in a history text written decades after the fact was something a great deal more significant to the poor souls who actually had to do the mopping up with loaded rifles and as steady a set of nerves as they could manage. To the individual, a single bullet can be as fatal as a round-the-clock bombing campaign. Again, a one- or five-star rating isn't intended to suggest that any one action of the war was more or less important than another. It's provided simply to give the modern traveler an idea of the extent of the physical evidence remaining at a given location.

World War II travel is especially rewarding, if only for providing perspective on the very different ways in which countries weave the mythology of the historic conflict into their national identity.

To whatever degree travel provides a connection to the past, it's 100 times more a connection to the present. With a computer, television or library card, one can gather plenty of information on a foreign location. But nothing compares to actually being there. World War II travel is especially rewarding, if only for providing perspective on the very different ways in which countries weave the mythology of the historic conflict into their national identity. The photograph of the Eisenhower monument in Normandy that opens this introduction reflects a solidly American point of reference for the war. A day or two in London, however, and the Martian observer might well conclude that a handful of Hurricane and Spitfire fighter planes alone decided the entire war in the skies above St. Paul's Cathedral in 1940. Never mind the Allies, the Queen's own forces in France, Norway, North Africa, Italy and particularly the Far East barely rate a mention there.

In Russia, matters are more complicated. The bulk of Soviet World War II history was written and memorialized—on an impressively grand scale—by the Communist Party during the Cold War. In this version of events, which the Russians know as the Great Patriotic War, the Western allies, when spoken of at all, are usually referenced only grudgingly. Or with a

smirk. A telling example is a wartime propaganda poster on display at the Defense of Moscow Museum (page 134). One half juxtaposes a bare Soviet fist knocking teeth and blood from a Nazi mouth vis-à-vis the gentler gloved hand of the American-British allies politely displacing a German's helmet with an effete slap. One can't entirely fault the Russians for their version of the war. The unfathomable toll of what the Germans called *der Russland Krieg* (the Russia War) far eclipsed anything that occurred in the West. Yet most Americans know little of the savagery and scale of that battlefront.

For all this, Russia is in the midst of a social and political sea change that includes a reexamination of World War II informed by a candor that until recently would have been unthinkable. On a tour through the tank battlefield near Kursk, the longtime curator of a local museum, my guide for the day, spared few opportunities to share with me epic, propagandist tales of the courage and patriotism of Red Army soldiers that enabled the Soviet Union to win the war. "At this place," she said, with typical awe, "our soldiers allowed themselves to be shot en masse so that their corpses would form a human wall behind which their comrades could pass unharmed by German bullets."

Throughout the day our driver—a heavyset, rough-looking guy in his mid-50s who kept a rifle near the front seat—had barely bothered to subdue his skepticism at these sorts of anecdotes. With this pronouncement, he finally was moved to set the record straight. "They were all drunk, that's why they did it!" he declared, tipping his thumb to his mouth and winking at me across the van while the curator fell into a black silence in the back seat. "The officers got the men drunk before a big battle and threatened to shoot them themselves if they didn't follow orders. I should know, I was in the Soviet Army for two years. As was my father!"

One imagines it was this sort of impertinence that the American GIs who first linked up with the Soviets on the Elbe River (page 242) in 1945 found so engaging. A young Andy Rooney, then a U.S. Army war correspondent, went so far as to describe the Red Army soldiers that day as "the most carefree bunch of screwballs that ever came together in an army." It's unlikely the average Wehrmacht foot soldier would have found much in Rooney's statement with which to agree. Indeed, in light of the decades that followed, Rooney's assessment always seemed to me to be one of the most profoundly absurd of the war. But you travel to a place, walk the ground, talk to the people, meet the veterans—and there are plenty of them still around, despite what you've been told—and you develop an appreciation of historical events that might otherwise be unattainable.

It should be noted that much (though not close to all) of the information in this book appears in some form or other in a number of sources—brochures, asides in travel guides, websites and small books, usually published privately or within small locales. Such books have long been the domain of war buffs,

> **This book is about the tangible materials that lift the war off textbook pages, television and movie screens and provide a tactile connection to the great story of the 20th century.**

local historians and inveterate artifact hunters. But what few copies of these materials exist tend to concentrate on small areas. Furthermore, they're hard to come by, often involving a trip to whatever region they cover and some amount of chance. For the war's larger campaigns—D-Day, Battle of the Bulge, Operation Market-Garden—a number of specialty guides have been published (the best are noted in the appropriate chapters of this book). But no single guidebook attempts to cover a comprehensive list of European war sites, weed out the existing mountain of misinformation or present details in a way that might lead the casual traveler to places both historically significant and intrinsically fascinating.

This is not a book for war buffs. It's a book for travelers. Though it's hoped that those with a more intense interest will find the book useful, its main concern isn't with whether it was Army Company A or B that took Hill 57 (or was it Sector X?), or whether the SB2A dive bomber that supported the mission was colloquially known as the Buccaneer or the Helldiver, or whether the 75 mm A/T guns the company carried had a range of 5,500 or 9,000 yards, or even what A/T stood for. (Anti-tank, as it turns out, as well as the Buccaneer, built by Brewster, and 9,000-plus yards.) With respect to the personnel who built and used that equipment and served in those battles, their families and anyone else interested in such detail, the technical end of the war has already been covered more thoroughly and expertly than I could ever hope to fake. As for the essential narrative thread, documentaries from the classic Laurence Olivier–narrated *The World at War* to Ken Burns' *The War*—which follows the experiences of men and women from a handful of typical American towns—have covered the plot points large and small in fine detail. Though major figures, weapons, technology and battles provide the framework, this book is more interested in the beaches, battlefields, cities, artifacts, museums and monuments left behind. In other words, the tangible materials that lift the war off textbook pages, television and movie screens and provide a tactile connection to the great story of the 20th century, a story still firmly in charge of shaping the century that followed it.

A NOTE ON DIRECTIONS, DRIVING, DISTANCES AND GUIDES

Like any travel guide, this one strives to present information with a certain level of consistency. Unfortunately, the terrain it covers—the battlefields of World War II—can hardly be regarded as uniform. In many places, traditional street addresses and directions are easy to provide and simple to follow—Washington, D.C., and London come to mind. Other sites present greater challenges, necessitating the sort of "walk south 100 yards from the big rock" landmark-based instructions normally found on a child's treasure map. In each case, and at the regrettable expense of consistency, I've provided the type of direction that seems to best suit the area concerned.

Outside of major cities and a few noted exceptions, the best way to efficiently visit the battlefields and sites covered in this book is by car. As in the United States, driving across all of continental Europe is on the right side of the road, overtaking on the left. Highways and city roads are almost without fail well-maintained (conditions deteriorate in eastern Europe). All major American car rental companies operate across the continent and in Great Britain. As of this writing, National Car Rental (800-227-7368) consistently offered the best rates of any U.S. company operating in Europe. Better rates are often available through Auto Europe (888-223-5555 in U.S.; 00-800-223-55555 toll-free from anywhere in Great Britain and Europe). Europcar (www.europcar.com or through Auto Europe at 888-223-5555) is a major European company with competitive rates. Booking and paying for a rental car in the United States before arriving in Europe almost always ensures a better rate. Commercially available Michelin road maps (used by the German command to plan many World War II operations) are invaluable.

Distances are listed in miles or kilometers, following both the convention of the country to which they apply and the assumption that travelers will be using local road signs and possibly odometers to get from point to point. If signs and other indicators in a given location are listed in kilometers, it seems counterproductive to list mileage (and vice versa) no matter what the nature of one's native familiarity with such measurements. In this regard the rule is ancient—do as the Romans do. All walking distances, however, are presented in feet, yards and miles, units most familiar to the largely American audience anticipated for this book. Many of the distances (particularly for walking or general orientation) are estimates and shouldn't be considered precise unless stated as such (1.2 km, 138 feet, 96 steps, and so on).

To the degree that this book has been written to aid independent travel, every effort has been made to direct the reader to sites without the assistance of a human guide. Numerous companies do, however, operate excellent historical battlefield tours. For the benefit of those interested in escorted or group travel, local guides and tour companies are listed in chapters where they seem most helpful.

1

Normandy I

Utah • Omaha

FRANCE

Utah Beach

THE WAR YEARS

Noise. Fire. Smoke. Confusion. Accounts of the June 6, 1944, Allied D-Day invasion of Normandy, France, typically impose a sense of narrative order upon events of the most historic day in American arms. But the experience of what was at the time the largest amphibious assault ever mounted is best understood in terms of the anarchy that prevailed on the beaches of Normandy for much of the first day. As one GI disembarking onto a corpse-littered Omaha Beach put it: "I became a visitor to hell."

It wasn't supposed to have been that way. To meet the unprecedented scale of the assault on Adolf Hitler's heavily defended Fortress Europe, Operation Overlord, the Allied invasion of northwestern Europe (D-Day being the initial attack on Normandy), produced the most detailed document ever prepared by an armed force. Delivered by a galaxy of ships—4,000 landing craft, 3,500 amphibious vehicles, 284 major warships—five Allied armies (two American, two British, one Canadian, with Free French, Polish and other nationalities participating) were to establish a foothold at five beaches along a 50-mile front, thus beginning the great drive to Berlin. Overall command rested with American General Dwight Eisenhower, a career staff officer who'd seen little battlefield action, but whose uncanny organizational and political skills disguised a mental ruthlessness perfectly suited for the job. By war's end, virtually all agreed that no other Allied commander could have performed the delicate and difficult job given to Eisenhower.

The landings on the American beaches—Utah and Omaha—were preceded by a midnight invasion of 13,000 paratroopers from the U.S. 82nd and 101st Airborne Divisions. Dropped into enemy territory behind Utah, the paratroopers were to destroy German artillery positions and seal roads and bridges against German counterattack. After a majestic armada of 822 C-47 transports carrying the airborne soldiers took off from English airfields, heavy German antiaircraft fire created havoc in the skies. Paratroopers were scattered as far as 35 miles off target, left in the dark, literally and figuratively. "The majority were lost, lonely and afraid," wrote historian John Keegan, but their efforts to regroup, achieve some (not close to all) objectives and thoroughly confuse German defenders remains among the most inspiring chapters of the war.

German positions were further softened by pre-invasion aerial and naval bombardment that shook the countryside for hours. Their contributions often overlooked, the U.S., British and Canadian Navy's heavy bombardment from battleships and other vessels was notably accurate in places such as Crisbecq. Though most aerial bombs dropped "harmlessly" behind the coast—the campaign killed thousands of civilians and slaughtered Normandy's dairy herds—air superiority throughout D-Day was decisive. Against 8,000 aircraft, the decimated Luftwaffe managed to get barely 100 aircraft aloft. "The outstanding factor both before and during the invasion was the overwhelming air superiority of the enemy," German officers reported after the war.

Perhaps the most distinguishing feature of the U.S. Army was its inexperience. Most landing at Normandy had never seen combat—they were "as green as growing corn," said one Navy officer—and spent seaborne approaches in rough English Channel waters woozy and vomiting. More than anything, the U.S. Army was a menagerie of "civilians in uniform"—teachers, grocers, truck drivers, engineers, farm kids—who stood in sharp contrast to the traditional soldiers fielded by the more hidebound militaries of

Britain and Europe. This casual "civilian" demeanor would make the final achievements of the Americans against the "professional" German military all the more remarkable (and inspire the title of historian Stephen Ambrose's *Citizen Soldiers*). But early on D-Day, their inexperience would show.

Four-mile-long Omaha, where two-thirds of the 58,000-strong U.S. force landed, was by far the bloodiest of the five beaches. Inexpertly launched 12 miles from shore, American landing craft were pounded by artillery and underwater mines long before they reached land. Twenty-seven of 32 "floating" tanks sank, leaving soldiers pinned on open beaches with no supporting armor. From low bluffs, the best of Germany's Normandy defenders raked wide, sandy Omaha with interlocking fire. A paralyzing dread swept over men who huddled behind German beach obstacles and other minimal cover. This was brute, frontal assault, on par with eastern war combat, best described by those who fought it: "Within 10 minutes of the ramps being lowered, (the leading company) had become inert, leaderless and almost incapable of action. Every officer and sergeant had been killed or wounded." "People were yelling, screaming, dying, equipment was flying everywhere, men were bleeding to death, crawling, lying everywhere, firing coming from all directions." "The beach was literally covered with the bodies of American soldiers."

Through acts of suicidal heroism, small groups of GIs under direct fire crawled to German positions and dropped grenades and other explosives into pillboxes. Miraculously, by nightfall, Americans occupied the main heights above the beach (the area now occupied by a large American cemetery). In all, 156,000 Allied troops would come ashore across Normandy within 24 hours, but not before 2,500 casualties were sustained on Omaha.

Of all invasion beaches, operations at lightly defended Utah went the smoothest. Landings were marred by soldiers who, loaded with as much as 70 pounds of gear, disembarked from landing craft only to be pulled beneath the surf and drown. Nevertheless, of the 23,250 men who came ashore at Utah on D-Day, only 197 were killed, wounded or missing. The rest quickly secured the beachhead from thinly dispersed, second-tier German defenders before moving several miles inland.

Gaps between the five invasion beaches were closed June 12—well behind schedule— and the Allies spent almost two months bottled up in Normandy by fierce German resistance. Still, as one German officer remarked after inspecting a set of captured plans describing the invasion: "In my entire military life, I have never been so impressed. At this moment, I knew Germany was going to lose this war."

SOURCES & OTHER READING

Six Armies in Normandy: From D-Day to the Liberation of Paris, Keegan, John, Jonathan Cape, 1982

The Longest Day: June 6, 1944, Ryan, Cornelius, Simon & Schuster, 1959

D-Day, June 6, 1944: The Climactic Battle of World War II, Ambrose, Stephen, Simon & Schuster, 1994

Crusade in Europe, Eisenhower, Dwight D., Doubleday, 1948

Major and Mrs Holt's Battlefield Guide to the Normandy Landing Beaches, Holt and Holt, Leo Cooper, 2001 (revised)

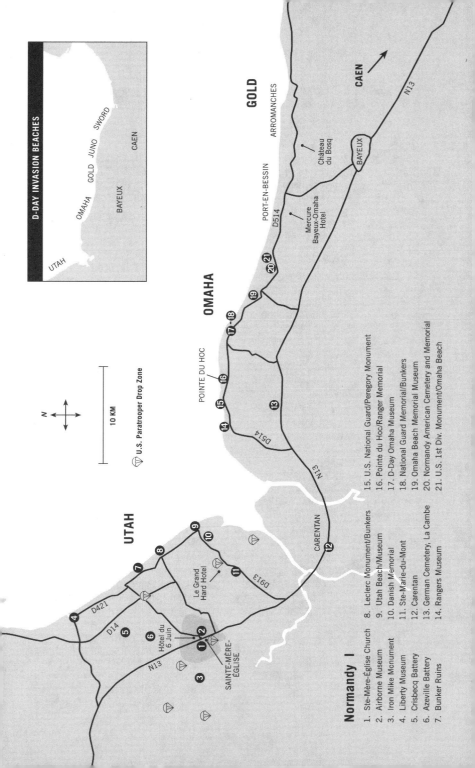

D-DAY INVASION BEACHES

UTAH · OMAHA · GOLD · JUNO · SWORD

BAYEUX · CAEN

N

10 KM

⊕ U.S. Paratrooper Drop Zone

UTAH

OMAHA

GOLD

CAEN

POINTE DU HOC

CARENTAN · N13

Le Grand Hard Hôtel

Hôtel du 6 Juin

SAINTE-MÈRE-ÉGLISE

D421 · D14 · N13 · D913

ARROMANCHES

PORT-EN-BESSIN

D514

Mercure Bayeux-Omaha Hôtel

Château du Bosq

BAYEUX

N13

Normandy I

1. Ste-Mère-Église Church
2. Airborne Museum
3. Iron Mike Monument
4. Liberty Museum
5. Crisbecq Battery
6. Azeville Battery
7. Bunker Ruins
8. Leclerc Monument/Bunkers
9. Utah Beach/Museum
10. Danish Memorial
11. Ste-Marie-du-Mont
12. Carentan
13. German Cemetery, La Cambe
14. Rangers Museum
15. U.S. National Guard/Peregory Monument
16. Pointe du Hoc/Ranger Memorial
17. D-Day Omaha Museum
18. National Guard Memorial/Bunkers
19. Omaha Beach Memorial Museum
20. Normandy American Cemetery and Memorial
21. U.S. 1st Div. Monument/Omaha Beach

NORMANDY TODAY

Population: 115,000 (Caen); 15,000 (Bayeux); 1,500 (Ste-Mère-Église); 600 (Arromanches) • Country Code: 33 • €1 = $1.36/£0.67

Though Americans associate Normandy with the historic invasion, Europeans also know it as a seaside vacation ground (or second-home territory for middle-class Parisians) filled with wide beaches, ancient Romanesque villages and, because this is France, excellent bistros, patisseries and outdoor cafes. Summer visitors to the five D-Day invasion beaches will find themselves sharing space with sunbathers, swimmers and families on holiday. Many beach tourists come from Britain, with the result that English is widely spoken in the region. Normandy beaches aren't particularly beautiful—Arromanches (near Gold Beach) has the best one—but they're all accessible and easy to walk. Normandy has 340 miles of coastline and even travelers intent on history will find that leaving swimsuits at home is a mistake—in summer, temperatures can reach the 90s.

Post-war Allied funds helped rebuild Normandy's war-ravaged towns (many wrecked by pre-invasion Allied bombardment), a job largely completed by the early 1950s. In smaller towns, efforts were made to rebuild in the traditional style. Most are now as picturesque as they were

before the war. Beyond the coastline are gentle hills, farmland and some industry. July and August (the crowded, high-travel season) are typically dry and warm. November to January is rainy and chilly and many museums are closed.

Central to all five invasion beaches, Bayeux is the best base of operations. It's large enough to provide ample visitor services, small enough to get in and out of quickly. The first town liberated, Bayeux suffered little battle damage, leaving it one of the most atmospheric small towns in northern France, so many of which were leveled by the war. Larger Caen, totally destroyed by contrast, has Normandy's major World War II museum, a magnificent castle (Château de Caen, established by William the Conqueror in 1060) and commerce and traffic in equal measures. Carentan, Ste-Mère-Église and Ste-Marie-du-Mont are small towns located closer to Utah Beach.

If one simply wants to walk the beaches, all five can be visited briefly in a single day. To spend more time and have a look at the museums, two full days are needed to cover sites in the Normandy I chapter, two to three days for Normandy II sites.

POINTS OF INTEREST

Hundreds of small markers and historic points are scattered throughout the Utah and Omaha area. This chapter presents the highlights on a route that travels past many roadside monuments, and so on. Driving distances are approximate.

1. Sainte-Mère-Église Church ★★★★

City center. From N13, D67 or other roads, follow signs to town square and park near large, central church.

The large Catholic church in the center

of town gained enduring fame when American paratrooper John Steele got hung up in its steeple on his June 6 jump into enemy territory. Steele played dead to avoid German capture. His exploit was re-created in 1962's *The Longest Day*. In summer, an effigy of Steele suspended by a parachute hangs from the steeple. It's a favorite stop for visitors, one of D-Day's more recognizable icons. Bullet scars are still visible on the church's exterior. Outside the church is the famous pump from which villagers passed buckets of water to extinguish a house fire on the night of the invasion—in the midst of their work, locals, long under the heel of Nazi occupation, were stunned to find American paratroopers descending around them. A large stained-glass window at the rear of the church depicts the Virgin Mary surrounded by American paratroopers.

One of the first French towns liberated in June 1944, Ste-Mère-Église has established a 15-point "Circuit Historique" tracing important local events of the liberation. Points include American flags and liberation markers, U.S. glider landing spot and Milestone 0 of the Liberty Way route that runs from here to Bastogne (a French KM Zero milestone beginning a route to Paris can be found at Utah Beach). Brochures and circuit maps are available from the Office de Tourisme (6 rue Eisenhower, 02-33-21-0033). With plenty of good cafes and shops, Ste-Mère-Église is a pleasant walking town, worth a couple of hours.

2. Airborne Museum (Musée Airborne) ★★★★

14 rue Eisenhower, Ste-Mère-Église
(across street from Point 1)
T: (0)2-33-41-4135
Daily, 9:30 a.m.-noon, 2-6 p.m.,
February-March, September-November,
(9 a.m.-6:45 p.m. April-September)
Closed December, January
Adult: €6; Child (6-14): €3

One of the better museums in the American zone, the two buildings shaped like open parachutes advertise the prevailing airborne theme here. Excellent displays in 32,000 square feet of gallery space recount the daring paratrooper drops that preceded amphibious landings. A Sherman tank and 90 mm American anti-aircraft gun stand outside, but the high points are an original, accessible Waco glider used to transport 12 men (plus pilot and copilot) and a restored C-47 Dakota troop carrier that brought the bulk of the paratroopers to Normandy and also towed gliders. Members of the U.S. 82nd and 101st Airborne Infantry donated many of the items on display. American airborne troops suffered the highest casualty ratios during the invasion, with 2,499 killed, wounded or missing. Their story has been recounted in such films as *The Longest Day* and *Band of Brothers*. The title character played by Matt Damon in *Saving Private Ryan* was a fictional member of the 101st Airborne.

3. Iron Mike Monument ★★★

Off D15, 4 km southwest of Ste-Mère-Église. Kitty-corner from the U.S. flag and liberation marker at Ste-Mère-Église's main square, turn left on D15 toward Chef du Pont. After 0.5 km fork right and follow D15 toward Mémorial des Parachutistes. Proceed 3.5 km to memorial parking lot on right side of road.

One of the more impressive Normandy memorials, this larger-than-life bronze statue of a rugged American paratrooper composite ("Iron Mike") was dedicated in 1997. A large orientation table shows the area of fighting from June 6 to 9. The site overlooks the "Fierce Cauquigny" battlefield, a crucial route across a flooded marsh. A plaque recalls Pfc. Charles DeGlopper, a member of the 82nd Airborne, who died near this spot on June 9, 1944, while providing covering fire for comrades during a savage German attack. DeGlopper's Medal of Honor citation reads like over-the-top Hollywood war fiction: "Scorning a concentration of enemy automatic weapons and rifle fire, he walked from the ditch onto the road in full view of the Germans, and sprayed the hostile positions with assault fire. He was wounded, but he continued firing. Struck again, he started to fall; and yet his grim determination and valiant fighting spirit could not be broken. Kneeling in the roadway, weakened by his grievous wounds, he leveled his heavy weapon against the enemy and fired burst after burst until killed outright."

4. Liberty Museum (Musée de la Liberté) ★★

Avenue de la Plage, off D42 in Quineville, 25 km northwest of Ste-Mère-Église
T: (0)2-33-21-4044
Daily, 10 a.m.-6 p.m., mid-March-May,

October-mid-November
Daily, 9:30 a.m.-7:30 p.m.,
June-September
Adult: €5.50; Child: €4

Beyond the northern end of Utah Beach, Quineville was the location of a German regional command post and large gun installations. There were no Allied landings here, but some 82nd Airborne paratroopers came down in the vicinity. It's a bit out of the way, but the 10,000-square-foot beachfront museum built over a German bunker impressively re-creates life during the Occupation. Interesting items include a baby's gas mask, a vintage wireless set, several 1940s vehicles, handmade American flags and 400 "unpublished" photos including a moving enlargement of a French housewife greeting an American soldier with her arms flung wide open.

5. Crisbecq Battery (Batteries de Crisbecq) ★★

Near intersection of D14 and D69 (follow signs for Batteries de Crisbecq), 6 km south of Point 4

Also called St. Marcouf Battery, this gun emplacement commanding Utah Beach sea approaches housed 155 mm coastal-defense guns. The Allies bombed the site prior to and during D-Day landings, but the guns remained untouched and were responsible for sinking an American destroyer off Utah. Return fire by the USS *Nevada*, which had been badly damaged at Pearl Harbor and refitted for service in time for D-Day, scored a direct hit. The battery was taken on June 12 only after its crew evacuated. No guns remain, but visitors can walk on top (no interior entry) of the intact casemates.

6. Azeville Battery (Batteries d'Azeville) ★★★

La rue in Azeville. From D69 follow signs for Batteries d'Azeville et de Crisbecq to D269, then follow signs for Batteries d'Azeville. About 2 km south of Point 5
T: (0)2-33-40-6305
Daily, 2-6 p.m., April-May
Daily, 11 a.m.-6 p.m., June-September

(closed at 7 p.m., July, August)
Irregular hours, January-March. Call ahead.
Last entry 30 minutes before close
Adult: €4; Student/Child: €1.60

Refurbished in 2002, these four large gun casemates were an integral piece of Normandy's Atlantic Wall defenses. After several attempts, the position and its 170-man crew were captured on June 9 when Private Ralph Riley, finding his way through a protective minefield, torched one of the buildings with a flamethrower, igniting ammunition inside. Visitors can wander through the large, concrete structures.

7. Bunker Ruins ★★

Along beach side of D421, 9 km southeast of Point 5

Ruins of German coastal-defense bunkers along the beach road can be entered. The view from inside looks straight down the Utah landing beach. U.S. forces were supposed to have come ashore at this heavily defended position on June 6. Fortunately for them, they mistakenly landed farther down the beach near what was to become the main Utah landing area.

8. Leclerc Monument/Bunkers (Leclerc Comité de Débarquement) ★★★

Along beach side of D421, 2.5 km southeast of Point 7

A well-preserved half-track, an armored car, several bunkers and a large blockhouse surround an impressive stone monument and NTL (Normandie Terre-Liberté) interpretive totem—the blue-and-white markers emblazoned with a dove logo are found throughout Normandy—where the French 2nd Armored Division led by General Philippe Leclerc came ashore well after the initial D-Day invasion. The French force joined the U.S. 3rd Army in the breakout campaign from Normandy. A true French hero, Leclerc (who led a Free French force across the Sahara to join the British 8th Army in Libya in 1942) accepted the German surrender of Paris in August 1944. Nearby dunes and bunkers are on private property (across a wire fence), but accessible German bunkers can be found at various points along this stretch of D421.

9. Utah Beach/Museum (Utah Beach Musée du Débarquement) ★★★★★

Intersection of D421 and D913, at Ste-Marie-du-Mont, 4.5 km southeast of Point 8
T: (0)2-33-71-5335
Daily, 9:30 a.m.-7 p.m., May-September
Daily, 10 a.m.-12:30 p.m., 2-6 p.m., April, October
Weekends, holidays, 10 a.m.-12:30 p.m., 2-5:30 p.m., November-March
Adult: €5.50; Child: €2.50
Beach access free, charge for museum only

Large American and French flags herald the entrance to the westernmost D-Day landing beach. Here, 865 ships of "U" (for Utah) Force approached, the U.S. 9th Air Force began bombing at 5:20 a.m., and D-Day's first assault troops waded ashore at 6:30 a.m. By noon the Americans controlled the beach and at day's end they occupied a section of the coast to an inland depth of 6 to 10 km. By nightfall, 23,250 men and 1,700 vehicles had been brought ashore. Eventually, 836,000 service personnel would enter Europe from this point.

Built around a German blockhouse at the center of the American landing zone, the modern, two-story museum tells the story of the landings with an impressive collection of photos, a 12-minute film, maps, models, relics, weaponry, vehicles and landing craft. Outside are an LCVP Higgins boat landing craft used by assault troops, a Sherman tank and many plaques and memorials. The beach here is wide and soft, with a low rise of dunes behind it. Among the five D-Day beaches, it attracts the fewest sunbathers. It's easily accessed from behind the museum—the full length can be walked without difficulty.

The central flag station, pointedly built atop a German bunker, shows directions and distances to major campaign points: Ste-Mère-Église (10 km), Paris (265 km), Bastogne (505 km), Berlin (1,100 km), and so on. It also points to the position from which Pearl Harbor veteran USS *Nevada* successfully fired on German batteries. Surrounded by a stone wall, the oldest house at the north end of the beach somehow survived the torrid pre-invasion shelling. In 2001, in the grassy area across from the stone-pillar monument, an enormous tent theater was erected for the premier of the HBO film *Band of Brothers*. Many veterans of the 101st Airborne Easy Company upon whom the series was based (many of the men parachuted into points behind Utah) attended the ceremony. The Le Roosevelt cafe and bar across the parking lot isn't named for the American president, but for 57-year-old Brigadier General Theodore Roosevelt, Jr. (son of President Theodore Roosevelt), who, brandishing a .45 Colt and clutching a wooden cane, was the oldest D-Day officer to land with the first wave of assault forces. Also here is Liberty Milestone "KM Zero," starting point of the famed Liberty Highway that the U.S. 4th Division and Leclerc's 2nd Armored Division forged from Utah Beach to Paris and other points.

10. Danish Memorial ★

Along D913, 2 km inland from Point 9

This roadside memorial commemorates the approximately 800 Danish soldiers who participated in Utah action, many of them serving aboard ships.

11. Ste-Marie-du-Mont ★★

On D913, 6 km inland from Point 9

On the roadside, next to the Liberty Milestone, an NTL totem—emblazoned with a poignant photo—tells the story of the 101st Division "Screaming Eagles" airborne troops, led by General Maxwell Taylor, who landed around the town (by mistake) in the early hours of June 6. With great skill and courage, the scattered paratroopers regrouped in the dark and began attacking German positions. Ten or so historical signs describing local actions can be found around the small town. Bullet scars are visible in some of the older buildings in the town center.

12. Carentan ★★

Off N13, 10 km south of Point 11

At the Hôtel de Ville (City Hall) in the center of town (on the main road), a large stone marker, NTL totem and 101st Airborne "Screaming Eagles" plaque commemorate the Allied liberation of Carentan. A key road junction linking Utah and Omaha beaches (the first meeting of troops from the two beaches occurred northeast of town at Brévands), Carentan was the scene of June 6 to 12 fighting that involved a rare American bayonet charge under cover of smoke bombs. The 101st Airborne sustained significant losses—Stephen Ambrose devotes a full *Band of Brothers* chapter to the Carentan battles of Easy Company. Just behind the Hôtel de Ville, the Notre Dame church has a stained-glass window dedicated to the 101st. Small memorials and markers are placed throughout the town.

13. German Cemetery at La Cambe (Cimetière Militaire Allemand) ★★★★

Off N13 at La Cambe, 20 km east of Point 12. Take La Cambe exit and follow signs for Cimetière Militaire Allemand. No gates, but 8:30 p.m. closing time posted

Dominated by a massive, black stone cross and two human forms (mourning parents) atop a mass burial mound, the sprawling cemetery contains the graves of 21,115 German soldiers. From the top of the mound—accessible by stairs—visitors can view the entire field. Here as elsewhere in Europe, several characteristics differentiate German and American military cemeteries. Dark stones embedded in the ground mark graves shared by four, six or more German soldiers. Clusters of low, granite crosses are symbolic—they don't mark graves. On the gravestones, the names of those buried are engraved along with dates of birth and death (American

headstones list only date of death), revealing the ages of fallen soldiers. As one follows the Allied advance eastward across Europe, the ages of German war dead drops into the teens—15- and 16-year-olds can be found in a number of German military cemeteries—a reflection of Nazi Germany's declining fortunes and desperation. A number of cemeteries contain graves of navy personnel who, in another sign of desperation, were pulled off ships to serve in infantry regiments. A name accompanied by "Strm" indicates "storm trooper" or SS soldier. The men in this cemetery were largely in their 20s and 30s during the Normandy battles, but 18- and 19-year-olds can be found. The information house and museum has English brochures explaining the cemetery and German People's Organization (Volksbund Deutsche Kriegsgräberfürsorge) that maintains German war cemeteries across Europe. There are six German cemeteries in Normandy (this is the largest), including the nearby Orglandes German Cemetery (off D24, 12 km west of Ste-Mère-Église) where 10,152 are buried.

14. Rangers Museum (Musée des Rangers) ★★

Quai Crampon, in Grandcamp-Maisy, 8 km north of Point 13. From D514 or D113 heading toward Grandcamp-Maisy, follow signs to "le port." From port parking area, walk 200 yards to the museum on the street (Quai Crampon) abutting the ocean. T: (0)2-31-92-3351
Tuesday-Sunday, 9:30 a.m.-1 p.m., 2:30-6 p.m., mid-May-October
(1-6 p.m. mid-February-mid-May)
Closed Monday and all other months
Adult: €3.05; Student: €2.30; Child: €1.50

Pointe du Hoc was supposedly the strongest German position on the invasion front in Normandy and it had to be taken. With numerous photos, text, artifacts, uniforms and various displays, this small museum recounts the unit of elite and specially trained men who captured the hill (Point 16) in one of the most daring actions of the invasion. An 18-minute film runs continuously.

15. U.S. National Guard/PeregoryMonument ★★

On D514, 1.5 km east of Point 14

The roadside monument honors National Guardsmen who fought in Normandy, with tribute paid to Medal of Honor recipient Technical Sergeant Frank Peregory, whose unit faced stiff German opposition in this area. The Virginian's heroic MOH citation in part reads: "Encountering a squad of enemy riflemen, he fearlessly attacked them with hand grenades and bayonet, killed eight and forced three to surrender. Continuing along the trench, he single-handedly forced the surrender of 32 more riflemen, captured the machine gunners, and opened the way for the leading ele-ments of the battalion to advance." Peregory was later killed in action on June 14. He's buried in plot G-21-7 at the Normandy American Cemetery (Point 20).

16. Pointe du Hoc/Ranger Memorial ★★★★★

Off D514, 3.5 km east of Point 15. Follow signs for La Pointe du Hoc.

At 7:10 a.m. on June 6, 225 U.S. Rangers scaled the 90-foot cliffs at Pointe du Hoc to neutralize six 155 mm German guns, capable of firing on Allied beaches. With grappling hooks and rope ladders, the Rangers forged upward even as enemy troops above unleashed a blizzard of fire and grenades upon them. Within an hour, 150 survivors of the climb seized their objective, only to find that the guns, much feared by invasion planners, had been relocated long before D-Day. Nevertheless, for two days the Rangers held this position against close-quarters enemy attacks. By the time they were relieved, on June 8, only 90 Rangers were alive, many badly wounded.

Now carpeted with low grass, the 30-acre Pointe du Hoc area is punctured through-out by deep bomb craters—most created by shore bombardment from the USS *Texas*—producing a surreal, undulating moonscape. The Rangers spent much of their time here taking cover inside the

craters. Massive, concrete casemates and remains of German defense works litter the field. The focal point is a stone memorial spire that crowns a German bunker at cliff's edge. From this position the visitor gets panoramic views of the cliffs and English Channel approaches to the Normandy beaches (Omaha to the right, Utah to the left). It's one of the most evocative spots in all of World War II Europe.

17. D-Day Omaha Museum (Musée D-Day Omaha) ★★

On D514 in Vierville-sur-Mer, 7 km east of Point 16
T: (0)2-31-21-7180
Daily, 10 a.m.-12:30 p.m., 2-6 p.m., April, May, September-November 11
Daily, 9:30-7:30 p.m., June-August
Closed November 12-March 31
Adult: €5; Child: €3

A phalanx of American anti-aircraft guns greets visitors to this musty Quonset hut packed with original weaponry, uniforms and much more. The *pièce de résistance* is a German Enigma cryptographic machine. Other interesting items at this 1997-opened private museum include a naval mine, a German Goliath remote-controlled vehicle, a U.S. Navy telescope, an American searchlight and a tiny British motor scooter. There's a lot to see, if you know what you're looking at. Signage is in French, and not extensive at that, though the chatty curator is often on hand.

18. National Guard Memorial/Bunkers ★★★★★

On coast toward western end of Omaha Beach in Vierville-sur-Mer (on road toward beach from Point 17)

French and American flags fly at this large, bunker-like structure (built on top of a German blockhouse) that reveals the history of the U.S. National Guard and June 6 capture of this German gun posi-tion. Invaders at this beach (code named Dog Green) sustained some of D-Day's highest casualty rates. Many of the 23 men from Bedford, Virginia (wartime population 3,000), lost on D-Day died here, among them three sets of brothers. Though producers and scriptwriters have consistently insisted their story is fictional, the opening assault scenes in *Saving Private Ryan* were based on action at this point. A regimental history written by men who came ashore just below the National Guard Memorial will resonate with those familiar with the film: "The first ramps were dropped at 0636 in water that was waist deep. As if this had been the signal for which the enemy waited, the ramps were instantly enveloped in a crossing of automatic fire which was accurate and in great volume." Don't bother looking for exact filming locations—because Omaha Beach is a protected historical landmark, and changed to a degree since 1944 with the addition of such landmarks as the huge American cemetery, Steven Spielberg shot the Omaha landing scenes on beaches in County Wexford, Ireland. Subsequent scenes of the battered French village were filmed at an abandoned airfield, 45 minutes north of London, with massive sets built in Los Angeles and shipped to England. Opening and closing scenes at the cemetery were filmed on location at the American cemetery above Omaha (Point 20). A lode of interesting *Saving Private Ryan* historical information can be found in the British journal *After the Battle,* issue 103, "Spielberg's D-Day," published in 1999.

A short walk along the beach (eastward) are a memorial at the site of the first U.S. burials in Normandy, a plaque commemorating the unsuccessful 1942 Operation Aquatint raid by British commandos, a marker commemorating the U.S. 1st Infantry Division, 166th Regimental Combat Team and boundary between Dog and Easy beaches and, a bit farther on, a bunker in which 40 Germans were killed.

19. Omaha Beach Memorial Museum (Musée Mémorial Omaha 6 Juin 1944) ★★

On D514 (follow signs) in St-Laurent-sur-Mer, 2.5 km east of Point 17
T: (0)2-31-21-9744

Daily, 10 a.m.-12:30 p.m., 2:30-6 p.m., February 15-March 15
Daily, 9:30 a.m.-6:30 p.m., March 16-May 15, September 16-November 15
Daily, 9:30 a.m.-7 p.m., May 16-September 15 (closed at 7:30 p.m., July, August)
Closed November 16-February 14
Adult: €5.20; Senior/Student: €4.20

This private, medium-size collection of photos, uniforms, vehicles and arms (mortars, rifles, Sherman tank, landing craft, U.S. 155 mm "Long Tom" cannon) has good displays describing the war in Normandy, from German occupation to the French Resistance to the D-Day landings. French and English signage helps an already nicely organized presentation.

20. Normandy American Cemetery and Memorial ★★★★★

Off D514 (follow signs to American Cemetery) in Colleville-sur-Mer
T: 703-696-6897 (Arlington, Virginia)
Daily, 8 a.m.-6 p.m., April 16-September 30
Daily, 8 a.m.-5 p.m., October 1-April 15

Covering 172.5 acres of beautifully manicured ground—workers spend early hours scrubbing the 9,387 headstones—this breathtaking cemetery is the second-most-visited attraction in Normandy (behind Mont St-Michel). Even for those familiar with the Normandy battle and its remorseless statistics, the seemingly endless rows of perfectly aligned white marble crosses and Stars of David—laid out in the form of a Latin cross—come as shocking testimony to the carnage American men suffered here. At the head of the long, narrow field is a reflecting pool and memorial, a semicircular colonnade with huge battle maps at each end of a 22-foot bronze sculpture titled "The Spirit of American Youth Rising from the Waves." The maps and lengthy accompanying text describe Allied landings in Normandy and the subsequent drive across western Europe. Behind the memorial, 1,557 names are inscribed on stone tablets in the Garden of the Missing. Nearby, an observation deck and orientation table overlook Omaha Beach. Opposite the memorial are a pair of flagpoles—the Stars and Stripes fly every day on this land given to the United States by France. On a cliff overlooking the ocean—U.S. forces captured these heights late on June 6—the cemetery is framed by heavy Austrian pine, Whitebeam, Russian olive, Japanese rose, French tamarisk, elm, cypress and other trees and plants. Visitors enter the site via a 10,000-square-foot visitor center. Opened in 2007 and built largely underground, the impressive center has displays of weaponry, artifacts, photos and video. As at all American Battle Monuments Commission cemeteries, this sad yet beautiful site invariably summons in visitors a mood of somber reflection. For Americans, it's the centerpiece of all Normandy war sites.

21. U.S. 1st Division Monument/Omaha Beach ★★★★★

Off D514, just below cemetery. From Point 20 parking lot, rejoin D514 east. After just less than 1 km turn left at sign for Plage d'Omaha and continue downhill. After 1.5 km, the right fork leads to beach parking, the left fork leads uphill to the monument (follow signs for Monument de la 1ère Division).

Though the dominant landmark is a 25-foot stone pillar commemorating the famed "Big Red One" U.S. 1st Infantry Division—soldiers waded ashore directly in front of the pillar—there's plenty more to see. Next to the monument are accessible German bunkers. Down the hill the Fifth Engineers monument sits atop another bunker. To the east one can see Port-en-Bessin, the demarcation point between British and American beaches, and to the west, the expanse of Omaha Beach. Walking amid the concrete ruins of German defense works, one gets a clear sense of the superior German positions and incomprehensible task facing their attackers. An NTL totem in the parking lot recalls the struggle: "As soon as landing ramps were lowered men were greeted by murderous fire ... 'Two kinds of people are staying on this beach, the dead and those who are going to die. Now let's get the hell out of here!' This cry from Colonel Taylor sums up the situation." From here it's possible to walk (or drive) to the shore, walk the beach, perhaps wade into the water to face the German-held beach with the same view assault troops had on June 6.

The west-to-east tour of D-Day beaches and battlefields continues with Point of Interest 1 in the Normandy II chapter.

RELATED SITES BEYOND UTAH AND OMAHA

Cherbourg

Fort du Roule Liberation Museum (Musée de la Libération) ★★★

Fort du Roule, Cherbourg, 30 km northwest of Ste-Mère-Église
T: (0)2-33-20-1412
Daily, 10 a.m.-noon, 2-6 p.m., May-September
Closed Sunday and Monday mornings
Wednesday-Sunday, 2-6 p.m., October-April

Though not part of the June 6 D-Day assault, the large port at Cherbourg (population 25,000), on the western tip of the Cotentin Peninsula, was vital to the success of Operation Overlord. In addition to being an off-loading port for troops and supplies, Cherbourg was significant as the terminus of PLUTO, the Pipeline Under the Ocean that brought vital fuel to advancing Allied armies. Actually four pipelines, PLUTO ran from Britain via the Isle of Wight to Cherbourg, which was captured by American troops on June 30 after harsh combat. In a fortress built by Napoleon III and captured in 1940 by German General Erwin Rommel, the excellent museum has flags, photos, weapons, uniforms (many donated by U.S. veterans) and audiovisual displays recounting the German occupation, 1944 liberation and role of the sea and navies in wartime.

Dead Man's Corner Museum ★★★

2 Village de l'Amont, Saint-Côme-du-Mont, between Carentan and Houseville, just west of E46 (Cherbourg-Paris highway)
T: (0)2-33-42-0042
Daily, 10 a.m.-6 p.m. Closed Sundays in September-May and closed December 23-January 2

In the early morning of June 6, 1944, paratroopers of the 101st Airborne Division became the first Allied soldiers to touch French soil. A vital intersection in the town of St. Côme-du-Mont was defended by a crack German unit. Here, the 101st was committed in the first large-scale attack launched during the invasion. The intersection later became known as "Dead Man's Corner." A house at the intersection served as Allied head-quarters and aid station. The moving museum is located inside the house. With an impressive collection of German and American airborne artifacts, it's the initial entry in the ambitious Carentan Historical Center system. Three more WWII museums are planned. Updates can be found at www.paratrooper-museum.org.

OTHER AREA ATTRACTIONS

Bayeux Tapestry

At Musée de la Tapisserie de Bayeux
Rue de Nesmond, Bayeux
T: (0)2-31-51-2550
Dating to 1077, the 230-foot-long stitched fabric chronicles the story of William the Conqueror's 1066 victory at the Battle of Hastings and Norman conquest of England that changed the course of world history. The 58 panels illustrate everything from major historical figures to common household items of the day. On display in its home of Bayeux, the price-less tapestry was taken to the secure environs of Le Mans before June 1944.

Étretat

A staple of French postcards, the rippled white cliffs that plunge into the surf at Étretat are one of the country's most famed landmarks. About 85 km east of Caen (on D940), tiny Étretat (population 1,600) is jammed with tourists on summer weekends. At any other time, it's certainly worth an afternoon trip.

GETTING TO AND AROUND NORMANDY

From many U.S., Canadian and European cities, dozens of airlines fly nonstop to Paris' Roissy-Charles-de-Gaulle Airport (page 126). Continental (800-231-0856), American (800-433-7300) and Delta (800-241-4141) are among airlines that offer nonstop flights from the United States.

Normandy cities can be reached via a one-to-two-hour train ride from Paris. Visit France's national railway website, www.sncf.com for schedules and information. SNCF reservations assistance and telephone information in English is available at (0)8-36-35-3539. Trains can be booked from the United States through RailEurope (800-782-2424, or at www.raileurope.com).

Unless you travel with an organized tour, a car is essential for touring the beaches and battlefields. The D-Day invasion beaches are two to three driving hours from Paris (see Driving, page xv). Most major roads head toward the hub of Caen. The countryside has a network of good two-lane roads. Beyond larger population centers (notably Caen and Bayeux, where summer parking can be quite aggravating), getting around is easy and parking isn't a problem. The essential road map is Michelin's "Battle of Normandy" (Michelin map Number 102), available in larger U.S. bookstores and on the internet. Once in Normandy, a number of D-Day and/or Battle of Normandy maps are available at most museums. These have less road detail, but are easier to read. A good choice is the "Historic Map of D-Day and the Battle of Normandy" published by France-based OREP (info@orep-pub.com). Running east-west along the coast, Route

D514 skirts four of the five invasion beaches (D421 parallels Utah Beach) and many of the attractions listed here.

Normandy has enough World War II history and points of interest to fill an entire book and, indeed, several guides devoted solely to the region are available. The authoritative and exhaustive guidebook to war sites is the U.K.-published Major and Mrs Holt's Battlefield Guide: Normandy Landing Beaches. It's jammed with historic background, battle minutiae and directions to the smallest of markers and memorials. Overwhelming in detail for the casual visitor, it's an invaluable guide for many others. Lonely Planet's Normandy isn't satisfactory for those interested in World War II, but,

with many maps of small towns and insightful cultural notes, it's the best general guide to the area.

Guided tours of D-Day beaches and Normandy battlefields are widely available. California-based Valor Tours (800-842-4504 or 415-332-7850; www.valortours.com) runs an excellent, longstanding "D-Day Normandy Invasion" tour (as well as other highly recommended tours of World War II sites across Europe and the Pacific). In Normandy, Battlebus (02-31-22-2882, www.battlebus.fr) and D-Day Tours (02-31-51-7052, or at www.normandywebguide.com) offer half- and full-day tours with English-speaking guides.

ACCOMMODATIONS

Port-en-Bessin

Hotel-Restaurant Mercure Bayeux-Omaha Beach

Chemin du Colombier
T: (0)2-31-22-4444 F: (0)2-31-22-3677
www.mercure.com
70 rooms
From €115

For those wanting to stay near the beach, this relatively upscale resort (with golf course, pool, workout room) is the best choice. Five km from the Normandy American Cemetery and Memorial, it is central to American and British and Canadian beaches. Only 27 of the chain-hotel–style rooms are air-conditioned—request one in summer.

Commes

Château du Bosq

Off D514
T: (0)2-31-92-5277 F: (0)2-31-92-2671
www.chateau-du-bosq.com
12 rooms
€30-80

Though creaky and frayed at the edges, the château gives budget travelers a chance to escape cramped hotel rooms for a country estate. The property is near the beach, between Port-en-Bessin and

Arromanches. The €80 rooms have private baths.

Ste-Mère-Église

Hôtel du 6 Juin

11 rue des Clarons
T: (0)33-21-0718 F: (0)2-33-21-3755
www.hotel-du-6-juin.com
8 rooms
€49

A converted house; all rooms at this two-star, family-run hotel have private bathrooms, phone and TV. It's all very simple, but clean. Free parking is a plus in Ste-Mère-Église, which gets crowded in summer.

Ste-Marie-du-Mont

Le Grand Hard

La Rivière
T: (0)2-33-71-2574 F: (0)2-33-71-0280
www.le-grand-hard.club.fr
14 rooms
€70-130

Individually decorated rooms at this stylish inn are spacious and modern. The salon and outdoor dining area should please anyone looking for a French country experience, but the hotel is largely recommended for those wanting quick access to Utah Beach.

Normandy II

Gold · Juno · Sword

FRANCE

Montgomery Statue

THE WAR YEARS

The decades since the June 6, 1944, invasion of Normandy have given rise to a fallacy that "Bloody Omaha" was alone among the five D-Day beaches in presenting the Allies with any genuine difficulty. The notion betrays a perhaps understandable prejudice—without doubt Omaha attackers faced the fiercest German defense on D-Day and sustained the most casualties. But it would be absurd to presume anything other than that, as one historian has written, "there were moments of violent intensity and horror on the British beaches as shattering as anything that happened on Omaha." If German soldiers weren't as heavily entrenched at Gold, Juno and Sword—the British, Canadian, British beaches, respectively—they were every bit as determined to prevent the Allies from piercing Fortress Europe in their sector. The attackers themselves fought just as valiantly, though perhaps with different motivations.

"For the British people far more than for the Americans, the invasion represented a rebirth, a return, a reversal of all the humiliations and defeats that they had endured since 1939," wrote British journalist Max Hastings. Though American General Dwight Eisenhower was named Supreme Commander of Allied Forces, each of his three primary subordinates—in charge of all land, sea and air operations—were British. "This was the final occasion of the war on which British officers achieved such a measure of authority over Americans, and Americans bowed to British experience," wrote Hastings.

Commanded by General Bernard Montgomery, the firebrand son of a clergyman and Britain's most talented general, the British-Canadian land invasion began with a daring midnight airborne operation. About 8,000 British 6th Airborne Division troops descended in the darkness just beyond Sword Beach, securing the easternmost flank of the Normandy battlefield and seizing two bridges. The capture of Pegasus Bridge over the Orne Canal went particularly smoothly, with glider-borne "Red Berets"—lead by Major John Howard the "Ox and Bucks" (Oxford and Buckinghamshire Regiment)—landing within 50 yards of the target. In short order, 180 commandos earned the first Allied victory in German-occupied France, taking the critical bridge with little difficulty. "Pegasus" remains among the most perfectly executed airborne operations in history.

Suffering intense distress on rough seaborne approaches—ships tossed like corks, men violently ill, landing craft exploded by submerged mines—British and Canadian troops stormed the beaches at approximately 7:30 a.m. Some units rushed across the shore unscathed. Unlucky others absorbed crushing losses. Sword Beach was the "easiest," and though it lacked the carnage of Gold and Juno, its forces were stopped by determined resistance well short of their Day One objective of Caen. Behind Gold Beach, British troops fought through torrid defense, reaching Bayeux on June 7, making it the first French city to be liberated. Of approximately 60,000 British troops who landed on D-Day, 3,000 were killed, wounded or missing.

The Allied force that achieved the most substantial measure of its first-day objectives was the 3rd Canadian Division—15,000 Canadians, augmented by British, Belgian, Dutch and Polish troops. Despite losing 20 of 24 initial-wave landing craft along four-mile Juno Beach (one company of 175 men was abruptly cut down to 26), the Canadians rallied against second-tier German defenders—"Not the physical equivalents of the magnificent young Canadians," wrote historian John Keegan—to secure the beach within two hours. Canadian teams pushed seven miles inland to the Caen-Bayeux railway line. Canada suffered 1,000 casualties on D-Day, including 335 dead, but won an important victory. "Nothing in the day's news brought as much satisfaction as the account of the Canadian landing," wrote Keegan. "At the end of the day its forward elements stood deeper into France than those of any other division."

If a single feature distinguished British beaches, it was the presence of ingenious if not quirky British technology mostly eschewed by the Americans. Under Major-General Percy Hobart, British engineers modified a number of vehicles to facilitate the landings. "Hobart's Funnies" included Crocodiles (flamethrowing tanks), DD or duplex-drive tanks (propellers and flotation screens got them from sea to shore) and Crabs (tanks equipped with rotating drums and flailing chains to detonate mines). These strange vehicles well assisted the successful advance of British and Canadian forces, but the most important British development was the Mulberry Harbor, enormous modular pieces floated across the English Channel which, when connected, served as a massive, temporary port. "The Mulberries were the most fantastic plan of its kind ever used in warfare," wrote American historian Louis Snyder. Two Mulberries were constructed. The first, at Omaha, was destroyed in a terrific storm in mid-June, but the second, at Arromanches near Gold, remained intact. By month's end, more than half a million troops and countless tons of supplies had passed over the port and onto the beaches. The outcome of the Battle of Normandy depended largely upon which side could resupply faster. In this endeavor, the importance of the Mulberry Harbor at Arromanches was irrefutable.

From 156,00 attackers, Allied D-Day casualties on all five beaches were 10,724, with 2,132 killed. Though initial German response to the invasion was confused—German General Erwin Rommel, in charge of French coastal defense, was at his home in Germany on June 6—defenses were quickly reorganized. The Allies' anticipated rapid advance inland proved optimistic—front lines remained largely stagnant for almost two months—but by June 30, 850,279 men, 148,803 vehicles and 570,505 tons of supplies had landed in Normandy. Bitter combat lay ahead, but after years of unimpeded domination of western Europe, the Third Reich was in mortal peril for the first time. Declaring Normandy "not the end, but the beginning of the end," British Prime Minister Winston Churchill put words to a euphoria that swept across a continent finally united in the belief that nearly a half decade of Nazi rule soon would be put to an end.

SOURCES & OTHER READING

Six Armies in Normandy: From D-Day to the Liberation of Paris, Keegan, John, Jonathan Cape, 1982

D-Day: The Greatest Invasion—A People's History, Van Der Vat, Dan, Bloomsbury, 2003

June 6, 1944: The Voices of D-Day, Astor, Gerald, St. Martin's Press, 1994

D-Day 1944 (3) Sword Beach and British Airborne Landings, Ford and Gerrard, Osprey Publishing, 2002

D-Day 1944 (4) Gold and Juno Beaches, Ford and Lyles, Osprey Publishing, 2002

Overlord: D-Day, June 6, 1944, Hastings, Max, Michael Joseph, 1984

Marching as to War: Canada's Turbulent Years 1899-1953, Berton, Pierre, Anchor Canada, 2002

Major and Mrs Holt's Battlefield Guide to the Normandy Landing Beaches, Holt and Holt, Leo Cooper, 2001 (revised)

D-DAY INVASION BEACHES

UTAH

OMAHA GOLD JUNO SWORD

BAYEUX

CAEN

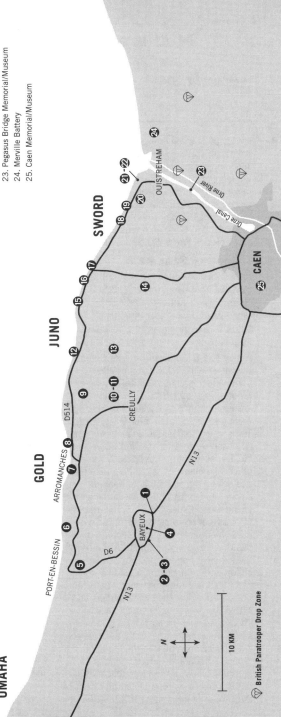

Normandy II

1. Eisenhower Statue
2. Bayeux Memorial Museum
3. Bayeux War Cemetery
4. De Gaulle Memorial and Museum
5. Museum of Underwater Wrecks
6. Longues Battery
7. Arromanches/D-Day Museum/Mulberry Harbor
8. 360° Cinema/Gold Beach Orientation Table
9. America/Gold Beach Museum
10. Green Howards Monument
11. Montgomery Headquarters
12. Juno Beach Memorial/Tank
13. Canadian War Cemetery
14. Radar Museum
15. Juno Beach at Bernières
16. Juno Beach at St. Aubin
17. Juno Beach at Langrune-sur-Mer
18. Sword Beach at Lion-sur-Mer
19. Sword Beach at Hermanville
20. Montgomery Statue/Sword Beach
21. No. 4 Commando Museum/Sword Beach
22. Atlantic Wall Museum/Sword Beach
23. Pegasus Bridge Memorial/Museum
24. Merville Battery
25. Caen Memorial/Museum

OMAHA

PORT-EN-BESSIN

GOLD

ARROMANCHES

D514

JUNO

CREULLY

SWORD

OUISTREHAM

Orne Canal

Orne River

BAYEUX

N13

D6

N13

CAEN

N

10 KM

British Paratrooper Drop Zone

NORMANDY TODAY

See Normandy I, page 4.

POINTS OF INTEREST

Hundreds of small markers and historic points are scattered throughout the Gold, Juno and Sword area. This chapter presents the highlights on a route that travels past many roadside monuments. Driving distances are approximate. Some might wish to begin the itinerary with the Caen Memorial and Museum (Point 25), which chronicles all World War II, not just D-Day.

1. Eisenhower Statue ★★★

Eisenhower Roundabout, east end of Bayeux. From Caen, follow N13 to Bayeux, taking Bayeux exit onto D613 and roundabout. From other directions, follow Bayeux ring road to Eisenhower Roundabout.

A nine-foot-tall bronze statue of General Dwight Eisenhower, Supreme Allied Commander, stands resolutely in the center of a large traffic roundabout at the eastern entrance of Bayeux, the first French town liberated after D-Day. Born in Texas, raised in Kansas, Eisenhower was an obscure figure for the first 50 years of his life, even within the Army. A career officer, he made an astounding meteoric rise during the war, from lieutenant-colonel in 1941 to Supreme Commander of the Allied Expeditionary Force in 1944, in charge of the most powerful force ever assembled under one man. Among qualities that made him the natural choice for the job were imperturbability, public charm and an uncommon political touch that smoothed the often-contentious relations among rival field commanders and within the Anglo-American alliance. Though he likely never fired a shot in anger, by war's end he was a five-star general and genuine hero in the United States, Britain and Europe. Courted by both the Democrat and Republican parties, he served as Republican president of the United States from 1953 to 1961.

2. Bayeux Memorial Museum (Musée Mémorial de la Bataille Normandie) ★★★★

Boulevard Fabian Ware, Bayeux
T: (0)2-31-51-4690
Daily, 9:30 a.m.-6:30 p.m.,
May 1-September 14
Daily, 10 a.m.-12:30 p.m., 2-6 p.m.,
September 15-April 30
Closed January 1, last two weeks of January, December 25. Closed mornings of January 2, December 26
Adult: €6.50; Military/Senior: €3.80; Student/Child: €3.80; WWII Veteran: Free

With separate galleries dedicated to Americans, British, Canadians and Germans, this 24,000-square-foot museum covers the entire 77-day Battle of Normandy. Photos, newspapers, more than 100 uniforms, personal items—everything here is presented in modern, professional fashion (with English signage). Highlights include numerous restored vehicles from both sides of the battle—a rare self-propelled Sexton gun used by the 1st Polish Armed Division, U.S. half-track, Daimler "Dingo" armored car, monstrous 1944 Caterpillar bulldozer and much more. This is the finest museum devoted to the Normandy campaign. A two-hour visit is recommended, including time for the excellent 30-minute film that shows in English five times daily—10:30 a.m., noon, 2 p.m., 3:30 p.m., 5 p.m.

3. Bayeux War Cemetery ★★★★

On D572, 200 yards west of Point 2 (easiest to walk from Point 2)

Containing 4,648 graves (3,935 from the United Kingdom), this immaculate site is the largest British World War II cemetery in France. Across the street is the Bayeux Memorial to the Missing with No Known Graves. It's inscribed with 1,805 names of Commonwealth soldiers, all of whom likely perished in the Battle of Normandy.

4. De Gaulle Memorial and Museum ★

10 rue Bourbesneur, at Place de Gaulle, Bayeux. From Point 2, return to Eisenhower Roundabout, proceed toward Centre Ville, fork right toward Office de Tourisme. Park near tourist office (1.5 km from Eisenhower Roundabout) and get city map. Memorial and Museum is about six blocks away, off Rue St-Loup. Walking through town not only eliminates driving and parking hassles amid the narrow streets of Bayeux, it takes the visitor through a historic town that escaped wartime destruction.

T: (0)2-31-92-4555
Daily, 9:30 a.m.-12:30 p.m., 2-6:30 p.m., June-August; Daily, 10 a.m.-12:30 p.m., 2-6:30 p.m., March-May and September-November
Closed December-February
Adult: €3.50; Student/Child: €2

This small museum is dedicated to the famous speech General Charles de Gaulle delivered upon his June 14, 1944, return to France after exile in England: "We will all, together, overwhelmed with emotion, feeling joy, pride and hope in our nation, climb out of the abyss we have known." A collection of de Gaulle's personal items is displayed. France's great 20th-century soldier, patriot and statesman, de Gaulle became president of France in 1959 and served for 10 years. The government of liberated France was installed inside this Renaissance building.

5. Museum of Underwater Wrecks (Musée des Épaves Sous-Marines du Débarquement) ★★

On D6, 1 km south of Port-en-Bessin. From Point 4, follow signs toward Port-en-Bessin/D6.
T: (0) 2-31-21-1706
Daily, 10 a.m.-noon, 2-6 p.m., June-September
Adult: €6; Student/Child: €3

This small, private museum has a unique assortment of rusted war materials salvaged by divers off the Normandy coast. The most interesting pieces are in the yard outside.

Items include a P-38 Lightning aircraft engine, German torpedoes and mines and, most exceptionally, an intact Sherman DD or duplex-drive floating tank with twin propellers still attached. Of 32 such tanks launched at Omaha Beach, only two operational "Donald Duck" tanks reached the beach. The rest sunk quickly with their crews inside or were otherwise disabled.

6. Longues Battery (Batteries de Longues) ★★★★

Off D514 in Longues-sur-Mer. From Point 5, proceed north on D6 to General Montgomery/PLUTO Roundabout—the spherical sculpture represents the undersea world, the pillars represent the remarkable Pipeline Under the Ocean (PLUTO) that brought fuel via Cherbourg to the Allied armies. Veer right on D6a toward Toutes Direction and Office de Tourisme. Veer onto D514 toward Arromanches then Longues s/Mer and proceed 0.8 km on side road to battery.

A threat to Gold and Omaha landings, the four heavy German guns installed here had a range of more than 12 miles. Guns from the battery exchanged fire with at least five ships on June 6 before being knocked out. On June 7, British troops took its 120-man garrison prisoner and occupied the battery. Today, all four well-preserved casemates are accessible. Three contain the original guns. From the tops of the bunkers and separate commandant's post, the visitor gets unrestricted views of approaching sea lanes, a good place to imagine the colossal invasion armada that stunned German observers. This is one of Normandy's best existing relics from the war.

7. Arromanches/D-Day Landings Museum/Mulberry Harbor (Musée du Débarquement) ★★★★★

Place du 6 Juin, Arromanches (also Arromanches-les-Bains). On D514 (follow signs to Musée du Débarquement), 7 km east of Point 6.
T: (0)2-31-22-3431
Daily, 9 a.m.-7 p.m., May-September (closed 6 p.m. in September)
Daily, 10 a.m.-12:30 p.m., 1:30-5 p.m.,

February, November, December
Daily, 9:30 a.m.-12:30 p.m., 1:30-5:30
p.m., March, October
9 a.m.-6 p.m., Easter weekend
Open 10 a.m. Sundays, excepting
June-August (9 a.m.)
Last entry 30 minutes before close
Closed January, December 24, 25, 31
Adult: €6.50; Child: €4.50; beach access
free, charge for museum only

With large-scale models, dioramas, photos, and other displays, the museum presents a thorough examination of the Mulberry Harbor for which Arromanches gained fame. The "artificial harbor" concept is often credited to Winston Churchill, who ordered its development after the Allies' disastrous amphibious assault at Dieppe in 1942. This Mulberry was as large as the permanent harbor at Dover, England. Each structural component was constructed in England, towed across the English Channel in sections and assembled here with what can only be described as technical genius. Up to 40 ships could unload simultaneously, moving a daily average of 7,000 tons of goods into France. The "Mulberry" designation was meaningless— a random code word assigned to the project. Intended to last 100 days, large pieces of the harbor can still be seen on the beach in front of the museum. The museum also has uniforms, vehicles, bombs, mines, a large Bofors gun and a short film on the conception, achievement, transport and use of the Mulberry Harbor. Rimmed by sheer bluffs, the pretty beach and town make Arromanches one of the more picturesque spots on the coast. British forces landed just east of the museum and captured the town not via frontal sea assault but from the hills to the east.

8. 360° Cinema and Gold Beach Orientation Table ★★★★

On D514 in St-Côme, 1 km east of Point 7
T: (0)2-31-22-3030
20-minute movie begins 10 and 40 minutes after each hour, generally from 10 a.m. to 5, 6 or 6:40 p.m. (depending on season)
Closed in January
Adult: €4; Child: €3.50; World War II
Veteran: Free
No charge for roadside Orientation Table

An unabashed tourist attraction, the 360° Cinema—projected onto a circular screen—is nevertheless a very good one. There's no narration to the 20-minute film, *The Price of Freedom*—only somber music and battle sounds accompany a whirl of moving images from 1944 combat on all Normandy fronts to present-day peace. Included is rare war correspondents' footage and aerial shots of important D-Day locations. The film ends with a stunning flight over the seemingly endless rows of marble crosses at the Normandy American Cemetery and Memorial at Omaha Beach. Violent in spots, the film is tasteful and very well produced, a good way to mix up activities on a D-Day circuit. It's not necessary to buy a ticket to climb the small rise next to the theater for a look at the orientation platform, which offers panoramic views over Gold and Juno beaches, with detailed maps showing the locations of landings and combat. British commandos came ashore just below this spot. Troop memorials and German bunkers are located nearby. It's a fantastic place to get an unobstructed view of the battlefield.

9. America/Gold Beach Museum (America/Gold Beach Musée) ★

2 Place Admiral Byrd in Ver-sur-Mer. From Point 8, follow D514 east 7 km, turning right at signs for Green Howards Memorial and Crepon, then following signs for Musée.
T: (0)2-31-22-5858
Daily, 10:30 a.m.-1:30 p.m., 2:30-5:30 p.m., May-October (closed Tuesdays in May, June, September, October)
Closed all other months
Adult: €4; Child: €2.40

The name of this museum can be misleading. Most of the compact display is dedicated to the first transatlantic airmail flight between France and New York in 1927. Because Paris was fogged in, the flight landed in Ver-sur-Mer. That's the "America" part. The sparse Gold Beach section has a small collection of artifacts, photos and text related to D-Day.

10. Green Howards Monument ★★★

Off D65 in Crepon, about 0.5 km beyond Crepon roundabout. From D54 or D112 follow signs for Green Howards War Memorial.

Of the many small-unit memorials in Normandy, this larger-than-life bronze sculpture of a contemplative soldier at rest, hand on knee, propping up his rifle, is one of the more dramatic. It commemorates the storied Green Howards Regiment—participants in most major British campaigns and wars since the 17th century—which landed with the first assault wave on Gold Beach. By nightfall they'd fought to the villages of Crepon and Creully, among the farthest points of Day One Allied advance.

11. Montgomery Headquarters (Château de Creullet) ★

Off D65, 300 yards northwest of Point 10

Heading toward the coast from Point 10, the large building on the left side of the road (on the north side of a small bridge) is the Creullet Château. Here British Field Marshal Bernard Montgomery—in command of all Allied land forces on D-Day—set up tactical headquarters on June 9, 1944. Winston Churchill met here with Montgomery on June 12. Charles de Gaulle came on June 14. Monty stayed until June 22, when he moved to Blay, 10 km west of Bayeux. A monument near the intersection of D96 and D206 marks the location of his Blay headquarters.

12. Juno Beach Memorial/Churchill Tank ★★★★★

Off D514 in Graye-sur-Mer (follow signs to Juno Beach Memorial), 11 km from Point 8

A 12-foot-tall stone pillar on the beach marks this as the place where "On the 6th June 1944 Europe was liberated by the heroism of the Allied forces." A formidable network of bunkers, machine-gun nests, flamethrowers, mines and booby traps greeted attackers along this section of beach. On D-Day, it was stormed by, among others, Canada's Royal Winnipeg Rifles, which suffered 128 casualties, placing it among the hardest-hit Canadian regiments on D-Day. Today, it's a popular beach for swimmers and sunbathers and is easily accessed from the parking lot. A small rise of dunes behind the beach gives a good sense of the defenders' strong positions. Near the line of Canadian and French flags is the hulking remain of a German bunker, overtaken on June 6. The nearby Churchill tank has never left the beach. It was originally stopped about 100 yards from its present position. A plaque tells the story of its crew, some of whom survived the battle, some of whom didn't. Also nearby is an NTL (Normandie Terre-Liberté) interpretive totem—the blue and white markers emblazoned with a dove logo and explanatory text are found throughout Normandy—and massive Cross of Lorraine, symbol of the French Resistance. Churchill came ashore here on June 12. This is also the spot where Charles de Gaulle first returned to French soil.

13. Canadian War Cemetery ★★★★

On D35 in Bény (also Bény-sur-Mer), 1 km west of intersection with D79. About 5 km south of Point 12.

Aligned in perfect rows, the white headstones with raised maple leaves are surrounded by trees, a chapel and an elegant memorial cross and landscaping typical of Commonwealth War Graves Commission cemeteries. Of the 2,049 graves, 2,044 are Canadian. Many of those buried here were killed on D-Day. Nearby is a plaque dedicated to the Regina Rifle Regiment.

14. Radar Museum (Musée Radar de Douvres) ★★

Off D83 just south of Douvres (also Douvres-la-Délivrande), 5.5 km southeast of Point 13. From D404 (heading south from coast) follow signs for Musée Radar de Douvres. Note: An alternate route to the museum is signposted near Point 18 at intersection of D514 and D221.
T: (0)2-31-37-7443
Tuesday-Sunday, 10 a.m.-6 p.m., June 15-September 15 (last admission 5:30 p.m.)
Open select weekends in May, June
Adult: €5.50; Child (10-18): €5

This important German radar station, manned by a crew of 200, wasn't captured until June 17. The position, relatively near the shore, indicates just how slow and difficult Allied progress was after the successful D-Day landings. Housed within a pair of large bunkers, the museum traces the history of radar. The highlight is a large Würzburg-Riese radar dish, a well-preserved battlefield relic.

15. Juno Beach at Bernières ★★★

On D514 in Bernières, 5 km from Point 12

Along the beach are Allied flags, various monuments to Canadian soldiers and a house "liberated at first light on D-Day" by Canadian troops. Down the beach 200 yards is a German bunker crowned by Allied flags. A bronze maple leaf commemorates 800 men of the Queen's Own Rifles who rushed ashore and, at great cost, overwhelmed the lethal bunker. There's also a plaque honoring the 8th Brigade 3rd Canadian Infantry with a map showing progress from Normandy through European operations, including the Rhineland campaign of 1945.

16. Juno Beach at St. Aubin ★★★

On D514, 2 km east of Point 15

A line of Allied flags, an NTL totem and a German bunker stand at the site where several hours of particularly chaotic D-Day combat took place. Survivors recall the hellish scene of the beach here, covered by a smoky haze, littered with dismembered corpses and wrecked equipment. The 48th Royal Marine Commandos were among groups who stormed the rocky "awkward beach" (according to signage). Other memorials are dedicated to soldiers of the Fort Garry Horse, North Shore Regiment, other combat units and civilians killed or wounded on D-Day.

17. Juno Beach at Langrune-sur-Mer ★★★

On D514, 2 km east of Point 16

Allied flags and a stone memorial mark the scene of an unsuccessful June 6 assault by the 48th Royal Marine Commandos, who suffered violent losses while trying to break through machine-gun positions in an effort to bridge the gap between Juno and Sword beaches. The 48th sustained 100 casualties—half its attacking force—in hand-to-hand fighting.

Tanks broke up the German position on June 7.

18. Sword Beach at Lion-sur-Mer ★★★★

On D514, 4 km east of Point 17

At this western end of Sword, British commandos faced determined German defenders, who held out until June 7. The site where commandos pushed ashore under heavy mortar and artillery fire is marked by a well-preserved Churchill tank, a large sun-dial monument and a plaque inscribed with President Franklin Roosevelt's four essential freedoms—freedom of speech and worship, freedom from want and fear. The town square was renamed Place du No. 41 Commando in honor of the liberators.

19. Sword Beach at Hermanville ★★★★

Just off D514, 2 km east of Point 18. Proceeding east from Point 18, turn left in front of red British telephone box, continue straight 0.3 km to tank on roadside.

An NTL totem and a Churchill tank stand at the approximate center of Sword Beach, which runs about 1.5 miles in either direction. This lightly mined beach was subjected to the heaviest pre-landing bombardment of any invasion beach. The attack on stunned German defenders was assisted by 21 DD Sherman tanks. Within two hours, most of the beach was cleared and forces were advancing toward their Day One objective of Caen (which wouldn't be captured until July 9). The beach is long, sandy and popular with summer tourists. It's easily accessible and can be walked without difficulty. On the beach a marble monument has been erected in memory of the Royal, Merchant and Allied Navy men who fought in Normandy.

20. Montgomery Statue/Sword Beach ★★★

Off D514 in Colleville-Montgomery, 1.5 km east of Point 19. At traffic light at Colleville-Montgomery Plage, turn right on D60a, proceed to square.

With the Union Jack flying overhead and "Monty" carved into the base, this bronze statue of the famed British commander was dedicated in 1996. Of major Allied figures, Montgomery has the legacy that is perhaps the most difficult to sort out. Openly criticized if not despised by a number of American peers and rivals—notably General George Patton—the 56-year-old (during the Normandy campaign) Montgomery was an insatiable glory hound (though no more so than Patton), often as not criticized by historians, both American and British. But he was highly respected by German General Erwin Rommel—whom he defeated in North Africa, giving the Allies their first significant land victory of the war—and beloved by those who fought under him. Montgomery had his failures, but the source of much criticism leveled at him was simply a matter of philosophical differences. Noted for his work on *The World at War* BBC documentary series, historian Mark Arnold-Forster offers the best summary of the rub: "Most American generals believed that in most military situations the right time to attack was always and that the right place to attack was everywhere. Montgomery's general belief was more subtle. He was a consistent seeker-out of weak places in the enemy line. If no weak place existed Montgomery would try to create one. Time and again he would tempt his opponent to reinforce one part of his line at the expense of another. Montgomery would then attack the weaker part." The method was effective, but could seem maddeningly slow to observers. Nevertheless, Monty carried on, certain of his tactics. He's now undeniably among the first rank of British military heroes. Behind the statue, the road provides access to Sword Beach, where markers recall the first British graves in Normandy, British commando efforts and Colleville-sur-Mer's decision to adopt the name Colleville-Montgomery.

21. No. 4 Commando Museum/Sword Beach (Musée No. 4 Commando) ★★★

Place Alfred Thomas (across from casino) in Ouistreham, 2 km east of Point 20. In Ouistreham, turn left on Boulevard Winston Churchill, right at sign for Musée de Débarquement Sword and go 0.3 km.
T: (0)2-31-96-6310
Daily, 10:30 a.m.-6 p.m., mid-March-mid-October

Adult: €4; Student/Child: €2.30; Under 10: Free

This small museum recounts the story of the first British commandos to reach Sword Beach, intent on destroying the area's formidable defenses (Point 22) and (successfully) relieving the paratroopers who'd captured Pegasus Bridge. Among these commandos were the only French soldiers who participated in the first wave of D-Day assaults to liberate France. Exhibits include an interesting scale model of the attack, uniforms, maps, photos, personal items, berets and other items unique to commandos. One of Sword's enduring legends was born here when Brigadier Lord Lovat of the 1st Special Service (Commando) Brigade ordered Pipe Major William Millin to play his bagpipes even as German machine guns rattled, tanks burned and men crouched for cover on the beach. Millin played "Highland Laddie" and "The Road to the Isles," though not to everyone's satisfaction. "What the hell are you playing at, you mad bastard?" shrieked one airborne sergeant. "Every German in France knows we're here now!" Millin's bagpipes can be seen in the museum at Point 23. Despite the "easy" conquest of Sword, the terrain was hellish on the exposed No. 4 Commandos, who quickly took 40 casualties. Across the street, the battle at the casino—used as a German machine-gun position and captured by the British—was depicted in 1962's *The Longest Day* (as was Millin's piping).

22. Atlantic Wall Museum/Sword Beach (Le Grand Bunker Musée Le Mur de l'Atlantique) ★★★★★

Avenue du 6 Juin in Ouistreham, 0.5 km east of Point 21
T: (0)2-31-97-2869
Daily, 10 a.m.-6 p.m., February 1-November 15 (9 a.m.-7 p.m., April-September)
Closed November 16-January 31
Adult: €6.50; Child (6-12): €4.50

This 52-foot-high bunker is among Normandy's few major German defense installations left almost entirely intact. The massive, reinforced concrete walls were built to withstand even the most punishing assault. The nerve center of area defenses, it was attacked on June 6 by British and French forces, who were quickly repelled by machine-gun fire. It was finally captured on June 9 when four British engineers blew open the armored door—a job that took four hours—and accepted the surrender of the 52 besieged Germans inside. Now a museum, it has exhibits located in various rooms—generator room, gas filters room, ammo dump, radio room, and so on—but the point is simply to climb the cramped stairs and ladders through this massive tower. The observation post on the top floor overlooks the epic sweep of Sword Beach and the English Channel. Perhaps more than at any other place in Normandy, a visit here reinforces the scale and seeming insurmountability of the task that faced Allied troops on June 6, 1944.

23. Pegasus Bridge Memorial/Museum of British Airborne Troops (Musée des Troupes Aeroportes Britanniques) ★★★★

Avenue du Major Howard in Ranville. Off D514 (follow signs for Memorial Pegasus), 7 km south of Point 22.
T: (0)2-31-78-1944
Daily, 9:30 a.m.-6:30 p.m., May-September
Daily, 10 a.m.-1 p.m., 2-5 p.m., February-April, October-November
Closed all other months
Adult: €5; Student/Child: €3.50

The first important D-Day engagement took place at this crossing of the Orne Canal, where British commandos were to capture and hold a vital bridgehead at the eastern extreme of the D-Day invasion. (From here, Utah Beach is 47 miles away.) Just after midnight on June 6, gliders landed and 6th British Airborne Division soldiers seized the now-famous bridge, which they named Pegasus after the winged-horse emblem on their shoulder patches. It was, as signage here testifies, "one of the most skillful and courageous

operations of World War II." With a roof shaped like a glider wing, the museum opened in 2000. There's lots of fascinating commando paraphernalia and concise explanation of the operation. Features include photos, uniforms, a scale model, a 15-minute film (in English) and more. Bill Millin's original D-Day bagpipes are here (Point 21) along with the original "Pegasus Bridge" sign handwritten on a piece of wood by soldiers in June 1944. Behind the museum is the original Pegasus Bridge—replaced in 1984 by a look-alike—a bland, industrial span of no great beauty but of tremendous importance. Around it are several restored military vehicles and artillery pieces. A plaque down a path from the Allied flags marks the landing spot of the leading glider. Across the road is the new bridge and Pegasus Bridge Café Gondrée, which bills itself as the first house in France to be liberated, and serves simple meals.

24. Merville Battery (Musée de la Batterie de Merville) ★★★

Off D514 then C5 in Merville-Franceville, 9 km northeast from Point 23. Directions are signed along road.
T: (0)2-31-91-4753
Daily, 10 a.m.-7 p.m., June-September (closed at 6 p.m. March 15-May and September-November 15)
Adult: €5; Child: €3; Under 10: Free

German officer Rudolph Steiner called the capture of this battery "one of the most daring feats by Allied soldiers." Thought to contain heavy 150 mm guns capable of harassing invasion forces along the coast, the position was highly worrisome to D-Day planners—so much so that a full-scale model of it was built in Britain for pre-invasion training purposes. In the real event, numerous unforeseen problems forced the British 9th Parachute Battalion to improvise its attack, which succeeded only after gruesome, close-quarters fighting. To the victors' disappointment, the battery contained no heavy guns, just light cannons. Today, a small museum is housed inside one of the concrete casemates. In the middle of a field, the site and several large bunkers are preserved exactly as they were at the time of the invasion.

25. Caen Memorial/Museum (Le Mémorial de Caen) ★★★★

Esplanade Dwight-Eisenhower in Caen
T: (0)2-31-06-0644
Daily, 9 a.m.-8 p.m., summer (closed 6 p.m. in winter, 7 p.m. in spring, fall)
Adult: €17; Student/Child (10 to 18): €15.50 World War II Veteran: Free
Also known as the Peace Museum, this World War II exhibition is on par with the best war museums in the world. Its circuit begins with the aftermath of World War I, the global economic crisis of the 1930s and Adolf Hitler's rise to power, augmented by the first of many short videos and archive films that play throughout the museum. The path symbolically spirals into a lower level of darkness, where the Nazi's Nuremberg rallies are presented with powerful photographic enlargements. From here, numerous videos and high-tech displays cover the shocking fall of France, the Battle of Britain, the Eastern Front, the Holocaust and French collaboration. There's even a section devoted to the Pacific War (rare in Europe), including an elaborate five-foot-long model of the fully loaded aircraft carrier USS *Intrepid* (now docked in New York City). There's much more to see. Opened in 1988 to promote peace, the museum concludes visits with an examination of the United Nations. During busy times, lines form shortly after opening—it's wise to arrive just before 9 a.m. Allow two to three hours to see the museum.

OTHER AREA ATTRACTIONS

See page 12.

GETTING TO/AROUND NORMANDY

See page 12.

ACCOMMODATIONS

Bayeux
Churchill Hotel

14 rue St-Jean
T: (0)2-31-21-3180 F: (0)2-31-21-4166
www.hotel-churchill.com
32 rooms
€85-160

The hotel evokes a traditional feel. The rooms come with satellite TV. Reliable service and good location make it one of Bayeux's more popular hotels. Reservations should be made well in advance.

Novotel

117 rue Ste-Patrice
T: (0)2-31-92-1611 F: (0)2-31-21-8876
www.novotel.com
77 rooms
€90-125

Rooms at this business-class hotel are clean and functional. Good service and English-fluent staff are dependable.

Caen
Best Western Hôtel Le Dauphin

29 rue Gémare
T: (0)2-31-86-2226 F: (0)2-31-86-3514
www.le-dauphin-normandie.com
37 rooms
€80-115

In the center of Caen, this lovely hotel— polished floors, exposed wood beams—has a good restaurant and, perhaps even more important in congested Caen, a parking lot. Rooms are the basic, three-star variety.

3

London

ENGLAND

St. Paul's Cathedral

THE WAR YEARS

The London Blitz—the German Luftwaffe's terror bombing of the British capital—began by mistake. Among Germany's gravest errors of the war, it was
compounded by Adolf Hitler's typical disregard for military logic. In the
eyes of many Britons, it ranks among those rare events upon which the fate
of worlds is decided.

Through the opening weeks of the Battle of Britain (page 101), London was a forbidden target for Luftwaffe bombers. On August 24, 1940, however, several German aircraft misread their positions and dropped their payloads on London. Little damage
was done, but, mistake or not, the civilian war had begun. On August 25, Britain's
Royal Air Force (RAF) retaliated with a week of reprisal attacks on Berlin. These confused raids barely scratched the German capital. But they enraged Hitler to such a
degree that he shifted Battle of Britain tactics from attacks on RAF airfields—necessary preparatory steps for Operation Sea Lion, the invasion of England scheduled for
mid-September—to a campaign of sheer punitive violence on London. "We will raze
their cities to the ground, so help us God!" Hitler promised his nation.

The Blitz began on September 7, 1940, with a 900-plane attack on London's East
End, and continued for 57 consecutive nights. The British were largely powerless to
resist the night raids by massed Nazi bombers. Yet as London burned—its firefighters
outmatched, thousands left homeless, 13,000 eventually killed—its spirit soared.
"London can take it!" became the slogan as residents resurrected a communal spirit
long vanished in what was then officially the world's largest city. Citizens famously
endured air raids in crowded Underground stations, though most simply carried on
with a stereotypical stiff upper lip since passed into legend. Above all, miraculously
unscathed amid the glowing orange of nightly fires, St. Paul's Cathedral became the
beacon of resiliency. "Surrounded by fire ... it stood there in its enormous propor-
tions—growing slowly clearer and clearer, the way objects take shape at dawn," wrote
war correspondent Ernie Pyle. "It was like a picture of some miraculous figure that
appears before peace-hungry soldiers on a battlefield."

If St. Paul's was the symbol of London's defiance, 65-year-old Prime Minister Winston
Churchill was its heart. Refusing to accept "the logic of defeat," Churchill willed his
countrymen to withstand the onslaught of "the Hun." An inveterate boozer with an
imperialist taste for war, Churchill set his jaw in bulldog position and never let it slip.
He met frequently with his war cabinet to discuss strategy, but it was as an orator that
his value to the national cause was most apparent. (Not unlike Hitler, one might
note.) Amid the Blitz and Battle of Britain, Churchill said of Englishmen, "This was
their finest hour." In tribute to RAF fighter pilots he declared, "Never in the field of
human conflict has so much been owed by so many to so few."

With London refusing to break, Hitler indefinitely postponed the invasion of England
on October 12 and eventually called off the nightly raids. It was Nazi Germany's first
true defeat of the war. Though prevailing wisdom suggests that a German victory
would have led to certain occupation—in 1940 "Germany appeared sinister and brilliant and quite unstoppable," according to authors Tim Clayton and Phil Craig—recent
assessments suggest that a German invasion was never realistic. True, 150,000 soldiers and a powerful German invasion fleet was anchored in France, just 22 miles

across the English Channel. But logistical problems associated with such a grand operation were apparent even to Hitler. Whether or not Sea Lion was the war's greatest bluff remains open to debate.

London survived the Blitz (which continued sporadically into 1941), but residents had little chance to celebrate. Swaths of the city were reduced to rubble. Food rationing became severe. Kept from the door, the wolf was very much at large across the Channel. Yet against this gloom, London bustled as countless American and Allied troops assembling for the great invasion of Europe poured into the country. Their nationalities advertised by exotic shoulder badges—USA, Australia, Belgium, Canada, Czech, Denmark, Free French, India, New Zealand, Norway, Poland—they turned London into a melting pot of rowdy soldiers, many away from home for the first time.

"The blacked-out streets were teeming with allied servicemen and more than enough 'ladies of the night' to go around," according to an unofficial history of the U.S. 94th Bomb Group stationed outside the city. "Only speculation and the Flight Surgeon could estimate the number who indulged in these sensations of ... the Piccadilly campaign." There were less-enthusiastic members of the military crowd in England—J.D. Salinger's short story "For Esmé—with Love and Squalor" offers a sobering reminder—but, by and large, the 94th Bomb Group author describes the popular image of wartime London.

Germany would blast London again in 1944-45, this time with a barrage of V1 and V2 rocket-propelled weapons, an example of indiscriminate bombing at its worst. About 2,340 flying weapons hit London, killing 5,475 and injuring 16,000. Yet in diverting resources to his marginal special weapons—neither accurate nor strategically successful—Hitler was again pursuing a fool's errand. London's legacy had been determined in 1940. Had Germany not redirected its Battle of Britain attacks from RAF installations to London, Germany's capable pilots might well have won the battle. England might have fallen under Nazi control, rendering the 1944 D-Day invasion of Europe impossible. All of this, perhaps, but for the navigational error of a few German pilots, and the legendary will of a defiant island tribe whose only hope for survival, as Churchill well knew, was to hang on. As Clayton and Craig put it: "Britain could not win the war alone, but in 1940, she refused to lose it."

SOURCES & OTHER READING

Finest Hour: The Battle of Britain, Clayton and Craig, Hodder and Stoughton, 1999

London's Burning, FitzGibbon, Constantine, Ballantine Books, 1970

"The London Blitz, 1940," Eyewitness to History, eyewitnesstohistory.com, 2001

The London Blitz, Johnson, Davis, Stein and Day, 1980

Churchill: A Life, Gilbert, Martin, Heinemann, 1991

Hitler on the Doorstep: Operation Sea Lion, Kieser, Egbert, Naval Institute Press, 1997

Operation Sea Lion: German Plans for the Invasion of England, 1939-1942, Wheatley, Ronald, Clarendon Press, 1958

Invasion Scare 1940, Glover, Michael, Leo Cooper, 1990

"For Esmé—with Love and Squalor" (included in *Nine Stories*), Salinger, J.D., Little, Brown, 1953

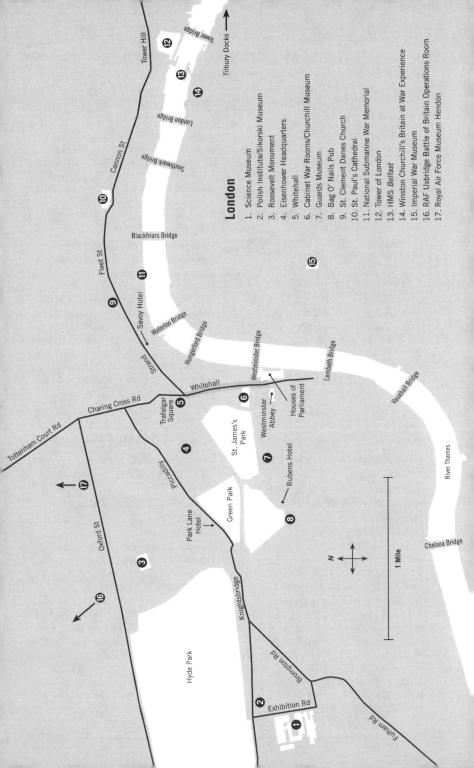

London

1. Science Museum
2. Polish Institute/Sikorski Museum
3. Roosevelt Monument
4. Eisenhower Headquarters
5. Whitehall
6. Cabinet War Rooms/Churchill Museum
7. Guards Museum
8. Bag O' Nails Pub
9. St. Clement Danes Church
10. St. Paul's Cathedral
11. National Submarine War Memorial
12. Tower of London
13. HMS *Belfast*
14. Winston Churchill's Britain at War Experience
15. Imperial War Museum
16. RAF Uxbridge Battle of Britain Operations Room
17. Royal Air Force Museum Hendon

LONDON TODAY

Population: 7 million • Country Code: 44 • £1 = $2.02/€1.48

Spread along 620 square miles of the banks of the River Thames, London is this book's most rewarding city to visit, if only because the British are the world's great historic preservationists. Visitors will have no difficulty locating authentic, visceral reminders of the time when Great Britain stood alone against Nazi Germany. Blocks of stunning architecture highlighted by renowned landmarks—Buckingham Palace, Big Ben, St. Paul's Cathedral, Tower Bridge—keep the rest of the city's 2,000-year history in plain view.

Still, it's the hum of the modern metropolis—crowded pubs, screaming tabloid headlines, anxious lines at theater box offices—that fires the imagination. Areas such as Westminster (government), St. James (royal history) and Covent Garden (theater) deserve attention for their obvious attractions. This is a city of empire, with superb Indian, Chinese, Caribbean and international restaurants, as well as a "British fusion" culinary renaissance. It's not a place to go hungry, but it might be one in which to go broke— without question London ranks among the world's most expensive cities.

There remains here a somewhat myopic view of the war and London's place in it— a week in the city and one might conclude the entire war was fought and won by Spitfires and Hurricanes alone in 1940. Nevermind the Allies, the Queen's forces in Africa, Italy and particularly the Far East largely seem to have been forgotten. Despite this, the city's four- and five-star attractions are worthy of full afternoon visits. Four days are needed to cover all sites—two days for the highlights.

POINTS OF INTEREST

U denotes nearest Underground or rail station

1. Science Museum (★★ for World War II exhibits, ★★★★ otherwise)

Exhibition Road
U: South Kensington
T: (0)870-870-4868
Daily, 10 a.m.-6 p.m.
Closed December 24-26
Entry fee only for IMAX theater

The Flight section of this sprawling museum—five floors covering the history of technology—has a decent World War II aviation section. Aircraft include a Hurricane (which took part in the Dunkirk evacuation), Spitfire, V1 flying bomb and 163B-1 Komet German jet fighter. The large collection of aircraft engines includes a Daimler-Benz V-12 from a German Me-109 and Rolls-Royce Merlin, versions of which powered the Spitfire and Hurricane.

2. The Polish Institute and Sikorski Museum ★★

20 Princes Gate
U: South Kensington
T: (0)207-589-9249
Monday-Friday, 2-4 p.m.
First Saturday of every month,
10 a.m.-4 p.m.
Or by appointment

A 10-minute walk north of Point 1, this multiroom museum has numerous military pieces including personal items of General Wladyslaw Sikorski, military hero and leader of the Polish government exiled in London during the war. The museum highlights little-known Polish contributions to the war, among them, that one in 10 RAF pilots in the Battle of Britain were actually Polish Air Force regulars.

3. Roosevelt Monument ★★

Grosvenor Square
U: Bond Street

In an area known as "Little America" during wartime, an American flag and 15-foot-tall statue of U.S. President Franklin Roosevelt stand watch over a peaceful park, once used as a dumping ground for downed German aircraft. Opposite Roosevelt, a monument commemorates the 244 American pilots of the RAF's Eagle Squadrons who flew in combat for Great Britain more than a year before the United States officially entered the war in December 1941. General Dwight

Eisenhower is commemorated by a fine statue outside the U.S. Embassy. Also in the park is a memorial dedicated to victims of the September 11, 2001, terrorist attacks in the United States.

4. Eisenhower Headquarters ★

Norfolk House 31, on St. James Square

A plaque on the six-story brick building reads: "At this site, General Eisenhower … directed the Allied Expeditionary Forces against Fortress Europe, 6 June 1944." (Ike in fact moved to Southwick House near Portsmouth, page 106, just before the actual D-Day invasion.) A separate plaque notes this site as Eisenhower's HQ for Operation Torch, the Allied campaign in North Africa.

5. Whitehall ★★★★★

U: Charing Cross

Then as now, the literal and symbolic center of the British government was housed along the great street of Whitehall. Walking the street from Trafalgar Square to Westminster Abbey requires less than an hour and takes in the heart of Britain's administrative power, from colonial times through the Churchill era and present.

From Trafalgar Square, walk south on Whitehall (noting the large Admiralty Arch to the immediate right). About 300-400 yards down the street on the left, just south of Whitehall Place, is the former **War Office Building ★★**. Built in 1898, it remains part of the renamed Ministry of Defense (a new headquarters was built around the corner after the war), but isn't open to the public. A statue of the Duke of Cambridge on horseback stands directly in front of the building.

Across the street, 20 yards south, is the Horse Guards headquarters (opposite Horse Guards Avenue). Walk through the Horse Guards archway to the open parade ground. The imposing brick and marble building to the right is the old **Admiralty**

Building ★★ from which the Royal Navy was governed. Now part of the Foreign and Commonwealth Office, it's closed to the public. To the left, the ivy-covered **Citadel ★★**, used as a wartime bunker, is the place where Churchill reportedly planned to make his last heroic stand against the Germans should the need have arisen.

Back on Whitehall, about 150 yards south, on the same side of the street as the old War Office Building, stands a statue of **Field Marshal Sir William Slim ★★** with binoculars and Australian bush hat. Hero of the Burma campaign (1943-45), Slim was one of the most capable, beloved (by his men) and underappreciated British generals of any century. He served as commander of Australian forces from 1953-60.

About 75 yards south, across the street from Slim, is Downing Street and **Number 10 Downing ★**, official residence of prime ministers, including Churchill. The street and house are closed to the public. (A signed path to the Cabinet War Rooms, Point 6, is south of Downing Street on the same side of the street, just beyond the

Cenotaph.) In the center of the street, 50 yards south of Downing Street, is the 30-foot-high stone **Cenotaph** ★ dedicated to "The Glorious Dead" of both world wars.

Another 250 yards south, a larger-than-life statue of **Winston Churchill** ★★, looking typically resolute, faces the Big Ben clock tower. The statue is on Parliament Square, where Whitehall becomes Parliament Street. About 150 yards south are the magnificent **Houses of Parliament** ★★★★, the seat of the British government. Visitors can wait in line—sometimes for several hours—to watch proceedings of the House of Commons. Tours are given between July and October—contact First Call (0870-906-3773) for dates or check regulations/times at www.parliament.uk. A monument to "The Few" was unveiled here by the Queen in May 2005.

Across the street is the monumental **Westminster Abbey** ★★★★, coronation and funeral site for more than 1,000 years of British royalty. Spectacular architecture and history make it one of London's most popular attractions. Its World War II history is commemorated by the Battle of Britain chapel—the small, arched area at the farthest end of the Henry VII chapel. RAF figures are found in the stained glass. Names of famed officers—Dowding, Harris, Tedding, and so on—are inscribed below. To the left of Douglas' name is a hole encased in glass left from a wartime air raid. Also inside the abbey is a commemorative stone to Churchill (next to the Tomb of the Unknown Soldier in the Nave) and, in the outer walkway around the cloisters, a trio of statues representing the World War II submarine corps, commandos and airborne forces. Westminster Abbey (0207-654-4900) is open Monday-Friday, 9:30 a.m.-3:45 p.m. (Wednesday late opening, 6-7 p.m.) and Saturday 9:30 a.m.-1:45 p.m. Closed Sunday. Guided and audio tours available. Admission is £7.50 (adult), £5 (senior/student/under 15). Nearest Underground stations are Westminster and St. James Park.

6. Cabinet War Rooms/Churchill Museum ★★★★★

Clive Steps, King Charles Street
U: Westminster, St. James Park
T: (0)207-930-6961
Daily, 9:30 a.m.-6 p.m. (open 10 a.m., October-March)
Last entry 5:15 p.m.
Closed December 24-26
Adult: £11; Senior/Student: £9;
Under 16: Free

Preserved in its 1940 state, the extensive, subterranean labyrinth where Churchill and his cabinet conducted the business of war is one of the most engaging original attractions left from the war. Displays carrying visitors from the Battle of Britain to the war's conclusion include the Trans-Atlantic Telephone Room (a converted broom closet that gave Churchill a direct line to Roosevelt) and Chiefs of Staff Conference Room. In Churchill's private quarters, a massive wall map of Europe faces the bed—even in sleep one senses the Prime Minister could feel the Nazi menace closing in. Memorabilia includes Churchill's chrome-plated air-raid helmet and bottles of his favorite vintage champagne. Videos, audio loops, photos, interpretive signage—there's much to see. Audio guide available and highly recommended. Using part of the underground complex, the excellent Churchill Museum, opened in 2004, is dedicated to the entire life of the man many regard as the greatest Briton ever. Allow two hours.

7. Guards Museum ★

Wellington Barracks, Birdcage Walk, 200 yards east of Buckingham Palace
U: St. James Park
T: (0)207-414-3271
Daily, 10 a.m.-4 p.m.
Last entry 3:30 p.m.
Closed December 25, all January, ceremonial days
Adult: £2; Senior/Student/Child: £1

With weaponry, art, flags, bric-a-brac and displays, this colorful museum recounts the history of the red-coated Foot Guards, from the days of 1600s swordsmen to the present. The modest World War II section includes weapons and mementos of action from Egypt, Italy, France, Norway and other far-flung battlefields.

8. Bag O' Nails Pub ★★

6 Buckingham Palace Rd.
U: Victoria
T: (0)207-828-7003

Allied soldiers turned countless pubs into their homes away from home. Across from the Rubens Hotel (see Accommodations), this one was known as a gathering point for airmen of all nationalities, identified by the array of colorful insignias on their sleeves. No decorations commemorate the war—the pub simply looks much as it did in the 1940s, though with a good, modern menu (chicken-and-salsa wrap, and so on) alongside traditional English fare.

9. St. Clement Danes Church ★★

Intersection of Fleet Street with Strand and Aldwych
U: Temple
T: (0)207-242-8282
Closed during services

Almost totally destroyed during the Blitz then rebuilt in 1958, this small but graceful church is now the Central Church of the Royal Air Force. Flanking the main entrance are larger-than-life statues of Air Chief Marshal Lord Hugh Dowding (commander of RAF Fighter Command during the Blitz and Battle of Britain) and Sir Arthur "Bomber" Harris, commander of RAF Bomber Command from 1942-45, the man most responsible for the controversial bombing of Dresden, Germany, in February 1945. The plaque for Dowding reads: "He was among the first to appreciate the vital importance of R.D.F. (radar) and of an effective command and control system for his squadrons." (For more on Dowding, see pages 35, 101.) The marble floor inside is inlaid with squadron insignias. A trophy case holds various RAF mementos.

10. St. Paul's Cathedral ★★★★★

St. Paul's Churchyard, off Cannon Street
U: St. Paul's
T: (0)207-236-4128 or (0) 207-246-8350 (general information);
(0) 207-246-8347 (visiting information)
Monday-Saturday, 8:30 a.m.-4 p.m.
(Galleries, 9:30 a.m.-4 p.m.)
Guided tours (90 minutes) at 11 a.m., 11:30 a.m., 1:30 p.m., 2 p.m.
Adult: £9.50; Student: £8.50; Child (6-16): £3.50; Family: £22.50
Guided tours cost £3 and depart throughout the day. Audio tours cost £3.50.

At more than 300 years old, the Christopher Wren-designed church survived the Blitz to become the symbol of hope and victory to beleaguered Londoners (not to mention the future venue for the wedding of Prince Charles and Princess Diana). Inside, the American Memorial Chapel is located at the extreme east end of the Cathedral (below the spot where a bomb exploded in October 1940). Moved by the idea of an American chapel, General Dwight Eisenhower offered U.S. assistance in its construction, but British representatives declined on the grounds that the chapel was to be a tribute from the people of their country to their American brothers-in-arms. The chapel's three stained-glass windows are bordered with insignias of the 50 states and branches of the U.S military. On a marble pedestal is the Roll of Honor, presented by Eisenhower after the war, inscribed with names of more than 28,000 Americans who gave their lives aiding the United Kingdom during World War II. Another copy of the book is available by request, for visitors to be shown names, which are listed alphabetically followed by rank and service. Elsewhere in the church are memorials to Burma commander General William Slim and Indian and Gurkha soldiers. The Golden Gallery—more than 300 feet above street level and reached by 530 stair steps—offers panoramic views of London. On January 30, 1965, the cathedral was the site of Winston Churchill's monumental state funeral, attended by representatives of 110 nations—"My old friend, farewell," said Eisenhower—and watched by millions on international television.

11. National Submarine War Memorial ★

Victoria Embankment, just east of inter-section with Temple Place

This 12-foot-high stone wall bears relief images of submariners at work and names of all these submarines lost during both world wars.

12. Tower of London ★★★★ (★ for World War II significance)

At Tower Bridge
U: Tower Hill
T: (0)870-756-6060
Daily, 9 a.m.-6 p.m. (open 10 a.m. on Sunday, Monday), March-October
Daily, 9 a.m.-5 p.m. (open 10 a.m. on Sunday, Monday), November-February
Last entry one hour before closing
Closed December 24-26, January 1
Adult: £16; Student: £13; Child (5-16): £9.50; Family: £45

The fortress/prison founded in 1066 includes the cell where, following one of the war's more bizarre episodes, Nazi Deputy Führer Rudolph Hess was impris-oned after he parachuted into Scotland in May 1941 with a secret plan to negotiate a peace treaty without Hitler's consent. Hess was tried at Nuremberg after the war and given a life sentence. He died in 1987 in Berlin's Spandau Prison.

13. HMS *Belfast* ★★★★

Morgan's Lane, Tooley Street
U: London Bridge
T: (0)207-940-6300
Daily, 10 a.m.-6 p.m., March-October
(Closed 5 p.m., November-February)
Last entry one hour before closing
Closed December 24-26
Adult: £9.95; Senior/Student: £6.15; Under 16: Free

Permanently docked between the London Bridge and Tower Bridge, the cruiser HMS *Belfast* is the only surviving example of the Royal Navy's big-gun World War II ships. Built in 1938 to counter Japanese ambitions in the Pacific, the *Belfast* served as a supply-convoy escort to Russia through frigid arctic waters. Her crowning glory came on December 26, 1943, at the Battle of North Cape (in the Barents Sea off northern Norway) when she took part in the sinking of the German cruiser *Scharnhorst*. She also participated in the massive shore bombardment that ushered in D-Day in Normandy in 1944. Visitors have full access to the 613-foot-long ship—bridge, shell rooms, magazine, triple gun turrets, mess halls, surgery, sleeping quarters, boiler and engine rooms. With wax figures, original plots and audio loop, the Operations Room re-creates the sinking of the *Scharnhorst*.

14. Winston Churchill's Britain at War Experience ★

64-66 Tooley St.
U: London Bridge
T: (0)207-403-3171
Daily, 10 a.m.-6 p.m., April-September (closed 5 p.m., October-March)
Adult: £9.95; Senior/Student: £5.75; Child: £4.85; Family: £25

This less-than-authentic re-creation of London civilian life during wartime has some interesting objects—gas masks, propaganda posters, facsimile of an air-raid shelter—but exhibits are marred by such ghoulish and amateur additions as random, plastic mannequin limbs meant to represent Blitz carnage. This popular school field-trip destination might be worthwhile for parties with kids under 12. Otherwise, it's a pricey tourist trap.

15. Imperial War Museum ★★★★

Lambeth Road
U: Lambeth North, Elephant and Castle
T: (0)207-416-5320
Daily, 10 a.m.-6 p.m.

The vast museum's collection examines the means and spoils of colonial British warfare. World War II exhibits are exten-sive and impressive. The main gallery is dominated by large equipment including a Spitfire, U.S. P-51 Mustang fighter plane,

German jagdpanzer tank destroyer, Soviet T-34 tank, various armored cars and the American-made Grant tank used by British General Bernard Montgomery at the Battle of El Alamein. Separate exhibits—Second World War, Holocaust, Blitz Experience, Monty: Master of the Battlefield—are of the highest standard. One of many fascinating pieces is a large, bronze eagle ripped by Russian soldiers from the Reichs Chancellery at the fall of Berlin in 1945. Plan two to three hours for a visit.

16. RAF Uxbridge Battle of Britain Operations Room ★★★★★

RAF Uxbridge base, Uxbridge, Middlesex
U: Uxbridge
T: (0)189-581-5400
Weekdays, by appointment only, at least two days in advance, contact curator Hazel Crozier

The Fighter Control station for the Battle of Britain's all-important RAF Number 11 Group, this plotting room—60 feet underground—is one of the most evocative relics of World War II. The moment one enters the room—preserved to specifications of 11:30 a.m., September 15, 1940, when Churchill was here—the ghosts and echoes of war are almost palpable. The huge tote board displaying squadron status ("Available 30 Minutes," "Refueling," "Enemy Sighted," and so on) dominates the room from which much of the Battle of Britain was controlled. (Germany had no equivalent "real time" command center.) A remarkable painting depicts the room in wartime, with its 85 percent female WAAF (Women's Auxiliary Air Force) crew who used croupier sticks to move markers around the giant plotting table. From here, controversial Air Chief Marshal Hugh Dowding coordinated radar reports, invented fighter coordination and more than any single man helped win the Battle of Britain. His innovations laid the foundation for aerial-combat control in use

today. Despite this, he was harshly criticized—few understood his genius or difficult personality—and forcibly retired in 1941. In addition to Churchill, the King and Queen, Eisenhower, Montgomery, Charles de Gaulle and many luminaries visited the room. Actor Rex Harrison (known by WAAFs as "Sexy Rexy") was an operations officer here. June 6, 1944, D-Day fighter operations were also controlled from the room. The adjacent museum includes a number of relics, uniforms, photos and mementos. Little publicized, this is one of the great sites from the war—more than worth the 70-minute train ride to London's outskirts.

17. Royal Air Force Museum Hendon ★★★★

Grahame Park Way, North London
U: Colindale
T: (0)208-205-2266
Daily, 10 a.m.-6 p.m.
Closed December 8-17, 24-26, January 1

Second only to the Imperial War Museum at Duxford (page 168), this 10-acre complex displays about 80 planes in a huge indoor hall built on the site of former RAF Station Hendon from which Hurricane fighters took off to defend London during the Battle of Britain. Aircraft range from biplanes to modern jets. The World War II section is the centerpiece. Mint-condition aircraft include, but are not limited to, a Spitfire, Lancaster bomber, Hawker Typhoon, Lockheed Hudson, Supermarine flying boat, Wellington bomber, B-17 and B-25 bombers and many German aircraft. The much-feared "Stuka"—the dive bomber that terrorized Poland and Western Europe in 1939-40 with its "Trumpets of Jericho" sirens—looks menacing even sitting still. A good amount of original ground vehicles, videos, photos, text and other displays. If you can't get to Duxford, this facility is well worth the hour train ride from central London.

Tilbury Docks ★

London's East End
U: Canary Wharf

There's no real wartime evidence here
—though talk of a memorial is circu-
lating—and development is transforming
the former-blue-collar area into a fashionable residential/shopping district. The site
is included for being the primary port—
famed during colonial days for sending
ships East of Suez—heavily damaged
during the opening night of the Blitz.

Royal Engineers Museum ★★★★

Prince Arthur Road, Gillingham, Kent,
about 50 km southeast of London
U: Gillingham
From London by car, stay with the A2 by
turning off left where the M2 begins. Follow
signs for Chatham and Historic Dockyard
(brown sign with image of an anchor).
Proceed past the Dockyard and continue up
the hill to a roundabout. Turn hard left at
the roundabout (first exit). Brompton
Barracks (School of Military Engineering) is
about 275 yards on the left. Don't turn into
main gate, but take first left and follow
road downhill to museum.

T: (0)163-482-2839
Tuesday-Friday, 9 a.m.-5 p.m.
Saturday, Sunday, 11:30 a.m.-5 p.m.
Closed Mondays, Christmas week
Adult: £6.35; Student/Child: £3.30
Family: £16

One of the country's best military museums, this enormous collection tells the
story of the Corps of Royal Engineers (aka
Sappers), one of the most innovative and
versatile elements in the British armed
forces. The use of specialized armor in
World War II resulted in a massive amount
of experimental work leading to the formation of three armored engineer regiments
for D-Day. These forces served throughout
the European campaign with great success
—just one of the many fascinating stories
chronicled in the museum's 26 galleries
charting the history of military engineering. From here the famed Mulberry Docks
(floating harbors) were conceived, built
and floated to Normandy after the June 6,
1944, D-Day landings. Other notable
items include Chinese embroideries given
to General Charles "Chinese" Gordon and
Zulu shields from Rorke's Drift in South
Africa. A quick tour takes 90 minutes;
detailed visits can last up to four hours.

Chartwell (Winston Churchill Home) ★★★

Chartwell, Westerham, Kent, about 3.2 km
south of Westerham. Turn off the A25 onto
B2026 and fork left after about 2.5 km
T: (0)173-286-8381
Wednesday-Sunday, 11 a.m.-5 p.m.,
late March-early November
Also open Tuesdays in July, August
Adult: £9.80; Child: £4.90; Family: £24.50

Just southeast of London, in the county of
Kent, this is the home Churchill occupied
from 1924 until his death in 1965.
Preserved rooms reflect the time when this
was the family home. Churchill possessions on display include books, photos,
furniture, wardrobe, hats, cigars and his
own paintings. The spacious grounds and
gardens are beautifully maintained. A
must for Churchill fans and historians.

GETTING TO/AROUND LONDON

Dozens of airlines fly nonstop to London's
two primary airports—Heathrow and
Gatwick—from U.S., Canadian and other
international cities. British Airways (800-
247-9297) and its partner American
Airlines (800-433-7300) operate dozens
of daily flights from North America.

Heathrow Express trains depart that airport
every 15 minutes (from 5:30 a.m.-11:30
p.m., with service ending about 10:30
p.m. on Sundays) nonstop for Paddington
Station in central London. The trip takes
less than 30 minutes and costs £14.50
(Child: £7.20). The 25-km taxi trip to the

city center costs about £35. From Gatwick, the Gatwick Express departs every 15 minutes (from 5:30 a.m.-11:30 p.m., with service ending about 10:30 p.m. on Sundays) nonstop for Victoria Station in central London. The trip takes 30 minutes and costs £14.90 (Child: £7.45). The 35-km taxi trip to the city center costs about £60.

Renting a car in congested London is pointless. The city's Underground covers the city. Day passes valid for zones 1 and 2 (covering almost all tourist sites) cost £4.10. All-zone day passes (including Uxbridge and Hendon museums) cost £5.10. Pocket Underground and city maps are available at Underground stations and hotel desks.

For information on rail trips outside of London, visit any primary Underground station or contact BritRail (0845-748-4950; www.britrail.net).

Leger Holidays (0845-458-5604) offers four-day Walking the Blitz tours.

ACCOMMODATIONS

Park Lane Hotel Sheraton

Piccadilly
U: Green Park
T: (0)207-499-6321 F: (0)207-499-1965
www.sheraton.com/parklane
302 rooms
£160-260

A Starwood luxury property, this is one of London's best examples of art deco architecture (including marble bathrooms in most guest rooms). The artistic Palm Court bar serves afternoon tea and evening cocktails. The ballroom has been featured in film and television shows including "Jeeves and Wooster" and *The Winds of War*. Guest rooms are modern and spacious. Good fitness center. Within walking distance of Buckingham Palace. One of London's top hotels.

The Rubens at the Palace

39 Buckingham Palace Rd.
U: Victoria
T: (0)207-834-6600 F: (0)207-233-6037
www.redcarnationhotels.com
179 rooms
From £160-400

Directly across from the Bag O' Nails Pub (Point 8) and Buckingham Palace, the high-quality Rubens was an RAF air-crew hostelry and housed a Canadian air officers club during the war. Its Cavalry Bar today has a British military theme. Rooms are individually decorated. The restaurant is popular, and the staff is justly known for attentive service.

The Savoy

The Strand
U: Covent Garden
T: (0)207-950-5492 F: (0)207-950-5482
www.savoy-group.co.uk
263 rooms and suites
From £280-1,800

Well outside most travelers' budgets, the landmark, five-star hotel has a proud legacy. During the Blitz, its basement was used as a bunker. Its kitchen staff provided catering for, among others, the code breakers at Bletchley Park (page 166). Theatres, opera, ballet and shopping of the West End and Covent Garden are located nearby. There are few more legendary or exclusive hotels in the world—from public areas to rooms to staff, this one generally lives up to its gilded reputation.

4

Auschwitz-Birkenau

POLAND

HALT! STÓJ!

Auschwitz I

THE WAR YEARS

W hen he ascended to power in 1933, Adolf Hitler almost certainly did not envision the industrialized liquidation of the Jewish race in Europe. The infamous death camps at Auschwitz-Birkenau represented merely the culmination of Nazi ideology regarding the "Jewish question" and the attendant series of official, progressively brutal measures meant to solve it. The first "solution," begun in 1933, was the relocation of German Jews from small towns to cities, followed by encouraged emigration; the third was the establishment of the ghetto system in 1939; *Einsatzgruppen* death squads, set loose in 1941 in German-controlled USSR and eastern Europe, comprised the fourth solution—about one-quarter of all Jews killed in the Holocaust were shot by these "mobile killing squads." The fifth and final solution was the establishment of a vast network of camps into which entire Jewish populations from around Europe were herded and slaughtered. In 1933, 9 million Jews lived in continental Europe. Within a dozen years, two of every three would be dead.

Located in southwestern Poland near the Czech border, Auschwitz-Birkenau comprised two camps. The smaller "Auschwitz" camp was established in early 1940 to hold political prisoners. The "Birkenau" camp was built a mile and a half away in March 1942. It was to become the largest of all Nazi death camps, but despite the numbers killed there, Auschwitz-Birkenau also functioned as headquarters of Germany's slave labor system. Upon arrival, those who could work at one of the area coal mines or for a recently relocated German company immediately relinquished their clothes and anything else they carried. Their heads and bodies were shaved. They were directed to a showers chamber, where streaming water might provide the first sanitary drink in days. They received a camp uniform and wooden shoes. Each prisoner was registered, photographed and, beginning in 1943, tattooed with an ID number on the forearm (Auschwitz was the only camp to tattoo its prisoners).

Prisoners deemed unfit to work—including almost anyone very young, very old or sick—by one of the doctors that greeted each transport were immediately loaded onto trucks and delivered to one of several gas chambers, the largest of which could fit 2,000 people. SS officers attempted to keep prisoners as calm as possible by directing them to the "showers" with gentle words and promises of soup afterward. Any prisoners who couldn't fit into the chamber were shot on the spot. Once the prisoners were inside, canisters of lethal Zyklon B (hydrogen cyanide, a nerve agent) were dropped into vents in the ceiling. The killing was over within two minutes. After 30 minutes, guards opened the doors to find bodies with their mouths wide open, half-sitting or curled up, covered with excrement, vomit and blood. *Sonderkommandos*, Jewish prisoners chosen for special work detail, quickly went to work shaving the heads of the dead (the hair was used for textiles) and pulling out gold teeth, which was later melted into gold bars.

Initially, the dead were buried. But after concentration camp administrator Adolf Eichmann began directing that all traces of the extermination be obliterated, corpses were burned in the open air. In the fall of 1942, the *Sonderkommand* was responsible for digging up and burning 107,000 previously buried corpses. Eventually, five large crematoriums would burn as many as 8,000 bodies a day. Collected by the *Sonderkommandos*, the ashes were either dumped in rivers or used as fertilizer in camp farms. To leave no evidence of the killings, these special Jewish workers were liquidated regularly.

For prisoners, work was a means of saving one's self. Once reveille was sounded, laborers rushed to roll call. Primo Levi described the scene in his remarkable memoir, *Survival in Auschwitz:* "Some, bestially, urinate while they run to save time, because within five minutes begins the distribution of bread ... the holy grey slab which seems gigantic in your neighbor's hand, and in your own hand so small as to make you cry." The workday, which began at 4 a.m., included farming, loading and unloading of supplies, construction and work at the gravel pits, as well as work for German companies under Nazi contract at one of almost 50 subcamps around Auschwitz. Prisoners injured while working were killed. The labor program, as well as the inhuman living conditions, were a conscious means of exterminating prisoners.

In addition to its role as liquidation site and slave-labor headquarters, Auschwitz-Birkenau was an important center of Nazi medical experimentation. Thirty-two-year-old Josef Mengele personally carried out experiments on twins, in hopes of finding a key to creating a master race. He ordered any prisoners with physical abnormalities to be killed to provide specimens—he personally murdered patients by injecting them with poison.

The medical program at the camp was one element of an immense web of killing, held up by a complex bureaucracy and vast infrastructure. According to historian Robert S. Wistrich: "At places like Auschwitz-Birkenau ... the entire apparatus of the modern German state—the resources of its bureaucracy and military-industrial complex—were put at the disposal of the SS in order to carry out streamlined executions. All the skills and techniques of modern technology, of scientific and medical expertise, as well as precise railway scheduling, were enlisted in the service of racial murder."

In the days before Soviet soldiers liberated the camp on the afternoon of January 27, 1945, the Germans evacuated thousands of prisoners for transport to other labor camps, leaving piles of charred documents and the remains of burned-out crematoria in their wake. The soldiers found only 7,000 prisoners—walking dead—scattered among the camp's hundreds of buildings. This meager population was all that was left to represent the 2.5 million people deported to Auschwitz-Birkenau from March 1942 to January 1945, 2.25 million of whom were murdered.

SOURCES & OTHER READING

Auschwitz: Nazi Death Camp, Piper and Swiebocka (eds), Auschwitz-Birkenau State Museum, 1996

Survival in Auschwitz, Levi, Primo, Touchstone, 1958

KL Auschwitz as Seen by the SS, Höss, Broad and Kremer, Auschwitz-Birkenau State Museum, 2002

Hitler and the Holocaust, Wistrich, Robert S., Modern Library, 2001

The Origins of the Final Solution, Browning, Christopher R., University of Nebraska Press, 2004

The Holocaust: The Jewish Tragedy, Gilbert, Martin, Collins, 1986

Babi Yar: A Document in the Form of a Novel, Kuznetsov, Anatoli, Farrar, Straus & Giroux, 1970

Auschwitz-Birkenau (Oswiecim) Today

Population: 44,000 (Auschwitz); 770,000 (Krakow)
Poland Country Code: 48 • 1 zloty = $0.36/£0.18/€0.26

Though nearly all of its half-million annual visitors come to tour the Auschwitz-Birkenau complex, the small town of Auschwitz—known locally as Oswiecim (OWS-VEE-ENCH-EM)—does have a few minor attractions. Founded in the early 1300s and eventual capital of the Duchy of Oswiecim, the area is anchored by the Castle of Oswiecim, with a large Gothic turret dating to the 14th century. From the tree-lined banks of the Sola River, the town looks pleasant

enough. Sadly, that largely sums up the secondary attractions of this industrial town—chemical works, construction material, technical gases—in which one stays the night only if the last bus or train to Krakow has departed. It isn't a good sign when local tourist brochures trumpet the town's chief employer by announcing that "Firma Chemiczna Dwory was removed from the disreputable list of 80 greatest polluters in Poland." There are five hotels in town and a handful of restaurants, most of which close early. The better option is Krakow, traditional center of Polish culture and one of Europe's unsung treasures. As no battles or major bombing campaigns took place here, Krakow survived the war as Poland's only large city with a wealth of original architecture. Most of this is found in the largely car-free Old Town—the center of tourist activity has a medieval Market Square, dramatic cathedrals and numerous museums.

The area covered by Auschwitz I and particularly the Auschwitz II-Birkenau camp is enormous. It's difficult to see all of both camps in less than four hours. Typical visits last five to six hours.

POINTS OF INTEREST

This area's immense size, the extreme nature of the Holocaust and Auschwitz-Birkenau's role in it renders this book's established rating-system format inappropriate. A brief description of the two camps is the preferred alternative. Due to the intensely graphic and disturbing images inside, children under 14 officially aren't allowed into either camp, though this regulation is rarely enforced.

Officially called the Auschwitz-Birkenau State Museum, the former concentration camp is divided into two sections. Auschwitz I (established in 1940) is the general starting point for visitors. It houses the main museum, information center and exhibits. Entry is free. This is the place to arrange and begin guided tours with the reputable and generally good English-speaking private guides assembled at the entry. Guides cost about 30 zlotys per person. The English "Auschwitz-Birkenau Guide Book" pamphlet sells for 3 zlotys in the bookstore. It offers thorough explanations of most points of interest. The museum and exhibits include English signage.

Three km west of Auschwitz I is Auschwitz II-Birkenau (completed in 1942), usually included as part of guided tours. Entry is free. There's a bookstore and small reception area, but few exhibits and only sparse signage. What the visitor finds at Auschwitz II-Birkenau are simply the stark and extensive remains of the "Birkenau" camp.

Auschwitz I

Leszcynskiej Street (off Route 933) in Oswiecim, 54 km west of Krakow
T: (0)33-843-2022
Daily, 8 a.m.-3 p.m.
December-February
March, November 1-December 14,
8 a.m.-4 p.m.
Daily, 8 a.m.-5 p.m., April, October
Daily, 8 a.m.-6 p.m., May, September
Daily, 8 a.m.-7 p.m., June, July, August
Closed January 1, Easter Sunday,
December 25

At the entry to the museum is a bookstore, information desk, restaurant and small theater that shows a harrowing 15-minute introductory film on the camp. From here visitors pass outside and into the camp through the main gate bearing the infamous Nazi inscription, *Arbeit Macht Frei* ("Work will make you free"). The camp remains as it was built, with original, bleak blocks of prisoner barracks surrounded by gates, barbed wire and watchtowers. Exhibits are located inside many of the blocks.

Block 4

Exhibits here deal with the development of the full network of Nazi death camps, ensuing deportation process and instruments of mass killing such as Zyklon B gas pellets, a collection of which is inside. Among the more disturbing displays is half of a very long room filled with female hair discovered upon the camp's liberation. The hair was shaved from victims' heads and used to make thick tailor's fabric (haircloth), bolts of which are displayed. Haircloth formed the basis of a profitable Nazi trade.

Block 5

Chronicling "Material Proofs of Crime," this block has separate rooms filled with piles of possessions seized from prisoners. One room contains a huge assortment of shoes, another thousands of pieces of luggage heartbreakingly hand-marked with names and anticipated destinations, another an unending pile of pots, pans and kitchenware, another is packed with eyeglasses. Most unsettling is the room filled with prosthetic limbs from murder victims. The sheer number of items reinforces both the massive scale and individual tragedy of the Holocaust.

Block 6

Hundreds of startling prisoner "mug shots" begin an exhibit documenting the arrival, processing and horror of daily life of prisoners at Auschwitz. Newcomers had clothes confiscated and hair shaved. They were sprayed with disinfectant, given a registration number and, beginning in 1943, labeled with tattoos. Graphic photos attest to the horrific conditions, hard labor, unsanitary barracks, tiny food rations and ceaseless misery.

Block 11

Isolated from the rest of the camp, the "Death Block" was the scene of thousands of executions (mostly of Poles) carried out by the SS. Floggings, hangings and other punishments were meted out here. The

ground floor includes a re-created SS office and Gestapo Police Court. Underground prison and torture cells can be seen in the cellar.

Blocks 15-21

These buildings are devoted to national exhibits from countries that experienced Nazi repression. The range of presentations is fascinating. The Austrian exhibit (Block 17) includes large stained glass depicting the Holocaust. France and Belgium (Block 20) recount the Nazi invasion of their countries in traditional museum fashion. The Italian exhibit (Block 21) is simply a boardwalk through a long, circular Holocaust mural that consumes three full rooms.

Block 27

Dedicated to the Martyrdom of the Jews, this small museum uses film, photography and other exhibits to present the story of Jews who suffered oppression around the world. It also includes sections on Jewish resistance and Jews in combat against Nazi Germany.

Crematorium and Gas Chamber

"You are in a building where the SS murdered thousands of people." This signage offers a chilling introduction to the most inhuman (if such a thing can be measured) section of the camp. Outside the main fence, the largest room of the crematorium was the mortuary. Inside are two furnaces (rebuilt from original elements destroyed by the Nazis toward war's end) that could burn approximately 350 bodies a day.

Auschwitz II-Birkenau

From Auschwitz I, catch the free shuttle (in season) or turn right out of parking lot, proceed 0.8 km and turn left just before the first traffic roundabout. Follow the highway overpass road the remaining 2.2 km to the camp in the village of Brzezinka.

Encompassing 425 acres, 67 of this enormous camp's original 300-plus buildings stand today amid a broken wilderness of

smokestacks and brick ruins left from demolished wooden barracks. The smokestacks are remains of fireplaces from primitive prisoner barracks. There are no elaborate displays or presentations at this very large site—simply fields of foundations, roads, railroad tracks and occasional buildings, all bearing stark testimony to the vastness of the Nazi operation.

The camp was (and is) divided into several sectors. A map in front shows the location of various sites along a marked route. Walks begin at the main SS watchtower where recorded commentary in 12 languages is available. Below is the "Gate of Death" where prisoners were unloaded, following long, paralyzing journeys by train. What follows are the sites (some destroyed, some remaining) where a roll call of Nazi horrors took place: roads along which prisoners were herded to labor and then death; a storehouse for property taken from murdered victims; ruins of the crematoria and gas chambers; hatches through which Zyklon B pellets were poured; dissection rooms used for autopsies and human experiments performed by Nazi doctor Josef Mengele, with a separate barrack used for experiments on children; pits where bodies were burned; mass graves of Soviet POWs; a pond into which human ashes were dumped; crude, cold latrines and washrooms with the command *Verhalte dich ruhig* ("Keep quiet") still etched on the walls; a barrack for sterilization experiments; another where women and babies born in the camp were "murdered by phenol injections into the heart." A final barrack has crude wall art—a sunny day, a soldier—drawn by captive children. A more deeply disturbing place is difficult to imagine.

RELATED SITES BEYOND AUSCHWITZ-BIRKENAU

Schindler's Factory/Plaszow Concentration Camp

ul. Lipowa 4, Krakow

Made famous by the film *Schindler's List*, Oskar Schindler's enamel factory is currently a Krakow electronics plant. It's closed to the public, but the large, three-story facility can be seen on Lipowa Street in Krakow. A 15-minute walk or short cab ride from Krakow-Plaszow station, an enormous and stunning stone memorial on a large hill overlooks the site of Plaszow Concentration Camp. As depicted in the film, many of Oskar Schindler's factory workers lived here. There's nothing left of the original camp.

See also Auxiliary Sites, Poland (page 247).

GETTING TO/AROUND AUSCHWITZ (OSWIECIM)

"Auschwitz" (the German spelling) is actually "Oswiecim." Virtually all highway and local signage appears as Oswiecim.

The nearest major airport is Krakow Airport, about 55 km due east of Oswiecim. Most visitors come to the museum and camp as a day trip from Krakow, or from as far away as Prague. Several trains a day depart Krakow's (main) Glowny Station for the 90-minute trip to Oswiecim Station. Trains run even more frequently from Krakow-Plaszow Station, about 15 km outside the city center and reached from downtown Krakow via tram line number 9. In Poland, dial the four digits 9436 from anywhere for English information on trains. A number of buses and mini-buses also run frequently between Krakow and the Auschwitz I museum and camp. Call (0)33-876-1107 for information (in Polish) on express mini-buses, which are much faster than the train.

Auschwitz I is a 20-minute walk south of the Oswiecim Station. Taxis and other transport are available. By car, Auschwitz I is just off Route 933, south of A4 and east of E75, about 54 km west of Krakow. A free shuttle runs the 3 km (northwest) between Auschwitz I and Auschwitz II-Birkenau April 15-October 31. Otherwise, it's necessary to walk, drive or cab between the two camps. The Auschwitz guidebook available at the Auschwitz I museum has a map. Directions also can be obtained at the Auschwitz I museum.

The Oswiecim tourist office (Leszcynskiej Street at corner of Spoldzielcow Street, across from Auschwitz I, 033-843-0091, English spoken) is open 365 days a year, the same hours as the Auschwitz I museum. Krakow's tourist office (012-421-7706) is located in the Cloth Hall on Rynek Glowny and open weekdays (9 a.m.-6 p.m.) and Saturdays (9 a.m.-2 p.m.).

In Krakow, Jarden Jewish Bookshop (ul. Szeroka 2, 012-421-7166) operates

Auschwitz-Birkenau day trips as well as a two-hour "Schindler's List Tour" that takes in many sites featured in the film. The bookshop sells a *Schindler's List* guide-book for those wishing to see the sites without the organized tour. Orbis Travel (Rynek Glowny 41, 012-422-4035) and Intercrac Travel (ul. Krupnicza 3, 012-422-5840) also offer Auschwitz-Birkenau tours. From Prague, a 15-hour day trip is operated by Wittmann Tours (420-222-25-2472, www.wittmann-tours.com).

ACCOMMODATIONS

Oswiecim
Miedzynarodowy Dom Spotkan Mlodziezy
ul. Legionow 11
T: (0)33-843-2107 F: (0)33-843-2377
www.mdsm.pl
37 rooms
120-240 zlotys

In a quiet woodland setting on the Sola River, this seasonal lodge, with restaurant and meeting facilities, is the nicest place in town. It also serves as the International Youth Meeting House. An easy 15-minute walk to Auschwitz I.

Hotel Olimpijski
ul. Chemikow 2a
T: (0)33-842-3842 F: (0)33-847-4194
50 rooms
100-280 zlotys

This just-the-basics hotel on the east edge of town has a decent restaurant, friendly staff and reasonable rooms, especially for the price. Close to the city center, but a 30-minute-plus walk to Auschwitz I.

Krakow
Hotel Copernicus
ul. Kanonicza 16
T: (0)12-424-3400 F: (0)12-431-1140
29 rooms
750-1,500 zlotys

At the foot of Wawel Hill, the hotel occupies a pair of gorgeous Gothic buildings that stand out even on this very atmospheric street (the oldest in Krakow). Among the city's most elegant hotels, the updated decor includes painted wooden ceilings from the 14th century. Air-conditioned rooms have satellite TV, internet access and mini-bar. The rooftop bar is a summertime favorite. Ten minutes by taxi from the main train station, a five-minute walk from Market Square.

Hotel Campanile
ul. Sw Tomasza 34
www.campanile.com.pl
T: (0)12-424-2600 F: (0)12-424-2601
105 rooms
From 330 zlotys

Part of a reliable French hotel chain, the relatively new Campanile is a good value with an Old Town location, two minutes from Market Square and a five-minute walk from the main train station. Rooms are basic, with satellite TV and air-conditioning. Some have internet connections.

5

Bastogne

Battle of the Bulge I

BELGIUM

Place McAuliffe

THE WAR YEARS

F
or an overview of the Battle of the Bulge, see Belgium and Luxembourg chapter, page 56.

"Nuts!" As the defiant response to a German surrender demand, the simple epigram became the second-most-famous four-letter word of World War II. Eventually, it would come to symbolize the mythic American defense of the Belgian town of Bastogne—part of the Battle of the Bulge—an action that would invent the legend of one general ("Nuts!" author Anthony McAuliffe), gild another's (George Patton) and, through freezing temperatures and terrifying artillery barrages, test the endurance of some of the United States' most elite soldiers.

The Battle of the Bulge is best understood as a number of separate defensive actions by Allied troops (overwhelmingly American) against a massive German assault launched on December 16, 1944, on Luxembourg and the Ardennes forest of Belgium. As U.S. forces fell to the surprise onslaught, a triangle-shaped "bulge," roughly 50 miles wide and 65 miles deep, was created in American lines. Within the Bulge, the only territory eventually not in German control was a small defensive perimeter surrounding the suddenly critical crossroads town of Bastogne, where 40,000 Germans were aligned against 18,000 Americans and 3,000 Belgian civilians. Bastogne became an ulcer in the belly of the German Bulge that, while completely surrounded, refused to be subdued.

"By direct assault, the enemy armored corps tried to gain the city," reads today's major American memorial in Bastogne. "Its men and metal were driven back at every point." Many doing the driving back were part of the U.S. 101st Airborne Division—immortalized in the Stephen Ambrose book and HBO television series *Band of Brothers*—but the U.S. 10th Armored Division, 705th Tank Destroyer Battalion and many others played just as vital roles in Bastogne's defense.

Following Germany's offensive, American troops were rushed to Bastogne in a panic—many without supplies, winter clothing or ammunition. As temperatures dropped into the teens, ill-equipped defenders found themselves shivering through wet, frigid nights in snow-lined foxholes in the woods around town. The battle was as much against savage winter elements as it was against German artillery bombardment.

"Tank turrets froze (and) had to be chipped free to regain traversing action," according to a U.S. 6th Armored Division history. "M-1s refused to function until bolts were beaten back and forth with grenades. Feet froze. Men became so cold they 'burned.'"

Desperate for action, Allied Supreme Commander General Dwight Eisenhower called on American General George "Old Blood and Guts" Patton to break the German stranglehold on Bastogne. Headquartered 40 miles southeast in Luxembourg City, Patton immediately reorganized his massive 3rd Army for a counter-strike to his rear—it was a logistics miracle. But his battle plan, which called for close-in air support of tank and infantry forces, was halted by ever-worsening weather that kept his planes grounded.

On December 22, with the defensive situation in Bastogne seemingly hopeless, four German soldiers approached American lines bearing a white flag. After being blindfolded and taken to a nearby farmhouse, the envoys presented a letter demanding Bastogne's surrender. The communiqué was relayed to Brigadier-General Anthony McAuliffe, an unknown, former desk officer nicknamed "Old Crock" and now acting commander of the 101st Airborne. McAuliffe considered the message and then typed "N-U-T-S" on a sheet of paper. Back at the farmhouse, Colonel Joseph Harper translated the message for the Germans, who were confused by the terse reply. "It means the same as 'Go to hell!'" Harper explained. "(And) if you continue to attack, we will kill every goddamn German that tries to enter this city." Within hours, Luftwaffe aircraft punished Bastogne with a curtain of bombs.

In Luxembourg, the exasperated Patton delivered his now well-known Patton prayer for fair weather. "Almighty and most merciful Father, we humbly beseech Thee ... to restrain these immoderate rains with which we have had to contend," read the opening line of the prayer (actually composed by 3rd Army chaplain James O'Neill). Whether by luck or Providence, the skies cleared. Thousands of Allied C-47 transport planes dropped supplies into Bastogne, and Patton launched his attack. While the Luftwaffe bombed Bastogne, Americans in the field ate cold white beans for Christmas dinner, but the turn in the weather provided a much-needed morale boost. On December 26, after intense hand-to-hand fighting—"a clubbing, beating melee," according to one account—Lieutenant Charles Boggess led a small group of Sherman tanks through the rear of a weakened German position at the village of Assenois, just south of Bastogne. Hunkered in foxholes facing the Germans, American GIs rushed out to meet the tanks. The German line had been breached. For five days the Germans attacked in furious bursts, but the walls of Patton's narrow corridor held. Bastogne was relieved.

In all, at least 642 Americans died in Bastogne, 3,743 were injured or missing. Belgian casualties are unknown, though it's widely remembered that locals did everything from fight on the lines to strip their beds of white sheets to provide U.S. troops with camouflage. When Patton died in a car accident in December 1945, near Mannheim, Germany, the triumph at Bastogne was listed among his remarkable career's crowning glories. It had been the perfect stage for the brash general's inestimable skills as both strategist and leader. At Bastogne, Patton displayed the genius for war that sealed his reputation as the ablest and most feared commander the Axis faced on the Western Front and, arguably, in the entire war. It was the suffering "dogface" soldiers, however, who, "through guts and blood," according to historian Louis Snyder, turned Bastogne into a legend surpassed by no other in the pantheon of American military victories.

SOURCES & OTHER READING

Seven Roads to Hell: A Screaming Eagle at Bastogne, Burgett, Donald, Presidio, 1999

Bastogne, Marshall, S.L.A., Center of Military History, U.S. Army, 1988 (originally published 1946)

A Time for Trumpets: The Untold Story of the Battle of the Bulge, MacDonald, Charles B., Morrow, 1985

Band of Brothers, Ambrose, Stephen E., Simon & Schuster, 1992

Patton and the Battle of the Bulge, Green and Green, MBI Publishing, 1999

War as I Knew It, Patton, George S., Houghton Mifflin, 1947

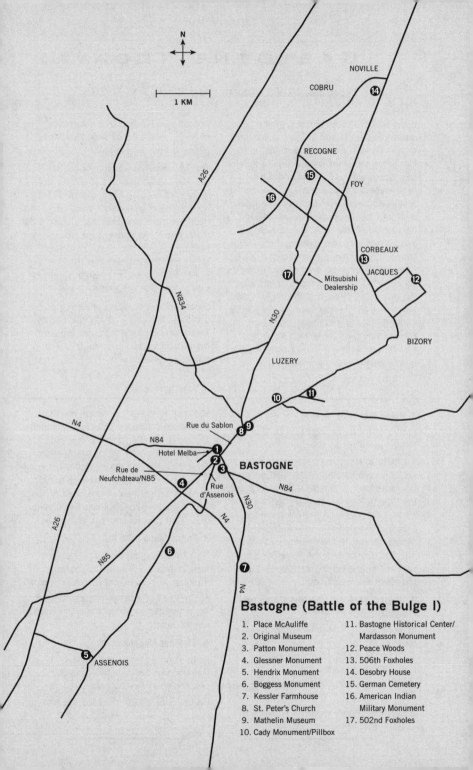

Bastogne (Battle of the Bulge I)

1. Place McAuliffe
2. Original Museum
3. Patton Monument
4. Glessner Monument
5. Hendrix Monument
6. Boggess Monument
7. Kessler Farmhouse
8. St. Peter's Church
9. Mathelin Museum
10. Cady Monument/Pillbox
11. Bastogne Historical Center/ Mardasson Monument
12. Peace Woods
13. 506th Foxholes
14. Desobry House
15. German Cemetery
16. American Indian Military Monument
17. 502nd Foxholes

BASTOGNE TODAY

Population: 10,000 • Country Code: 32 • €1 = $1.36/£0.67

If the rest of the Ardennes region relies on scenic beauty and outdoor adventure to lure visitors, Bastogne remains firmly "an American town" (according to at least one local), with U.S. flags and other reminders of its American connection readily apparent. Rebuilt after wartime devastation, the town's square—designated Place McAuliffe, after the famed general—is a busy commercial zone with shops, cafes, bars, a tourist office, a Sherman tank and a bust of McAuliffe (lit up at night). American tank turrets guard the entrances of each of the major roads into town. Businesses bear names such as Le Nuts Cafe and White House Hotel. The surrounding (and replanted) Ardennes looks much as it did in 1944-45. Rather than a single, unbroken forest, the Ardennes is typified by thick groves of trees, separated by wide meadows, plateaus and river valleys.

Though no battle was fought in the Belgian capital (and the country's main entry port), Brussels (population 1.1 million) is one of the world's great cities and deserves more attention than travelers normally give it. As home of the EU, the modern Upper Town is as "Eurocratic" as locals love to complain it is. But the old Lower Town is as architecturally impressive as any part of Europe.

Bastogne's major sites can be toured in two days. Including an afternoon at its world-class military museum, Brussels merits at least two or three days as a tourist destination.

POINTS OF INTEREST

1. Place McAuliffe ★★★

Center of Bastogne, bordered by Rue du Sablon and Rue de Marche

A tribute to Bastogne's American defenders, this commercial square features a Sherman tank, a Liberty Milestone (part of the Liberty Highway marking various Allied routes across Europe from Normandy) and a bust of Brigadier-General Anthony McAuliffe next to the main tourist office. The first six notes of the "Star-Spangled Banner" chime from church bells down the street every half-hour.

2. Original Museum (Au Pays d'Ardenne l'Original Museum) ★★★

20 Rue de Neufchâteau, 75 yards south of Point 1
T: (0)61-21-4911
Daily, 9 a.m.-5 p.m.
Closed December 25-January 1
€3

This small, private museum is jammed with battlefield relics—weaponry, Nazi decorations, personal effects. The unique feature is the shop in front that sells authentic, if pricey, World War II relics. Typical pieces and asking prices include a U.S. 60 mm mortar launcher (€1,050), German potato-masher grenades (€110), Nazi medals (€75-250) and GI helmets (€250). A find for souvenir collectors.

3. Patton Monument ★

Next to parking lot near intersection of Avenue Albert 1er and Rue Joseph Renquin, about 250 yards south of Point 1

At the head of a 50-yard grass corridor, the contentious general's face is carved in marble relief.

4. Glessner Monument ★

From Point 1, turn right on Rue de Neufchâteau (eventually called N85) and proceed (past Point 2) about 1 km.

On the right side of the road is a tank turret and monument to Ernest Glessner, the first American killed in Bastogne (debatably) on this spot in September 1944.

5. Hendrix Monument ★

From Point 4, continue south on Rue de Neufchâteau/N85 about 4 km. Turn left at sign for 1 Assenois (just past highway turnoff for Arlon and Luxembourg City). Follow this windy road 1.5 km past the cemetery into village of Assenois.

In front of a church, a small monument recalls Medal of Honor recipient James Hendrix who alone attacked a German gun position, killing two and capturing the rest of its crew on December 26, 1944. The area was the site of horrendous artillery bombardment, an estimated one shell per square meter falling here.

6. Boggess Monument ★★

From Point 5, proceed 40 yards east to T intersection. Turn left and proceed 2.5 km.

On the right side of the road is a bunker where the Bastogne encirclement was broken on December 26, 1944, by an assault of six (possibly eight) U.S. tanks led by 33-year-old Lieutenant Charles Boggess. His "Cobra King" tank is now on display at the Rose Barracks U.S. Army installation in Vilseck, Germany, 50 miles northeast of Nuremberg.

7. Kessler Farmhouse ★★

Follow N30 south out of Bastogne. After N30 merges into N4, make a U-turn at first safe spot after the retaining wall, then proceed back toward Bastogne, following the exit for N30.

Directly across from the N30 exit sign for Bastogne and Diekirch is the white, three-story Kessler farmhouse where German envoys delivered their surrender demand and then received McAuliffe's "Nuts" reply. The house is now a private residence.

8. St. Peter's Church ★★

Rue du Sablon, five-minute walk north of Point 1

Occupied by U.S. troops during the battle, the badly damaged Romanesque (exterior)

and Gothic (interior) Catholic church was rebuilt after the war. A stained-glass window in front features a U.S. flag. GIs were also cared for inside the long brick girls school next door (at 336 Rue de Sablon).

9. Mathelin Museum (Maison Mathelin) ★★★

1 Rue Delperdange, next to Point 8
T: (0)61-21-3287
Tuesday-Saturday, 10 a.m.-noon, 1-5 p.m., July and August only; other times by appointment
€3

This three-story, 17th-century house is crammed with worthwhile memorabilia—uniforms, maps, flags, weaponry—as well as World War I relics. The large, ivy-covered monument across the street is dedicated to Belgian casualties of the war.

10. Cady Monument/Pillbox ★★

Just less than 2 km northeast of Point 9 on road to Clervaux (Rue Delperdange)

The pillbox is named for Corporal Emile Cady, the first Belgian soldier killed in the defense of Bastogne in 1940.

11. Bastogne Historical Center/Mardasson Monument ★★★★

Colline du Mardasson
About 200 yards beyond Point 10, fork right and follow signs for Mardasson and the Historical Center.
T: (0)61-21-1413
Daily, 10 a.m.-5:30 p.m., March-April, October-December
Daily, 9:30 a.m.-6 p.m., May-September
Closed January 1-February 14, December 24, 25, 31
Adult: €8.50; Senior/Student: €7; WWII veteran: Free

Bastogne's official war museum, this is by far the area's most slick and professional presentation. In a comfortable screening room, visits begin with an excellent 30-minute documentary recounting the superhuman defense of Bastogne. With interpretive text, photos and maps, presentations in the large, airy museum include life-size battle re-creations and pieces ranging from tanks to a wartime Harley-Davidson motorcycle to the coat worn in the battle by German General Hasso von Manteuffel (donated by the general himself after the war). Lots of weaponry, good gift shop. Across the parking lot is the enormous, 40-foot-tall Mardasson Monument, built in the shape of a five-pointed American star with tributes to all 50 states. Massive panels inscribed with gold letters tell the story of the battle. Sixty steps ascend to the top of the monument, where orientation maps augment views of the historic battlefield. The tall radio tower in the distance is located at the approximate location of McAuliffe's headquarters. Behind the U.S. and EU flags is a crypt with three mosaics representing the Protestant, Catholic and Jewish religions. Visits to the Museum and Monument last 90 minutes to two hours.

12. Peace Woods (Bois de la Paix) ★★

From fork in road described in Point 11, veer left for Bois de la Paix, then left again after about 3 km, then follow small brown signs. About 5 km from point 11.

In a large field that occupied the battle's front line, or no man's land, signs next to newly planted trees (donated by various international cities) tell the tragic stories of such war-torn places as Warsaw (Poland), Cassino (Italy), Kiev (Ukraine) and Stalingrad (Russia).

13. 506th Foxholes ★

From Bastogne, take N30 north (toward Liege) 5 km to the village of Foy. Turn right (southeast) at the crossroads of the main paved road between Foy and Bizory. After about 1 km, a dirt or mud tractor path on left side of road leads into woods. Foxhole remnants can be found 10 or so feet from the road near this path.

Difficult to find without a guide, indentations in the woods here mark the spot where the Easy Company "Band of Brothers" popularized by the Stephen Ambrose book and HBO series of the same name dug in, enduring hellish weather and artillery attacks.

14. Desobry House ★

On N30 (toward Liege), at south end of Noville, about 7.5 km north of Bastogne. Entering the village it's number 15, the fourth house on left.

The two-and-a-half-story stucco house was headquarters of American General William Desobry, who led the defense of Noville from December 18-20 before being captured. German forces then occupied Noville during the battle. Signage across the street describes events here. About 150 yards up the road on the right, a plaque on the side of a church recalls German soldiers who fought here.

15. German Cemetery ★★★

From Point 14, return toward Bastogne along N30. After 2 km turn right at sign for Recogne 2 (a left turn here leads to Point 13) and follow the road 1 km. The cemetery is 5 km north of Bastogne.

Low gray crosses mark the shared graves of 6,807 German soldiers, most of whom died during the Bulge. The desperation of the German military is evident in the ages of those buried (many teenagers) as well as ranks—naval graves indicate the severe manpower shortages at this stage of the war that forced German sailors onto front lines. A small chapel and low wall of red sandstone enclose the north side of the cemetery. See page 8 for more information on German military cemeteries.

16. American Indian Military Monument ★

About 300 yards beyond Point 15, take first possible left turn (toward signs for La Ferme des Bisons). After 1 km, take first possible right turn (just beyond fenced meadow) and proceed 120 yards. The small monument is on left side of road.

At the edge of a bison ranch and American Indian Museum, this simple, unique monument was erected by a Belgian man "in the loving memory of the American Indian soldiers fallen for the liberation of Belgium."

17. 502nd Foxholes ★★★

From Point 16, return 120 yards, crossing main road and continuing straight along potholed, dirt road into woods. After 1 km turn right at first crossroad. Follow this road 1.5 km to where it breaks out of woods, with wire fence and open fields to the right. At the wire fence is a rough dirt road leading right, into the woods. Park car and walk this road about 100-120 yards, then cut into the woods (just past where road begins to dip downhill). About 10 yards into the woods, a large field of foxholes begins.

Directions from Bastogne: Follow N30 north toward Foy and Noville. After about 3 km, note the large, ball-shaped water tower on left. Make first possible left turn on unmarked road, directly opposite faux-stone, two-story building with yellow trim. (If you see the Mitsubishi dealership, you've gone just past it.) Follow this road about 200 yards (around a 90-degree curve) to the edge of the woods. Park at the wire fence and dirt road on left and follow previous directions.

This large field of more than 50 foxholes was the command area of the 101st Airborne's 502nd Regiment. The foxholes here are deeper, more numerous and easier to find than the 506th foxholes (Point 13) and, in the quiet woods, do more than most sites to impart a visceral sense of the battle experience.

RELATED SITES BEYOND BASTOGNE

Fort Fermont ★★★★★

See Auxiliary Sites, France: Maginot Line (page 237).

Brussels

Eight days after Germany launched its May 10, 1940, attack on Belgium, Luxembourg, the Netherlands and France, Belgian King Léopold III surrendered to German occupation, which lasted until September 1944. The capital of Brussels suffered little damage during the war. The occupation was generally peaceful, the city's beauty and largely friendly locals making it a prized R&R spot for German soldiers. As a result, Brussels' wartime history is often overlooked by travelers—a mistake for anyone passing through the city on the way to Bulge sites to the east. Concentrated in the old Lower Town, the following bold-faced sites can be located with the aid of the Map of Brussels (Stadtplan-Brüssel) and walked in a short afternoon. The map is issued by Brussels International Tourism and Congress (BITC) and available at the tourist office at Grand Place (in Hôtel de Ville, 02-513-8940, daily in summer, 9 a.m.-6 p.m., Monday-Saturday in winter, 10 a.m.-2 p.m.). Rosemary Van Peer (03-888-5928) is an English-speaking guide with an exceptional knowledge of Brussels and its World War II sites.

On May 18, 1940, at **City Hall (Hôtel de Ville) in Grand Place ★★★★**, the mayor of Brussels formally handed control of the city to German Lieutenant-General Joachim von Kortzfleisch. The same mayor returned control of the city here to British liberators on September 4, 1944. British General Bernard Montgomery took part in a formal ceremony here four days later. (A statue of Monty stands in front of the Montgomery Metro station, one stop beyond the royal military museum.) Across the square, the house now occupied by **El Greco restaurant ★** was a military recruiting station for Nazi sympathizers. Just south, at the corner of Rue de l'Étuve and Rue du Chêne, the nationally famous, irreverent bronze fountain **Manneken-Pis ★** features a naked boy urinating into a pool. Each September 3 and 4, the statue is dressed in the uniform of the Welsh Guards, the division that liberated the city. A few blocks south, at Place Rouppe, the five-story, Art Deco–style building on the northwest corner was used as the **German Police headquarters ★**. A five-minute walk southeast, at 126 Rue des Tanneurs, are unmarked gray gates that were (and are) the back entrance of the **Capucines Catholic cloister** ★ where many Jews were hidden or given aid. About 23,000 Jews were deported from Brussels during the occupation—fewer than 20,000 live in the entire country today. Around the block, the cloister's façade is fronted by a daily flea market. A few blocks east, at 62 Rue des Minimes, is the **Church of Minimes** ★★. Inside, the Martyr of Loreto Chapel is dedicated to Allied pilots who reportedly prayed here before missions—many of their names are inscribed on the walls. Just south, at Place Poelaert, is the magnificent **Palace of Justice** ★★★★. Still a courthouse, the building can be entered on weekdays from 9 a.m.-3 p.m. As a World War I soldier, Adolf Hitler passed through Brussels. More than two decades later, his singular memory was of this huge 19th-century structure, which he considered among the most impressive in all Europe. Hitler returned in June 1940, and the building became Brussels' Nazi headquarters. In front is a monument to veterans of both world wars. A few-minutes walk northeast, at Place Royale Konningsplein, is the grand **Royal Palace** ★★★, open to the public from late June through the first weekend in September. Per arrangement with Léopold III, the Germans didn't occupy the palace, though an enormous swastika flag flew from its rooftop throughout the occupation. Around the corner at Place du Trône, the six-story, marble-and-stone building served as **Headquarters of the Oberfeldkommandatur** ★★, the highest-ranking German officer in Belgium.

Royal Museum of the Army and Military History (Musée Royal De l'Armée et d'Histoire Militaire) ★★★★★

Parc du Cinquantenaire 3, Brussels
Metro: Merode
T: (0)2-737-7833
Tuesday-Sunday, 9 a.m.-noon, 1-4:45 p.m.
Closed Mondays, January 1, May 1, November 1, December 25, election days

Among the largest and best military museums in the world, this monumental attraction—housed in a massive hall opened in 1910—is loaded with more than 100,000 military artifacts. Armor, weapons, uniforms, even sleds used in pre-mechanized northern campaigns— from the Middle Ages through Napoleon and both world wars, if it was used in battle, it's probably represented here. Having undergone major renovations in 2003, the absorbing World War II gallery includes multimedia presentations in addition to collections focusing on all major combatant nations in Europe. Mint-condition tanks include many American models (M24 Chaffee, Sherman "Jumbo" and "Firefly"), as well as a British Mark IV Churchill, a Soviet T-34 and IS-3 Stalin, and a German panzer. Aircraft include a De Havilland Mosquito, a Hawker , a Supermarine Spitfire and others. One could spend an entire day in this museum. The World War II gallery is worth a full afternoon. A site not to be missed.

Breendonk Fort National Memorial (Mémorial National du Fort de Breendonk) ★★★

Off A12, halfway between Brussels and Antwerp
Brandstraat 57, Willebroek
T: (0)3-860-7525
Daily, 9:30 a.m.-5:30 p.m.
(last entry 4:45 p.m.)
Closed January 1, last Sunday of August, December 25
Adult: €6; Senior/student/child: €5

Dating to 1906, this Belgian Army fort became a detention camp during the German occupation. It's now one of the most striking and well-preserved historical remnants of Nazi terror in Belgium. Numerous videos, photographs and audio effects re-create Breendonk's terrible past. The tour, updated in 2003, takes about two hours.

OTHER AREA ATTRACTIONS

Grand Place, Brussels

With intricately detailed guildhalls dating to the 17th century, this public square is the pride of Belgium and one of Europe's architectural wonders. Filled with tourists, this is the first stop for anyone spending even just a day in Brussels.

Waterloo Battlefield and Wellington Museum (Musée Wellington)

147 Chaussée de Bruxelles, Waterloo
Off N5, 18 km south of Brussels.
T: (0)2-357-2860
Daily, 9:30 a.m.-6:30 p.m, April-September
Daily, 10 a.m.-5 p.m., October-March
Closed December 25, January 1

Adult: €5; Student: €4; Child (6-12): €2

The site of the battle where 50,000 died and Allied forces defeated Napoleon on June 18, 1815, draws more than one million visitors annually. In the center of Waterloo (population 20,000), the museum is housed in British commander the Duke of Wellington's headquarters and includes 14 rooms displaying weapons, battle plans and other items. The actual battlefield lies about five km south of Waterloo in the village of Mont-St-Jean. The 226 steps to the top of the Lion's Mound memorial provide instructive views of the battlefield.

GETTING TO AND AROUND BASTOGNE

Bastogne is 171 km southeast of Brussels, almost all on fast highway. Visitors should pick up a copy of the Bastogne walking map (published by Institut Géographique National) at the Tourist Information office (061-21-2711) on Place McAuliffe. A retired Belgian Army officer and fluent English speaker, Henri Mignon (061-21-3502) is an energetic, highly professional guide and leading local authority on the Battle of the Bulge. For general information on Bastogne and Belgium travel (airlines, maps, and so on), see Belgium chapter, page 67.

ACCOMMODATIONS

Bastogne
Best Western Hotel Melba

49-51 Avenue Mathieu
T: (0)61-21-7778 F: (0)61-21-5568
www.hotel-melba.be
34 rooms
From €67-146

With a good location about 100 yards from Place McAuliffe, this clean, comfortable hotel is the best in town. The restaurant and buffet breakfast are excellent, the English-fluent staff extremely accommodating. Fitness room and sauna available to guests. Free parking.

Hotel Collin

8-9 Place McAuliffe
T: (0)61-21-4358 F: (0)61-21-8083
www.hotel-collin.com
16 rooms
€85-140

With a central Place McAuliffe location, this small hotel has nice, tidy rooms. Its restaurant, called 1900, is worth a visit even if you're not a hotel guest.

Brussels
Hotel Metropole

31 Place de Brouckère
T: (0)2-217-2300 F: (0)2-218-0220
www.metropolehotel.com
306 rooms
From €359-389

This first-class hotel is located within a few blocks of Grand Place and Old Town's many shops, pubs and outdoor cafes. A Metro station (direct line to the Army Museum) and good internet cafe are a block away. Elegant lobby bar and restaurant. Rooms facing the century-old Brouckère Square are best.

6

Belgium

with LUXEMBOURG

Battle of the Bulge II

Houffalize

THE WAR YEARS

I n autumn 1944, with Allied forces marching with impunity across western Europe and Germany clearly losing the war, Adolf Hitler was desperate for a victory. Turning his eye toward the scene of one of Nazi Germany's great triumphs—the 1940 blitzkrieg through the so-called Low Countries—Hitler concocted a plan he called *Wacht am Rhein* (Watch on the Rhine), a grand counteroffensive against the Allied armies now massed along or just inside Germany's western border. German forces would carry a surprise attack west through the dense Ardennes forest, considered an unlikely place for a renewed German offensive. *Wacht am Rhein*'s strategic objective was the recapture of Antwerp, Belgium, liberated by the Allies in September 1944. In regaining this critical port city, Hitler believed he could drive a flanking wedge through enemy lines. This, in turn, would heighten bickering among Allied chiefs, thereby provoking the inevitable dissolution of the testy American-British alliance.

The idea was Hitler's own, and vigorously questioned within the *Oberkommando der Wehrmacht* (OKW). In a November 1944 communiqué to Field Marshal Karl Gerd von Rundstedt, General Alfred Jodl frankly admitted that the Antwerp objective "appears to be disproportionate to our available forces." Jodl's concerns would be vindicated, but not before an appalling battle that would enter the pantheon of American military actions as the Battle of the Bulge—named for the large indentation or "bulge" in U.S. Army lines created by charging German troops. (In Europe, the battle is generally referred to as the Battle of the Ardennes.) Fought between December 1944 and January 1945, across a front roughly 50 miles wide and 65 miles deep, it would become, in terms of combatants, the largest single battle in which the United States has ever fought, including Gettysburg.

The initial phase of the German attack achieved total surprise. On December 16, 1944, 300,000 men arranged into three armies—6th SS Panzer Division (north), 5th Panzer Army (center), 7th Army (south)—poured into Allied lines along a front stretching from the German town of Monschau in the north to Echternach in Luxembourg. Led by mercurial and highly decorated 29-year-old Colonel Jochen Peiper, 4,800 men and 117 tanks of the northern forces charged toward the Meuse River and Antwerp, reaching La Gleize (more than 20 miles inside Belgium) in two days. Resting and newly arrived American troops were overrun with ease. In the central Ardennes, 7,000 men of the U.S. 106th Infantry Division were taken prisoner—the most American POWs captured in a single action by the Germans. December 23, 1944, marked the extreme point of German advance at Dinant (roughly 65 miles inside Belgium) on the banks of the Meuse. This was the western end of the "bulge," which, drawn on a map, with its base along Germany's Belgian and Luxembourg borders, resembles a jagged arrowhead.

Early Wehrmacht victories notwithstanding, the battle quickly devolved into a series of heroic and unconnected holding actions by Allied troops (largely American). Fought from snow-lined foxholes amid the relentless chill of the worst winter in memory—a New Year's Day 1945 temperature of 13 degrees was recorded by one American unit—these determined defensives came to define the Battle of the Bulge. Rushed into combat following the surprise attack, many soldiers fought without winter clothing, in some cases without even weapons or ammunition.

"Shivering was as normal as breathing," wrote Stephen Ambrose in *Band of Brothers*, the book and later television series that added yet another layer to the battle's mythic legacy. "The men looked like George Washington's army at Valley Forge, except that they were getting fired upon, had no huts, and warming fires were out of the question." Many spent freezing weeks outdoors, never once entering the inside of a building.

Ambrose's "brothers," members of the U.S. 101st Airborne Division, took part in the famed defense of Bastogne (see Battle of the Bulge I). Less publicized but as strategically important were stands at isolated points across the front, in places such as St. Vith, Rocherath, Krinkelt and Stoumont, by members of the often uncredited 1st, 2nd, 9th and 99th Infantry Divisions, among many others.

"Most accounts of the fighting turn on the 101st Airborne and its defense of Bastogne," according to *The Oxford Essential Guide to World War II*. "But the key position in the Battle of the Bulge was Elsenborn Ridge. The holding of it ... against attackers that outnumbered (the Americans) five or more to one, was the outstanding achievement of the battle."

Hampered by traffic jams and fuel shortages, Germany's offensive stalled toward the end of the year. After a massive "Great Blow" Luftwaffe air attack on January 1, which damaged but didn't break Allied lines, the dramatic Wehrmacht advance was thrown into reverse. Hitler flew into a rage, but his apoplectic demands for defense were futile against the revitalized Allied charge. On January 11, American and British forces met up at La Roche-en-Ardenne in a symbolic victory. With the Allies largely back in control of the original front, the battle was declared over on January 28.

Although British, Canadian, Belgian, Luxembourg and French soldiers performed important and courageous roles, the Battle of the Bulge would be memorialized, as Winston Churchill immediately put it, as "the greatest American battle of the war." Of the almost 600,000 American soldiers who took part, about 20,000 were killed, 40,000 wounded, 16,000 taken prisoner. At least 800 tanks were destroyed. German losses to death, injury or capture totaled about 100,000, nearly a third of its attacking force.

Hitler's gamble to repulse the Allied advance on Berlin had failed. The Wehrmacht's last professional reserves were spent. The U.S. Army had emerged as unequivocal makeweight in Europe. Within months, the Third Reich's collapse would be complete.

See Bastogne chapter (page 46) for more on the Battle of the Bulge.

SOURCES & OTHER READING

A Time for Trumpets: The Untold Story of the Battle of the Bulge, MacDonald, Charles B., Morrow, 1985

Hitler's Last Gamble: The Battle of the Bulge, December 1944-January 1945, Dupuy, Trevor, HarperCollins, 1994

The Battle of the Bulge: The German View, Perspectives From Hitler's High Command, Parker, Danny S. (ed), Greenhill Books, 1999

A Tour of the Bulge Battlefield, Cavanagh, William, Leo Cooper, 2001

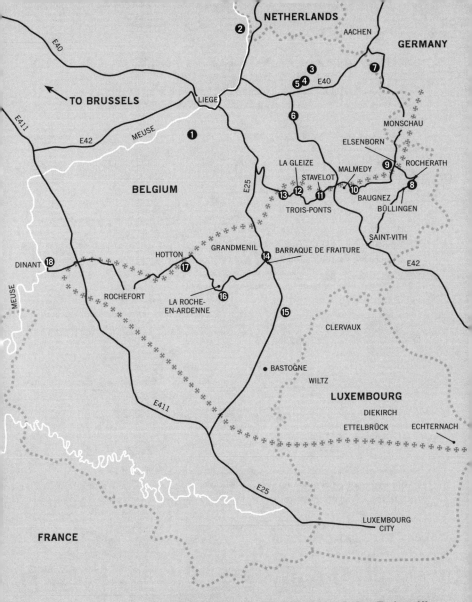

Belgium/Luxembourg (Battle of the Bulge II)

1. Ardennes American Cem. and Mem.
2. Fort Eben-Emael
3. Henri-Chapelle American Cemetery and Memorial
4. U.S. First Infantry Monument
5. Remember Museum
6. Envisal Historical Museum 1940-45
7. Siegfried Line "Dragon Teeth"
8. Krinkelt
9. Camp Elsenborn Museum
10. Malmedy Massacre Memorial
11. Stavelot/U.S. Halftrack
12. Dec. 1944 Hist. Museum/Tiger Tank
13. Stoumant
14. Parker's Crossroads
15. Houffalize
16. La Roche-en-Ardenne/Battle of Ardennes Museum
17. Hotton Commonwealth War Cemetery
18. Dinant/German Advance Monument

N

20 KM

BELGIUM (ARDENNES) TODAY

Population: 10.2 million (country); 4 million (Wallonia)
Country Code: 32 • €1 = $1.36/£0.67

With dense woodlands, rolling hills and rushing rivers, the Ardennes corner of eastern Belgium (part of the prosperous French-speaking region of Wallonia) is highly regarded for outdoor recreation and pastoral beauty. Its combination of scenery, visitor services and relaxed pace make it one of the most pleasant places to visit in Europe. English is widely spoken.

As the only large city in the area, the former industrial center of Liège (population 200,000) provides business-class hotels, rental cars and decent nightlife. Many U.S. troops were stationed here following the liberation of Belgium. Most other cities and villages have fewer than 10,000 residents. Hotels tend to be small, but clean, impeccably operated and located within picturesque villages and towns. With the exception of numerous tanks,

museums and monuments, there are few remaining traces of the ferocious battles waged here. Still, wandering the villages, fields and woods, it's possible to get a sense of the difficulties the terrain presented to combatants on both sides.

Two to three days are suggested to cover sites in this chapter. Add a day for Liège, another for visits to one or more of its forts. One could spend months cataloging the hundreds of historical markers and monuments spread throughout the countryside and in villages. The high points are presented here. For those with a more intense interest, William Cavanagh's *A Tour of the Bulge Battlefield* is the best guide devoted specifically to the area. Charles Whiting's *The Battle for the German Frontier* includes several chapters on touring Bulge battlefields.

POINTS OF INTEREST

1. Ardennes American Cemetery and Memorial ★★★★

On Route N63, 19 km southwest of Liège on the southeast edge of the village of Neupre (aka Neuville-en-Condroz)
T: 703-696-6897 (American Battle Monuments Commission, Arlington, Virginia)
Daily, 9 a.m.-5 p.m.
Closed December 25, January 1

Like all ABMC cemeteries, this exquisitely manicured field is poignant both for its beauty and the staggering number of crosses and Stars of David marking gravesites. Covering more than 90 acres, 5,328 graves of Americans who died primarily during the Battle of the Bulge are arranged in the form of a Greek cross (visible from the air). A rectangular memorial of limestone and granite dominates the field. The chapel includes three huge campaign maps with engraved battle histories. Despite the name, the cemetery is

not actually in the Ardennes, but this hardly detracts from its role as a pristine place for somber reflection.

2. Fort Eben-Emael ★★★★★

Off N671, in Eben-Emael, 23 km north of Liège
Rue du Fort, Eben-Emael
T: (0)4-286-2861
Open one weekend per month, March-October (consult www.fort-eben-emael.be or call for schedule). Tours at other times available by prior arrangement.
Adult €6; Senior/Student: €5; Child €3

Though not directly connected to the Battle of the Bulge, Fort Eben-Emael deserves a visit. The most famous of the Forts of Liège (see page 66), this gargantuan subterranean defense structure— including nearly four miles of corridors— was manned by 750 to 1,000 soldiers. Built between 1932-35, it was intended to be a primary safeguard against German invasion. It wound up becoming the object of the first glider attack in history when, on May 10, 1940, nine German gliders landed on its wide, flat roof. Combat engineers pierced its dense concrete with hollow-charge explosives, a technology largely unknown to the Belgians. The bulk of the fort fell to the Germans within a half-hour, though the official surrender didn't occur until the next day. It was one of the most dramatic and frightening episodes of the German blitzkrieg that swamped western Europe in 1940. German troops occupied the fort until September 11, 1944, when Americans captured it, along with six unfortunate German defenders who had not already evacuated.

Tours of the well-preserved structure last about two-and-a-half hours and include a number of stairs. It's the mammoth dimension of the fort, the miles of concrete and palpable certainty of German attack they betray, that leaves the strongest impression. It's always cold underground—sweatshirts are vital, even in summer. If time allows a visit to only a single Liège fort, this is the one.

3. Henri-Chapelle American Cemetery and Memorial ★★★★

On N3, 3.2 km northeast of Henri-Chapelle, 29 km east of Liège
T: 703-696-6897 (Arlington, Virginia); (0) 8-768-7173
Daily, 9 a.m.-5 p.m.
Closed December 25, January 1

This 57-acre cemetery contains the bodies of 7,989 American military dead, most killed during the Bulge and 1944-45 American advance into Germany. From the highway that passes through the reservation, the visitor gets good views of the rolling countryside, once a battlefield. Along with seemingly endless rows of brilliant marble crosses and Stars of David, the dominant feature is a massive colonnaded monument, inscribed with state seals and names of 450 soldiers whose remains were never recovered or identified. Within the memorial, two maps carved in black granite show the progress of U.S. forces through Europe. A place of austere beauty and immense sadness.

4. U.S. 1st Infantry Division Monument ★

Along N3, about 1.5 km east of Clermont

The 25-foot-high obelisk is engraved with the insignia of "The Big Red One," the storied American Army division that liberated Liège in 1944. The site overlooks the edge of the Ardennes.

5. Remember Museum ★★★

4 Les Beolles, Thimister-Clermont.
Off N3, in Clermont, 2.5 km west of Point 4
T: (0)87-44-6181
First Sunday of each month, 9 a.m.-6 p.m., or by appointment for groups of 10 or more
€4

One of the better private museums in Belgium, this one was founded by gregarious owner Marcel Schmetz, a schoolboy during the German occupation and subsequent liberation. The museum occupies three rooms of his childhood house and farm, where 110 American soldiers briefly camped, leaving behind the material that would form the origins of the large collection here. Starting with the Sherman tank parked outside, the focus is on American liberators, but also includes rare, personal memorabilia, uniforms, Nazi flags, re-created battle scenes, a large truck from the Red Ball Express with an African-American mannequin at the wheel.

6. Envisal Historical Museum 1940-45 ★★★

Rue de la Saunerie 31, Envisal
Off Route E42, in Envisal, about 10 km south of Point 5, just south of Verviers
T: (0)87-33-9388
Last Sunday of the month, 10 a.m.-noon, 2-6 p.m.
Adult: €2; Child (12 and under): Free

Another private collection, this one belongs to an excavator who has unearthed aircraft and bodies of soldiers. It's also the home of the Center of Military Archaeology. Uniforms, weapons, aircraft parts, photos, personal items and much more occupy several floors. Odd items include a wedding gown made from parachute silk and a large display of pre-war currency from the devastated German economy that includes a 20-billion-mark note from 1933.

7. Siegfried Line "Dragon Teeth" ★★

At intersection of Schmidhof Strasse and Monschauer Strasse, in village of Schmidhof (Germany), 9 km south of Aachen along alternate road between Aachen and Monshau (not Route 258)

Remnants of the Siegfried Line (or Westwall) defense fortifications are visible at many points along Germany's western border. This is one of the best places near Bulge sites to see a long line of "dragon teeth" tank obstacles. Exactly at the intersection described above, a large field of the three-foot-high, pyramid-like obstacles can be seen directly along the road.

8. Krinkelt ★

Off N658 between Rocherath and Büllingen, 41 km south of Point 7

Along the main road in the village of Krinkelt, directly across from the Catholic church, are handsome marble memorials to the U.S. 2nd and 99th Infantry Divisions. Bitter, early Bulge defense by Americans in the twin villages of Krinkelt and Rocherath included hand-to-hand combat and allowed for a strategic retreat to nearby Elsenborn Ridge.

9. Camp Elsenborn Museum/Elsenborn Ridge ★★

At Camp Elsenborn (Belgian Army facility). Off N647, main entrance is 4 km west of Elsenborn (follow signs).
T: (0)80-44-2105
Monday-Thursday, 9 a.m.-4 p.m., Friday noon-4 p.m.
Closed on weekends.

Much of Elsenborn Ridge is now occupied by the Belgian Army. The on-base museum is generally not open to the public, but visits can be arranged by calling ahead. It's a decent museum with mannequins in uniforms, large guns, vehicles and battle maps showing various troop positions. Amid low, rolling hills, the high point of the ridge (at 2,000 feet elevation, just east of the village) is difficult to discern.

Peiper's Route

The following four sites were part of Colonel Jochen Peiper's *Kampfgruppe* advance. Peiper's entire route can be followed along the main roads connecting Losheim, Honsfeld, Büllingen, Ligneuville, Stavelot, La Gleize and Stoumont, with side trips between Stavelot and Trois-Ponts and La Gleize and Werbomont. For biographies of Peiper, consult *Jochen Peiper* by Patrick Agte or *The Devil's Adjutant* by Michael Reynolds.

10. Malmedy Massacre Memorial ★★★

At intersection of N632 and N62, near Malmedy, 20 km southwest of Point 9. Look for signs to Baunez/Malmedy American Memorial.

One of the most notorious episodes of the Bulge was the December 17, 1944, Malmedy Massacre (also called the Baunez Massacre), in which about 150 unarmed American prisoners were lined up in a field, then swept with fire from German pistols, machine guns and tanks. Some were shot in the head at point-blank range. Some men ran as shots were fired, others played dead in the mud. At least 30 survived and made it back to Allied lines with their stories. Peiper earned the lifelong epithet "Butcher of Malmedy," though it's almost certain he neither ordered the slaughter nor was present for it.

A chapel, a large crucifix and a 100-foot-long stone wall (officially known as the Baugnez American Memorial) stand in memory of the event. The massacre took place across the road from the memorial (on Route N62) in the field to the left of the house with hedges lining the driveway.

11. Stavelot/U.S. Half-track ★★★

Off N68, 14 km west of Point 10. From town center, turn left at signs to Abbaye and Musées on Rue du Châtelet, then left at fork after about 0.5 km. The half-track is just across the bridge.

This half-track (a troop and supply vehicle with a combination of tires and tank treads) was relocated here in 1995. The vehicle bears the names of battalions that fought in Stavelot. The French plaque on the opposite side of the bridge notes this as the spot where, between December 18, 1944, and January 13, 1945, "Nazi troops of von Rundstedt were repelled by forces of the First American Army." With a lovely town square, Stavelot (population 6,500) is one of the nicer villages covered in this chapter.

12. December 1944 Historical Museum/Tiger Tank ★★★

Rue de l'Eglise 7, La Gleize-Stoumont. On N633, in La Gleize, 11 km west of Point 11. From N633, follow signs to Musée.
T: (0)80-78-5191
Daily, 10 a.m.-6 p.m.; March-late November;
Open weekends and holidays late November-February
Adult: €5; Student (12-18): €4; Child (6-11): €3

The highlight of the museum is the rare German Tiger tank parked in front (no admission needed). Limited by slow speeds and voracious gas consumption, the Tiger was nevertheless the largest and most intimidating tank built in World War II. William Cavanagh, author of *A Tour of the Bulge Battlefield*, calls this tank from the 501st Heavy SS Panzer Battalion "undoubtedly the most impressive relic on the battlefield today." The small museum has many pieces of original material— weaponry, field guns, uniforms, equipment. From roads around La Gleize, one can clearly sense how the terrain of deepening forest and ravines contributed to the fatal slowing of Peiper's tank advance.

13. Stoumont ★

On N633, 3 km west of Point 12

Behind the town's new church are plaques and a memorial honoring a priest who hid Jewish children inside his church, the town's American liberators and Stoumont's WWI and WWII dead. There's little evidence of the fighting here. The town is included for being the point where Peiper's advance was finally stopped.

14. Parker's Crossroads ★★

At intersection of N30 and N89 near E25, at Barraque de Fraiture

The intersection of the main roads between Bastogne/Liège and La Roche/St-Vith near the village of Barraque de Fraiture was the site of a ferocious, five-day Allied stand led by American Major Arthur Parker III. A German panzer division ultimately overran the position, but Parker's 500 men succeeded in pulling off an important delaying action along a major supply route against a much stronger force. At the crossroads now is a plaque and a 105 mm howitzer.

15. Houffalize ★

On N30 at junction of N860 and N826, about 15 km south of Point 14

Houffalize gained fame as the meeting point of the U.S. 1st and 3rd Armies on January 16, 1945, an event that effectively cut off the Bulge in Allied lines. In a small park along N30 is a panzer tank. The armies actually met outside town. From the center of town, follow N860 a few km toward La Roche-en-Ardenne. A plaque commemorating the armies' meeting is at the bridge crossing the Ourthe River.

16. La Roche-en-Ardenne (aka La Roche)/ Battle of the Ardennes Museum (Musée de la Bataille des Ardennes) ★★★

Rue Châmont 5, La Roche-en-Ardenne
On N89, about 16 km west of Point 15
T: (0)84-41-1725
Wednesday-Sunday, 10 a.m.-6 p.m., (closed weekdays January-March)
Closed December 25, January 1
Adult: €5.95; Child (12 and under): €3

This museum has an original German Enigma cryptographic machine, a good collection of uniforms and weaponry, a Hillerich and Bradsby baseball bat (left by U.S. troops) with Roger Hornsby's autograph emblazoned on the barrel. About 75 yards from the museum, at the corner of Rue de la Gare and Rue de Cielle, a plaque notes the spot where American and British forces met up on January 11, 1944. Virtually destroyed by Allied bombardment, La Roche-en-Ardenne is now a pretty town of 4,000 residents. Near the main church is a U.S. Pershing tank. Along the road on the hill overlooking town is a parking lot with a tank (an Achilles with Sherman parts added) dedicated to the British 1st Northamptonshire Yeomanry. From this tank, 100 yards along the road toward Marche, is a memorial to the U.K.'s 51st Highlanders.

17. Hotton Commonwealth War Cemetery ★

On N86, about 17 km northwest of Point 16. Enter town center. At T intersection, turn left at sign for 23 Rochefort. (On the small Ourthe River bridge is a plaque honoring the 51st Engineer Combat Battalion, which held the bridge against a fierce German assault on December 21, 1944.) After less than half a km, turn left at green sign for Hotton War Cemetery.

On this small plot are rows of headstones

marking the graves of 667 British and Commonwealth war dead, many killed in battle in the surrounding area.

18. Dinant/German Advance Monument ★★

On N94, about 40 km west of Point 17. Entering town from the east on N94 (off N97), turn right (toward town center) at the T intersection at Meuse River. Proceed 200 yards. The roadside monument is just past the spot where the road passes through a narrow cut in a tall rock.

A triangular rock monument marks the furthest point of the Nazi's "Bulge" advance, reached December 23, 1944, on the banks of the Meuse. Primary German objectives were to cross this river and advance on Antwerp. The monument is nondescript, but Dinant (population 13,000) is a superb city, with an impressive hilltop citadel and an afternoon's worth of crowded streets to walk. In the Citadel parking area (082-22-3670; summer, 10 a.m.-6 p.m.; winter, 10 a.m.-4:30 p.m.; €5) are a 40 mm anti-aircraft gun and a battered British Gloster Meteor Mark VIII (post-war model), the only Allied jet fighter to see WWII action.

LUXEMBOURG (GRAND DUCHY DU LUXEMBOURG)

An intense, often-overlooked Bulge battleground, Luxembourg (population 437,000) is one of Europe's most scenic countries. Perched above a spectacular river valley, Luxembourg City (population 80,000), with Old World architecture and sublime views, shouldn't be missed.

Luxembourg City

Excepting the American and German cemeteries, the following sites are within walking distance of each other or just outside Luxembourg City's pedestrian-only center.

Three miles due east of Luxembourg City center and five km southwest of the airport in an area called Hamm (from A1, follow exits to Aéroport past the terminal, then follow signs for Cimetières Militaires) the **Luxembourg American Cemetery and Memorial** ★★★★ (daily, 9 a.m.-5 p.m., closed December 25, January 1) is

impressive, and not simply because General George Patton is buried here. Occupying a 50-acre glade, the resting place of 5,076 American soldiers is dominated by a massive square chapel of white stone. Officers and enlisted men aren't separated in American military cemeteries—Patton's grave is the single exception. At the head of the burial field—halfway between the flagpoles—his plot was moved because sites around it were being trampled by visitor traffic, and also, reportedly, because his wife wanted him eternally placed front and center. About 1.5 km from the cemetery (follow signs for Deutscher Soldatenfriedhof) is **Sandweiler German Cemetery** ★★★, where, of the 10,913 German soldiers at this vast plot, 4,829 are in a mass grave beneath a towering cross. A tour of

Luxembourg City can begin at **Patton's Headquarters** ★★, now the Pescatore Foundation building, at end of Avenue Pescatore, just outside the no-vehicles zone of the city center. A plaque at the entrance of this magnificent orange stone building marks it as Patton's place from December 21, 1944, to March 27, 1945. Inside he planned the 3rd Army's decisive breakthrough at Bastogne during the Bulge and delivered his famed prayer for favorable weather. Visitors may wander the courtyard, but the building is closed to the public. Attached to the City Palace (Cercle Municipal) at Place d'Armes is a **Liberation Plaque** ★ commemorating the American capture of the city, September 10, 1944. The **National Monument of Luxembourg Solidarity** ★ is located on Boulevard F.D. Roosevelt at Plateau du St-Esprit. Inaugurated in 1971, this circular concrete eyesore recalling resistance during the Nazi occupation has the distinction of being perhaps the least attractive public monument ever constructed in memory of World War II. At **Place Winston Churchill** ★★, about eight blocks west of the city center, stands an eight-foot-tall statue of the British leader. South of the city center, opposite the main train station, the **Hotel Alfa** ★★ (Mercure Grand Hotel Luxembourg Alfa, 16 Place de la Gare, 352-49-0011, from €140) gained fame as Patton's residence during the Battle of the Bulge. With a stunning beaux-arts façade, the business-class hotel has been thoroughly modernized.

Diekirch ★★★★
Diekirch National Military History Museum
10 Bamertal, 100 yards from town center
T: 352-80-8908 or 352-80-4719
Daily, 10 a.m.-6 p.m., (opens at 2 p.m. November-March) Last entry 5:15 p.m.
Adult: €5; Student: €3

By far the most important Bulge museum anywhere, this incomparably complete collection resembles a war buff's fantasy garage. If it was used during the Bulge, chances are it can be found here. It holds innumerable vehicles, uniforms and photos.

Lacking the spit and polish of the Historical Center in Bastogne, the collection is nonetheless several magnitudes larger and better. A must for Bulge historians.

Ettelbrück ★★
Next to a Sherman tank, the replica of the **Patton statue** at West Point (on right side of main road entering Ettelbrück from Diekirch) has been called the most important Patton monument in Europe. In town, the **General Patton Memorial Museum** (5 Rue Dr. Klein; 352-81-0322, daily, 10 a.m.-noon, 1-5 p.m., July 1 to September 15, Sundays only, 2-5 p.m., September 16-June 30, Adult: €2.50; Child: €1.25) more extensively recaps the Battle of the Bulge than it does Patton.

Clervaux ★★★
In the city center at Château de Clervaux, the **Battle of the Ardennes Museum** (352-92-1048, daily, 11 a.m.-6 p.m., summer only, €2.50) has an excellent display of uniforms including a U-boat commander mannequin in menacing black leather body suit, GIs in winter whites and several WAC dress outfits. Also here are aircraft models, weaponry and assorted relics. Clervaux is an outstanding medieval market village, sunk into a narrow valley and surrounded by rugged hills and forest. It's a great spot to spend a day. A five-minute walk from the city center, the **Golf-Hotel Claravallis** (3 Rue de la Gare, 352-92-1034, www.claravallis.lu, from €60) is a clean, well-run hotel. It served as a regimental headquarters commanded by American Colonel Hurley Fuller. During the German capture of the village in December 1944, Fuller and his staff escaped by scaling the steep rock wall behind the hotel. Alas, they were later captured west of Clervaux.

Wiltz ★★
Entering Wiltz from Bastogne, follow signs to Vieux Château and Ville Haute. Up the hill is an 80-foot-tall monument dedicated to civilians slaughtered here or sent to concentration camps in 1942. A few hundred yards up the street is the **Battle of the**

Ardennes Museum (Château de Wiltz, at Square Eisenhower, 352-95-7442, daily, 10 a.m.-noon, 1-5 p.m., summer only). The square is named for General Dwight Eisenhower, who visited the town. Across the street is a keystone memorial to the U.S. 28th Infantry Division, which liberated the town in September 1944. Inside the castle, the two-story museum has a medium-size collection of artifacts.

RELATED SITES WITHIN BELGIUM

Liège ★★

On the Meuse River, Liège was one of wartime Belgium's critical industrial and transportation centers, and later a base for thousands of post-liberation Allied soldiers. It was also the epicenter of the Belgian Resistance and is now home to the **National Resistance Monument** (along Avenue Rogier in Parc Avroy, just across Albert Bridge). The monument consists of four 12-foot-high limestone figures, dressed in trench coats, carrying machine guns and generally looking stealthy. A few minutes walk behind the monument (away from the river) is **The Educational Center for Tolerance and Resistance**, known locally as Les Territoires de la Mémoire (86 Blvd. D'Avroy, 04-232-7040, open weekdays 9 a.m.-4 p.m., first and third Saturday of each month, noon-3 p.m., closed Sundays and holidays, adult €2.50, child €2). Established in 1993, the highly political museum presents a credible and absorbing view of Nazi persecution of Jews, Gypsies, political dissidents and others. Entirely in French, the 45-minute, self-guided exhibit includes film, photography (graphic) and a replica rail car in which visitors are locked in tight quarters for five minutes. Those under 12 are not admitted. At Blvd. La Constitution 41, a plaque on the outer wall of the **St-luc Liège school** notes it as the "site occupied by the 56th General Hospital U.S. Army" in the post-liberation period. At Parc de la Citadelle, the brick remains of the **Liège Citadel** overlook the city. The Germans used the Citadel as a prison. On the grounds is a cemetery for political prisoners executed by Nazi troops. Within the Citadel's inner ring is an altar and tall hedge, behind which prisoners were tied to wooden posts and shot. The holes where the posts stood remain at this sobering location.

Forts of Liège ★★★★

To protect Liège from German onslaught, eight massive concrete fortresses were constructed in a ring around the city in the late 1880s and 1890s. These forts were used during World War I, then updated between the world wars. In addition, four new, larger and even stronger forts were constructed in the 1930s. Though they utterly failed to stop the 1940 German blitzkrieg, all 12 forts stand today as eerie evidence of a time when fear and hellbent industry gripped Europe. Most can be visited (call ahead for schedules). The best are **Fort Eben-Emael** (see Point 2) and **Fort Aubin-Neufchâteau** (site of an 18-day Belgian-German battle in May 1940), but each has unique characteristics. Walls as high as 25 feet above ground reveal simply the tips of these concrete icebergs, typified by miles of subterranean passageways. Multiple levels house every component of an underground city for up to 1,000 men. Information on each fort can be found in the comprehensive French-language "Les Forts 1914 & 1940" pamphlet published by Liège Province Tourist Federation (Blvd. De la Sauvenière 77, 4000 Liège, Belgium, 04-232-6510, ftpl@prov-liège.be). Running clockwise around the city, the accessible forts are: Eben-Emael (04-286-2861), Aubin-Neufchâteau (04-86-26-6240), Barchon (04-387-4364), Battice (087-67-9470), Tancrémont (087-31-5532), Embourg (04-343-9928) and Flémalle (0498-38-5838). On Liège's western flank, three *petit* forts in use during World War II (still massive and fascinating) are Hollogne (04-234-0950), Loncin (04-246-4425) and Lantin (04-246-5544).

GETTING TO/AROUND BELGIUM

Brussels is the airline hub of Europe and capital of Belgium and the European Union, so it's hard to find a major airline that doesn't fly there. As of this writing, Continental Airlines (800-231-0856) offers the best fares from the United States.

Getting around Brussels is easy by foot, taxi, Metro (subway) and train. Belgian Railways (in country at 02-555-2555; from the United States call Rail Europe, 800-438-7245) operates an extensive and excellent railway system that covers the entire country.

The only way to efficiently see the points of interest in this chapter is by car. (See Driving, page xv.) The drive from Brussels to Liège is about 100 km. Michelin's Benelux map covers Belgium, Luxembourg and the Netherlands. More detailed maps are Michelin 213 (includes Liège and northern section of this chapter) and Michelin 214 (includes Bastogne and southern section of this chapter). Either the Benelux or two numbered maps are recommended (many good competing maps are available in the country). The Office de Promotion du Tourisme Wallonie-Bruxelles (in Brussels, 02-504-0390, www.belgique-tourisme.net) publishes the Battle of the Ardennes Belgium map—it lacks detailed road information, but does provide a visual reference covering the entire Bulge battlefield. It's available at tourist offices, museums and major tourist points. Accredited and excellent, English-fluent guide Jacques Gilson (032-4367-6558) is a former Belgium Army tank officer with a thorough knowledge of Bulge battlefields and Liège forts.

ACCOMMODATIONS

Liège
Hotel Bedford
36 Quai Saint Léonard
T: (0)4-228-8111 F: (0)4-227-4575
www.hotelbedford.be
149 rooms
€210-235

On the banks of the Meuse River, this business-class hotel, opened in the 1990s, is among the best places to stay in this midsize city. The garden courtyard bar is nice, but the Convent restaurant on the first floor (above the lobby) is worth a look even if you're not staying the night. The all-brick room—a restored convent—is dominated by stunning ceiling arches.

La Roche-en-Ardenne
Hostellerie de la Claire Fontaine
Route de Hotton 64
T: (0)84-41-2470 F: (0)84-41-2111
www.clairefontaine.be
28 rooms
From €77-127

About two km outside scenic La Roche-en-Ardenne, the hotel sits on the Ourthe River, surrounded by green fields and forests. With chandeliers and lots of wood, the lounge and lobby exude an Old Europe feel. Rooms are basic (small but clean), and the service is good. The hotel's four-star rating is due in large part to its well-regarded French restaurant.

Stavelot
Romantik Hotel le Val d'Ambleve
Route de Malmedy 7
T: (0)80-28-1440 F: (0)80-28-1459
www.levaldambleve.be
Rooms: 20
€100-125

In a green Ardennes valley, this handsome, two-story country house built in 1937 was converted to a hotel and thoroughly renovated in 2001. The bright, stylish rooms are individually decorated and have large windows. Its four-star rating is a mild stretch, owing largely to the successful restaurant, which serves "refined cuisine."

7

Pas de Calais

Éperlecques Blockhouse

THE WAR YEARS

Often left off the roll of principal theaters of activity, France's Pas de Calais region was among the war's hardest-hit areas. Here, an Allied defeat inspired one of the century's greatest moments of oratory, Canada suffered its most profound loss of the war, Germany built the strongest points of its Atlantic Wall and Adolf Hitler based his technological gamble to end the war.

After launching Hitler's murderous blitzkrieg on western Europe on May 10, 1940—Belgium, Luxembourg and the Netherlands were swiftly overrun—German forces crossed the Meuse river on May 15, broke across France and rushed toward the overmatched and retreating French Army and 200,000 men of the British Expeditionary Force. At Dunkirk, on May 26, Allied remnants set up a defensive perimeter and prepared to evacuate the continent. Dubbed Operation Dynamo, the ugly retreat from Dunkirk's piers and beaches would come to be regarded in mythic scale across the Allied world. As aircraft dueled in the skies and German submarines lurked offshore, warships and a ragtag fleet of private British and French vessels—fishing boats, barges, small pleasure craft—made numerous 22-mile crossings from Dunkirk to Dover, ferrying soldiers to safety in England. In all, 861 vessels rescued 338,226 men. The evacuation ended on June 4 when German soldiers broke the perimeter, capturing 40,000 prisoners and all of the Allies' heavy equipment, ammunition, artillery, vehicles and fuel.

From the maw of this burning humiliation, new British Prime Minister Winston Churchill (his term began May 10, 1940, the day Germany invaded the West) summoned his immeasurable powers of speech to spin the military disaster into a propaganda triumph. On June 4, his address to the House of Commons, drawing upon the spirit of Elizabeth I rallying her troops against invading Spaniards at Tilbury, concluded with a now familiar refrain: "We shall fight on the beaches, we shall fight on the landing grounds, we shall fight in the fields and in the streets, we shall fight in the hills; we shall never surrender!"

"The escape captured the minds and hearts of the British people at a time when it looked probable that we too would soon be invaded," wrote historian David Knowles.

Invasion of England was on Hitler's mind, but when that failed to progress beyond the aerial Battle of Britain (July-October 1940), his attention swung to the European coast-line bordering the English Channel. Here, it was widely believed, the inevitable Allied invasion of Europe would come. To thwart such an effort, Hitler ordered construction of the Atlantic Wall, a massive belt of interconnected fortifications along nearly 2,000 miles of coastline that included barbed wire, machine-gun nests, bunkers and monumental blockhouses protecting huge guns. By June 1944, 9,000 positions were complete, 5,700,000 mines had been laid in northern France. Between Calais and Boulogne, the wall was built to its most intense degree. Even after the June 6, 1944, D-Day landings, Hitler believed the "real" invasion would come here.

The first major test of Germany's hold on the French coast was Operation Jubilee, a raid by about 6,000 men (4,963 Canadians, 1,074 British, 51 U.S. Rangers) at Dieppe. Never intended to establish a permanent position on the continent, the operation nevertheless carried ambitious objectives—compel Germany to strengthen Channel defenses at the expense of the Eastern Front, gain experience in amphibious assault and test new equipment.

Launched on August 19, 1942, at five points around Dieppe—the main assault came along the town's rocky beach and promenade—the attack was an unmitigated failure. German machine gunners hidden in Dieppe's chalky cliffs enfiladed the wide, exposed beaches as men leapt ashore. Nearly all were instantly pinned down. Retreat was nearly impossible. The chaotic raid lasted nine hours. The Royal Air Force lost 106 aircraft to the Luftwaffe's 48. More than 900 Canadians were killed, that country's highest fatality total on any day of the war. Casualties including prisoners totaled 3,642.

"As an experiment in making a landing, Dieppe was extremely expensive," wrote historian Martin Marix Evans. "That it was a necessary experiment remains an open question."

Dieppe is somewhat the equivalent of Tarawa in the Pacific—a battle of dreadful consequence that many argue was a critical step toward the successful 1944 landings in Normandy. Churchill's assessment of the disaster reputedly inspired the idea for the temporary Mulberry Harbor used so effectively by the British in Normandy. (On September 1, 1944, Dieppe was liberated by Canadian troops.)

As Germany's fortunes declined, Hitler grew fanatical in his push for secret weapons, flying bombs (*Vergeltungswaffen*) designated as V1, V2 and V3. The V1 "buzz bomb" was essentially a (highly inaccurate) cruise missile, a 27-foot-long jet aircraft that carried a 1,875-pound warhead at more than 400 mph. The more fearsome V2 was a true rocket, 46 feet tall with a 2,150-pound warhead and a top speed of 2,500 mph. The monstrous V3, never completed, was a long-range cannon intended to fire a fin-stabilized shell up to 60 miles. The first V1 was launched against London on June 13, 1944. By war's end, 20,000 had been fired at Britain and Belgium. About 1,000 V2s were launched at Britain, Belgium and Luxembourg. Weapons of terror that achieved no military gain, each was developed, built and/or launched in the Pas de Calais region.

The special-weapons program's brilliant progenitor, Wernher von Braun (and about 100 of his colleagues), escaped prosecution after the war. Spirited out of Germany, they became key figures in the United States' nascent space program. Von Braun, who died in Virginia in 1977, became the chief architect of the Saturn V super-booster that propelled the Apollo spacecraft to the moon in 1969.

SOURCES & OTHER READING

Dunkirk: Anatomy of Disaster, Turnbull, Patrick, Batsford, 1978

Dunkirk: The Storms of War, Harris, John, David & Charles, 1980

The Miracle of Dunkirk, Lord, Walter, Viking Press, 1982

Dieppe: Tragedy to Triumph, Whitaker and Whitaker, McGraw-Hill Ryerson, 1992

Unauthorized Action: Mountbatten and the Dieppe Raid, Villa, Brian Loring, Oxford University Press, 1989

Hitler's Atlantic Wall, Saunders, Anthony, Stroud, Sutton, 2001

Smashing the Atlantic Wall: The Destruction of Hitler's Coastal Fortress, Delaforce, Patrick, Cassell, 2001

German Secret Weapons of the Second World War: The Missiles, Rockets, Weapons, and New Technology of the Third Reich, Hogg, Ian V., Greenhill Books/Stackpole Books, 1999

Pas de Calais

1. Historical Centre for Dunkerque
2. Allied Memorial/Evacuation Beach
3. *Princess Elizabeth*
4. Second World War Museum Calais
5. Memorial/Bunker
6. Cap Blanc Nez
7. Battery Todt
8. World War II History Museum
9. La Crèche Bunkers
10. Fort Mimoyecques V3 Base
11. Éperlecques Blockhouse V2 Base
12. La Coupole
13. Dieppe Memorial/Museum
14. Dieppe Assault Beach
15. Dieppe Canadian War Cemetery
16. Bunkers/Dieppe Secondary Beaches

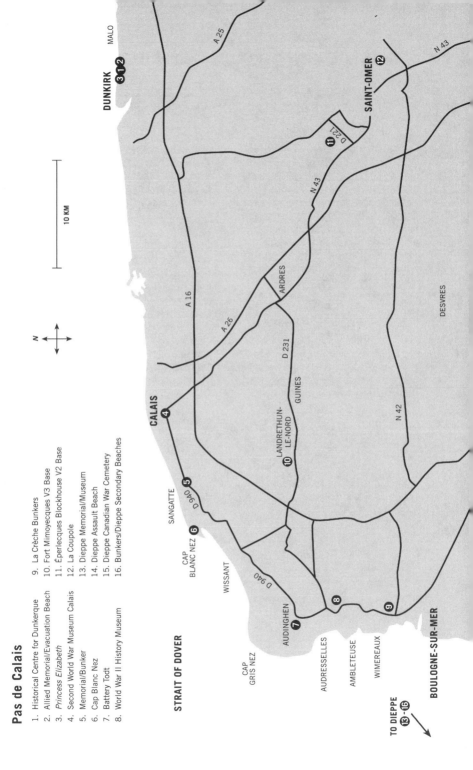

PAS DE CALAIS TODAY

Population: 80,000 (Calais); 73,000 (Dunkirk); 38,000 (Dieppe)
Country Code: 33 • €1 = $1.36/£0.67

Running across the northern tip of France, from the Belgium border near Dunkirk to the Authie river at Berck-sur-Mer, the Pas de Calais region is noted for sandy beaches, bracing breezes, rolling farmland and picturesque villages. France's trendy, swimming beaches might be in the south, but for laid-back beach atmosphere and ease of travel, this region is a find ... at least for Americans. With Calais just 22 miles from Dover, England (now the home of the Eurotunnel Terminal, it's the busiest ferry port in Europe), the area has long been a holiday retreat for British tourists.

With a busy shopping strip, lots of restaurants and a sandy beach, the centrally located Calais is the best place from which to base a visit. To the east, Dunkirk, with its large port and heavy industry (oil refining, textiles, machinery), is best done as a day trip. In the Haute Normandy region (southwest of Pas de Calais), friendly Dieppe's rocky beach doesn't discourage sunbathers, but there are enough walking, shopping and eating opportunities to fill a weekend.

Not to be missed is the remarkable Côte d'Opale, about 35 km of sandy beach that stretches westward from Calais to Boulogne-sur-Mer. Key spots are Cap Blanc Nez and Cap Gris Nez, dramatic cliffs that plunge into the sea. For travelers, this is also an area with several major Atlantic Wall points of interest—a perfect synthesis of outstanding travel and significant history. Three or four days are recommended to cover all the sites in this chapter.

POINTS OF INTEREST

Dunkirk

The three sites listed below merit a collective ★★★★ rating, based largely on Dunkirk's wartime significance. Negotiating this industrial, traffic-filled city is probably not worth the trouble for those with only a passing interest in Operation Dynamo.

1. Historical Centre for Dunkerque (Centre Historique de Dunkerque/Memorial du Souvenir) ★★

Rue des Chantiers (west end of beach, aka Plage des Alliés).
From highways entering Dunkirk, follow signs to Malo, then Malo les Bains and Plage des Alliés.
T: (0)3-28-66-7921

Daily, 10 a.m.-noon, 2-5:30 p.m., May-September (other times by appointment)
Adult: €3.50 Under 12: Free

This midsize museum recounts the evacuation with photos and relics, such as the intact engine of a British Spitfire shot down over Dunkirk. Large models of chaos on the beaches impressively bring life and perspective to the drama that unfolded here.

2. Allied Forces Memorial/Evacuation Beach ★★★

From Point 1, walk a few hundred yards toward the sea (roughly northeast), crossing the bridge spanning the canal.

At the western end of the long, sandy beach is a stone monument (12 feet high, 20 feet long) commemorating the sacrifices of the French and Allied armies. With its long esplanade (lined with touristy shops and restaurants), the beach, which is easy to walk, is crowded in summer with vacationers. Other than the memorial, little indicates the epic events that occurred here. Next to the monument is a km-long concrete quay, popular with walkers, that passes dock-side evacuation points. Opposite the quay, about 200 yards west of the monument and across the channel, is a small memorial dedicated to navy casualties of the evacuation—between 4,000 and 5,000 men were lost at sea, along with 250 craft (including 20 warships) and nearly as many Allied planes.

3. *Princess Elizabeth* ★★

Port Est, off Avenue de l'Université. From Point 1 parking lot, turn left (south) and proceed down Rue des Chantiers about 200 yards. Turn right at first opportunity. At first traffic circle, follow signs for Les Darses and Université. This road becomes Avenue de l'Université. After crossing two bridges and traveling 1.5 km, veer left at signs toward Ostende. Park at the Pôle Marine shopping complex. The ship is anchored behind it.
T: (0)3-28-65-8181

Restored and rented for private functions, this 1927 British paddle steamer made four trips between Dunkirk and Dover during Operation Dynamo, rescuing 1,763 men. The 195-foot-long ship was then used as a minesweeper and anti-air-craft vessel during the war.

4. Second World War Museum Calais (Musée de la Seconde Guerre Mondiale de Calais) ★★★

Parc St-Pierre, Calais
T: (0)3-21-34-2157
Daily, 11 a.m.-5 p.m., February-April, October, November
Daily, 10 a.m.-6 p.m., May-September
Call for reservations at other times.

Adult: €6; Student/Child: €5; Family (two adults, two children): €14

This excellent museum is spread through 21 chambers of a large, wartime bunker. Exhibits include those pertaining to nearby V1, V2 and V3 bases. Displays include a scale model of the Normandy invasion and exhibits on the Atlantic Wall.

Atlantic Wall/Route D940

Heading west from Calais, the two-lane D940 hugs the Côte d'Opale, passing some of the most impressive remains of the Atlantic Wall. For coastal scenery alone, it's one of the best drives in France. This drive along the Atlantic Wall merits a cumulative ★★★★★ rating.

5. Memorial/Bunker in Sangatte ★

In the small town of Sangatte, about 3 km west of Calais, a 20-foot-high mono-lith honors World War I and II soldiers. In Sangatte, concrete ruins of German defense bunkers are visible near beach

houses and sand dunes. One of the Atlantic Wall's largest fortifications, Battery Lindemann was located in Sangatte, from where it shelled England. Its remains have been nearly obliterated by Chunnel construction, landfill and other development.

6. Cap Blanc Nez ★★★

Three km west of Sangatte is the turnoff for Cap Blanc Nez (look for the stone tower on the hill), a viewpoint with breathtaking views of the coast and countryside. Numerous open bunkers and reinforced concrete positions are scattered near the main parking lot. Though it can be windy, this is a great picnic spot.

7. Battery Todt (Musée du Mur de l'Atlantique) ★★★★

On D940, in Audinghen, just west of Cap Gris Nez (look for large, white letters spelling "Musée" on side of concrete blockhouse), 21 km south of Point 6
Daily, 9 a.m.-7 p.m., June-September
Daily, 9 a.m.-noon, 2-6 p.m., October-May (weekends only December, January)
T: (0)3-21-32-9733
Adult: €5.50; Child: €2.50

Named for Fritz Todt, whose Todt Organization oversaw virtually all Third Reich construction projects, this battery was one of the seven largest Atlantic Wall bunkers. It protected a gargantuan 380 mm gun, which fired one-ton shells into England. The gun is no longer inside, but the intact blockhouse's size and density (walls and roof are 11 feet thick) are striking. The museum includes weapons, vehicles and other artifacts. The *pièce de résistance* is a fully preserved K5 280 mm German railway gun built in 1941. With a barrel almost 120 feet long, it had a range of 53 miles (with a special shell). The largest mobile guns ever built, railway guns were huge and slow loading (a train of 28 support cars accompanied the weapon) but used effectively by the Wehrmacht to demolish enemy defenses. The world's only other gun of this type is located at the U.S. Army Ordnance Museum in Aberdeen, Washington (410-278-3602).

8. World War II History Museum (Historique de la Seconde Guerre Mondiale) ★★★

On D940, in Ambleteuse, 4 km west of Point 7
T: (0)3-21-87-3301
Daily, 10 a.m.-6 p.m., April-mid-October (open weekends mid-October-November, March);
Closed December-February
Other months by appointment for groups
Adult: €5.50; Child: €3.80

A museum dealing with all of World War II, from Poland 1939 to Hiroshima 1945, this is, in terms of presentation and polish, the most impressive museum along D940. Covering 800 square meters, the collection is highlighted by life-size battle re-creations with more than 120 mannequins in uniforms. Though it includes some interesting pieces (e.g., a Japanese flight suit), the Pacific section is relegated to a small room.

9. La Crèche Bunkers ★

Along D940, 8 km south of Point 8
Fenced off, several large German bunkers rise above the grass on the inland side of the road. About 250 meters beyond the bunkers are signs for Terlinchtun Cemetery, the burial place of 4,534 Commonwealth soldiers, most from World War I.

10. Fort Mimoyecques V3 Base (Fortresse de Mimoyecques) ★★★

Off D231, in Landrethun-le-Nord. Follow signs for Base V3 Mimoyecques and Fortresse de Mimoyecques. About 22 km northeast of Point 9, or 20 km southwest of Calais
T: (0)3-21-87-1034
Daily, 11 a.m.-6 p.m., April-June, September 1-November 11
Daily, 10 a.m.-7 p.m., July, August
Closed all other times
Adult: €5.50; Child: €4

Construction of this 2,000-foot-long, subterranean tunnel housing V3 construction began in September 1943. Continuous Allied bombing forced the Germans to abandon the site in August 1944. The immense tunnel and 50-degree-angled launch shafts that were intended to support the approximately 415-foot-long gun tubes (no gun is inside, no V3 was ever fired in combat) have an eerie quality. The enormity of the project and history of the "London Gun" (the weapon here was intended to obliterate the British capital) are fascinating. The hour-long, self-guided tour explains the mechanics behind the V3. There's a memorial inside to Lieutenant Joseph Kennedy, brother of the future president, who died when his plane went down over the English Channel during a raid on the site. With a constant 50-degree underground temperature, warm clothing is recommended.

11. Éperlecques Blockhouse V2 Base (Le Blockhaus d'Éperlecques) ★★★★

Rue des Sarts, Éperlecques
Off D221, in Éperlecques, about 30 km southeast of Calais. From Calais follow N43 south to D221 east toward Éperlecques. Proceed through town of Éperlecques, turning left onto small Rue des Sarts. Follow signs for Blockhaus Éperlecques for 1 km (veering right at first fork). From Point 10, follow D231 east to N43 south and follow prior directions. About 35 km east of Point 10.
T: (0)3-21-88-4422
Daily, 2:15-5 p.m., March
Daily, 10 a.m.-noon, 2:15-5 p.m., April,October
Daily, 10 a.m.-7 p.m., May-September
Daily, 2:15-5 p.m., November
Closed December-February, holidays
Adult: €7; Student: €5.50; Child: €4.50

Beginning in March 1943, more than 35,000 men (mostly forced laborers) took a year to build this enormous complex for constructing and launching V2 rockets. The massive grounds (the self-guided audio tour takes about 90 minutes) include stations explaining the history and technology of the V2. Also on site is an original mobile V1 launch ramp with replica V1 on top. But it's the epic scale of the blockhouse—72 feet tall with 16-foot-thick concrete walls—that leaves visitors awestruck. Work at this facility, which could store 120 V2s (each about 46 feet tall), was eventually abandoned due to Allied bombardment. To stand before this behemoth is to stand before a frightening and visceral representation of Nazi Germany's grand ambitions and nearly commensurate abilities.

12. La Coupole ★★★★★

Off BP284, 5 km outside St-Omer. From Calais, follow A26 south (toward Paris/Reims) to exit 3 and follow signs for La Coupole for about 10 km. It's about 45 km southeast of Calais. From Point 11, drive west to A26 south and follow previous directions.
T: (0)3-21-12-2727
Daily, 9 a.m.-6 p.m., September-June
Daily, 10 a.m.-7 p.m., July, August
Closed late December to early January (dates vary) for annual maintenance.
Adult: €9; Child: €6; Family: €19.50

Pas de Calais' major military attraction, this concrete monster rises from the hillside like a primitive planetarium. The enormous dome—236 feet in diameter and almost 18 feet thick—was built to protect a launch site and underground work facility for the V2, the first missile to reach the stratosphere. Today, the dome holds two cinemas and exhibition galleries that recount the war and Germany's secret-weapons program. An elevator takes visitors to work areas below the dome. Exhibits draw a clear line from Hitler's war machine to the Nazi engineers who critically aided the triumphant American moon landing in 1969. Numerous short documentaries, audio-guided headsets, full-size reconstructions of the V1 and V2 weapons. Complete English signage. Allow two to three hours to tour.

Dieppe

One of the most poignant spots in the war for Canadians—the failed raid here was a national tragedy that cast a shadow over the Canadian military for years afterward—Dieppe today is one of the more pleasant and scenic towns on the French coast. The white chalk cliffs that tower above the main beach in front of town are photogenic, as is the small harbor. As in so many places in Europe, it's surreal to imagine such a charming place as the scene of terrible violence and loss.

13. Dieppe Memorial/Museum of August 19, 1942 (Dieppe Mémorial du 19 Août 1942) ★★

Le Petit Theater, Place Camille St-Saëns (just behind Hôtel La Présidence)
T: (0)2-35-40-3665
Daily, 2-6:30 p.m., May-September
Closed Tuesday and all other times
Adult: €2.30; Under 16: Free

In the main room of the ornate Le Petit Theater (occupied briefly by a handful of gritty Canadian troops), the museum recounts the Dieppe raid with blow-by-blow accounts of the fighting. The bell of the HMS *Berkeley*, sunk during the raid, is on display. The centerpiece is a permanent display of large black-and-white portraits of veterans who returned in 2002 for 60th-anniversary ceremonies.

14. Assault Beach ★★★

Along Boulevard Maréchal Foch

Though it attracts sunbathers in summer, the principal landing beach in front of the town and esplanade is rocky. The long, wide beach—one gets a terrifying look here at how badly the Canadians were exposed—is dominated by gorgeous, white chalk cliffs. Beneath the cliff-top castle is a stone plinth and flower beds

in the shape of maple leaves. On the beach in front of the three-star Hotel Aguado (30 Boulevard de Verdun, 02-35-84-2700) is a 10-foot-tall monument dedicated to French-Canadian troops.

15. Dieppe Canadian War Cemetery ★★

Rue des Canadiens, 4 km south of town. From the western end of the beach, take the main road (called Rue de Sygogne here and eventually Avenue Gambetta) south toward Paris and Rouen and follow cemetery signs.

In this small, peaceful plot are buried 707 Canadian and 232 British soldiers. Most died in the Dieppe raid. A plaque shows the landing beaches and describes the raid.

16. Bunkers/Secondary Beaches ★★

Leave town from the western end of the beach along the main road (called Rue de Sygogne here). After a few blocks, turn right on Rue Toustain toward Varengeville-sur-Mer and Pourville and follow road uphill. After two km, the remains of a German bunker are visible behind a fence (private property) on the inland side of the road. Just beyond this, the road begins a scenic descent into the village of Pourville and rocky landing beaches used by the South Saskatchewan Regiment and Cameron Highlanders of Canada. A Canadian flag flies at a small remembrance monument in the village. The road continues three km to Varengeville-sur-Mer, former site of the German Battery Hess, neutralized early in the raid by a daring and successful commando attack. The commando landing beaches, designated Orange I and II, are just west of the village. Another two km beyond is a memorial to French victims of both world wars.

GETTING TO/AROUND PAS DE CALAIS

From many U.S., Canadian and European cities, dozens of airlines fly nonstop to Paris' Roissy-Charles-de-Gaulle Airport. As of this writing, Continental Airlines (800-231-0856) offers the best fares from the United States. See page 12 for information on France's national railway.

The only way to efficiently see the points of interest in this chapter is by car. (See Driving, page xv.) The drive from Paris to Calais and/or Dunkirk is about 275 km. Widely available in France, De Rouck's France map is a good road map covering the entire country. More detailed local maps, including the national Office of Tourism's Tourist Map (Carte Touristique), are available at gas stations, convenience stores and major tourist points. The Calais Office of Tourism is located in Calais at 12 Blvd. Clémenceau (03-21-96-6240).

For cross-channel ferry information call Eurotunnel at 08-705-35-3535 (from U.K.) or 03-21-00-6100 (from France), or Hoverspeed seacat ferry service at 44-0870-240-8070 (U.K. reservations center) or 00800-1211-1211 (continental reservations center).

ACCOMMODATIONS

Calais
Metropol Hotel

45 Quai du Rhin
T: (0)3-21-97-5400 F: (0)-3-21-96-6970
www.metropolhotel.com
40 rooms
From €66

This nondescript traveler's hotel is a few minutes walk from Calais' main World War II museum (Point 4), train station and busy city center. Features include free parking and a stylish English pub in the lobby. Like much of Calais, the hotel is often filled with British travelers using the nearby car ferry and Eurotunnel Terminal from Dover.

Holiday Inn Calais Coquelles

Avenue Charles de Gaulle
T: (0)3-21-46-6060 F: (0)3-21-85-7676
www.holidayinncoquelles.com
118 rooms
€125-150

Equipped with a health center, meeting rooms and an excellent restaurant, this business-class hotel is the best in the area. It's located about two km outside the Calais city center.

Côte d'Opale

Vacation houses dot the scenic Côte d'Opale coastline in the Pas de Calais region. For rental information contact the Calais Office of Tourism (03-21-96-6240) or Borough of West Calais (03-21-85-5320).

Dieppe
Hôtel La Présidence

Boulevard de Verdun
T: (0)2-35-84-3131 F: (0)2-35-84-8670
www.hotel-la-presidence.com
89 rooms
€75-160

At the western end of Dieppe's main beach (next to the memorial and museum and casino), this is the town's top hotel. The restaurant is good, and the higher-priced rooms are large by European standards. Not a luxury hotel, it's still clean and comfortable, with a great location.

8

Berlin

G E R M A N Y

Topography of Terror

THE WAR YEARS

I n the 1920s, the National Socialist German Workers' Party (NSDAP or Nazi)
gained prominence in the raucous beer halls of Munich, but it was in the capital
of Berlin that the party seized control of the country. With the Nazis winning a
controlling bloc in the parliamentary elections of 1932 and Adolf Hitler installing
himself as chancellor on January 20, 1933, Berlin quickly became the administra-
trative and symbolic heart of the Third Reich. After a suspicious 1933 fire damaged the Reichstag building—traditional seat of the German government, loathed by
Hitler—Nazi chief architect Albert Speer, just 28 at the time, designed Hitler's new
Reichs Chancellery along Berlin's bristling government corridor of Wilhelmstrasse.
Completed in 1938, the imposing structure—ceremonial entries, extensive hallways,
quarry-loads of red marble—provided a template for Germania, the world-ruling city
Hitler envisioned as Berlin's future. This was the municipal foundation the Nazis carried
into the 1940s.

As Germany's war fortunes deteriorated, Berliners were among the hardest-hit civilians
in western Europe. By 1944, the city was subject to at least two air raids per day—
American bombers by day, British by night. Smoke, dust and fire ravaged the city.
"Berliners, gaunt from short rations and stress, had little to celebrate at Christmas
in 1944," wrote historian Antony Beevor.

Like London and other cities pummeled by air raids, Berlin didn't crumble. Trains operated. Factories remained open. People went about daily business. Still, as 1944 became
1945 and the much-feared Soviets closed from the East, a sense of desperation gripped
the city. Berliners' famed gallows humor never disappeared—the omnipresent acronym
LSR for *Luftschutzraum* (air-raid shelter) soon came to stand for *Lernt Schnell Russich*
(Learn Russian quickly). Jokes scarcely hid the truth. The avenging Red Army was being
primed by Soviet propaganda to sack Berlin without mercy as retribution for the horrors
visited upon Russia and eastern Europe by the SS and Wehrmacht. Discovery of scenes
such as those at Auschwitz-Birkenau only stiffened Russian bloodlust as the Soviet jug-
gernaut savaged crumbling German positions across eastern Europe.

Political maneuvering for post-war control of Berlin has emerged as one of the war's
most debated subjects. The Russians long regarded the German capital as their rightful
prize. Soviet leader Josef Stalin not only sensed symbolic power in Berlin, according to
Beevor, he secretly coveted the materials and scientists of Berlin's Kaiser Wilhelm
Institute, which housed Germany's atomic-research program. Deeply mistrustful of
Stalin, British Prime Minister Winston Churchill lobbied Allied Supreme Commander
General Dwight Eisenhower to seize Berlin before the Russians could arrive. Eisenhower
still receives censure for essentially ceding Berlin to the Soviets. The British were outraged at Ike's alleged naiveté, but Eisenhower wasn't the dupe many historians make
him out to be. Russia's claim to Berlin had been decided at the Yalta Conference in
February 1945 and, unlike the Red Army, Eisenhower simply couldn't justify the squander of countless lives for symbolic objectives. With their "human wave" strategy of
attack, the Soviets would lose between 70,000 and 100,000 men taking Berlin.

In the event, on April 25, 1945, U.S. Army patrols linked with Red Army soldiers near
Torgau, 70 miles south of Berlin, closing the pincers on the German Army. By that time,
the Soviets had the capital encircled. For the Battle of Berlin—the climax of the war in

Europe and one of history's largest battles—the Soviets amassed 1.5 million men and 5,000 tanks against fewer than 100,000 defenders, perhaps half of whom were old men or ill-equipped Hitler Youth. In a 10-day period, the Russians fired an unprecedented 1.8 million artillery shells on the city. As their ring of destruction tightened, Russian troops embarked on a rape and looting campaign perhaps without historical equal. "Nuns, young girls, old women, pregnant women, mothers ... were all raped without pity," wrote Beevor. Allied soldiers could be rapacious looters—the code name for the British-led crossing of the Rhine was the less-than-subtle Operation Plunder—and rape wasn't unknown in their ranks. But the scale and violence of the Red Army's "revenge" on the women of Germany was shocking. Western historians estimate two million German women were raped, 100,000 in Berlin alone. Most Russian historians refute the claims.

Berlin's defenders fought tenaciously, mostly from fear of capture by Soviets, or SS and Hitler Youth execution squads who until the very end roamed the streets in search of "cowardly" countrymen attempting to surrender or flee. But Soviet forces were over-whelming. On April 30, after a fierce room-to-room battle, Red Army soldiers raised the hammer-and-sickle standard atop the Reichstag in an event scripted for Soviet photographers. Not unlike the photo of U.S. Marines raising the American flag on Iwo Jima, the staged image stands among the most striking and enduring of the war.

Secluded for weeks in his subterranean bunker, an increasingly deranged Hitler married his mistress, Eva Braun, on April 28. She wore a black dress to the simple ceremony. On April 30, with cyanide and pistol, the couple committed suicide. To avoid Mussolini-style dismemberment, their bodies were soaked in gasoline and burned in the garden above the bunker. On May 2, German forces surrendered Berlin. With Hitler dead, national collapse came quickly. On the night of May 8-9, on the outskirts of Berlin, Soviet Marshal Georgi Zhukov accepted Germany's final surrender from a glowering Field Marshal Wilhelm Keitel.

In the 1930s, Hitler promised to eradicate Bolshevism from Europe. Instead, he'd brought it to the center of Germany. From a 1940 population of 2.2 million, just 193,000 Berliners were left (most having evacuated) by May 1945. The process would be slow and painful, but upon defeat Berliners would strive to reclaim a sense of normalcy. Three days after their surrender, the first Jewish religious service in Berlin was held in the synagogue of a former Jewish hospital in Iranischestrasse.

SOURCES & OTHER READING

The Fall of Berlin, Beevor, Antony, Viking Penguin, 2002

The Day the War Ended: May 8, 1945—Victory in Europe, Gilbert, Martin, Henry Holt, 1995

The Last Six Months: Russia's Final Battles With Hitler's Armies in World War II, Shtemenko, S.M., Kimber, 1978

Berlin Diary: The Journal of a Foreign Correspondent, 1934-1941, Shirer, William L., Knopf, 1941

Eisenhower and Berlin, 1945: The Decision to Halt at the Elbe, Ambrose, Stephen, W.W. Norton, 1967

The Villa, the Lake, the Meeting: Wannsee and the Final Solution, Roseman, Mark, Penguin, 2002

Berlin—The War, the Wall, Richison, Randy, Jaron, 2002

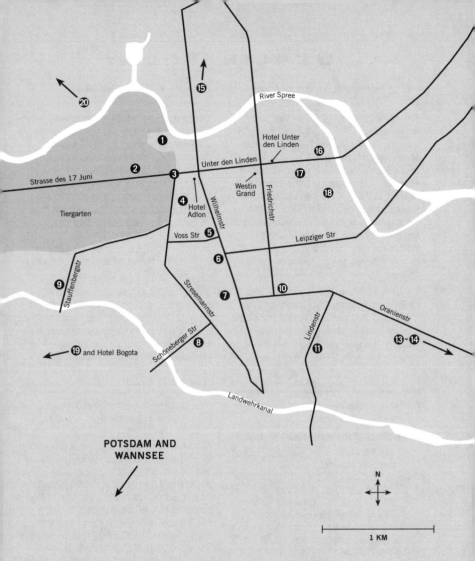

Berlin

BERLIN TODAY

Population: 3.4 million • Country Code: 49 • €1 = $1.36/£0.67

The demolition of the Berlin Wall on November 9, 1989, marked a new age for the city, but it was the 1999 completion of the national government's relocation to Berlin that accelerated the most radical changes. The reconstructed national parliament building—the glass-domed Reichstag has become a major tourist attraction—is but one of countless construction projects that have changed the look of the city. "East Berlin"—physically, at least—barely exists insofar as the visitor can see.

Berlin is an international cultural mecca—three opera houses, 150 theaters, 170 museums, 250 public libraries and countless cafes, pubs and restaurants where debates still rage about how, or even if, to preserve Germany's World War II and Cold War past. Those who want to build a new Berlin over the rubble of the old are often accused of denying the city's history. Complicating the issue is the lucrative business that surrounds that dark era. Berlin is Germany's leading city destination, and while many come for cultural attractions, others are drawn by the legacy of menace and oppression that took charge here. Cold War nostalgia as ubiquitous commercial enterprise is visible in book stores, trinket shops and museums.

Covering 343 square miles, Berlin is a sprawling city, but an extensive train, subway and bus system makes it easy to get around. Downtown sites can be walked in a single day, but a minimum of three days are needed to cover all war sites, with an extra day for Potsdam and Wannsee.

POINTS OF INTEREST

S or U indicates closest train (S-Bahn) or subway (U-Bahn) station

1. Reichstag (Parliament Building) ★★★

Platz der Republik
S: Under den Linden
Daily, 8 a.m.-10 p.m.
T: (0)30-22-62-9933 (Roof cafe)
T: (0)30-22-72-2152 (Chamber visits)
Daily, 8 a.m.-midnight (roof terrace)
Closed December 24.
Access to the visitor's gallery is offered when the Bundestag is not in session, and must be booked in advance. English tours every Tuesday at noon

In disrepair through the Cold War, the Reichstag (now Bundestag), symbol of the German government, reopened in 1999 with a glass dome placed atop its 19th-century stonework. At the southwest corner, 96 stones are inscribed with names of political opponents murdered during Hitler's reign.

2. Soviet War Memorial at Tiergarten (Sowjetisches Ehrenmal Tiergarten) ★★★

Tiergarten Park, along Strasse des 17 Juni, 300 yards west of Brandenburg Gate. Five-minute walk from Point 1.
S: Unter den Linden

A 40-foot-tall marble-and-brass semicircle topped with a victorious Red Army soldier stands within view of the Reichstag at the point where the Battle of Berlin ended. In front are a pair of T-34 tanks and artillery cannons. Many Germans would like to see Berlin's Communist monuments torn down, but the 1990 treaty that structured Soviet withdrawal stipulated that this memorial, along with the one at Treptower Park and Soviet cemetery at Pankow, would be maintained by the city. Built in 1873, the Victory Column (to the west) was repositioned by Hitler to line up with Brandenburg Gate, creating a grand boulevard for Nazi victory parades.

3. Brandenburg Gate (Brandenburger Tor) ★★

Pariser Platz
S: Unter den Linden

On January 30, 1933, columns of storm

troopers theatrically marched through Berlin's central landmark to herald Hitler's rise to power. Badly damaged in the 1945 battle, it was refurbished in the 1950s. In 1961, the Berlin Wall was erected a few yards away. The Gate and area east fell into East Berlin.

4. Memorial to the Murdered Jews of Europe (Denkmal für die ermordeten Juden Europas) ★★★★

Corner of Ebertstrasse and Behrenstrasse, 150 yards south of Point 3
S: Unter den Linden

Consuming a full square block in the center of Berlin, this massive, unforgettable memorial, a field of 2,700 concrete-slab "coffins," opened in 2005. With exhibitions on the Holocaust, an underground information center is located on the southeast corner. Development of the area (history park, monument) will continue until 2011. The memorial receives 450,000 visitors a year.

5. Hitler's Bunker/Reichs Chancellery Site ★

Near corner of Wilhelmstrasse and Voss Strasse
U: Mohrenstrasse

There were several entrances to the bunker beneath the Reichs Chancellery where Adolf Hitler and Eva Braun committed suicide. Thoroughly covered by new construction, the site's precise location is difficult to define. Before being destroyed in 1946, the Chancellery's main entry was located at 77 Wilhelmstrasse— the address is now occupied by restaurants and apartments. From here, one can walk south a few hundred yards and turn right on Voss Strasse. About 20 yards from the corner, a small school playground covers the former garden where the bodies of Hitler and Braun were burned. All exterior traces of the bunker have been destroyed. Though inaccessible, much of it remains intact more than 50 feet below ground. The site was marked in 2006 with an elaborate marker (English and German) at the parking lot at Gertrud-Kolmar-Stasse and In den Ministergarten, NE of the corner of Wilhelmstrasse and Voss Strasse.

6. Aviation Ministry Building (Reichsluftfahrtministerium)/Wilhelmstrasse ★★★

Leipziger Strasse 7 (corner of Wilhelmstrasse)
U: Mohrenstrasse

Wilhelmstrasse was the political equivalent of Washington's Capitol Hill or London's Whitehall, the nerve center of the Nazi administration. Almost nothing of it survived. This five-story, slate gray monolith—opened in 1936 as Hermann Göring's Aviation Ministry, it's still one of the largest office buildings in Berlin—is the sublime exception. In its undeniably powerful yet somehow sterile design, one can readily imagine Hitler's vision of the totalitarian Germania, the futuristic world capital he planned for Berlin to become. Closed to the public, the building is now part of the German Ministry of Finance. On the façade, the mural depicting a Socialist utopia is a fascinating leftover from East German times. Along this stretch of Wilhelmstrasse, Plexiglas historical markers (German text) note locations of Third Reich buildings and sites, virtually all vanished.

7. Topography of Terror (Topographie des Terrors) ★★★

Corner of Wilhelmstrasse and Niederkirchnerstrasse
U: Kochstrasse
T: (0)30-2548-6703
Daily, 10 a.m.-8 p.m. May-September
Daily, 10 a.m.-6 p.m. (or until dark), October-April

On the one-time location of Gestapo Headquarters, this outdoor exhibit of photos and text (all in German, English audio guide available at information center) chronicles Nazi oppression from book burnings to the Holocaust. In the shadow of the former Aviation Ministry and a 200-yard original section of the Berlin Wall, the site imparts a sense of Berlin's malevolent history. Construction of a large indoor center began in 2007. It will open in May 2010.

8. Anhalter Air-Raid Bunker (Bunker Anhalter Bahnhof/Gruselkabinett) ★★★

Schöneberger Strasse 23
S: Anhalter (3-minute walk from train station)
T: (0)30-2655-5546
Monday, Tuesday, Thursday, Sunday, 10 a.m.-7 p.m.
Friday, 10 a.m.-8 p.m.
Saturday, noon-8 p.m.
Closed Wednesday
Adult: €7.50; Student (15-18): €5.50; Child (up to 14): €5

Advertised as "the only World War II air-raid shelter permanently open in Berlin," this 38,000-square-foot, five-story bunker features a haunted house on two floors and a World War II museum on a third (two floors are inaccessible). One ticket is good for both attractions. Inside this concrete behemoth as many as 12,000 people (more than twice the structure's capacity) took refuge for weeks at a time. One display offers testimony from a woman who sat, ate and slept on a single stair for six days. The stench and claustrophobia was almost unbearable—the alternative outside was worse. Though distracting, the spook show keeps the bunker in business and is a worthwhile diversion for parties with kids who resent being dragged to historic sites. Cheesy as it is—scenes of medical dismemberment, corpses in creaky coffins, and so on—it actually produces a few decent scares. About 200 yards from the bunker along the way to or from Anhalter Station is the preserved brick and terra-cotta façade of the original Anhalter Station. Once among the largest and most beautiful stations in Europe, it was bombed to ruin.

9. German Resistance Memorial Center (Gendenkstätte Deutscher Widerstand) ★

Stauffenbergstrasse 13-14
S: Potsdamer Platz
T: (0)30-2699-5000
Weekdays, 9 a.m.-6 p.m. (until 8 p.m. Thursdays)
Weekends, holidays, 10 a.m.-6 p.m.
Closed December 23-26, December 30-January 1

Dedicated to the negligible German resistance movement, the museum is housed in the old German War Office where would-be Hitler assassin Claus von Stauffenberg worked. Von Stauffenberg successfully exploded a bomb in Hitler's Wolf's Lair command post in Poland, but Hitler survived and von Stauffenberg and co-conspirators were executed in the courtyard here. A memorial marks the spot. The exhibit is extensive but dry. It's all text (German only, 45-minute English audio guide available) and photos recounting many tragic stories.

10. Checkpoint Charlie Museum (Haus am Checkpoint Charlie) ★★★

Friedrichstrasse 43-35
U: Kochstrasse
T: (0)30-253-7250
Daily, 9 a.m.-10 p.m.
Adult: €9.50; Student: €5.50; Child (up to 14): Free

"You are leaving the American sector." Few during the Cold War could have imagined that the ominous message signposted for years at Checkpoint Charlie—the Cold War gate between the former East and West Berlin—would supply the central ethos of one of unified Berlin's top tourist attractions. The museum sits in front of a reconstructed Checkpoint Charlie—the original guardhouse is located in the Allied Powers Museum (see page 88)—and draws mixed reviews for its hodgepodge assembly of relics. There's much to see—and far too much to read—and the place does a commendable job of showing the many ingenious and sometimes tragic methods East German citizens used to escape to the West. Artwork, videos, photos and much East-West propaganda are inside. An 80-minute, 16-site audio walking tour (in German) of Cold War sites is available on CD at the ticket desk and gift shop (called "Hear We Go," it sells for €15).

11. Jewish Museum Berlin (Jüdisches Museum Berlin) ★★★★

Lindenstrasse 9-14
U: Hallesches Tor
T: (0)30-2599-3300
Adult: €5; Senior/Student: €2.50

Child (under 6): Free; Family: €10
Daily, 10 a.m.-8 pm. (closed at
10 p.m. Monday)
Last entry one hour before closing
Closed Rosh Hashanah, Yom Kippur,
December 24

Much of the point here is the building
itself—an unorthodox zigzag of colossal
expressionist architecture meant to disori-
ent and shift reality. Slanted walkways,
oddly placed windows and hallways that
veer at unexpected angles accentuate
exhibits of Nazi persecution of Jews.
Memorable features include the Holocaust
Tower, a dark, four-story vertical void that
creates a symbolic sense of confinement
and isolation. Gut-wrenching exhibits—
photos, text, videos, personal items—offer
graphic testimony to the suffering and
deaths of Jews killed under Nazi oppression. A familiar story told exceptionally
well in this super-sleek museum.

12. Tempelhof Airport (Flughafen Tempelhof) ★★

Off Tempelhofer Damm (200 yards from
U-Bahn station)
U: Platz der Luftbrücke

Small by modern standards, Tempelhof
Airport was once the largest building in
Berlin. The terminal is the city's largest
remaining example of Nazi architecture,
recognizable by its multitude of right
angles and flat surfaces. Rectangular pillars and a marble mezzanine dominate the
interior. In front of the main entrance is a
two-foot-high bronze eagle head, the only
surviving piece of the 15-foot-tall eagle
that adorned the roof from 1940 to 1962.
Between the airport and Metro station is
the Berlin Airlift Memorial, commemorating Tempelhof's role as the primary airport
used during the 1948 Berlin Airlift.

13. Soviet Memorial at Treptower Park (Sowjetisches Ehrenmal Treptower) ★★★

Along Puschkinallee. From Treptower
station, exit toward Treptower Park, walk
away from station (up Puschkinallee)
almost 1 km. Cross street at crosswalk in
front of marble arch.

S: Treptower Park

The Cold War is over, but the hammer and
sickle stand over Berlin at this largest
Soviet memorial in the city. The park is
dominated by a 35-foot-tall Soviet soldier
(baby in one hand, victory sword in the
other), an enormous gate of red marble
stripped from Hitler's Reichs Chancellery,
and a sculpture of a despairing Mother
Russia. About 5,000 Soviet soldiers killed
in the Battle of Berlin are buried here.
Sixteen 12-by-8-foot slabs are carved with
heroic scenes of battle. Soviet imagery is
emblazoned throughout the park. An
unforgettable Communist display in
modern Berlin.

14. German-Russian Museum Berlin-Karlshorst (Deutsch-Russiches Museum Berlin-Karlshorst) ★★★★

Zwieseler Strasse 4 (at corner of
Rheinsteinstrasse). From train station pro-
ceed right on Treskowallee (immediately
crossing Stolzenfelsstrasse) one block to
Rheinsteinstrasse. Turn right and follow
sign to Museum Berlin-Karlshorst, a
10- to- 15-minute walk from station.
S: Karlshorst
T: (0)30-5015-0810
Tuesday-Sunday, 10 a.m.-6 p.m.

Although a U.S.-led coalition accepted the
Third Reich's unconditional surrender in
Reims, France, on May 7, 1945, on
behalf of all the Allies, Josef Stalin insisted on a ceremony that would put the
USSR in the lead role. With all Allied
powers present, the Soviets accepted
Germany's full capitulation in this former
school building on the night of May 8-9,
1945. Soviet-flavored exhibits (all in
Russian and German, English guidebook
2) in 14 rooms tell the history of the war
in the East. Video loops feature astonishing battle footage. The Western Allies
merit only token mention. The surrender
hall is preserved in 1945 condition. It's an
impressive ceremonial chamber—high-
ceiling, formal seating, long tables—compared to the humble surroundings of the
makeshift map room of the Reims surrender (page 125). Outside are a Soviet T-34
tank, a Katyusha rocket launcher and

various German artillery. At one of Europe's most historic spots, this is a well-put-together museum.

15. Gesundbrunnen Bunker ★★★

Corner of Badstrasse and Böttgerstrasse, in front of Gesundbrunnen U station
S/U: Gesundbrunnen
T: (0)30-4991-0517

The graffiti-and-ivy-covered blockhouse is the entry to a vast subterranean air-raid complex designed for civilians. The entry is sealed off. For excellent tours of this and other Berlin bunkers, contact the Berlin Underground Association, a tremendous resource for World War II enthusiasts.

16. German History Museum (Deutsches Historiches Museum) ★★★

Unter den Linden 2
S/U: Friedrichstrasse, Hausvogteiplatz
T: (0)30-20-3040
Daily, 10 a.m.-6 p.m.
Closed December 24
Adult: €5; Youth (under 18): Free

The world-renowned museum—located in the grand 1730 Grand Prussian Arsenal—reopened in 2006 after an extensive restoration of its main building, the Zeughaus. On its ground floor, the museum features a large exhibit on the national socialist regime and the Second World War.

17. Bebel Platz (Book Burning Site) ★★

Unter den Linden at Universitätsstrasse
U: Hausvogteiplatz, Französische Strasse

Bebel Platz gained notoriety on May 10, 1933, as the site of the first mass burning of books deemed anti-Nazi. It now has a creative memorial—a window in the center of the square looking in on a collection of empty bookshelves. Surrounded by magnificent buildings—the gorgeous Opera House, domed St. Hedwig's Cathedral, Altes Palais from the 1830s, entrance to Humboldt University—it's the most photogenic square in Berlin.

18. Reichs Bank ★★

Werderscher Markt (corner of Werderscherstrasse and Kurstrasse), a five-minute walk south of Point 16

U: Hausvogteiplatz

This large building is regarded as Germany's first example of Third Reich architecture, and its right angles, austere façade and rigid features are unmistakable hallmarks of the Hitler and Nazi power aesthetic. It's now part of the federal Foreign Affairs office.

19. The Story of Berlin ★★

Kurfürstendamm 206
U: Uhlandstrasse
T: (0)30-8872-0100
Daily, 10 a.m.-8 p.m. (last entry 6 p.m.)
Adult: €9.80; Student: €8;
Child (6-14): €3.50; Family: €21

It's a bit of a tourist trap, but this 23-room, multimedia museum does a credible job of cramming 800 years of Berlin history into a single "audivisual experience." Rooms are dedicated to such phases as the Birth of a Metropolis and the Industrial Revolution. Then comes a descent into the dark basement of the Hitler years. There's a lot of text, photos, relics, wax figures, video, flashing lights, and so on. Exhibitions on Berlin's Cold War years as a "Divided City" are fair.

20. Plötzensee Memorial Center (Gedenkstätte Plötzensee) ★

Huttigpfad, off larger Saatwinklerdamm. Easiest way is train to Beusselstrasse then €5 taxi. Buses 123 or 126 leave Beusselstrasse station for the memorial.
S: Beusselstrasse
T: (0)30-344-3226 or info@gdw-berlin.de
Daily, 9 a.m.-5 p.m. (closes at 4 p.m., November-February)
Closed December 24-26, December 30, January 1
S/U: Beusselstrasse

This two-room memorial provides powerful witness to one of the Gestapo's ghastly killing grounds. The prison complex was used for more than 2,500 executions, initially by guillotine, then by multiple hangings from a row of meat hooks, a reconstruction of which is on display. English signage tells tragic stories of victims.

The very good **Battle of Seelow Heights Museum (Gedenkstätte Seelower Höhen)** ★★★ (Küstrinerstrasse 28a in Seelow, 033-4-6597), 70 km east of Berlin, is on the site of one of the last major battles of the war. An hour train ride north (to Fürstenberg Havel station), **Sachsenhausen Concentration Camp Memorial** includes a crematorium, a medical experimentation room and prison cells. Ninety km north at **Ravensbrück Concentration Camp** a memorial and small section of the original camp are all that exist. **The Olympic Stadium** ★★ of 1936 Games (Jesse Owens) fame is located west of the city at either Olympia-Stadion transit stop—Nazi statuary and architectural elements can be seen. The former Luftwaffe Gatow Airfield, also on the western outskirts, houses the excellent **Luftwaffen Museum** ★★★ (Kladower Damm 182, 030-811-0769), which has about 100 contemporary aircraft—of the five or so World War II aircraft, only the Me-163 is of German origin. See also **Dresden** and **Torgau** under Auxiliary Sites, Germany.

Southwest Berlin

The following sites can be visited along the same train lines (S7 to Wannsee then S1 to Potsdam), taking most of a day.

Grunewald Platform 17 Memorial (Grunewald Gleis 17) ★★★
Devil's Mountain (Teufelsberg)★
Grunewald Station

From Platform 17 at Grunewald Station (signposted *Gleis 17*), more than 50,000 Jews were deported to camps in the East. The football-field-long platform is now a unique monument lined with iron grates inscribed with the date, number of people deported and destination; for example, "12.3.1943/944 Juden/Berlin-Auschwitz." It's a moving, often overlooked memorial.

To walk to Devil's Mountain (30-45 minutes each way), exit the station at the opposite end of Platform 17 and head to the map and signpost at the start of Grunewald Forest just outside the station. Trails lead to the hill (by car, the mountain is off Teufelsstrasse). At 377 feet, Teufelsberg is the highest peak in Berlin. The entire "mountain" is actually a pile of bomb rubble deposited at the location during post-war cleanup, the largest of 14 such rubble hills around Berlin, covered with dirt, trees and brush: Its distinguishing feature is a series of space-age white towers at the top. These are the dilapidated remains of a U.S. military radar station that once monitored all of the Eastern Bloc. Closed in 1990, it's now a Cold War ghost town. The mountain itself is stirring evidence of how extensively Berlin was damaged.

House of the Wannsee Conference (Haus der Wannsee-Konferenz) ★★★
Am Grossen Wannsee 56-58 (ring bell for entry)
S: Wannsee
Catch bus 114 from Wannsee station to Haus der Wannsee-Konferenz. Taxis are usually in front of train station for the 10-minute drive.
T: (0)30-805-0010
Daily, 10 a.m.-6 p.m.
Closed national holidays

On January 20, 1942, 15 high-ranking Nazi officials, led by Reinhard Heydrich, met at this placid lakeside villa to discuss sterilization, deportation and other details concerning German Jews. "With breathtaking calmness," wrote author Mark Roseman, "details of the Final Solution to the Jewish Question that would affect 11 million people were discussed."

A synopsis of the conference—the so-called Wannsee Protocol—was prepared by attendee Adolf Eichmann and discovered in 1947. It's become a key and controversial piece of evidence concerning the Nazi's master plan of genocide. Almost exclusively through text and photos, the exhibit winds through 14 rooms, including the original conference and dining room, with photos of participants and original documents. The juxtaposition of cold-blooded inhumanity in such a gorgeous setting adds a surreal edge to visits. Built in 1914-15, the mansion and grounds were purchased by the SS in 1940.

Potsdam Cecilienhof Palace (Potsdam Conference Site) ★★★★

At north end of Neuen Garten, off Im Neuen Garten, a few kilometers north of Potsdam city center. Take Berlin transit to Potsdam Hauptbahnhof. Trams 92 and 95 leave from the station to Rathaus and Reiterweg/Alleestrasse stops. From either stop, bus 692 runs directly to Cecilienhof Palace. Taxis available at the Hauptbahnhof for the 10-minute drive to palace.

T: (0)331-969-4244
Tuesday-Sunday, 9:30 a.m.-12:30 p.m.; 1-5 p.m. (closes at 4 p.m., November-March). Closed Monday.
Adult: €4; Student/Child: €3

From July 17 to August 2, 1945, the Potsdam Conference (technically the Berlin Conference) that organized the political boundaries of post-war Europe (and decided surrender terms for Japan) was conducted in this half-timbered Tudor mansion. The resulting accords created the political landscape of a new Europe and set the stage for the Cold War. It takes 30 minutes to walk through the rooms used by the delegations (some English signage). Separate Soviet, American and British studies are accessible—with a large bay window and an octagonal breakfast room, the British got the best of these. The superbly preserved conference room (Great Hall) has a 40-foot-high vaulted ceiling and gorgeous views. Part of the mansion is occupied by the 41-room Schlosshotel Cecilienhof (0331-37-050; www.relexa-hotels.de). Rooms start at €150.

OTHER AREA ATTRACTIONS

Cold War Sites/Berlin Wall

The end of the Cold War brought the beginning of a curious tourist trade, epitomized by the **Checkpoint Charlie Museum** (Point 10). In addition to its large permanent collection, the museum offers guided walking tours of East and West sites. The excellent **Allied Powers Museum** (Clayallee 135, 081-8-1990) displays the original Checkpoint Charlie guardhouse along with exhibits on JFK's "Ich bin ein Berliner" speech, espionage and more. It's located on a former U.S. military base near the Oskar-Helene-Heim U-Bahn Station, in the area of Wannsee and Potsdam (see Related Sites). The **Stasi Museum** (Ruschestrasse 103, 553-6854) recounts the history of the much-feared East German State Security Ministry. One of the best places to see a long original stretch of the **Berlin Wall** is at the Topography of Terror (Point 7). The abandoned U.S. Radar Field Station Berlin atop **Teufelsberg** (Related Sites) is interesting for the adventuresome—a flashlight is helpful, along with a willingness to poke around in a fenced-off area—an open road does lead into the complex. The Image Network Company of Berlin publishes a Cold War pocket map showing the course of the now obliterated Wall, along with 11 sites of note. It's available at Berlin Story bookstore (see Getting To and Around Berlin).

Getting To and Around Berlin

Dozens of airlines fly nonstop to Berlin's Schönefeld and Tegel airports from U.S. and international cities. Transport from Schönefeld to the city is via Airport Express train (lines RE4 and RE5) every half-hour between 4:30 a.m. and 11 p.m. The ride takes 30 minutes and costs €2.10. Buses depart regularly for the Rudow U-Bahn station. Taxis to the city center cost about €35. Transport from Tegel to the central transit station at Potsdamer Platz is via JetExpressBus, which takes 30 minutes and costs €3.10. Buses depart regularly and take 25 minutes. Taxis to the city center cost about €30.

Berlin's rail-transit system (S-Bahn for above ground, U-Bahn for below) is comprehensive. Taxis are plentiful, but pricey. Fares (with tips) usually run €10-15. A rental car isn't worth the hassle. Die Bahn (national rail system) information number for travel throughout Germany is (0)180-599-6633.

Original Berlin Walks (www.berlinwalks.com) conducts historical tours in English (€12, three to four hours). The Berlin Story bookstore (Unter den Linden 10, 030-2045-3842) specializes in publications (many in English) devoted to WWII and Cold War sites. City maps are free at most hotels. Berlin Tourist Information (030-25-0025, www.berlin-tourist-information.de) has locations at Brandenburg Gate (Pariser Platz), Europa-Center (Budapester Strasse 45) and TV Tower (Alexanderplatz). Among its better deals is the Welcome Card—three days of public transportation and discounts at museums and other sites for €21.

Accommodations

Westin Grand Berlin

Friedrichstrasse 158-164
S: Unter den Linden
T: (0)30-2-0270 F: (0)30-2027-3362
www.westin.com/berlin
359 rooms
€150-300

This Starwood property is near Berlin's main attractions. Rooms are spacious, service is great. Conference center, indoor pool, fitness center.

Hotel Adlon Kempinski

Unter den Linden 77
S: Unter den Linden
T: (0)30-2261-1111 F: (0)30-2261-2222
www.hotel-adlon.de
382 rooms
From €420

The Adlon was once *the* elite hotel in Berlin—pre-war guests included Charlie Chaplin and Marlene Dietrich. The gutted structure was built from scratch in 1997 and again occupies a prestigious position across from Brandenburg Gate.

Hotel Bogota

Schlüterstrasse 45 (off Kurfürstendamm)
U: Uhlandstrasse, Kurfürstendamm
T: (0)30-881-5001 F: (0)30-883-5887
www.hotelbogota.de
130 rooms
€40-118

This war survivor was the residence of a magnate known for throwing extravagant parties. The Nazis used the building as the Reichs Cultural Department. British forces occupied it after the war. Today, good prices, old-style rooms and an attentive, English-fluent staff have earned the hotel a following.

9

Washington, D.C.

U N I T E D   S T A T E S

The White House

THE WAR YEARS

No bombs fell on its buildings. No fire engulfed its streets. No battle decimated its population. Yet as capital of the only country fully engaged in both the Atlantic and Pacific theaters of combat, Washington, D.C., was arguably the most important city in World War II.

Following the 1939 outbreak of war in Europe, the United States aided Britain and Russia by sending war materials through the Lend-Lease program. Yet as London burned, Soviet cities were overrun and reports of Nazi atrocities filtered in, the United States remained a spectator to war, bound by Neutrality Acts resulting from intense national recoil at the horror of World War I. Two decades of isolationist intransigence would be reversed by the December 7, 1941, Japanese attack on Pearl Harbor. On December 8, in the U.S. Capitol, President Franklin Delano Roosevelt delivered his "date which will live in infamy" speech. Adolf Hitler declared war on the United States on December 11. Isolationism vanished overnight. Plainly unfit to conduct a war, "the capital entered its grimmest period since the Civil War," wrote historian William Manchester. A 1940 ranking had placed the U.S. Army 18th in the world, behind even Portugal and Switzerland. The ease with which Japan struck Pearl Harbor and seized American possessions in the Pacific crystallized how staggeringly unprepared America was to fight.

Final victory would be earned by millions, but it fell to one man to guide the country not just into war, but through the most convulsive period of social change in its history. Age 59 when the war began, President Roosevelt was both loved and loathed by Americans for his 1930s New Deal reforms that radically altered the American governmental landscape, and a demeanor that was at once charming and coldhearted. Yet few doubted that the job of rearming the flagging country and selling a grand vision of world power to a wary public required a man possessing his singular manipulative skills. "The United States was not a European country; it was a different kind of nation, and no one represented it better than the American in the White House," wrote Manchester. Dedicated to his ritual cocktail hour—even through the war—FDR bore the public trademarks of warmth, humor and unflappable optimism. "He always gives the impression that to him nothing is impossible, that everything will turn out all right," wrote journalist W.M. Kiplinger. With war news worsening in 1942, the job ahead looked nothing less than impossible, but Roosevelt had already famously promised that America would become "the arsenal of democracy" and he now embarked on a mission to make it happen.

It was German General Erwin Rommel who said, "The battle is fought and decided by the quartermasters before the shooting begins." But the quote well might have belonged to Roosevelt, who headed an energized bureaucracy that nationalized the war effort under such newly created offices as the War Production Board and legions of new laborers, including women and African-Americans. Unleashed, America's production might was unfathomable, the irrefutable key to Allied victory in World War II. When the German Luftwaffe initiated the Battle of Britain in 1940, it had 2,250 bombers and fighters at its disposal—between 1940 and 1945, the United States built 296,429 warplanes. In 1940, Germany's production of 4,000 tanks per year was the world standard—in five years, America built 102,351 tanks and self-propelled guns. Starting with a decrepit naval fleet, the country launched 87,620 warships (including transports) and conquered two oceans.

The effects on the capital were astonishing. "By 1943, Washington was pretty much like any other boomtown during the war—its population had nearly doubled since 1940, decent housing was impossible to find, uniforms were everywhere," wrote historian Doris Kearns Goodwin. The torch of free-world leadership having passed from British Prime Minister Winston Churchill to Roosevelt, the Allied war was now being run from Washington. The government's budget for the entire war totaled $245 billion, more than all combined U.S. federal budgets between 1789 and 1940. "The military found a natural ally in big business," wrote Goodwin.

Stricken with polio and confined to a wheelchair from age 39, Roosevelt suffered a cerebral hemorrhage and died on April 12, 1945, in Warm Springs, Georgia. One of the largest crowds in Washington history gathered for the funeral procession. Six white stallions slowly dragged his flag-draped coffin from Union Station down Delaware Avenue, taking Constitution, 15th Street and Pennsylvania Avenue to the White House, where a simple funeral was held in the East Room. It was the quietest day in American history. All business stopped. AP and other wire services tapped out a lone message: S I L E N C E.

Few men have at first appeared less qualified for the job of commander in chief than Vice President Harry S Truman. The humble Missourian who succeeded Roosevelt delivered perhaps the presidency's most awkward "inaugural address" to a group of reporters: "I don't know if any of you fellows ever had a load of hay or a bull fall on him, but last night the whole weight of the moon and stars fell on me. ... Please pray for me!" Many did and perhaps with results, if the title of post-war essay by veteran Paul Fussell is to be believed: "Thank God for the Atom Bomb." On the day of FDR's death, Truman knew nothing of the world-altering weapon being developed in New Mexico, yet within four months, he would approve the dropping of atomic bombs on Hiroshima and Nagasaki (Germany surrendered less than a month after he took office). As suddenly as Truman had become president, the war was over. Transformed in less than four years into the world's wealthiest, most powerful nation—the only major combatant not severely damaged by war—the United States suddenly saw in her destiny a blank slate she was empowered to fulfill in any way she deemed just.

SOURCES & OTHER READING

No Ordinary Time: Franklin & Eleanor Roosevelt: The Home Front in World War II, Goodwin, Doris Kearns, Simon & Schuster, 1994

The Glory and the Dream: A Narrative History of America 1932-1972, Manchester, William, Little, Brown, 1974

Washington Goes to War, Brinkley, David, Knopf, 1988

Days of Sadness, Years of Triumph: The American People, 1939-1945, Perrett, Geoffrey, Coward, McCann and Geoghegan, 1973

FDR, the War President, 1940-1943: A History, Davis, Kenneth S., Random House, 2000

Franklin Delano Roosevelt: Champion of Freedom, Black, Conrad, Weidenfeld, 2003

Truman, McCullough, David, Simon & Schuster, 1992

Washington, D.C. Sightseers' Guide, Pitch, Anthony S., Mino Publications, 2002

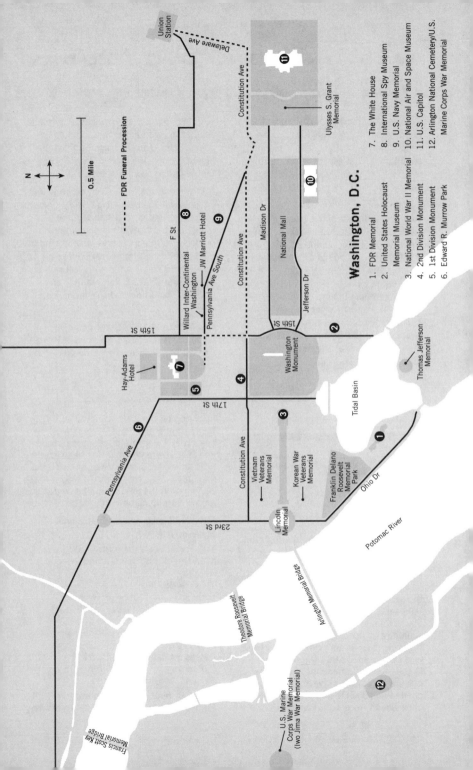

Washington, D.C.

1. FDR Memorial
2. United States Holocaust Memorial Museum
3. National World War II Memorial
4. 2nd Division Monument
5. 1st Division Monument
6. Edward R. Murrow Park
7. The White House
8. International Spy Museum
9. U.S. Navy Memorial
10. National Air and Space Museum
11. U.S. Capitol
12. Arlington National Cemetery/U.S. Marine Corps War Memorial

N

0.5 Mile

----- FDR Funeral Procession

Union Station

Delaware Ave

Constitution Ave

Ulysses S. Grant Memorial

F St

Willard Inter-Continental Washington

JW Marriott Hotel

Pennsylvania Ave South

Constitution Ave

Madison Dr

National Mall

Jefferson Dr

15th St

Hay-Adams Hotel

17th St

Pennsylvania Ave

Constitution Ave

Vietnam Veterans Memorial

Korean War Veterans Memorial

23rd St

Lincoln Memorial

Franklin Delano Roosevelt Memorial Park

Ohio Dr

Washington Monument

Tidal Basin

Thomas Jefferson Memorial

Potomac River

Theodore Roosevelt Memorial Bridge

Arlington Memorial Bridge

Francis Scott Key Memorial Bridge

U.S. Marine Corps War Memorial (Iwo Jima War Memorial)

WASHINGTON, D.C. TODAY

Population: 582,000 • Country Code: 01 • Area Code: 202 • $1 = £0.49/€0.73

Designed as the seat of government for a budding nation, Washington, D.C., is perhaps history's most successful planned community. That aspect makes visiting sites here comparatively easy yet also validates complaints of the city's sterile aura.

The primary area of interest is around the National Mall, which has been under the stewardship of the National Park Service since 1933. On or around the Mall are, in addition to most points of interest in this chapter, the U.S. capital's most recognizable landmarks—the White House, Washington Monument, Thomas Jefferson Memorial, Vietnam Veterans Memorial. The distance between the Lincoln Memorial, at the west end of the Mall, and the U.S. Capitol, at the east end, is two miles. The city is divided into four

sections—northwest, northeast, southwest, southeast—with the U.S. Capitol as the center point. The Beltway describes the highway loop—Interstates 95 and 495—that encircles the entire area.

Northwest of the Mall, Georgetown is the city's upscale neighborhood, with gorgeous old homes and good restaurants. Adams Morgan is the capital's bohemian neighborhood, with a collection of good ethnic restaurants amid former residences of such World War II luminaries as Dwight Eisenhower (2022 Columbia Rd.) and Douglas MacArthur (2853 Ontario Rd.).

The two weeks of spring when the capital's cherry blossoms bloom are generally regarded as the best time to visit. Primary sites in this chapter can be covered in one long or two relaxed days.

POINTS OF INTEREST

M indicates nearest Metro station

1. Franklin Delano Roosevelt Memorial ★★★

West Potomac Park, between Tidal Basin and Potomac River
T: 202-426-6841
M: Smithsonian
Daily, 8 a.m.-midnight
Closed December 25

Covering seven acres, this tribute to the man who served as U.S. president from 1933 to 1945 is one of the most expansive memorials in the nation. Rather than gawk at a single imposing structure, visitors walk through four open courtyards representing each of FDR's terms in office. The dominant feature is a larger-than-life sculpture of Roosevelt (with Fala, his trusty Scottie, at his side), but there are also statues of Eleanor Roosevelt, Depression-era Americans and, at the entry, a controversial (when the memorial opened in 1997) sculpture of a wheelchair-bound Roosevelt. Famous quotes are

inscribed on the walls along with FDR's four essential freedoms—freedom of speech and worship, freedom from want and fear. A simple engraving dedicated to FDR on a desk-size block of marble—the only monument he ever consented to—can be found on the grounds of the National Archives Building on Pennsylvania Avenue.

2. United States Holocaust Memorial Museum ★★★★

100 Raoul Wallenberg Place SW (next to 14th Street, just south of Independence Avenue)
T: 202-488-0400
Daily, 10 a.m.-5:30 p.m. (extended hours Tuesday, Thursday, April-June)
Admission free, but timed passes required. Contact www.tickets.com or 800-400-9373. Some same-day passes available at front desk.
Closed Yom Kippur, December 25
M: Smithsonian

In 1939, nine million Jews lived in Europe. Within a dozen years, two of every three would be dead. Gut-wrenching exhibits here tell the story of Nazi Germany's systematic genocide of Jews and other groups in unflinching detail. A 14-minute, introductory film discusses the unusual building—the significance of the twisted architecture of the entry Hall of Witness and other features—but the heart of the museum is the permanent collection. Covering three floors, it documents the rise of the Nazis, tepid world (and American) response, World War II and the Final Solution, with particular emphasis on the "Concentration Camp Universe." Through photos, video, audio testimonies and artifacts (Warsaw Ghetto cobblestones, German railcar, scale model of an operating gas chamber) other sections document the "Search for Refuge," "Terror Against the Poles" and other atrocities. A disquieting, unforgettable display. Average visits last two to three hours.

3. National World War II Memorial ★★★★

At Rainbow Pool, between Lincoln Memorial and Washington Monument
M: Smithsonian
T: 202-426-6841

The long overdue and controversial World War II Memorial was officially dedicated on May 29, 2004. Covering 7.4 acres, the large sunken plaza incorporates the pre-existing Rainbow Pool around a circular arrangement of 56 pillars (each 17 feet high) representing wartime states and territories. A pair of 41-foot arches emblazoned "Atlantic" and "Pacific" represent both fronts of the war. Each of the 4,000 stars on the Freedom Wall represents 100 Americans who died in the war, but the monument is meant to honor all American participants, including those on the home front. Critics have attacked the memorial's site (obstructing the National Mall) and its design as evocative of the Third Reich.

4. 2nd Division Monument ★

Constitution Avenue, near corner of 17th Street NW
M: Federal Triangle

Erected after World War I, this 30-foot-high rose-granite memorial was expanded to include all U.S. Army 2nd Infantry Division soldiers killed in battle. The division saw WWII action in Normandy, the Rhineland, Battle of the Bulge, Remagen, Czechoslovakia and other locations.

5. 1st Division Monument ★

17th Street NW, north of Pennsylvania Avenue South
M: Federal Triangle

This 60-foot granite tower topped by a golden figure was erected to honor WWI dead and later expanded. The legendary "Big Red One" saw WWII action in Algeria, Tunisia, Sicily, Normandy, northern France, the Battle of the Bulge, the Rhineland, Central Europe and other locations.

6. Edward R. Murrow Park ★

Intersection of Pennsylvania Avenue, 18th Street and H Street NW
M: Farragut West

The only remarkable thing about this small, grassy area is a plaque—embedded in the ground near the corner of 18th and H Streets—recalling the legendary broadcaster "whose clarity, humanity and courage helped his country and the world to know what America at its honest best could be." Murrow's eyewitness radio reports from the Battle of Britain and the London Blitz helped turn American popular opinion away from isolationism toward military engagement.

7. The White House ★★★

1600 Pennsylvania Ave.
Visitors Center at 1450 Pennsylvania Ave. South
T: 202-456-7041 (call for changing tour information)
Tuesday-Saturday, 7:30-11:30 a.m.
Tours must include 10 or more people and must be requested through one's Member of Congress.

"The Roosevelt White House during the war resembled a small, intimate hotel," wrote historian Doris Kearns Goodwin. Friends, foreign visitors and "permanent guests" were constantly in and out for everything from informal cocktail hours to war-strategy sessions. FDR's favorite room was the second-floor circular study on the south side of the house, just off his bedroom. On the night of December 7, 1941, he used the study to brief his Cabinet and Congressional leaders on the Pearl Harbor attack. During visits, Winston Churchill stayed in the Rose Room, also on the second floor. Roosevelt delivered radio fireside chats from the Diplomatic Reception Room on the first floor. Somewhat troublesome to arrange, White House tours are impressive, but with access limited to just 7 of 132 rooms, they don't take in sites terribly significant to the Roosevelt or Truman wartime administrations. (FDR's funeral was held in the East Room, which most tours include.) Still, as one of the most historic residences in the world, it's worth a look at least from outside.

8. International Spy Museum ★★★

800 F Street NW
M: Gallery Place-Chinatown
T: 866-779-6873
Daily, 10 a.m.-7 p.m. (closed at 5 p.m., November-March); last admission 2 hours before closing
Adult: $16; Senior/Active Military: $15; Child (5-18): $13
Time-specific advance tickets recommended for weekends and holidays (800-551-7328).

Exhibitions at this stylized museum containing "the world's largest collection of international espionage artifacts" run the gamut from Ninjas to the Cold War to modern efforts to infiltrate terrorist networks. The WWII section has an original German Enigma cipher machine and display on the British Bletchley Park effort that cracked its "unbreakable" code. Text, photos, inventive displays and touch-screen videos deal with the solving of Japanese codes prior to Pearl Harbor, the Pacific's Navajo Code Talkers and subterfuge surrounding the Manhattan Project. A small section is devoted to Operation Bodyguard, the astounding pre-D-Day counterintelligence campaign that, with inflatable tanks and vehicles, kept the Normandy landing times and places concealed from German command.

9. U.S. Navy Memorial ★

Pennsylvania Avenue and 9th Street NW
A seven-foot-tall sculpture of a sailor with his duffel bag stands in the center of this public plaza, which is ringed by six 75-foot flagpoles representing masts and 22 bronze bas-relief images depicting U.S. Navy history. Embedded in the ground is a 100-foot-wide world map.

10. National Air and Space Museum ★★★★★ for museum, ★★★ for World War II exhibits

Independence Avenue at 4th Street
M: L'Enfant Plaza
T: 202-633-1000
Daily, 10 a.m.-5:30 p.m.
Closed December 25

The most-visited museum in Washington chronicles the history of flight in 22 galleries. Highlights include the original Wright Brothers airplane that flew at Kitty Hawk, Charles Lindbergh's *Spirit of St. Louis* and the Apollo 11 command module, *Columbia*. Five World War II fighter planes are displayed in Gallery 205—an American P-51D Mustang, a British Spitfire, a German Me-109, an Italian Macchi Folgore and a Japanese Zero. Other World War II aircraft and parts—including a V2 replica—are displayed throughout the museum, but the museum's Steven F. Udvar-Hazy Center (see page 97) has the more impressive World War II collection.

11. U.S. Capitol ★★★★

Capitol Hill, east end of National Mall
M: Capitol South, Judiciary Square, Federal Center SW
T: 202-225-6827 (call for changes in tour information)
Monday-Saturday, 9 a.m.-4:30 p.m.
Tours begin every few minutes.
Closed on Thanksgiving and December 25

Washington law decrees that no building can exceed the height of this symbol of American government, the white-domed U.S. Capitol where senators and representatives convene. The building's most striking feature is the immense Rotunda (180 feet high, 97 feet across), topped by a nine-million-pound, cast-iron dome. Inside the House chamber, Roosevelt delivered his "date which will live in infamy" speech and Congress declared war in December 1941. The 30-minute tours (expect a line) deliver superb lectures on American history.

12. Arlington National Cemetery/U.S. Marine Corps War Memorial ★★★★★

Arlington, Virginia. From Washington, D.C., just across Potomac River via Arlington Memorial Bridge
M: Arlington Cemetery
T: 703-607-8000 (Cemetery)
T: 703-289-2500 (Marine Corps Memorial)
Cemetery: Daily, 8 a.m.-7 p.m. (closed at 5 p.m. October-March)

Covering 200 acres, the country's national military cemetery includes graves of soldiers from the Revolutionary War to the present. World War II burials include President John F. Kennedy, whose PT-109 heroics in the Solomon Islands added to his legend, and Texas farmboy-turned-hero Audie Murphy, who earned an unparalleled 28 medals. Other cemetery attractions include the ceremonial Changing of the Guard, every half-hour at the Tomb of the Unknown Soldier. Located at the cemetery entrance, the Visitors Center has maps, exhibits and information on grave locations.

On the northwest edge of the park (across the Theodore Roosevelt Memorial Bridge), the Marines Memorial (aka Iwo Jima Memorial) is one of the largest bronze sculptures ever cast. Though it re-creates the famous photo of six Marines raising the Stars and Stripes over Iwo Jima, it honors all Marines killed in battle since 1775.

RELATED SITES BEYOND WASHINGTON, D.C.

Pentagon ★★

Southwest of Washington, D.C., across the Potomac River in Virginia
M: Pentagon
T: 703-697-1776
Tours are available Monday-Friday, 9 a.m.-3 p.m. Group tours available by appointment. If group has fewer than 5 members, one must request a tour through one's Member of Congress.

The titanic Department of Defense headquarters is Washington's greatest surviving icon to the U.S. government's wartime expansion. Intended as a temporary structure to be torn down once the country's gargantuan war administration was no longer needed, it has evolved into a much larger entity. Completed in 1943 after just 16 months of work, its five floors include almost 18 miles of corridors.

National Air and Space Museum's Steven F. Udvar-Hazy Center ★★★

Chantilly, Virginia. Near Washington Dulles airport at intersection of Routes 50 and 28.
Daily, 10 a.m.-5:30 p.m.
Closed December 25
Shuttles operate between this center and the main National Air and Space Museum.

Twenty-eight miles from the Air and Space Museum's flagship building (Point 10), this facility houses 200-plus aircraft from all eras of flight. The World War II Aviation Hall is dominated by the B-29 *Enola Gay*, which dropped the atomic bomb on Hiroshima, but it also displays 10 or so aircraft, including a Curtiss P-40E Warhawk, a P-38 Lightning, a Grumman Hellcat and several Japanese fighters.

Navy Museum/Marine Corps Historical Center (Navy ★★★, Marines ★)

Washington Navy Yard, 9th and M Streets S.E.
M: Eastern Market
T: 202-433-4882 (Navy)
T: 202-433-3840 (Marines)
Non-military admitted only by appointment. Call for hours and access information.

The Navy Museum (Building 76) and Marine Corps Historical Center (Building 58) document the history of both service branches. By far the larger of the two, the 45,000-square-foot Navy Museum's World War II exhibits deal with the Atlantic, Pacific and home front. Sections on the Battle of the Atlantic, convoys and merchant shipping are housed in a gallery with angled walls representing icebergs. Sicily, Anzio, D-Day and other important naval actions are commemorated.

Overshadowed by the Marines who fought in the Pacific, 6,000 Marines nevertheless participated in the Atlantic, North African and European campaigns.

National Museum of the Marine Corps

18900 Jefferson Highway, Triangle, Virginia, 36 miles south of D.C., east of Interstate 95, and off U.S. Route 1.
T: 800-397-7585
Daily, 9 a.m.-5 p.m.

This recently opened museum chronicles Marine Corps history since its formation in 1775, through the World Wars and up to contemporary conflicts. The World War II section recalls the Marines' bloody Pacific campaigns. Wildcat and Avenger aircraft are on display. A Sherman tank is set up outside a Japanese-held cave. Also on display is one of the Corps' most iconic possessions: the Stars and Stripes raised by Marines over Mt. Suribachi on Iwo Jima. On three acres adjacent to the museum, the Semper Fidelis Memorial Park is dedicated to the service of all Marines in past and current conflicts.

National Archives at College Park

8601 Adelphi Rd., College Park, Maryland
Shuttles run on the hour, 8 a.m.-5 p.m., Monday-Friday, between National Archives buildings in downtown Washington (700 Pennsylvania Ave. NW) and College Park.
T: 301-837-2000
Monday-Friday, 9 a.m.-5 p.m.

Not necessarily a tourist attraction, this facility is the nation's primary repository for WWII records, including U.S. military plans, intelligence, seized enemy documents and more. It looks intimidating, but records and photos are pulled with admirable efficiency. Whether you seek 1943 U.S. Navy aerial surveys of obscure Southeast Alaska harbors, confiscated Gestapo directives or information on family or other veterans, this center is an invaluable resource.

Dumbarton Oaks ★

1703 32nd St. NW
T: 202-339-6401
Daily, 2-5 p.m. (garden); Closed holidays. Garden closed in inclement weather.
$1 suggested

At press time, the museum was closed for renovations. Check the Dumbarton Oaks website for updates (www.doaks.org). No house tours are offered, but by visiting the museum, visitors can see the 19th-century Georgetown mansion where the 1944 international Dumbarton Oaks Conference drew up preliminary plans for the United Nations. The most important meetings took place in the Music Room (visitors can take a look). As reflected by the museum collection and immaculate garden (open to the public), the estate now functions as a research center for Byzantine and pre-Columbian art and history, as well as landscape architecture.

National Cryptologic Museum ★★★

Colony Seven Road, Ft. Meade, Maryland. Near intersection of Maryland Route 32 and Baltimore/Washington Parkway (MD Route 295), near the National Security Agency, an hour north of Washington.
T: 301-688-5849
Monday-Friday, 9 a.m.-4 p.m.; open monthly on first and third Saturdays, 10 a.m.-2 p.m.

Closed federal holidays, December 26

With offerings from ancient cipher wheels to present-day espionage, this museum is the serious student's version of the International Spy Museum (Point 8). Its WWII section includes the U.S. Army's entire collection of captured Enigma machines along with encryption systems such as the Japanese "Jade" device and American Sigaba, the only machine code system to remain completely unbroken during WWII. There's also a display on the Native American Code Talkers, featured in the film *Windtalkers*.

OTHER AREA ATTRACTIONS

War Memorials

Amid the grandiose monuments and recognizable landmarks, a startling feature of the National Mall is the extent to which it functions as a vast war memorial. In addition to the National World War II Memorial, it offers the hypnotic, black granite wall of the Vietnam Veterans Memorial; the 19 lifelike soldiers wearing ponchos and leaning into a bitter cold at the Korean War Veterans Memorial; and the haunting, combat-weary faces of Civil War troops who flank the Ulysses S. Grant Memorial.

Getting To and Around Washington, D.C.

The nation's capital is served by three major airports—Ronald Reagan Washington National Airport, Washington-Dulles International Airport and Baltimore-Washington International Airport. Reagan National is nearest the city center (3.5 miles) and by far the most convenient. Cabs to the city center cost about $12. Trains to the city run from the airport's National Airport Metro station. Cabs from Dulles to the city center cost about $60. Cabs from Baltimore-Washington (32 miles from Washington, D.C.) cost $70-plus outside rush hours. The airport Rail Station (410-672-6169), with service to Washington, D.C., is located two miles from the main terminal at Baltimore-Washington.

Driving in Washington isn't hard, but parking is. For visitors, a car is generally more trouble than it's worth. Cabs are plentiful and operate on fixed rates between zones (no meters). Few rides cost more than $10. The Washington Metrorail subway is a clean, efficient way to get around. Tourmobile (202-554-5100) bus shuttles operate daily, 9:30 a.m.-4:30 p.m.,

between 17 major attractions around the Mall, including Arlington National Cemetery. Riders hop on and off the continuously running buses. Tickets can be purchased from drivers or select kiosks near points of interest. Old Town Trolley Tours (202-832-9800) operates narrated rides along a similar path—with on and off privileges between 25 marquee attractions—in turn-of-the-century-style, orange-and-green street trolleys.

The National Park Service's free "Washington: The Nation's Capitol" brochure is available at all NPS attractions—it has a simple-to-use walking map of the Mall and surrounding area. Available at bookstores, the pocket-size *Washington, D.C. Sightseers' Guide*, by Anthony S. Pitch, is a highly recommended walking guide. The D.C. Visitor Information Center offers a wealth of information (1300 Pennsylvania Ave. NW, 202-328-4748, Monday-Friday, 8:30 a.m.-5:30 p.m., Saturday, 9 a.m.- 4 p.m., in spring and summer; Monday-Friday, 9 a.m.- 4:30 p.m., in fall and winter).

Accommodations

Hay-Adams Hotel

1 Lafayette Square
www.hayadams.com
T: 202-638-6600 F: 202-638-2716
143 rooms
From $275

This elegant property regularly hosts entourages of visiting diplomats and politicians. Priding itself on "quiet luxury," the stately Hay-Adams has earned numerous *Condé Nast Traveler*'s "Gold List" inclusions among top hotels in the world.

Willard Inter-Continental Washington

1401 Pennsylvania Ave. NW
www.interconti.com
T: 202-628-9100 F: 202-327-0200
341 rooms
From $275

This is where Martin Luther King, Jr., composed his "I Have a Dream" speech while a guest. The Inter-Continental chain's top-drawer standards are exceeded here with three restaurants, large rooms and a staff that speaks nine languages.

JW Marriott Hotel Pennsylvania Avenue

1331 Pennsylvania Ave. NW
www.marriott.com
T: 202-393-2000 F: 202-626-1345
772 rooms
From $250

High-speed internet access in guest rooms, good restaurants and a swimming pool help make this a high-end Marriott property, but the White House area location and occasional internet specials are the selling points.

10

South Coast
of England

Hawker Hurricane

THE WAR YEARS

Difficult as it might be to fathom in a world overrun by global capitalism, in the summer of 1940, only a handful of democracies existed on a planet increasingly dominated by police states. Of these free nations, Great Britain stood alone in open defiance of the totalitarian menace that had swept across Europe with such violent efficiency.

With the astonishing fall of France in June 1940, Britain found itself just 22 miles from the frontier of the Third Reich—the distance across the English Channel from Dover to German-held Calais. Accordingly, Adolf Hitler had ordered Operation Sea Lion—the invasion of Great Britain—to commence in mid-September 1940. Aside from the Channel itself, all that stood between England and Nazi invasion was the Royal Air Force (RAF), which, if intact, could bomb an invasion fleet into ruin. The Battle of Britain thus began as Germany's attempt to destroy the RAF so as to clear the way for invasion.

"It is unlikely that there will ever be a parallel to the Battle of Britain where armies and navies, immobilized on either side of the Channel, watched a few thousand combatants meet in the air above," wrote historians Derek Wood and Derek Dempster, authors of the definitive text of the battle.

On paper, the battle belonged to the German Luftwaffe. When its air offensive began above Dover (the RAF recognizes July 10 to October 30, 1940, as official Battle of Britain dates) the experienced Luftwaffe had effortlessly dispatched all European rivals. It had about 2,250 fighters and bombers at its disposal, compared to Britain's 650 to 750 single-engine fighters. "There didn't appear to be anything that could save us in June 1940," recalled one Royal Navy officer.

But RAF Hurricane and Spitfire fighters were equal or superior to Germany's Messerschmitt Me-109 fighters (with Hurricanes eventually accounting for about 80 percent of British kills). For 114 days, the two air forces engaged in fatal, theatrical dogfights over the British coast while civilians and newsmen watched from below. Young, athletic, intelligent, rakish, British pilots became instant heroes. They were joined by Allied pilots from 14 nations (one each from Jamaica and Palestine, a full 10 percent from Poland), including a handful of Americans of the Eagle Squadrons, who fought for Britain more than a year before the United States declared war.

Miraculously, the RAF battled the Luftwaffe to a standstill, the effort aided by blustery rhetoric from Winston Churchill (see London chapter) and a new invention called RDF, or radar. In Air Chief Marshal Sir Hugh Dowding, Britain also had one of the few men in the world who knew what to do with the new technology. Dowding's brilliant synthesis of radar signals, field reports and radio communications allowed him to communicate "real time" commands to fighters in the sky from his underground Fighter Control command center at RAF Uxbridge (page 35). German pilots quickly grasped radar's implications, but, blinkered by the open-cockpit mentality he'd developed as a World War I pilot, Luftwaffe Reichsmarschall Hermann Göring halted attacks on coastal radar stations, oblivious to their value. Göring's ignorance "contributed perhaps more than anything to the Luftwaffe's undoing," according to Wood and Dempster. Time and again Germany sent massed formations of attackers at

Britain, hoping to lure the RAF into a huge, decisive battle. Hyper-aware of the paucity of his resources, Dowding scrambled his fighters with the thrift of a country parson.

Strategically, Dowding was a visionary. In company, he was stuffy, aloof and disliked by peers who appreciated neither radar nor Britain's critical shortage of pilots. For his heroics, Dowding was castigated—blamed for the unstoppable night bombings of London—and forcibly retired in 1941. Britain's official Air Ministry account of the Battle of Britain—considered won when Hitler indefinitely postponed Operation Sea Lion in October—failed to mention him by name.

"Dowding not only created Fighter Command from the ground up ... he out-thought and out-fought the enemy and thereby changed the course of history by making Great Britain an unsinkable platform from which the great assaults which would eventually topple Nazi Germany could be unleashed in the years ahead," wrote biographer Jack Dixon.

Dowding, a relative handful of pilots, largely invisible ground personnel and superior technology had dealt Germany its first defeat of the war, making possible the use of English shores for two more invasions. The first was the "friendly invasion" of hundreds of thousands of Allied troops (mostly Americans and Canadians). From Dover to Land's End, the Allied military took over the southern coast—many locals were forced from their homes for security reasons—to prepare for the greatest invasion armada ever assembled. British and Canadian troops were billeted east of Southampton, Americans were housed west of the city.

Though young soldiers created a party atmosphere during R&R in local pubs, the perilous nature of the job at hand was underscored by such events as Exercise Tiger. The massive U.S. Army and Navy D-Day practice exercise off Slapton Sands on April 18, 1944, was intercepted by a pack of German torpedo boats, which sunk two LST transport ships, sending 749 Americans to die in the icy Channel waters. It was among the costliest episodes of the war for U.S. troops, in combat or otherwise. Nevertheless, barely a month later, at Southwick House near Portsmouth, Supreme Allied Commander Dwight Eisenhower issued his famous order—"OK, we'll go." —setting in motion the June 6, 1944, D-Day invasion of Normandy. Over the following year, two million service personnel would depart the south coast of England for Europe, adding yet another chapter to the illustrious maritime legacy of a region already famous for names such as Francis Drake, *Mayflower* and *Titanic*.

SOURCES & OTHER READING

The Narrow Margin: The Battle of Britain and the Rise of Air Power 1930-1940, Wood and Dempster, Hutchison and Co., 1961

Finest Hour: The Battle of Britain, Clayton and Craig, Hodder and Stoughton, 1999

The Battle of Britain—Victory & Defeat: The Achievements of Air Chief Marshal Dowding and the Scandal of His Dismissal From Office, Dixon, Jack, Woodfield Publishing, 2001

The Forgotten Dead, Small, Ken, Bloomsbury, 1988

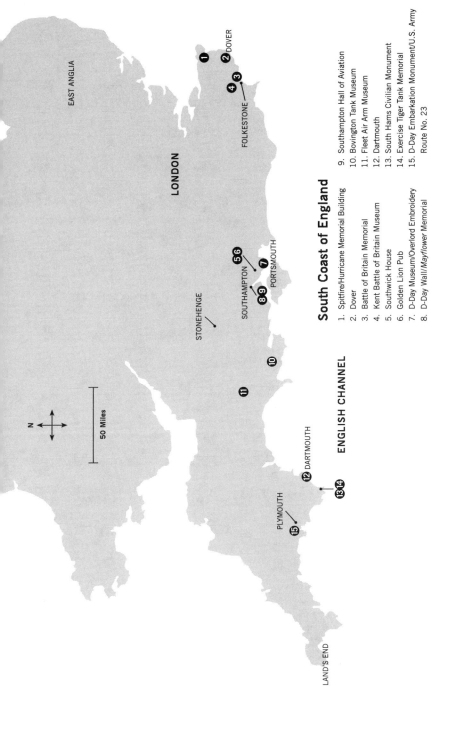

South Coast of England

1. Spitfire/Hurricane Memorial Building
2. Dover
3. Battle of Britain Memorial
4. Kent Battle of Britain Museum
5. Southwick House
6. Golden Lion Pub
7. D-Day Museum/Overlord Embroidery
8. D-Day Wall/*Mayflower* Memorial

9. Southampton Hall of Aviation
10. Bovington Tank Museum
11. Fleet Air Arm Museum
12. Dartmouth
13. South Hams Civilian Monument
14. Exercise Tiger Tank Memorial
15. D-Day Embarkation Monument/U.S. Army

Route No. 23

SOUTH COAST TODAY

Population: 33,000 (Dover); 211,000 (Southampton); 200,000 (Portsmouth); 6,000 (Dartmouth) • Country Code: 44 • £1 = $2.02/€1.48

Generally not considered a single political entity, the South Coast presents a number of faces to the visitor, momentous maritime history being its defining feature. The best hubs for visits are Dover, Southampton/Portsmouth, and Dartmouth.

Dover's location, 22 miles across the English Channel from Europe, has shaped its history as well as its present. Along with nearby Folkestone, it serves as Britain's primary port to France, with 16.5 million passengers coming in and out annually. The Dover Castle and famed White Cliffs are justly high on any traveler's checklist, but the town is more industrial than quaint. The central coast is dominated by larger and grittier ports. Portsmouth has a museum dedicated to favorite son Charles Dickens and the HMS

Victory, Admiral Lord Nelson's flagship from the 1805 Battle of Trafalgar. Both the *Mayflower* and *Titanic* (two eventual British tragedies) were launched from Southampton, a modern city rebuilt from the ashes of German bombing. For visitor appeal, the lush West Country is unequaled. In the area associated with Sir Frances Drake, the castles of Devon (0870-333-1181, English Heritage organization) are a major attraction. Dartmouth—old wharf buildings, crowded pubs, narrow alleys—is the most atmospheric and pleasant of the coast's small towns and home to the Britannia Royal Naval College.

By car or train, this chapter's highlights take four or five days to see.

POINTS OF INTEREST

1. Spitfire and Hurricane Memorial Building
★★★

Off A253, Manston Road, Ramsgate. Adjacent to Manston Airport (west of Ramsgate). Follow signs to Manston Airport and Spitfire Memorial. Nearest rail stations are Ramsgate and Margate. T: (0)184-382-1940
Daily, 10 a.m.-5 p.m., (closed at 4 p.m., October-March)
Closed December 25-27, January 1

This two-room hall houses one each of

Britain's legendary fighter planes—the Hurricane is rebuilt, the Spitfire is one of the few surviving with a wartime record. Displays include weaponry, civilian memorabilia, original diaries and the 12 'x 12' embroidered Battle of Britain Tapestry. The building is on the site of RAF Manston airfield, which, 10 flying minutes from France, bore the brunt of early Luftwaffe attacks in 1940. Subsequently expanded, it became a refuge for crippled Allied bombers returning from runs over Europe.

2. Dover

The Dover itinerary begins at Shakespeare Cliff. Proceed out of Dover on A20 south toward Folkestone. At final roundabout at edge of town, veer right at sign for Aycliffe/ Western Heights. Proceed 0.9 miles through Aycliffe neighborhood on Folkestone Road (old observation bunkers are visible from road) to sign describing "Drama on the White Cliffs." Follow adja-

cent footbridge over highway. At end of bridge, climb uphill, veering left. Shakespeare Cliff is at the top of the escarpment (extreme left point, closest to Dover) called the Western Heights, a 10-minute walk from the footbridge.

Without an aircraft, imposing **Shakespeare Cliff** ★★★ is as near as one can get to the Battle of Britain's aerial battlefield. From this vantage point ("a surreal grandstand to war"), BBC crews, American reporters Edward Murrow and Eric Sevareid and other spectators gathered to watch daily dogfights between British and German fighters. Even with the highway below, it's possible at this solemn place overlooking the famed cliffs and sea toward France to conjure the aerial ghosts of history. Hikers walking the length of the escarpment will find leftover WWII observation posts and remnants of an early radar station. The cliff is named for the probable setting for the scene in *King Lear* in which Gloucester throws himself off a cliff.

Back at the footbridge, continue around the U-turn in the road and proceed 0.3 miles to the apartment at 74 David's Ave., where a small trail leads to a steep, 10-minute climb uphill to the large concrete remains and three original gun mounts of **Citadel Battery ★★**, built 1898-1900 and manned throughout World War II.

Proceed from Aycliffe toward Dover, veering left at first roundabout onto South Military Road. Proceed 0.4 miles to parking lot at **St. Martin's Battery ★★★**, an 1800s brick-and-earth coastal-defense fort upgraded and manned through World War II. Original 1940s gun mounts are still in the ground; the cannons are gone; great ocean views remain.

Head back into Dover and follow signs for

Dover Castle (it's also signed from M20, A2 and city center). The immense **Dover Castle ★★★★**—one of the most powerful Roman fortresses in western Europe—is an attraction in its own right, commanding the sea link between the North Sea and English Channel, known in wartime as "Hellfire Corner." Within its secret tunnels, Vice Admiral Bertram Ramsey and Prime Minister Winston Churchill masterminded the Dunkirk evacuation. Naval personnel were stationed inside throughout the war. Today, the Command Centre and other rooms are preserved with maps, 1940s communications equipment and more. Audio loops re-create the menacing drone of bombers overhead. Located on Castle Hill Road, Dover Castle (0130-421-1067) is open 10 a.m.-6 p.m. (closed at 5 p.m., November-March). Closed December 24-26 and January 1. Adult: £9.80; Senior/student: £7.90; Children: £4.90.

In the town center, the **Dover Museum ★** has a small WWII exhibit concentrating on air-raid history. There's a 10-minute documentary on the Dunkirk evacuation, one of the more memorable events in Dover history. Located on Market Square, Dover Museum (0130-420-1066) is open, 10 a.m.-5:30 p.m. (closed Sunday). Adult: £2.50; Student: £1.50.

3. Battle of Britain Memorial ★★★

Off B2011, at Cape-le-Ferne, 1 mile northeast of Folkestone. From B2011 follow signs to Battle of Britain Memorial.
T: (0)130-325-3286
Daily, 11 a.m.-5 p.m., April-November 11

The centerpiece of this clifftop memorial is a sculpture of an RAF pilot facing the sea, white cliffs to his side. The pilot's seated pose suggests a contemplative yet vigilant mood. The park includes full-size Hurricane replica and a visitors lodge (open 11 a.m.-5 p.m., April-September).

4. Kent Battle of Britain Museum ★★★★

Aerodome Road, Hawkinge. Off A260, three miles north of Folkestone. From A260, follow signs to Museum.

T: (0)130-389-3140
Tuesday-Sunday, 10 a.m.-4 p.m., from Easter Friday to September 30
Last entry 4 p.m.
Closed Monday (except bank holidays) and from October to Easter Friday
Adult: £5; Senior/Student: £4; Child: £3.50; Under 6: Free

In five buildings on the site of an important Battle of Britain airfield, this excellent museum claims "the world's largest collection of Battle of Britain relics and related memorabilia." The lineup of full-size replica Hurricanes, Spitfires and Me-109s is impressive, but engines and other parts of more than 600 aircraft form the soul of the museum.

5. Southwick House (Eisenhower D-Day HQ) ★★★★

At Defence College of Policing and
Guarding in Southwick Park, off M27,
then B2177, just north of Portsmouth
T: (0)239-229-6905
Adult: £3

Weekdays by appointment only
Note: The Defence College of Policing and
Guarding is located on the site formerly
known as HMS Dryad Royal Navy Base.

Within a Royal Navy training school is
stately Southwick House, headquarters of
Supreme Allied Commander General Dwight
Eisenhower before and during Operation
Overlord's June 6, 1944, D-Day invasion of
Normandy. Inside is the preserved Wall
Map Room—Overlord's nerve center—still
dominated by the original 1,000-meter-
g-rid map of the English Channel and
French coast. It measures about 20' x 20'.
A painting shows the room as it looked on
June 6, a beehive of activity with frantic
personnel moving icons on the map, taking
calls and bustling about the room.

6. Golden Lion Pub ★★

High Street, Southwick (near Portsmouth)
T: (0)239-237-9134
From Point 5, proceed downhill from main
entrance to first right on High Street.
Open from 7 p.m. nightly

A 15-minute walk from Point 5, the pub
was a regular meeting place for Eisenhower,
British General Bernard Montgomery and
staff officers. According to the plaque outside, Ike usually ordered half pints of bitter while Monty "confined himself to
grapefruit juice." Unit insignias and war-
era posters decorate the pub.

7. The D-Day Museum and Overlord Embroidery ★★★★

Clarence Esplanade, Southsea,
Portsmouth
T: (0)239-282-7261
Daily, 10 a.m.-5:30 p.m., April-October
(closed at 5 p.m., November-March)
Closed December 24-26
Adult: £6; Senior: £5; Student/Child:
£4.20; Family: £16.20

This museum has a unique centerpiece:
comprised of 34 hand-stitched panels on
thick cotton fabric, the 272-foot-long, 10-
foot-tall Overlord Embroidery presents the
story of D-Day in riveting artistic fashion.
Panels depict various facets of the invasion, from embarkation along Britain's
southern coast to the bloody breakthrough
of German positions. The embroidery,
which occupies a circular gallery and took
five years to complete, must be seen to be
appreciated. Museum exhibits include D-
Day landing craft and a replica of the Wall
Map at Southwick House. The HMS
Victory is docked nearby along the historic
Portsmouth Waterfront.

8. D-Day Wall/*Mayflower* Memorial ★★

Off West Quay Road in Southampton, at
De Vere Grand Harbour Hotel

On the east side of the hotel is a small
section of brick wall upon which American
GIs carved their names before shipping off
on D-Day. The wall is referred to as the
"D-Day Wall," though the only dates visi-
ble among the now-faint lettering are from
December 1944, six months after D-Day.
A minute's walk east along the main West
Quay Road is the 30-foot-high Mayflower
Monument tower, which bears two of the
most profoundly coupled plaques in
American history. The first commemorates
the 1620 sailing of the Pilgrims to the
New World from Southampton. Above it, a
plaque recalls the two million American
service personnel who sailed from
Southampton to Europe in 1944-45, "in
order that the freedom for which their
Pilgrim Fathers strove should not be lost."
A few blocks away, a memorial commemo-
rates the departure point of the *Titanic*.

9. Southampton Hall of Aviation ★

Just off Canute Road, near Ocean Village
and Waterfront in Southampton
T: (0)238-063-5830
Tuesday-Sunday, 10 a.m.-5 p.m.
(open at noon on Sunday)
Closed Monday, December 24-26
Adult: £5; Senior: £ 4;
Child (5-16): £3

Twenty-six aircraft companies were once based around Southampton, including Supermarine Aviation Works, builders of the legendary Spitfire. This small hall pays tribute to the local industry. The lone Spitfire is a sleek example of the last version built in 1946.

10. Bovington Tank Museum ★★★★★ for tank enthusiasts, ★★★ otherwise

In Bovington. Take M27 to A31 (toward Bere Regis and Bovington), follow many signs to Tank Museum. Express train from London's Waterloo Station to Wool Station (a two-mile taxi ride to museum) takes an hour and 15 minutes.
T: (0)192-940-5096
Daily, 10 a.m.-5 p.m.
Closed Christmas week, January 1
Adult: £10; Child (5-16): £7; Family: £28

The revolving display of 160 to 180 tanks and armored vehicles from World War I to the present makes this one of the largest tank museums in the world. The WWII section includes some 70 tanks: German "King" Tiger, panzers, jagdpanzer, half-tracks, Soviet T-34s and virtually any Allied tank you can name. Many are rare and "one-off" prototypes. Most tanks are operational—summer Tuesdays and Thursdays are "Tanks in Action" days, with tanks engaging in mock battles in an outdoor arena. The tank-related gift shop is a find for enthusiasts. Allow three hours to visit.

11. Fleet Air Arm Museum ★★★

Royal Naval Air Station Yeovilton, Ilchester
Signposted on B3151, from A303 or A37
T: (0)193-584-0565
Daily, 10 a.m.-5:30 p.m.
(closed at 4:30 p.m., November-March)
Closed December 24-26
Adult: 10.50; Senior/Student: £8.50; Child: £7.50; Family: £32

On 6.5 hectares, this superb museum traces the development of naval aviation (mostly carrier-based aircraft) through four main halls. Of the approximately 60 aircraft, about 15 are from World War II, including a Grumman Hellcat and Avenger, a Fairey Swordfish II, a Hawker Sea Fury and a Fuji Ohka II.

12. Dartmouth/D-Day Embarkation Memorial ★★★

In center of town, along main quay between Dart Marina and Royal Castle hotels

A stone tablet on the waterfront recalls the "sailing from this port, on 3rd June 1944, of an amphibious force of 485 ships of the Royal Navy and United States Navy to take part in the invasion of Normandy…" Thirty yards away is a large, egg-shaped wartime naval mine. Behind the mine, in the Royal Avenue Gardens, a 15-foot cross bears names of locals who died in the war. Behind the gardens, on Duke street, the small Dartmouth Museum (daily, 10 a.m.-4:30 p.m., April-October; noon-3 p.m., November-March; closed Sundays and holidays; adult £1.50, child 50 pence) has some wartime memorabilia. All of this amounts to little tangible evidence of the massive pre–D-Day builup that took place here—one strains to imagine 485 warships crowding the narrow harbor—but Dartmouth might be the prettiest small port in England. It's included for tourist appeal as much as wartime legacy.

13. South Hams Civilian Monument ★

On A375, 7.5 miles south of Dartmouth. (A375 hugs the coast and is one of the most spectacular drives in all of England.)

The 20-foot stone tower on the beach erected by the U.S. Army in the 1950s honors locals who vacated their lands to provide a top-secret D-Day practice area for Allied troops.

14. Exercise Tiger Tank Memorial ★★★

On A375, 1.3 miles south of Point 13

In the early 1970s, Slapton-area beachcomber Ken Small, at the time in the throes of a nervous breakdown, uncovered evidence of the long-forgotten U.S. military Exercise Tiger tragedy. Small's biggest find was a Sherman tank sunk in 60 feet of water. Obsessed by "Tiger," he raised the tank and created this monument in 1984. In 1988, Small wrote a starkly personal book (*The Forgotten Dead*) about his experience, intimating that the Tiger deaths had been conspiratorially covered up by the U.S. government and General

Dwight Eisenhower. The claims created a small sensation before being convincingly refuted. "Tiger" had been publicly revealed by Eisenhower's office and explored in 1950s history texts (since out of print) before being essentially forgotten. Exercise Tiger remains a tragic and little-known episode. The tank stands as its memorial. Blackened by 40 years beneath the water and subsequent preservative coatings, it's more evocative and deathly than the well-preserved tanks generally found in Europe. This tank wasn't actually part of "Tiger"—it was lost during the prior Exercise Beaver.

15. D-Day Embarkation Monument/U.S. Army Route No. 23 ★★

Off A38, in Plymouth

At Saltash Passage, at the east end (Plymouth side) of the A38 bridge across Tamar River is a parking lot with views of the town of Saltash. To the left (facing the river) is a traffic circle signposted "Normandy Hill," aka U.S. Army Route No. 23, the road on which American troops marched and/or drove to the river to board transport vessels bound for Normandy in June 1944. The short walk down this road re-creates the final steps of invasion troops on English soil. At the bottom of the hill (veer left), a stone memorial commemorates the Operation Overlord departures.

Back atop the hill at the sign for Normandy Hill, one can cross the main road, walk 30 yards slightly uphill along the narrow, red-stone path onto wide Normandy Way. Lined with a low brick wall, this is a continuation of U.S. Army Route No. 23. A quarter-mile up the road is Cornwall's Gate Pub (71 Normandy Way; 0175-251-0902), site of a vicarage in 1944. In the parking lot, a plaque recalls U.S. Navy, Coast Guard, Marine Corps and Mercantile Services efforts in the war. Inside the pub is a small painting of the bridge area as it looked on June 6, 1944, jammed with men.

RELATED SITES BEYOND THE SOUTH COAST

Channel Islands

Ferries to England's Channel Islands of Guernsey and Jersey, rich in World War II relics, depart the British ports of Weymouth and Poole (both just southwest of Southampton). Because the islands are closer and easier to access from France, they're covered in the Auxiliary Sites chapter (page 235). See Getting To/Around section of this chapter for information on ferries to France.

OTHER AREA ATTRACTIONS

White Cliffs of Dover

National Trust Gateway to the White Cliffs Park
Daily, 10 a.m.-5 p.m., March-October
Daily, 11 a.m.-4 p.m., November-February
Closed December 25
T: (0)130-420-2756
Parking £2.50

On a sunny day, the famed 300-foot-high chalk cliffs are as impressive as legend suggests. The best place to photograph and hike around them is from the National Trust Gateway to the White Cliffs Park, accessed from Dover via Castle Hill Road. A bracing two-mile walk along the cliff tops to South Foreland Lighthouse offers superb views.

Stonehenge

2 miles west of Amesbury in Wiltshire, 90 miles west of London. Nearest rail station is Salisbury (9 miles), with service from London's Waterloo Station.
Adult: £6.30; Senior/Student: £4.70; Child: £3.20; Family: £15.80
For opening times, contact English Heritage (www.english-heritage.org; 0870-333-1181 for main office; 0117-975-0700 for Southwest region).

The ancient rock enigma of Stonehenge has drawn visitors for perhaps 5,000 years. No one knows how ancient man moved the massive stones used to build the monument, the heaviest of which weighs about 45 tons. Tourists from around the world come to marvel at the amazing feat of engineering and enduring mystery. During WWII, German bombers headed for Bristol used Stonehenge as a highly visible turning point.

GETTING TO AND AROUND SOUTH COAST

Sites in this chapter are located between 90 minutes and five hours from London, by car or rail. See Getting To and Around London (page 36) for flight information. See Getting To and Around East Anglia (page 171) for rental car information.

Trains depart London's Victoria Station for Dover's Priory Station. South-West line trains depart London's Waterloo Station for Portsmouth, Southampton and Dartmouth (the latter accessed via Paignton station, then connecting bus, ferry or about £35 taxi ride). For all train inquiries, call Brit-Rail (0845-748-4950; www.britrail.net).

Trains can also be booked from the United States through RailEurope (800-782-2424). From Paignton, Dartmouth also is accessed via the scenic Paignton & Dartmouth Steam Railway (0180-355-5872; www.paignton-steamrailway.co.uk) which runs the seven miles along the spectacular Torbay coast and costs £9.

From Dover/Folkestone, several companies offer passenger and car ferry or tunnel service to Calais, France. These include Eurotunnel (08705-35-3535), SeaFrance (0870-443-1686), P&O Ferries (0870-240-8282) and Hoverspeed (0870-240-8282).

ACCOMMODATIONS

Dover
County Hotel
Townwall Street
T: (0)130-450-9955 F: (0)130-421-3230
www.county-hotel-dover.co.uk
79 rooms
From £40

This clean, business-class hotel—fronting the sea, a block off Market Square Center—has large rooms and a good restaurant.

Portsmouth
Best Western Queen's Hotel
Clarence Esplanade, Southsea
T: (0)239-282-2466 F: (0)239-282-1901
www.bestwestern.com
75 rooms
£57-130

This historic hotel hosted soldiers and strategy meetings before the D-Day launch. It has one of the city's best restaurants.

Southampton
De Vere Grand Harbour Hotel

West Quay Road
T: (0)238-063-3033 F: (0)238-063-3066
www.deveregrandharbour.co.uk
173 rooms
£130-330

This is among the finest hotels on the south coast. Within walking distance of most historic attractions. Waterfront views with balconies, two restaurants and a bar.

Dartmouth
Dart Marina Hotel
Sandquay
T: (0)180-383-2580 F: (0)180-383-5040
www.dartmarinahotel.com
50 rooms
From £199

Built on the marina in 1996, this is Dartmouth's upscale hotel. A five-minute waterfront walk from the historic center. Some rooms have balconies, all overlook the picturesque harbor. A good lounge and restaurant with seafood specialties.

11

Cassino

ITALY

Abbey of Montecassino

THE WAR YEARS

W hen you see Italy today, it's nearly impossible to believe that anyone could have described it as Europe's "soft underbelly." The description seems particularly absurd from a man as worldly as Winston Churchill. The British prime minister had visited the peninsula on numerous occasions, including his honeymoon, yet these are the words he employed in making the case for mounting an attack on Fortress Europe through the Italian mainland. With narrow beaches abutted by close hills, and the treacherous Apennine Mountains running down the peninsula, the entire country is perfectly suited for military defense. It was a position from which German Field Marshal Albrecht Kesselring—considered in this campaign superior to his Allied counterparts—would mount an expert defense that produced some of the most terrible fighting of the war.

Whatever the fallacies of the initial decision and evident shortcomings of subsequent battle plans, the Allies launched the invasion of Italy's mainland from Sicily on September 3, 1943, with landings at Reggio di Calabria, followed by the British seizure of the port of Taranto and main Allied landings around Salerno on September 9. At Salerno, furious German resistance nearly pushed the Allies back into the sea—Hitler foresaw another Dunkirk—but an Allied beachhead was eventually established. In mid-September the Germans fell back—sacking Naples along the way—establishing eventual positions around Cassino known as the Gustav Line. Commanding approaches to Rome through the Liri and Rapido Valleys, Cassino, its rivers and 1,700-foot Montecassino (Mount Cassino) were linchpins of formidable German defenses. From January to May 1944, the Allies attempted to break the Gustav Line in a series of grim assaults known as the Four Battles of Montecassino.

The Alliance that fought the Nazis was truly global. Algerian, American, Brazilian, British, Canadian, French, Greek, Indian, Moroccan, Nepalese, New Zealand (including native Maori), Palestinian Jew and Senegalese soldiers suffered through the most bitter winter in memory in "Sunny Italy." Feet swelled with frostbite. Water froze in canteens. Unable to dig into frozen ground, soldiers piled bomb rubble around themselves for warmth and protection. "Once wet, nothing dried without fire, and there was no fire in the forward positions," wrote military historian Robert Rush.

The terrain forced primitive methods upon fighting men. Machinery that was supposed to make modern warfare mobile and efficient—trucks, tanks, self-propelled artillery—was useless in steep hills. Vehicles sunk to the axles in mud. Backs laden with supplies, men and mules carried the bulk of equipment uphill, their laborious progress making soldier and beast alike easy targets for German sharpshooters concealed above. This was mountain warfare at its harshest, with progress on both sides measured in feet, yards and staggering casualty figures.

Among the worst engagements was a January attempt by the seemingly fearless U.S. 36th "Texas" Division to cross the Rapido River near the base of Montecassino. The 36th was quickly surrounded. Three days of fighting left 1,000 Americans dead. The division's rescue was aided by the U.S. 442nd Regimental Combat Team, composed of Japanese-American soldiers, which became the most-decorated unit of its size in U.S. military history.

Towering above the battlefield, physically and psychologically, was the baleful and colossal Abbey of Montecassino. Repository of centuries of irreplaceable art, the Benedictine monastery founded in 529 A.D. by St. Benedict himself sat atop Montecassino, commanding all valley approaches and, most importantly, Highway 6 to Rome. Believing Germans were occupying the monastery, Allied commanders debated plans to bomb the complex. Most strident among bombing proponents was New Zealand Lieutenant-General Bernard Freyberg, whose troops, along with Indian soldiers, were to assault the mountain in the Second Battle of Montecassino. U.S. General Mark Clark eventually issued the order to bomb the Abbey—after the war he would regret the decision, disclaim responsibility and blame Freyberg for demanding it. Freyberg today generally receives the bulk of opprobrium for the attack.

Leaving the matter of responsibility open, on February 15, 1944, 254 Allied bombers soared over the monastery in an attack that would rank among the most infamous Allied actions of the war. As post-war testimony from resident monks would prove, German troops had never occupied the monastery. Only monks and civilians were inside when the air raid sent "great gusts of thunder ... along the vast stone passageways giving continuity to the crashes so that they were no longer a succession of explosions but a single great cataclysmic roar," according to Cassino veteran Fred Majdalany. The monastery was left nearly unrecognizable.

"Not only a crime against culture, the attack was also an outright blunder, because the Germans proceeded to fortify the rubble, making their positions even stronger," according to *The Oxford Essential Guide to World War II*. Germany pulled a propaganda victory from the wreckage, showing the world the barbaric treatment the Italian treasure had received from the Allies. Worse still, because the U.S.-led bombing was poorly coordinated with infantry movements, it "expended its fury in a vacuum, tragically and wastefully," according to Majdalany. "It achieved nothing, it helped nobody."

Montecassino would remain in German hands until May 18, when Polish troops, after two days of gory, attritional fighting, raised their tattered colors over the ruins of the monastery. The costly Polish charge was part of the final spasm of Operation Diadem, the spring offensive that finally broke the Gustav Line and catapulted Allied troops to Rome.

Within weeks, the D-Day invasion of Normandy would commence. The monastery and bombed-out town of Cassino would be left behind, a silent, smoking wasteland. Allied casualties for the entire Italy campaign (including Sicily) totaled 188,746, including 31,886 dead (including 19,475 Americans), and 156,860 wounded and missing (including 90,167 Americans). The once proud Axis power of Italy, its government in chaos, its army disintegrated, was left a dishonored, defenseless ruin.

SOURCES & OTHER READING

The Battle of Cassino, Majdalany, Fred, Houghton Mifflin, 1957

The Sideshow War: The Italian Campaign, 1943-1945, Botjer, George F., Texas A&M University Press, 1996

Cassino: The Hardest-Fought Battle of World War II, Parker, Matthew, Doubleday, 2004

Cassino: Anatomy of the Battle, Piekalkiewicz, Janus, Orbis, 1980

U.S. Infantryman in World War II: Mediterranean Theater of Operations 1942-45, Rush, Robert S., Osprey Publishing, 2002

Calculated Risk, Clark, Mark, Harper, 1950

"Quest for the Eternal City," Niderost, Eric, *World War II* magazine, July 2003

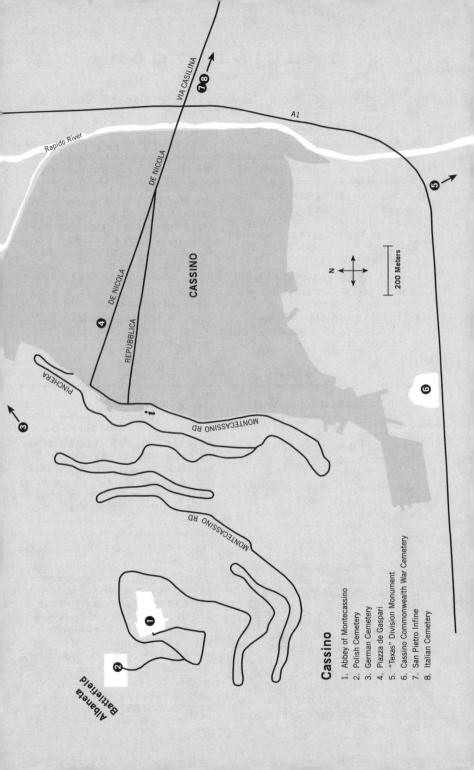

Cassino

1. Abbey of Montecassino
2. Polish Cemetery
3. German Cemetery
4. Piazza de Gaspari
5. "Texas" Division Monument
6. Cassino Commonwealth War Cemetery
7. San Pietro Infine
8. Italian Cemetery

CASSINO

Rapido River

VIA CASILINA

DE NICOLA

DE NICOLA

REPUBBLICA

PINCHERA

MONTECASSINO RD

MONTECASSINO RD

Albaneta Battlefield

A1

N

200 Meters

CASSINO TODAY

Population: 33,000 • Country Code: 39 • €1 = $1.36/£0.67

"Few battlefields reward careful study as much as that of Cassino," wrote British military historian Richard Holmes. Indeed, the drive alone into Cassino provides visitors with an appreciation of the rugged terrain that made fighting here such a terrible endeavor. The jagged peaks that were hell for soldiers are, however, breathtaking for modern travelers. In an area associated with tragedy, many are surprised to find intense natural beauty.

Cassino today is a nondescript modern town, entirely rebuilt downhill from the original site (the town was destroyed by a single Allied bombing raid in March 1944). Along primary streets are the kinds of piazzas, pastry shops, cafes and restaurants that make almost any Italian town a pleasure. But this is largely a factory community—the huge Fiat automotive plant being the largest local employer—with few evident attractions.

The rebuilt monastery is the biggest draw, but Cassino's proximity to other sites earns it a spot on the tourist map. In the shadow of Mt. Vesuvius, the ashen ruins of ancient Pompeii are an hour south by car. The Amalfi Coast is 90 minutes by car. Spectacular d'Abruzzo National Park provides mountain recreation to the north. Scenery, history and central location make Cassino a solid central base of operations. Cassino sites (including San Pietro Infine) can be covered in one (long) day.

POINTS OF INTEREST

1. Abbey of Montecassino (Abbazia di Montecassino) ★★★★

At top of serpentine, 8-km-long Montecassino Road (from Cassino follow hill/signs to Abbazia di Montecassino)
T: (0)776-31-1529
Daily, 8:30 a.m.-12:30 p.m.; 3:30-5 p.m.
(Closed 6 p.m. in summer)
Abbey open but museum closed November 1-March 21
Abbey admission: Free
Museum admission: €2
Visitors in shorts, sleeveless shirts or otherwise inappropriate dress will not be admitted. No flash photography.

Prior to 1944, the world-famous Abbey had been destroyed three times—twice by invaders (Lombards in 577 A.D., Saracens in 884 A.D.), once by earthquake (1349). The latest reconstruction efforts began immediately after the war, with meticulous attention to original plans. Though largely completed to almost perfect pre-war specifications in 1964, detailing efforts are ongoing. Inside the main entry, a statue of St. Benedict marks the spot where the monastery's founder died and the first Allied bombs fell. With its vaulted ceilings and ornate detail, the church is a masterpiece of gold inlay, mosaic, alabaster and original artwork—paintings, statues, altars, the original tabernacle—that survived the bombing. The museum has a large collection of original items salvaged from the rubble—chalices, crucifixes, ivory carvings, handwritten prayer and music books, much more.

The straight-walled Abbey is impressive less for aesthetic beauty than for its sheer size and dramatic mountaintop setting. Soldiers often spoke of the gloomy hulk lurking over them. Many were happy to see it demolished. No matter what one's response to the building, it remains among Italy's most important symbols of post-war reconstruction. Along the winding road up the hill are parts of the monastery's ancient subfortress and a hideous post-modern sculpture from 1984 representing an exploding bomb. Vistas inside offer open, edifying views of the treacherous battlefield. The story of its destruction attracts many, but the monks who live inside insist it's the process of rebuilding and renewal that makes the monastery relevant. So does all this reconstruction amount to the "real" Abbey, or is this simply an impressive replica? The monks who remain (the Abbey is now a national shrine owned by the government) have a simple reply and motto: "*Succisa Virescit.*" The Abbey will never die.

Albaneta Battlefield

Near the Abbey and Polish cemetery is the Albaneta area, site of vicious fighting. Permission to access the area must be obtained from the Abbey information office or by prior arrangement with a guide (see Getting To and Around Cassino). On the battlefield is a 40-foot marble tower commemorating Polish soldiers and a relief map showing troop positions and landmarks. From the hilltop behind the tower, called Calvary Hill during the battle, a crumbling house in which 60 German soldiers and Polish POWs remain entombed is visible. Along nearby Cavendish Road, a Sherman tank with turret blown off and treads refashioned into a crucifix recalls a battlefield description from Polish Lieutenant-General Wladyslaw Anders: "Corpses of Polish and German soldiers, sometimes entangled in deadly embrace, lay everywhere. ... There were overturned tanks with broken caterpillars and others standing as if ready for attack, with their guns still pointing towards the monastery."

2. Polish Cemetery ★★★

Off Montecassino Road, just below Abbey
Daily, 9-11:45 a.m.; 3-5:45 p.m.,
May 16-September 30
Daily, 9-11:45 a.m.; 2-4:45 p.m.,
October 1-May 15

A large staircase leads to a huge monument in the center of this most impressive of the area's war cemeteries. In the shadow of the monastery—Polish troops eventually seized the destroyed Abbey—the cemetery's 1,052 graves are dug into a wide bowl. This is a good spot for telephoto pictures of the monastery.

3. German Cemetery ★★★

In Caira area, about 3 km north of city center. From town, follow signs to "Cimitero Militare Germanico," "Cimitero tedesco" or "Deutscher Soldaten Friedhof." From 8 a.m. in summer (9 a.m. in winter) to 6 or 7 p.m. in summer (4 p.m. in winter).

The remains of 20,058 soldiers are interred in this hillside cemetery. Olive trees and hedges give it the feel of a city park. Many buried here were in their teens when killed in action. For more on German military cemeteries, see page 8.

4. Piazza de Gaspari ★

In the downtown square sit a Sherman tank, a PAK-40 artillery piece and a broken pillar (an area symbol). On the square is the bookshop Cartolibreria (Piazza de Gaspari 36-37, 0776-31-1143) owned by editor Federico Lamberti. A boy in Cassino during the war, the enthusiastic, English-fluent Lamberti leads battlefield tours.

5. "Texas" Division Monument/Rapido River ★★

At small bridge on Via Biffontaine

At the site where the U.S. 36th "Texas" Division and others lost more than 1,000 men trying to advance across the Rapido River (also called the Gari River), a French plaque honors the fallen Americans. The stone bridge is rebuilt to resemble its pre-war state. A large platform and freedom bell were installed in 2007.

6. Cassino Commonwealth War Cemetery ★★★

The largest British Commonwealth cemetery in Italy contains 4,265 graves, including those of Canadian, Indian and New Zealand troops. Etched on 15-foot granite slabs surrounding a reflecting pool and central monument are the names of 4,000 missing in action.

7. San Pietro Infine ★★★★★

From Cassino, follow Via Casilina Sud about 10 km southeast to small signs for San Pietro Infine. Entering village, turn left at roadside statue of Padre Pio (holding crucifix) and follow road uphill toward ruins. Museum admission: €5

Untouched since the war—a rarity in Europe—this large, important ghost town allows visitors to wander amid the ruins of a battle made famous by John Huston's 1944 documentary, *Battle of San Pietro*. Sent to Italy by the U.S. government to produce a film that would rally the American home front, Huston instead delivered a stark account of the torrid battle with a realism that shocked many. Through layers of propaganda, the film showed graphic scenes of death, young Americans being loaded into body bags, the obliteration of San Pietro (wartime population 1,412) by U.S. artillery and, perhaps worst of all, an inconclusive battle. One of only two films banned by the Office of War Information during the war (both by Huston) it's lived on, according to *The New York Times*, "standing alone in the history of documentary filmmaking."

As the vast wreckage testifies, the picturesque stone village was tragically gutted. Along original cobbled streets (lots of hills and stairs) are empty houses, businesses, piles of rubble. Half the central church dome remains torn open—the violent

damage it sustained clearly evident—hovering above the town in eerie, naked solitude. Caves where civilians and soldiers took refuge (depicted in the film) are accessible (flashlight helpful). The town was rebuilt downhill from the old ruins. This is one of the most poignant, evocative sites in all Europe—similar to France's Oradour-Sur-Glane (page 238) though without as much surrounding tourist infrastructure. For decades, the abandoned town was ignored by locals, but a museum was opened and an entry fee introduced in 2007. Excavation continues to unearth buildings and artifacts. This is a remarkable, important area.

8. Italian Cemetery (Sacrario Militare di Montelungo) ★★★

Along Via Casilina in Montelungo (on the hill, just before the village when arriving from Cassino), 3.5 km south of San Pietro Infine
Monday-Saturday, 9 a.m.-5:45 p.m., Sunday, holidays, 8:15 a.m.-1:15 p.m., May 16-September 30
Monday-Friday, 9 a.m.-3:30 p.m., Saturday, 9 a.m.-5:15 p.m., Sunday, holidays, 8:15 a.m.-1 p.m., October 1-May 15

A colonnaded monument and sculpture of Jesus above a dying soldier dominate this small cemetery, which occupies the site of the first major battles between Italian and German troops following Italy's withdrawal from the Axis alliance. Across the road is some interesting equipment, including tanks and field artillery.

RELATED SITES BEYOND CASSINO

Paestum (Salerno) Landing Beaches ★

Though U.S. Rangers and British commandos conducted operations along the Amalfi Coast and at Salerno, principle Allied landings at Salerno (Operation Avalanche) took place south of the city, along the 20-mile stretch of white sand fronting the Gulf of Salerno. British forces landed roughly in front of the town of

Battipaglia, just south of Salerno, on adjacent beaches code-named Uncle, Sugar and Roger. U.S. troops landed 37 km south of Salerno at small Paestum. At Paestum, the medieval Torre di Paestum (Paestum Tower)—the stone-built landmark used by the U.S. Navy to guide landings—stands at almost dead center of the American landing beaches. From SS18 at

Paestum, follow signs to Lido di Militare then Torre di Paestum. Between the tower and beach is a small park with a 10-foot, rose-granite obelisk commemorating the landing. Nearby is a small memorial to the 45th and 186th Infantry Divisions. These are the only markers recalling the invasion. A minute's walk from the obelisk, the beach is wide, flat, sandy and, in summer, filled with tourists who crowd the hotels and camper/trailer parks that line the coast.

OTHER AREA ATTRACTIONS

Amalfi Coast/Pompeii

Ninety minutes south of Cassino, the Amalfi Coast is famous for its succession of picturesque towns built into sheer cliffs and astonishing, panoramic views of the azure Tyrrhenian Sea below. The scenic road runs between Sorrento and Vietri sul Mare. Amalfi is the primary stopping point. Like all the tourist towns along the windy, busy, slow road, it's filled with shops, cafes, restaurants and views that rank among the best in the world. Just north, off A3/E45, are the accessible ruins of Pompeii (another major tourist attraction with commercial buildup), buried by the 79 A.D. eruption of Mt. Vesuvius.

GETTING TO/AROUND CASSINO

Cassino is about 115 km south of Rome (page 206 for flight information). Once beyond Rome's ring road, it's reached in an hour via Highway A1/E45 (see Driving, page xv). Cassino is also reached by regular train service from Rome's Termini Station. Trips take a little less than two hours. Timetable available at www.trenitalia.com.

City maps are available at hotels and the Tourist Information Office (Via G. Di Biasio 54, 0776-2-1292). Compact Cassino is easy to walk, but since taxis are scarce and most attractions are outside of town, and up steep hills, it's best to have a car. Hotels can also arrange rides. Local guides can be extremely helpful. Guide Michele Di Lonardo (338-814-2414 or 0776-33-7101 or micheledilonardo@hotmail.com) is unsurpassed in his knowledge of the Abbey, battle and local terrain. He's thorough, speaks excellent English and can get access to the Albaneta area.

ACCOMMODATIONS

Cassino
Hotel Ristorante al Boschetto

Via Ausonia 54
T: (0)776-3-9131 F: (0)776-30-1315
www.hotelristorantealboschetto.it
82 rooms
€80

This three-star hotel has a friendly staff, comfortable rooms and a large restaurant, with seating for up to 400. The regional specialties are popular. Free parking.

Forum Palace Hotel

Via Casilina Nord
T: (0)776-30-1211 F: (0)776-30-2116
www.hotelforumpalace.it

104 rooms
€120

Cassino's four-star hotel is a short walk from downtown. The rooms are good and the English-speaking staff is efficient.

Paestum (Salerno)
Savoy Beach Hotel

Via Poseidonia, Paestum
T: (0)828-72-0100 F: (0)828-72-0807
www.hotelsavoybeach.it
42 rooms
€65-180 (Imperial Suite, €750)

The 2001-opened hotel is slick, secluded and spacious. Close to the beach, it has tennis courts, spa, pools and fine dining.

12

Paris

F R A N C E

Hôtel National des Invalides and Eiffel Tower

THE WAR YEARS

I n a war fueled as often by propaganda as by bullets, Paris was an unequaled icon of conquest. Symbolically, its capture provided Adolf Hitler with his greatest triumph. Sparking one of the century's greatest celebrations, its liberation signaled to the world that the end of the war was within reach.

In May 1940, as 75 German divisions launched the war in western Europe by smashing though Belgium, Luxembourg, the Netherlands and northern France, the river of refugees entering Paris from the north swiftly gathered locals into its current. As "the Hun" closed on the city, the exodus of civilians created a chaotic, 400-mile-long traffic jam to the south. In 1939, Paris' population stood at about five million. By the end of June 1940, it was 1.9 million.

To save it from ruin, French leaders declared Paris an open city on June 12. On June 14, German troops entered the eerily silent streets—almost no one ventured outside to watch—marching through Napoleon's great Arc de Triomphe and down the famed Champs-Elysées. Within hours, enormous swastikas hung from every important building and monument—during four years of German rule, the Eiffel Tower was never seen without it.

"Once the Germans took Paris, it was evident that the conflict in western Europe was over," wrote *New York Times* correspondent C.L. Sulzberger.

The French government agreed. After Premier Paul Reynaud resigned on June 16, his successor, World War I hero Marshal Henri Pétain, immediately asked for armistice, leading to one of the most bizarre and humbling surrender ceremonies in history. Near the town of Compiègne, the railway car in which Germany had been forced into signing its own humiliating surrender at the end of World War I had been preserved as a French museum. Now, with Hitler, Göring, Hess and other high-ranking Nazis in attendance, the car was, as Sulzberger aptly described it, "wheeled out of its shed to serve as the parlor for France's funeral." The day following the June 22 surrender, Hitler made his only visit to Paris, taking in the Opera, Eiffel Tower, Napoleon's Tomb and Notre-Dame Cathedral, complaining about Sacré-Coeur ("appalling" was his verdict) and comparing the city unfavorably to Berlin.

In time, Paris life regained a sense of normalcy. Residents returned and by and large made peace with their new masters. With almost none of the pillage that accompanied German campaigns in the East, Paris was considered an enviable posting for German soldiers, a peaceful place to relax in cafes, meet women, enjoy fine meals.

Still, reality was never far from view. "The overriding fact of the occupation was that *feldgrau* (field grey) was everywhere ... and Parisians were expected to remember who had conquered whom," wrote historian Robert Cole in *A Traveller's History of Paris*. The Germans introduced curfews, censorship and blackouts. Private cars were banned, severe rations on all staples could be tyrannically enforced. And the darker side of the Nazi agenda was fulfilled. Jews were banned from public life, not to be seen in restaurants, theaters, libraries, museums, sporting fields and most shops. Aided by police and locals, 160,000 French were deported to Nazi camps throughout the war. Of the 76,000 deported Jews, only three percent survived.

Resistance activity in the French capital was negligible for most of the war, though it increased dramatically after the June 6, 1944, Allied landings at Normandy. Preceded by a week of strikes, local communists led a violent public uprising on August 19. A rival political group loyal to General Charles de Gaulle seized the Prefecture of Police building. Meanwhile, Hitler issued orders to sack the city. "Is Paris burning?" he demanded impatiently. Despite bloody street fighting—Parisians against Germans but also brutal killings of French collaborators—Paris' military commander, General Dietrich von Choltitz, who'd presided over the destruction of Rotterdam in 1940 and Sevastopol in 1942, defied the order. Paris was to be spared.

Initially, Supreme Allied Commander General Dwight Eisenhower intended to bypass Paris in the Allied march across France, preferring to save resources and leave the Germans the headache of feeding and administering the vast city. But with pressure from de Gaulle, the communist uprising and mounting human tragedy, the Allies were, in the words of historian Mark Arnold-Forster, "obliged to take Paris." Led by Lieutenant-General Jacques Philippe Leclerc and the 2nd French Armored Division, the first Allied tanks rumbled into Paris on August 24. "Parisians hysterical with relief ... kissed everything in uniform," wrote Cole. "It was a common sight to see soldiers fighting street to street with lipstick smeared over their faces."

On August 25, with U.S. troops supporting Leclerc's forces, von Choltitz surrendered Paris intact, with 10,000 troops. The public delirium that followed continued without pause for three days. De Gaulle entered the city late on the 25th, himself reaching for symbolism. Marching stiffly down the Champs-Elysées to thunderous cheers, he addressed the city in emphatic tones: "Paris! Paris outraged! Paris broken! Paris martyred! But Paris liberated!"

The street party and de Gaulle's position as the leader of France were sealed on August 27 when Eisenhower entered Paris, acknowledged the leadership of the future French president and reviewed Allied troops marching yet again, with powerful imagery, through the Arc de Triomphe and along the Champs-Elysées. Each subsequent Allied victory signaled a war nearer its end. But even though its liberation had delayed the advance on Germany, Paris, the first Allied capital rescued in Europe, provided emblematic proof that the Nazi stranglehold on Western civilization would not last.

SOURCES & OTHER READING

Paris in the Third Reich: A History of the German Occupation, 1940-1944, Pryce-Jones, David, Holt, Rinehart & Winston, 1981

The Fall of France: The Nazi Invasion of 1940, Jackson, Julian, Oxford University Press, 2003

The Fall of Paris: June 1940, Lottman, Herbert, HarperCollins, 1992

Is Paris Burning?, Collins and Lapierre, V. Gollancz, 1965

A Traveller's History of Paris, Cole, Robert, Interlink Books, 1998

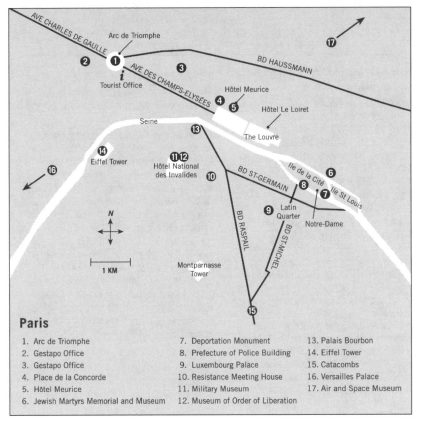

Paris

1. Arc de Triomphe
2. Gestapo Office
3. Gestapo Office
4. Place de la Concorde
5. Hôtel Meurice
6. Jewish Martyrs Memorial and Museum
7. Deportation Monument
8. Prefecture of Police Building
9. Luxembourg Palace
10. Resistance Meeting House
11. Military Museum
12. Museum of Order of Liberation
13. Palais Bourbon
14. Eiffel Tower
15. Catacombs
16. Versailles Palace
17. Air and Space Museum

PARIS TODAY

Population: 12 million (metro area) • Country Code: 33 • €1 = $1.36/£0.67

The capital of the country and center of the great Paris Basin, Paris is the heart from which all historic, political, economic and cultural blood flows through France. Nearly one-fifth of the country's population lives in the city and its suburbs. Paris is best known for its cuisine and unsurpassed architecture. Every street corner brings a building, sculpture or edifice worth study—or an outdoor cafe good for a drink. The city and its famed landmarks—the Eiffel Tower, Louvre, Sacré-Coeur, many more—were largely spared wartime destruction. It has thus retained its position as the one must-see city on any world traveler's list.

Paris is beset by troubles typical of the world's mega-cities—traffic, panhandlers, crowds, sanitation and excessive prices among them. The result among travelers is a love-it-or-hate-it reputation that extends back for centuries. Still, Paris is impossible to ignore.

Three or four days are needed to visit all the sites covered in this chapter (not including Compiègne and Reims), but major points can be visited in one or two days. Robert Cole's *A Traveller's History of Paris* includes a 20-page section on WWII in Paris and is invaluable for anyone with a deeper interest in this spectacular city.

POINTS OF INTEREST

M indicates nearest Metro or transit station

1. Arc de Triomphe ★★★

Place Charles de Gaulle
M: Charles de Gaulle-Étoile
T: (0)1-55-37-7377
Daily, 10 a.m.-11 p.m. (closed
10:30 p.m., October-March)
Last entry 30 minutes before close
Adult: €8; Student (18-25): €5;
Under 18: Free
284 stairs to top. Elevator for disabled only.

Built by decree of Napoleon Bonaparte to celebrate the victories of his Grande Armée, the Roman-style arch was the scene of the most wrenching image of the war to the French, when German troops paraded beneath it upon entering Paris. Each day of the occupation, a battalion of German soldiers marched around the arc and down the Champs-Elysées. Today the arch remains a resolute landmark and center of a major traffic roundabout. Views from the top are worth the climb, but the museum is small and disappointing. It costs nothing to walk through the arch at street level. Here, the eternal flame to the unknown French soldier of World War I remained ablaze throughout the occupation.

2. Gestapo Office ★

74 Avenue Foch
M: Charles de Gaulle-Étoile,
Porte Dauphine

This private mansion was used as a Gestapo interrogation and torture center. "At night, screams coming from [this building] often made sleep difficult for next-door neighbors," wrote historian Robert Cole.

3. Gestapo Office ★

9 Rue de Saussaies, between Rue du Faubourg St-Honoré and Rue de Penthièvre, a few blocks northeast of the Palais de l'Elysée
M: Miromesnil, St-Philippe-du-Roule

One of several infamous local Gestapo centers for interrogation, this six-story yellow-stone apartment building is next to a Ministry of the Interior office.

4. Place de la Concorde ★★

At west end of Jardin des Tuileries
on Rue de Rivoli
M: Concorde

This area was the scene of awful fighting on June 25, 1944. The Hôtel Crillon—an important German administrative center—was badly damaged. Once the Germans were vanquished, crowds turned on collaborators. Women with German boyfriends had their heads shaved. Others were killed outright. Today, at 258 Rue de Rivoli, a plaque marks the site of Hotel Talleyrand as the place where the post-war American Marshall Plan for the reconstruction of Europe was administered "against hunger, poverty, desperation and chaos." Directly across the street are 10 plaques bearing the names of French combatants who died in the August 25 fighting.

5. Hôtel Meurice ★★

228 Rue de Rivoli
M: Tuileries
T: (0)1-44-58-1010

The hotel served as headquarters for Paris military commander General Dietrich von Choltitz. On August 25, after refusing Hitler's order to destroy Paris, von Choltitz reportedly ate lunch, then—upon the arrival of the liberators—signed Paris' surrender on a billiard table. Completely restored, it's now a first-class hotel.

6. Jewish Martyrs Memorial and Museum (Mémorial de la Shoah) ★★

17 Rue Geoffrey-Asnier
T: (0)1-42-77-4472
M: Pont Marie
Sunday-Friday, 10 a.m.-9 p.m.
Closed Saturdays, national and
Jewish holidays

With archives and permanent exhibitions, this historical research center specializes in the fate of the Jews during World War II. The large memorial in front is dedicated to the six million Jews throughout Europe who died during the Nazi reign.

7. Deportation Monument (Mémorial des Martyrs de la Déportation) ★★

Extreme east end of Ile de la Cité, just across the Pont de l'Archevêché. From the back of Notre-Dame Cathedral, follow signs to Monument de la Déportement.
M: St-Michel Notre-Dame, Cité
T: (0)1-46-33-8756
Daily, 10 a.m.-noon, 2-7 p.m. (closed at 5 p.m., October-March)

This large memorial, established by Charles de Gaulle in 1962, is intended to recall the concentration camp experience of Jews and other persecuted groups. Grim features include narrow passageways, spiked gates and cramped concrete cells.

8. Prefecture of Police Building ★

Rue de la Cité
M: Cité, St-Michel Notre-Dame

The scars of bullet holes can be seen along the façade of the building—it directly faces Notre-Dame Cathedral—reportedly from fighting that occurred here during the final week of Nazi occupation.

9. Luxembourg Palace (Palais du Luxembourg) ★★

15 Rue de Vaugirard
M: Luxembourg (RER)
T: (0)1-42-34-2000

One of Paris' finest buildings, the Italianate palace, built 1615–30, served as Luftwaffe headquarters during the occupation. Today it's the seat of the French Senate, open to the public by appointment one Saturday per month. Open to the public, its extensive garden (now popular with joggers) was used as a parking lot for German tanks.

10. Resistance Meeting House ★

41 Rue de Bellechasse
M: Rue du Bac, Varenne

A plaque on this nondescript six-story apartment building notes it as the place where members of local and national resistance groups helped plan the uprising of August 19, 1944.

11. Military Museum (Musée de l'Armée) ★★★★★

129 Rue de Grenelle (inside Hôtel National des Invalides)
M: Latour-Maubourg, Invalides, Varenne
T: (0)1-44-42-3877
Daily, 10 a.m.-6 p.m., April-September (Closed at 5 p.m., October-March)
Closed January 1, May 1, November 1, December 25 and first Monday of each month
Adult: €8; Student: €6 (includes all four museums)

One of the top military attractions in the world, this museum is part of the sprawling Invalides complex, which houses four museums, including the grand tomb of Napoleon Bonaparte (definitely worth a stop). With purportedly the largest collection of arms and armor in the world, it has extensive sections covering medieval warfare, Napoleonic campaigns and World War I. The centerpiece is the three-floor, World War II section that traces the war from the rise of fascism in Europe to the atomic bombing of Hiroshima. A section is dedicated to nearly every campaign in Europe. Arms, hardware, relics and extensive interpretive text (English included) are supported by large video screens throughout the museum. These continuously loop engrossing footage and present short documentary pieces. Rare, enlarged photographs—panzers massed along the Belgian border in 1940, the beach at Dieppe littered with Canadian bodies—are chilling. Just a few of the thousands of artifacts include a German Enigma cryptographic machine, original iron and concrete beach obstacles from Normandy, a German Goliath remote-controlled mini-tank, goggles worn by General George Patton, full-size replicas of V1 and V2 weapons and much more. But for a larger section on the Pacific War and collection of large weapons—aircraft, tanks and the like are largely absent—this might be the finest World War II museum in the world. As it is, it's near the top and deserves a full afternoon visit.

12. The Museum of the Order of the Liberation (Musée Ordre de la Libération) ★★

Location: see Point 11
T: (0)1-47-05-0410
Hours: see Point 11
Closed January 1, May 1, June 17, November 1, December 25 and first Monday of each month
Admission: see Point 11

In November 1940, General Charles de Gaulle created the "Order of the Liberation" to reward efforts to liberate France and her empire. The two large galleries honoring recipients—photos, text and personal items ranging from guns to guitars—are well done. Other displays include the hubcap from Hitler's Mercedes and a graphic exhibit dealing with the Holocaust. The museum is worthwhile, though not at the expense of Napoleon's Tomb or other Invalides museums.

13. Palais Bourbon (Assemblée Nationale) ★★

At Pont de la Concorde on the Quai d'Orsay
M: Assemblée Nationale

Now the seat of the National Assembly, this magnificent Italianate building on the banks of the Seine, built in the early 1700s, was headquarters of the German Military Administration 1940–44. The building is open every Saturday for guided tours at 10 a.m., 1 and 5 p.m. (visitors must have passports).

14. Eiffel Tower ★★

Avenue Gustave Eiffel
M: Champ de Mars-Tour Eiffel
T: (0)1-44-11-2323
Daily, 9 a.m.-12:45 a.m. (mid-June-September)
Daily, 9:30 a.m.-11:45 p.m. (September-mid-June)
Elevator: first level (€4.50), second level (€7.80), top level (€11.50)
Stairs to first and second levels: €4

Hitler reportedly considered tearing down this landmark in order to salvage its 7,300 tons of iron. Perhaps he preferred its symbolic value. The giant swastika flag that hung from the top was a particularly grating insult to Parisians. After the war, the Tower Restaurant functioned briefly as an American enlisted men's club.

15. Catacombs ★★

Place Denfert-Rochereau
M: Denfert-Rochereau
T: (0)1-43-22-4763
Tuesday-Friday, 9 a.m.-4 p.m.; Saturday-Sunday, 9-11 a.m.

If you've ever wondered what six million skulls and bones stacked end to end look like, this is your place. Among the world's most bizarre attractions, this site is included because members of the Resistance used it for clandestine gatherings and movements. The tour requires descending many stairs into the ghoulish, dimly lit passageways.

16. Versailles Palace (Château de Versailles) ★★★

At Grand Canal, Versailles, 15 km southwest of Paris
T: (0)1-39-24-8888 (Versailles Tourist Office)
Tuesday-Sunday, 9 a.m.-6:30 p.m. (closed 5:30 p.m., November-March)
Last entry 30 minutes before close.
Adult (18 and over): €20; (€16 November-March); Under 18: Free
Audio guide: €6

Various price packages available. Those listed here allow access to most of the grounds, including the Hall of Mirrors.

The lavish palace of Louis XIV and others is an essential Paris tourist stop. The hour-long, self-guided tour winds through gilded rooms jammed with priceless furniture and art. In the Hall of Mirrors—its 17 arched windows overlooking the gardens are opposed by 17 matching mirrors—the 1919 peace treaty ending World War I was signed, its unfavorable terms for Germany setting the stage for Hitler's rise. The palace is magnificent, though visits are diminished by the snaking, jostling, yammering crowds who make appreciating details a chore. See the Trianon Palace hotel in the Accommodations section for another Versailles point of interest.

17. Air and Space Museum (Musée de l'Air et de l'Espace) ★★★

Aéroport de Paris-Le Bourget, 8 km north-east of Paris
M: Le Bourget
T: (0)1-49-92-7062
Tuesday-Sunday, 10 a.m.-6 p.m.
(closed 5 p.m., November-March)
Closed December 25, January 1
Adult: €7; Student: €5; Under 18: Free

Due to its outskirts location and limited publicity, many Paris visitors never hear about this major attraction, widely considered one of the world's great air museums. It's located at what was the main Paris airport during World War II, also the airfield where Charles Lindberg touched down to complete the first solo transatlantic flight in 1927. Large and extremely impressive galleries deal with early flight, World War I aircraft, modern flight and space travel. For all this one would expect a monumental exhibition of WWII aircraft. One would be disappointed. While the museum possesses a large collection of WWII airplanes, lack of space prevents it from displaying all but 9 or 10. That said, the collection includes rarities and mint-condition specimens—an original V1 missile, an He-162 "Volksjäger" (the Luftwaffe's last operational jet fighter, of which 116 were produced), a British Spitfire, an American B-26G Marauder and P-51 Mustang and others. The planes are housed in the Concorde Hall, which includes a Concorde jet that visitors can walk through.

RELATED SITES BEYOND PARIS

Compiègne Armistice Memorial and Museum (Compiègne Ville de l'Armistice) ★★★

Off D546, 7.5 km east of Compiègne, about 75 km northeast of Paris
From Compiègne, follow N1 (it becomes N31) toward Soissones/Reims, then follow signs for Clairière de l'Armistice
T: (0) 3-44-85-1418
Daily, 9 a.m.-12:15 p.m., 2-6:30 p.m.
(closed at 5:30 p.m. mid-October-March)

The histories of both world wars are inextricably intertwined, nowhere more visibly than here. At this site on November 11, 1918, in a railway car belonging to French Marshal Ferdinand Foch, "the criminal pride of the German Empire" succumbed to the Allies (according to the central memorial). The car was later inaugurated as a national museum. Hitler pointedly chose it as the spot for the French surrender on June 22, 1940, dancing a victory jig to complete his "masterpiece of revenge." As historian Louis Snyder wrote: "He, the lonely corporal of World War I, would grind the French noses into the dirt of Compiègne at the very spot of Germany's humiliation." The car was displayed in Berlin until 1945, when it was destroyed shortly before Germany's own capitulation. A precise replica of Foch's original car is the centerpiece of the small museum that stands in this historic clearing in the woods. It's possible to look through the windows of the car to view the arrangement of its 1918 condition. The museum has small displays of World War I and II items—mostly newspapers, photos, uniforms and small weapons.

Museum of Surrender at Reims (Musée de la Reddition à Reims) ★★★

12 Rue Franklin Roosevelt, Reims
T: (0)3-26-47-8419
Daily, 10 a.m.-noon, 2-6 p.m.
Closed Tuesdays, January 1, May 1, July 14, November 11, December 24-25
Adult: €1.50; Under 16: Free

On May 7, 1945, Colonel-General Gustav Jodl, leading a small German contingent, met with a dozen Allied officers and formally signed Germany's surrender, ending more than five years of war. The surrender took place in this former school building. Because no German officer of equal rank was present, Eisenhower skipped the ceremony. The following day, news of the signing was announced simultaneously in all Allied capitals—May 8 thus became the globally acknowledged date of surrender, as well as the date of a Soviet-led surrender ceremony in Berlin. The building is now a museum. The Map Room, where the surrender took place, is preserved behind Plexiglas, with original surrender table and humble school chairs surrounded by the original enormous Allied battle maps (before the Germans entered, this was one of the most secret rooms in the world). The collection includes a 10-minute film (in English), photos, uniforms and small items. The museum is small but stirring.

About 150 km northeast of Paris, Reims (population 187,000), the center of the Champagne region and industry, is one of the more charming cities in France. Its World War II sites include Eisenhower's residence—a plaque at 17 Blvd. Lundy marks the building as the general's home from February 20 to May 25, 1945—and a large Resistance monument in front of the Gare SNCF rail station. The city's magnificent architecture is anchored by the monumental Reims Cathedral, built 1211–1280. In this mesmerizing Gothic church, President Charles de Gaulle and German Chancellor Konrad Adenauer sealed the reconciliation between France and Germany on July 8, 1962.

The Reims Office of Tourism (2 Rue Guillaume, next to the Cathedral, 03-26-77-4525) has brochures on touring the great champagne houses and their underground storage caves, including those belonging to Veuve Clicquot, G.H. Mumm, Taittinger, Louis Roederer and others.

OTHER PARIS ATTRACTIONS

Montparnasse Tower (Tour Montparnasse)
33 Ave. du Maine
M: Montparnasse-Bienvenue
T: (0)1-45-38-5256
Elevator: Adult: €9.50; Youth (16-20): €6.80; Child (7-15): €4; Under 7: Free Daily, 9:30 a.m.-11:30 p.m. (closed at 10:30 p.m. October-March)
Last entry 10 p.m.

The Eiffel Tower is fine to go up (usually after a long line), but no view of Paris is complete unless the Eiffel Tower is *in* it. The problem is solved by the mostly featureless, modern Montparnasse Tower. In 38 seconds, its elevators reach the 56th-floor observation lounge, restaurant and access to a superb outdoor rooftop vantage point. Attached to the front of the building on the north side of the Montparnasse Tower (occupied by the C and A store at ground level, facing the Boulevard Montparnasse), a plaque notes the location as the site where von Choltitz officially surrendered to General Leclerc. Reputable sources, including the British journal *After the Battle*, dispute this signage, saying the actual signing took place at the Police Prefecture. This claim is, in turn, disputed by the story that says von Choltitz signed the surrender at the Hôtel Meurice.

GETTING TO/AROUND PARIS

From many U.S., Canadian and European cities, dozens of airlines fly nonstop to Paris' Roissy-Charles-de-Gaulle Airport (Continental, 800-231-0856; American, 800-433-7300; Delta, 800-241-4141). From the airport, the most efficient way into the center of Paris is via the RER B train, which departs from Terminals 1 and 2 (trip takes about 45 minutes, €8.20) and terminates at the Châtelet-Les Halles Station, not far from the Louvre. Also from Terminals 1 and 2, Air France buses depart every 12 minutes (from 5:45 a.m. to 11:30 p.m.) and stop at Porte Maillot and Arc de Triomphe (trip takes about 45 minutes, €14). Taxis into Paris cost €35-€50 and take 30 minutes to an hour, depending on traffic.

Renting a car in congested Paris is pointless. (If you're driving in, hotels will park your car or direct you to a nearby lot. Parking costs €20-40 for 24 hours.) Paris' subway and train network covers the entire city. Available at ticket windows at almost all Metro stations, Paris Visite passes grant full access to central Paris public transit for three days (€18.60) or five days (€27.20). A passport must be presented upon purchase. Taxis are easy to find. Meters drop at €2.10 with a minimum charge of €5.60. A typical fare within Paris is €8 to €12.

Good walking maps of the city's streets (with subway and train routes) are available at virtually all hotels. Maps can also be picked up at the main Paris Tourist Bureau (127 Ave. des Champs-Elysées, 08-92-68-3112), located at the Arc de Triomphe at Metro stop Charles de Gaulle-Étoile. Also available at the tourist office and major Metro stations and museums is a Paris museum pass, which allows unlimited access and head-of-the-line privileges to 70 museums. The cost is €15 for a one-day pass, €30 for a two-day pass and €45 for a four-consecutive-day pass and €60 for a six-consecutive-day pass.

Accommodations

Paris
Hôtel Meurice
228 Rue de Rivoli
M: Tuileries
T: (0)1-44-58-1010 F: (0)1-44-58-1015
www.meuricehotel.com
Rooms: 160
From €580

Centrally located, this former headquarters of Paris' German military commander General Dietrich von Choltitz is one of the city's landmark properties. Built in 1814, it's been thoroughly modernized, with spa, fitness facility and other luxuries. Many rooms have panoramic views of the city and/or the Eiffel Tower. The restaurant and bar are outstanding. Internet rates are often available for substantially less than price listed above.

Le Loiret
5 Rue des Bons Enfants
M: Palais Royal-Musée du Louvre
T: (0)1-42-61-4731 F: (0)42-61-3685
www.hotelleloiret.com
Rooms: 31
€100-190

This decent hotel is located in the Palais Royal area, within walking distance of the Louvre and other central sites. It's clean, air-conditioned and has private bathrooms.

Versailles
Trianon Palace
1 Blvd. de la Reine, Versailles
T: (0)1-30-84-5000 F: (0)1-30-84-5001
www.westin.com
Rooms: 195
From €350

It's pricey, but this Westin property, renovated in 2001, puts visitors in the lap of history—from September 1944 to the spring of 1945 the town was the site of Allied headquarters. Eisenhower's office was in the hotel for much of that period. Now an exclusive property with spa, business facilities and rooms decorated in Louis XV style, it's a short walk to the Versailles Palace.

Reims
Best Western Hôtel de la Paix
9 Rue Buirette, Reims
T: (0)3-26-40-0408; 800-428-2627 (in U.S.)
F: (0)3-26-47-7504
www.bw-hotel-lapaix.com
106 rooms
€115-350

Steps from Reims' central pedestrian mall—lots of shops, outdoor cafes, restaurants, bars—this reliable hotel is part of Best Western's vast European network. Rooms and beds are larger than one normally finds in Europe.

13

MOSCOW

RUSSIA

St. Basil's Cathedral

THE WAR YEARS

"It is possible to predict from experience how virtually every soldier of the Western world will behave in a given situation—but not the Russian." With these words, German General Erhard Rauss began a post-war essay discussing lessons learned by the German Army during the course of its *Der Russland Krieg* (The Russia War) odyssey. Russia was "a different world," noted Rauss. "He who steps for the first time on Russian soil is immediately conscious of the new, the strange, the primitive."

With few on his staff offering such caution, Adolf Hitler launched his invasion of the Soviet Union (Operation Barbarossa) on June 22, 1941. Barbarossa's goals were deceptively simple. In a four-month blitzkrieg—four to five million soldiers, 47,000 artillery pieces, 5,000 aircraft, 2,800 tanks—German forces would advance in three sections across a 2,000-mile front, capturing the cities of Kiev and Leningrad and the capital of Moscow. All before winter. In the process, the Red Army would be demolished, allowing Hitler to turn the full might of his military on western Europe. So confident of rapid success were Hitler and his commanders that neither winter clothes nor long-term provisions were issued to troops.

The Nazis weren't completely delusional. Soviet leader Josef Stalin had purged three-quarters of the Red Army's senior-officer ranks in the "Great Terror" of 1937-38, castrating a military now considered bottom-of-the-barrel across the globe. The army's dismal performance in expanding its Finland frontier in 1939-40 (a mitigated success) simply reinforced the notion of a weak Soviet machine. The "scarily odd" Stalin—as cagey as he was demented—was little understood and easily underestimated.

Barbarossa began well for the Germans. Achieving complete surprise, Wehrmacht troops rolled virtually unimpeded across the Russian steppe. Soviet formations surrendered en masse—an astonishing three million soldiers by one count. In two months, German forces advanced 750 miles. Kiev fell. Leningrad was surrounded and nearly starved to death. Slowed and bloodied at Smolensk, German troops nonetheless closed within 40 miles of Moscow by mid-October. Advance units would draw to within 20 miles, close enough to see the spires of the Kremlin.

Panic consumed the capital. The Bolshoi Theater and other landmarks were covered with enormous tarps, weak camouflage against expected air attacks. (Effective anti-aircraft fire and other factors limited Luftwaffe damage to Moscow.) Selected government offices were relocated far south. Stalin reeled with shock. "Crowds were looting bakeries and food stores as the usual stern order crumbled into chaos," wrote *New York Times* correspondent C.L. Sulzberger, witness to the scene. "Every inch of the (railway) platform ... was littered with huddled families and their pitiful belongings."

Martial law was declared on October 19 and the exodus of citizens forbidden. Having regained his composure, Stalin announced he would remain in the city, then appointed General Georgi Zhukov to take charge of Moscow's defense. A child of poverty with fanatical devotion to the Red Army, Zhukov was a ruthless, abusive and widely disliked commander who was nevertheless to become Stalin's miracle worker, among the few allowed to argue with the party leader and perhaps the greatest general of World War II (in Russia called the Great Patriotic War). Zhukov reorganized defenses, put thousands of civilians to work digging antitank trenches outside Moscow and, in the words of Sulzberger, "waited for his ally, 'General Winter.'"

Bogged down in knee-deep mud, the Germans also looked to winter for salvation, when frost might again make roads hard enough to allow their tanks and trucks to advance. But with a white fury, the Russian winter descended suddenly and completely on the ill-prepared invaders. Temperatures dropped to minus-20 degrees. Many soldiers had no gloves, no winter shoes. Guns wouldn't fire, radio batteries seized (limiting communications), oil froze in crankcases. In a few weeks, the Germans recorded 133,000 cases of frostbite. Frozen to death, 100,000 horses were summarily eaten by starving troops.

The Russians seemed not to notice the elements. Their diesel tanks ran as tirelessly as their fur-coated infantry. On December 6, 1941, bolstered by reserves from Siberia, Zhukov unleashed a carefully plotted counter-offensive, his men "falling upon the Germans like wolves from the woods," according to one historian. Hitler refused his generals' request to withdraw, then approved it. Thousands of frozen German corpses were left in the wake of the Wehrmacht's pathetic retreat. The war wasn't over—Hitler's 1942 campaign in Russia would nearly succeed—but for the first time since 1939, the German military, done in by poor planning, superior generalship and a savage environment, had given up ground in Europe. The threat to the critical Allied capital had been lifted.

Through the remainder of the war, Stalin would leave Moscow just three times—twice to meet with Allied leaders (in Tehran, 1943, and Yalta, 1945) and once to inspect a Red Army post far from the front. But his "statesmanship of the madhouse," as described by historian Robert Service, grew increasingly more paranoid and bizarre. Following the United States' entry into the war and large shipments of Lend-Lease equipment to the USSR, the totalitarian regime invented a new crime—the "praising of American technology" was punishable by a sentence in the gulag. More sinister, Stalin had untold thousands of returning Russian POWs arrested or executed as spies, cowards or otherwise tainted by their association with the Germans. "Stalin's reputation as a blood-soaked monster is not legend but fact," declares *The Oxford Essential Guide to World War II*. In such circumstances, Moscow life returned to normal as the war dragged on, and the Red Army forced ever more distance between its capital and the German front. Upon his death in 1953, Stalin was buried alongside Vladimir Lenin in Moscow's Red Square. He was removed from the tomb in 1961 after being denounced by Communist Party General Secretary Nikita Kruschev, himself a notorious wartime commissar in Stalingrad.

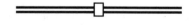

SOURCES & OTHER READING

Operation Barbarossa: The Battle of Moscow, Seth, Ronald, A. Blond, 1964

Fighting in Hell: The German Ordeal on the Eastern Front, Tsouras, Peter G. (ed), Ivy Books/Ballantine, 1995

The Second World War (5): The Eastern Front 1941-1945, Jukes, Geoffrey, Osprey Publishing, 2002

Stalin: Triumph and Tragedy, Volkogonov, Dmitri, Weidenfeld and Nicholson, 1991

Russia: A History of the Twentieth Century, Service, Robert, Penguin, 1997

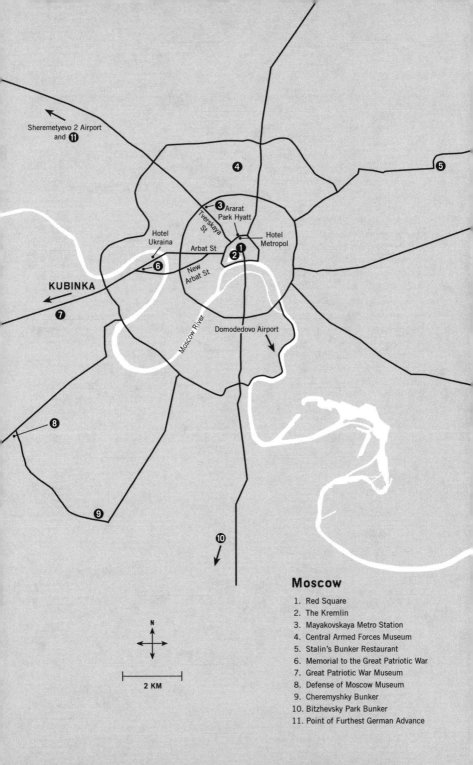

Sheremetyevo 2 Airport and **11**

4

5

3 Ararat Park Hyatt

Tverskaya St

Hotel Metropol

Hotel Ukraina

Arbat St

1

2

6

New Arbat St

KUBINKA

7

Moscow River

Domodedovo Airport

8

9

10

N

2 KM

Moscow

1. Red Square
2. The Kremlin
3. Mayakovskaya Metro Station
4. Central Armed Forces Museum
5. Stalin's Bunker Restaurant
6. Memorial to the Great Patriotic War
7. Great Patriotic War Museum
8. Defense of Moscow Museum
9. Cheremyshky Bunker
10. Bitzhevsky Park Bunker
11. Point of Furthest German Advance

Moscow Today

Population: 10 million • Country Code: 7 • 100 rubles = $3.50/£1.80/€2.70

At the fore of the New Russia of capitalism and epic social change, Moscow is a city like no other in the country. Dynamic and relatively prosperous, Moscow is a brightly lit metropolis where, whether tastes run to McDonald's or caviar, Western visitors will find few obstacles to comfort. Hotels are good (or superb), restaurants lively, nightclubs plentiful, streets jammed with cars. It's a stunning change for Muscovites who recall the dour Cold War times of empty shops, endless bus lines and streets darkened by nightfall.

The Moscow River winds through the city, which is arranged around four ever-widening ring roads. These emanate from the physical and spiritual center of the Kremlin and Red Square. A 10-minute walk west of Red Square is New Arbat Street (running diagonally off larger Arbat Street), a pedestrian-only mall filled with shops, restaurants and street vendors.

It's the best place to find souvenirs, including small Soviet-era military memorabilia (technically illegal to take out of the country).

Moscow historically draws little comparison to Las Vegas, but its titanic architecture and wide boulevards recall the 20-minutes-to-cross-the-street-and-navigate-the-stairs-promenade-and-gates exhaustion of the Nevada city. This is a place laid out for dictators accustomed to being chauffeured about town, not proles forced to hoof its great distances. Fortunately, the subway system is superb and taxis are plentiful. Outside the center, the city devolves into a phalanx of grimy, unattractive neighborhoods and slapdash shopping centers of little aesthetic note.

Moscow's war sites can be seen in two very busy days, though three or four are better due to reliable traffic delays.

Points of Interest

M indicates nearest Metro station

1. Red Square (Krasnaja Ploshhod)
★★★★★

Outside Kremlin's northeast wall, city center
M: Ploshhod Revolutsii

Fearful of German air attack, military parades were suspended in the 1,600-foot-long public center for much of the war. The exception was a dramatic November 7, 1941, parade at which Josef Stalin made a rare public appearance to rally soldiers heading directly to the front on the outskirts of the city: "The whole world is looking to you as the force capable of destroying the plundering hordes of German invaders. Be worthy of this mission!" Then as now, the square was

anchored by the mausoleum housing the viewable body of revolutionary leader Vladimir Lenin. The body was moved to Siberia during the war to prevent it from falling into Nazi hands. One can only imagine the way in which Hitler might have chosen to defile the corpse of the communist icon.

Just outside the square (at the end opposite St. Basil's Cathedral) stands a large statue of General Georgi Zhukov on horseback (the animal's hooves trampling German flags), an homage to his legendary victory lap around Red Square on a white charger in 1945. Nearby is an eternal flame at the Tomb of the Unknown Soldier with round-the-clock honor guard (known as Post Number One in the Russian Army). A row of blocks is inscribed with the names of Soviet Hero Cities (Minsk, Kiev, Odessa, Leningrad, and so on) that lost a majority of their populations or took part in important battles of the Great Patriotic War. In terms of symbolism and world renown, Red Square is Russia's top attraction.

2. The Kremlin (Kreml) ★★★

Main entry/ticket office in Aleksandrovsky Garden off Manezhnaya Square
M: Aleksandrovsky Sad
T: (0)95-203-0349 or (0)95-921-4720
Friday-Wednesday, 10 a.m.-6 p.m.
Ticket office closed 4:30 p.m.
Closed Thursday
Adult: 300 rubles (access to the cathedral square); 350 rubles (access to Armoury)

Those expecting a behind-the-scenes look at the Soviet (and current) Russian government will be disappointed with the limited access here, but a Kremlin visit remains worthwhile and memorable. Enclosed by high walls that run a mile and a half around (Kremlin literally means "fortress"), the highlights are commanding views of Moscow, seven ancient churches and the Armory, which houses a collection of swag gathered by centuries of Russian military men—plenty of diamonds, jewels and art. Inside the main entrance, to the right of Trinity Gate Tower, is Poteshny Palace (not accessible) where Stalin resided. Allow at least two hours.

3. Mayakovskaya Metro Station ★★

Off Tverskaya Street (formerly Gorky Avenue)
M: Mayakovskaya

Moscow's opulent subway stations were used as wartime hospitals and air-raid shelters. The most important station during the war was Mayakovskaya, where Stalin appeared at a massive party rally on November 6, 1941, the eve of celebrations in Red Square marking the Bolshevik revolution. Built in the mid-1930s (not as an air-raid shelter as some claim), it's one of the longest and widest of Moscow's subway stations. The gorgeous ceiling is decorated with 33 mosaic scenes.

4. Central Armed Forces Museum (Muzey Vooruzhronnih Sil) ★★★★

2 Sovietskoy Armii St.
M: Novoslobodskaya
T: (0)95-281-6303
Wednesday-Sunday, 10 a.m.-5 p.m.
Closed Monday, Tuesday
Adult: 30 rubles; Student: 15 rubles; Child: 10 rubles

One of the world's finest military museums offers an exhaustive look at the entire history of Soviet and Russian Federation militaries. The majority of the 24-room museum is devoted to the Great Patriotic War. A fraction of the highlights (the museum can display just 10 percent of its one million items): the original Soviet victory flag raised over Berlin's Reichstag in 1945, a half-ton bronze eagle from Berlin's Reichs Chancellery, a case with at least 1,000 captured Iron Crosses forged for expected German victors in Russia, personal effects belonging to Stalin, Hitler and other important figures, endless displays of weaponry and other material. Post-war sections document the nuclear- and space-age Soviet military, including a large piece of Gary Powers' U-2 spy plane "crushed" and brought down over the USSR in 1960 (it's been on display here ever since). Outside are 150 weapons and battle vehicles, mostly post-war items (jet fighters, bombers, ICBMs, tanks, modern artillery), with a few World War II tanks and other vehicles. The museum's only drawback is lack of English signage, but it's still worth a two-hour visit.

5. Stalin's Bunker Restaurant (Bunker Stalinaya, also Komandnye Punk Stalinaya) ★★

80 Sovetskaya
M: Ismailovsky Park
T: (0)95-166-3846 F: (0)95-166-1563
Lunch, dinner or tours, by appointment only. Appointment requests must be made by fax. Price depends on group, meal, and so on

Should the Germans have entered Moscow, Stalin was to have conducted the war from this large underground command center northeast of the city (connected to the Kremlin by a tunnel wide enough to drive a T-34 tank through). Stalin probably never set foot inside, but a section of the tunnel is accessible, along with "Stalin's" study, meeting hall, various corridors and gallery of exhibits. The imposing construction (now surrounded by a busy local marketplace) provides a unique and historic setting for an upscale version of cuisine from Stalin's native Georgia.

6. Memorial to the Great Patriotic War (Memorial Velekoy Otechestvennoy Voyny) ★

Kutuzov Avenue, about 1 km southwest of Hotel Ukraina
M: Kievskaya

This 50-foot obelisk is emblazoned with the Order of Lenin and flanked by large stone figures representing a mother (farmer), father (worker) and son (soldier).

7. Great Patriotic War Museum (Muzey Velekoy Otechestvennoy Voyny) ★★★★★

10 Bratev Fonchenko St. at Poklonnaya Hill, off Kutuzov Avenue
M: Park Pobedy
T: (0)95-142-4185
Tuesday-Sunday, 10 a.m.-7 p.m. (closed at 6 p.m. in winter)
Closed holidays
Adult: 120 rubles; Student/Child: 70 rubles

This lavish palace—chandeliers, frescoes, marble—is Russia's official museum dedicated to the Great Patriotic War. The museum is located at Poklonnaya Hill where, in 1812, Napoleon waited (in vain, at the spot of today's flower clock) for the keys to Moscow to be delivered to him. Nearby, a 328-foot stele—shaped like a bayonet and carved with heroic battle images—sets an appropriately grandiose tone. Inside, the Hall of Memory and Sorrow is draped with 2.6 million brass chain links with crystals at the ends representing tears for the official Russian count of the country's 27 million lives lost in the

war. Amid many exhibits (with English signage) are large dioramas depicting major battles (Moscow, Stalingrad, and so on), the spectacular Hall of Glory (inscribed with the names of 12,000 Heroes of the Soviet Union), a display on Soviet POWs (unthinkable during Soviet times), documentaries (accompanied only by music and sound effects), a substantial art gallery (most visitors make the mistake of skipping it) and a nod to contributions from the Western Allies (still generally regarded as negligible and half-hearted in Russia), including images of U.S. General George Patton and U.S. Marines raising the Stars and Stripes over Iwo Jima. Behind the museum are weaponry, fortification and naval exhibits, including tanks, aircraft and ship sections surrounded by water in a large moat. The colossal armored train car and railway gun are memorable. All in all, this is totalitarian symbolism at its demagogic peak.

8. Defense of Moscow Museum (Muzey Oborony Moskvy) ★★★

3 Olympic Village (on Muchurinsky Avenue)
M: Yugo-Zapadnaya
T: (0)95-430-0549
Tuesday-Saturday, 10 a.m.-6 p.m.
Closed Sunday, Monday
30 rubles

Located outside the city near the 1941 front lines—now an ugly residential neighborhood, the 1980 Olympics area was forest and swamp in wartime—this two-story museum dedicated to the Battle of Moscow isn't as large, but is every bit as impressively put together as other Moscow museums. Tracing all aspects of the battle, its many items include an original railcar for Soviet troops, the then-outdated though widely used Mosin rifle, 37 mm anti-aircraft gun, a moving display on women digging enormous antitank trenches (many were killed by German strafing while they shoveled), truck-mounted Katyusha rockets, Soviet GAZ jeep and uniforms from German officers (thin rabbit fur) and Russian infantry (heavy coats, leather knee boots), amply illustrating the Wehrmacht's lunatic lack of preparation for the merciless Russian winter. The second floor documents the Soviet counter-offensive and propaganda. One poster juxtaposes a bare Soviet fist knocking teeth and blood from a Nazi mouth vis-à-vis the gentler gloved hand of the British-American Allies politely displacing a German's helmet—a Soviet interpretation of the Anglo-American war contribution still widely accepted as fact across Russia. It's a worthwhile stop.

9. Cheremyshky Bunker ★

On Obrucheva Street, directly in front of huge (two football fields long), seven-story gray building. Walk 5 to 10 minutes along the street (uphill) from Kaluzhskaya station. M: Kaluzhskaya

In the Nouye Cheremyshky area, this is one of the few preserved bunkers from the Battle of Moscow. The concrete walls are about 10 feet long and 6 feet high. Entry is sealed off. Nearby memorial pieces include a pair of hedgehog tank obstacles and an engraved remembrance stone.

10. Bitzhevsky Park Bunker ★

On Novoyasenevsky Avenue, in Bitzhevsky Park residential area. From Yasenevo station proceed uphill (away from nearest

traffic light) about 1 km to bunker on left side of road.
M: Yasenevo

The white, concrete walls are about 10 feet long and 6 feet high. Entry is sealed off. Nearby memorial pieces include a pair of hedgehog tank obstacles and engraved remembrance stone. It is exactly the same as Point 9.

11. Point of Furthest German Advance ★

Off Leningradski Avenue, 5 km south of Sheremetyevo 2 airport, in suburb of Himky, 35 km northwest of Moscow center

In a small park, this monument more or less at the site where the German advance on Moscow was halted in 1941 features three huge hedgehog tank-obstacle statues and a memorial wall with soldiers sculpted in relief. In the near distance are Soviet-era communal high-rises and a sprawling IKEA. This is one of a handful of city landmarks (Red Square is another) visited by newlyweds on their traditional post-vow limo rides around the city. Be here on a Friday or Saturday and you'll likely see some champagne uncorked. For most, however, it's probably only worth keeping an eye out for along the right side of the main road (Leningradski Avenue) into Moscow from Sheremetyevo 2 airport.

Related Sites Beyond Moscow

Kubinka Tank Museum ★★★★★ for tank enthusiasts; ★★★ for others

On Mozhaisky Avenue (off M1/E30) in Kubinka, 64 km southwest of Moscow. Entry road marked by tank on M1/E30 roadside—turn in direction of tank and proceed toward long white hangars in distance.
T: (0)95-544-8611
Wednesday-Sunday, 10 a.m.-5 p.m.
Closed holidays
Advance appointment required
Admission: $20
(photo permission additional $20)

At least three museums lay tacit claim to housing the world's largest collection of

tanks—this one, England's Bovington (page 107) and France's Saumur Tank Museum (page 238). It's a close call, but Kubinka appears to hold the title. The seven-hangar behemoth displays about 300 tanks and armored vehicles, but it's the quality and rare models that inspire awe. Half the museum is dedicated to World War II, with separate hangars for vehicles from the USSR; United States, United Kingdom and Canada; and Germany. The latter includes panzers, Tigers and Elephants alongside the world's only Mouse (a 180-ton monster) and an unbelievably huge 600 mm cannon called Adam (its since-destroyed twin was named Eve). The presentation is no-frills—tanks are lined up track-to-track in huge hangars with little or no English signage—but it'd be tough to name a World War II tank not represented (including eight Japanese tanks). The entire collection takes in World War I to present day. Visitors can fork over $500 for the unique privilege of taking a brief ride in a Soviet T-34, German Panzer IV or contemporary tank. The museum is connected to a Russian Federation military post, hence the advance permission needed to visit.

Museum of Military Air Forces (Muzey Voenno-Vozdyshnyh Syl) ★★★

On Nyzhy Novgorod (off Gorkovskoy Shosse highway) on the grounds of the pilot academy at Monino Air Force Base, 38 km west of Moscow

T: (0)95-526-3327
Monday, Tuesday, Thursday, Friday, 9:30 a.m.-1:30 p.m., 2:15-5 p.m., Saturday 9 a.m.-noon.
Adult: $14; Student: $8; Child: $3
Foreign visitors require advance clearance

Covering 20 hectares, this largest aviation museum in the territory of the former USSR houses more than 170 aircraft. The slick, professional presentation consistently earns rave reviews from visiting Western military and commercial aviators. Airplanes, helicopters, gliders, missiles, rockets and bombs stand among many exhibits. The 10 or so World War II aircraft are of Soviet design, including a Po-2, Yak-9u and DB-3.

OTHER AREA ATTRACTIONS

Red Square

Outside Kremlin's northeast wall, in city center
M: Ploshhod Revolutsii

World War II registered but a blip on this five-centuries-old center of Moscow commercial, social and political activity. The "Red" has nothing to do with communism—the modern word for "red" doubles for "beautiful" in archaic Russian. The dominant landmark is St. Basil's Cathedral. Completed in 1561, its wildly colored, spiraled onion domes are recognized

across the globe. In Lenin's Tomb, the corpse of the founder of Soviet Russia can be viewed 10 a.m.-1 p.m. (closed Monday and Friday). The 1,600-foot-long, brick-paved square was the place where ICBMs and military parades were rolled out for the inspection of poker-faced Soviet officials lined up atop Lenin's mausoleum. Today, the only military parades are held on May 9, to commemorate victory over Germany in 1945. The square often appears smaller than many visitors imagine. Access is free, though entry fees are being considered.

GETTING TO/AROUND MOSCOW

Americans must arrange visas before traveling to Russia. New York's Russia National Group (212-575-3431) is one of many private companies that handle visa processing.

Two airports—Sheremetyevo 2 and Domodedovo—service most flights to Moscow. Delta Airlines (800-241-4141) flies nonstop daily to Domodedovo from New York's JFK airport. Russia's national airline Aeroflot (095-753-5555 in Moscow; regional U.S. offices include New York at 212-245-1100 and Los Angeles at

310-281-5300) flies direct to Moscow and around Russia from many international cities.

The trip from Sheremetyevo 2 to the city center takes a little more than an hour by minibus (departures every half-hour from a point about 200 yards in front of the terminal) and involves a change to the subway at Rechnoy Vokzal Metro station on the northern edge of the city. Taxis cost about $60 for the 45-minute ride to the city center. Express trains depart Domodedovo twice an hour for Paveletsky

Station. The trip takes 45 minutes and costs less than $2. Taxis to the city center cost about $50.

Moscow's Metro subway-and-train system is cheap and efficient—the best way to move around town. Taxis are plentiful, but so is traffic. Moscow has no official tourist office. Hotels have city and subway maps.

Moscow is easy enough for the independent traveler to deal with. Outside of the city (Volgograd, Kursk, and so on), difficulties increase exponentially. It's possible to drive in Russia (see Driving, page xv; for car rentals in Moscow call Budget at 095-737-0407 or Hertz at 095-937-3274), but it's expensive and often difficult. Even a command of the Cyrillic alphabet is use-less on rural highways that are often as not unmarked.

A local guide can save hours, in some cases days, of frustration. Moscow-based Three Whales travel agency (095-420-8441; www.threewhales.ru) is a trust-worthy, professional service operated by English-fluent Oleg Alexandrov. The agency's excellent and unique Great Patriotic War Tour takes in Moscow, St. Petersburg (Leningrad), Volgograd (Stalingrad) and Kursk, and includes pre-arranged access to military base museums covered in this chapter, insight from local experts and lunch with Great Patriotic War veterans (a high point). Individual tours also available. Highly recommended.

ACCOMMODATIONS

Hotel Metropol

1/4 Teatralny Proezd
T: (0)99-501-7800 F: (0)99-501-7810
www.metropol-moscow.ru
367 rooms
From $400

With the best location in Moscow—a few minutes walk from Red Square, the Kremlin and Bolshoi Theater—this legendary turn-of-the-century property was thoroughly updated in the 1990s. The "style modern" architecture is best appreciated in the glass-ceiling restaurant (Lenin delivered speeches from its balcony). Most rooms are spacious and elegantly furnished. Full range of services includes a gym, pool, casino, theater-ticket booth, night club and travel agent. Famous guests have included Leo Tolstoy, George Bernard Shaw and John F. Kennedy. Still *the* place to stay.

Ararat Park Hyatt Moscow

4 Neglinnaya St.
T: (0)95-783-1234 F: (0)95-783-1235
www.moscow.park.hyatt.com
219 rooms
From $700

The location just behind Hotel Metropol makes the five-star Hyatt almost as convenient to major tourist sites (important in congested Moscow). Rooms are spacious, with modern decor. Most have marble bathrooms, heated floors and high-speed internet connection. Three restaurants, two bars, fitness center.

Hotel Ukraina

2/1 Kutuzovsky Ave.
T: (0)95-299-8301 F: (0)95-933-6978
www.ukraina-hotel-ru
930 rooms
$170-$250

This very popular 1957-built hotel was conceived as a Communist Party gathering point in the "Stalin Classicism" style. Massive lobby, big rooms, high ceilings, deep tubs and many rooms with views across the Moscow River to the city center. The crowning tower makes it, at 675 feet, Russia's tallest hotel. For price and Cold War–era nostalgia, it's a good deal. Drawbacks are distance from Red Square (30-minute walk) and nearest Metro station (10-minute walk) and service that sometimes retains a chilly Soviet feel. Five restaurants, business center.

14

Normandy III

The Breakout

FRANCE

Avranches

THE WAR YEARS

A fter the dramatic June 6, 1944, landings on the Normandy coast of France, the Allied invasion of Europe quickly sputtered. Some territorial milestones were achieved. Cherbourg was captured on June 26, Caen on July 10, St-Lô on July 18. But by late July, Operation Overlord—the invasion of northwestern Europe—was six weeks behind schedule, mired in stalemate amid Normandy's thick *bocage*, low-lying country with four- and five-foot-tall hedgerows that restricted Allied movement.

To force a badly needed "breakout," U.S. General Omar Bradley devised Operation Cobra, a major offensive that commenced July 25, 1944, with prolonged carpet-bombing along a five-mile stretch of front west of St-Lô in the Cotentin peninsula. The punishing air attack resulted in 600 American friendly fire casualties—including the death of Lieutenant-General Lesley McNair, the highest-ranking U.S. officer killed in the war—but left the Germans trembling with shock. "Several of my men went mad and rushed into the open ground until they were cut down by splinters," reported one German officer. By July 31, the Cobra infantry offensive had reached south to Avranches.

With room to maneuver, the Battle of Normandy now became a general's war, a contest of strategy and tactics. No commander cast a greater shadow over the battle than American General George Patton. Though often mistakenly credited for playing a dominant role in the initial breakout—biographer Stanley Hirshson calls it "one of the most misinterpreted episodes in Patton's military life"—the 58-year-old took charge of the newly formed U.S. 3rd Army on August 1. Patton's relentless demand for action showed itself immediately at Pontaubault, just south of Avranches, where the only route east across the Selune River, a narrow bridge, presented a potentially fatal bottleneck to a charging army. "Defying every rule of staff college logistics, his seven divisions were got into the new theater of operation in 72 hours," wrote historian John Keegan. The feat displayed Patton's talent for operational detail beyond the simple battlefield ferocity that earned him the nickname "Old Blood and Guts."

With Patton, a master of mobile warfare, at the helm, the Allied campaign evolved into the largest tank battle fought in western Europe. For two weeks, across 800 square miles, 20 armored divisions (10 Allied, 10 German) clashed in a battle of armor surpassed in numbers only by the leviathan tank fight at Kursk in the Soviet Union. Spearheaded by a lightning thrust of tanks and aircraft—some historians have likened it to Germany's 1940 blitzkrieg—the Allied plan was simple: From Avranches, Patton's 3rd Army would move eastward beneath the main body of German troops in Normandy. From Caen, Canadian and Polish troops would sweep southward. The three groups would meet east of Falaise, enveloping the entire German 7th Army in a gigantic set of pincers.

Outnumbered two-to-one and running short of fuel and supplies, Adolf Hitler nevertheless forbade German withdrawal. Instead, he ordered a massive August 6 counter-strike at Mortain, where heights above the village—called Hill 317 by the small American occupying force—offered commanding views of the open countryside. For a week, German forces assaulted U.S. positions. Aided by virtually uncontested air support and Ultra intelligence that alerted the Allies to enemy plans, 700 American GIs made a determined stand. Some 300 would die on the wooded slopes of Hill 317, but the German thrust was repulsed. Patton roared east, hooking north just past Falaise.

Descending from the north, Canadian and Polish troops were fighting savagely to settle scores. Early in the campaign, a division of Hitler Youth had slaughtered a group of Canadian prisoners. The Polish II Corps, organized from forces who'd escaped the Nazi and Soviet devastation of their homeland, had developed into what Keegan called "one of the great fighting formations of the war." On August 19, they linked with American forces at Chambois—the first time soldiers from the two countries had ever met on the battlefield, a Polish officer happily noted—completing the encirclement of the German 7th Army in the Falaise gap (or pocket). The Germans were herded into the gap for one of the decisive slaughters of the war. Aircraft, tanks, artillery and mortars rained upon the trapped, exhausted and starving soldiers. "For sheer ghastliness in World War II, nothing exceeded the experience of the Germans caught in the Falaise gap," wrote historian Stephen Ambrose. "Dead cows, horses and soldiers swelled in the hot August sun, their mouths agape, filled with flies. ... Tanks drove over men in the way—dead or alive. Human and animal intestines made the roads slippery." The carnage ended on August 22. Two days later, Supreme Allied Commander Dwight Eisenhower called the Falaise battlefield "a scene that could be described only by Dante. It was quite literally possible to walk for hundreds of yards at a time, stepping on nothing but dead and decaying flesh."

The rout might have been worse. Historians have criticized American and Canadian commands for failing to close the Falaise gap fast enough, allowing 20,000 to 40,000 Germans to escape, certainly prolonging the war. Still, Germany had suffered a grievous defeat. From an initial force of one million men in Normandy, 240,000 had been killed or wounded since D-Day. In the Falaise gap alone, 10,000 were killed, 50,000 taken prisoner. Equipment losses included 20,000 vehicles, 3,500 artillery pieces and 1,500 tanks. From an invading force of two million in Normandy, the Allies suffered 209,672 casualties, including 39,796 dead.

The countryside itself was devastated—more than half of Normandy's towns were damaged in the battle. But, as Ambrose wrote, "the Battle of France had been won (in fact did not even have to be fought) thanks to the Battle of Normandy." On August 25, Allied troops liberated Paris and the Wehrmacht was in headlong retreat for Germany.

SOURCES & OTHER READING

Six Armies in Normandy: From D-Day to the Liberation of Paris, Keegan, John, Jonathan Cape, 1982

Breakout and Pursuit, Blumenson, Martin, Office of the Chief of Military History, U.S. Department of the Army, 1961

Clash of Arms: How the Allies Won in Normandy, Hart, Russell A., Lynne Rienner, 2001

Operation Cobra 1944: Breakout from Normandy, Zaloga, Steven J., Osprey Publishing, 2001

Saving the Breakout: The 30th Division's Heroic Stand at Mortain, August 7-12, 1944, Featherston, Alwyn, Presidio, 1993

Citizen Soldiers, Ambrose, Stephen, Simon & Schuster, 1997

General Patton: A Soldier's Life, Hirshson, Stanley P., HarperCollins, 2002

War as I Knew It, Patton, George S., Houghton Mifflin, 1947

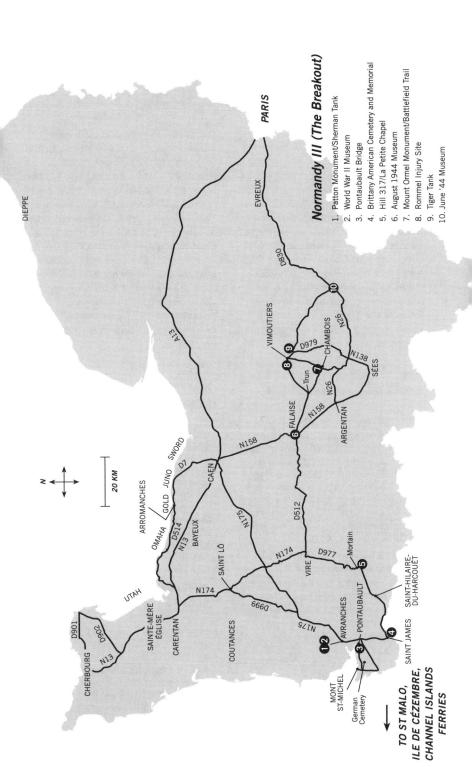

Normandy III (The Breakout)

1. Patton Monument/Sherman Tank
2. World War II Museum
3. Pontaubault Bridge
4. Brittany American Cemetery and Memorial
5. Hill 317/La Petite Chapel
6. August 1944 Museum
7. Mount Ormel Monument/Battlefield Trail
8. Rommel Injury Site
9. Tiger Tank
10. June '44 Museum

NORMANDY TODAY

Population: 10,400 (Avranches); 8,300 (Falaise); 4,100 (Pontorson)
Country Code: 33 • €1 = $1.36/£0.67

Aside from coastal areas famous for the D-Day invasion, Normandy is essentially an area of rural farmland, with medium- or small-size communities linked by a maze of slow, two-lane roads. More than half of Normandy's towns were damaged by the war. Some were destroyed by Allied artillery and aerial bombardment meant to clear terrain and drive out the Germans. Like those on the coast, almost all inland towns were restored by the early 1950s, thanks largely to Allied nations' funding and painstaking local efforts to rebuild following traditional designs. The result for the traveler is a bonanza of picturesque villages alongside nondescript tracts of farmland, with pockets of industrial development. Its famed hedgerows all but obliterated by modern agribusiness, Normandy is renowned for cheese (it's the home of Camembert, both the town and cheese) and mildly alcoholic ciders made from pears and apples. It's also the home of Calvados—the central region of apple orchards that runs from the D-Day beaches in the north to Falaise at its southern end—which lends its name to the famed apple brandy. Two days are necessary to visit all war-related sites in this chapter. An additional day is recommended for Ile de Cézembre (see page 236), accessed via St-Malo.

POINTS OF INTEREST

1. Patton Monument/Sherman Tank ★★
Exit N175 at Avranches, follow signs to city center and central traffic roundabout

The center of Avranches is dominated by a Sherman tank and a three-story-high stone monument commemorating the July 31-August 10, 1944, "Percée d'Avranches" by the "Glorieuse Armée Americaine du General Patton." Points of the star-shaped base indicate "breakout" campaign destinations—Saint-Nazaire, Falaise, Paris, Reims, Berchtesgaden, and so on.

2. World War II Museum (Musée de la Seconde Guerre Mondiale) ★★
Le Moulinet, Le Val St-Père in Avranches. Just off N175 (museum visible from road). Take Avranches Centre exit, follow signs to Musée or COBRA La Percée toward Pontaubault.
T: (0)2-33-68-3583
Daily, 9:15 a.m.-12:15 p.m., 2-6:15 p.m., April 1-November 11
Daily, 9 a.m.-7 p.m., July-August
Closed all other times.

Adult: €7; Child (5 to 10): €4

This interesting collection—German equipment, a grappling hook used by U.S. Rangers at Pointe du Hoc near Omaha Beach—is marred by poor signage. As at so many European museums, the many store mannequins in uniform convey the impression that all troops in battle were of medium height, thin and vaguely dashing. The large scale model of Patton's army crossing the bridge at Pontaubault is worth a look. It provides a clear sense of how that dramatic operation unfolded. A 30-minute film (in English) runs several times daily.

3. Pontaubault Bridge ★★★
Entry and exit to Pontaubault on D42

Moving an army across this narrow bridge—maybe 75 yards end to end—was one of the great logistical feats of the war. With General Patton directing traffic, up to 160,000 men, plus tanks, vehicles and supplies, moved into the battlefield in just three days. While this was "the most important bridge in the world," the surrounding area had been entirely flattened by bombardment. Today, a pleasant picnic area has tables overlooking the bridge and Selune River. Built in 1793, the span has been repaired and widened, but it's the same bridge Patton's men hustled across.

4. Brittany American Cemetery and Memorial ★★★★

On D250, 1.5 km southeast of St-James (20 km south of Avranches)
T: 703-696-6897 (Arlington, VA)
Daily, 9 a.m.-5 p.m., Closed January 1, December 25

At the point where American forces broke out of Normandy's hedgerow country into the plains of Brittany, 4,410 American war dead rest amid exquisitely manicured grounds. Though smaller and less visited than the American cemetery at Omaha Beach, this cemetery similarly stuns the visitor into contemplative silence with its epic sweep and perfectly aligned rows of marble crosses and Stars of David. The dominant feature is the granite Memorial Chapel and huge campaign maps.

5. Hill 317/La Petite Chapelle ★★★

In Mortain, 37 km northeast of Point 4. From entrance of town on D977 follow signs to top of hill. **Note: This hill is alternately called and locally signed "Hill 314."**

Overlooking the town of Mortain, 700 Americans absorbed a nearly 60 percent casualty rate, but managed to halt a furious German attack on Hill 317. At the top of the hill is La Petite Chapelle, a memorial to the U.S. 30th Infantry Division, orientation map, magnificent views of the battleground and an NTL (Normandie Terre-Liberté) interpretive totem (the blue-and-white markers emblazoned with a dove logo and historical text are found throughout Normandy). From this rocky peak, one gets a visceral sense of the military value of the high ground.

6. August 1944 Museum (Musée Août 1944) ★★★

Chemin des Rochers in Falaise. From principal roads follow signs to Falaise and Musée Août 1944.
T: (0)2-31-90-3719

Wednesday-Monday (closed Tuesdays), 10 a.m.-noon, 2-6 p.m., from first Saturday of April-November 11
Daily, 10 a.m.-noon, 2 p.m.-6 p.m., June-August

This exceptional private collection of rare and meticulously restored military vehicles is mostly displayed behind glass walls. Vehicles include many tanks and trucks, a colossal German Demag D7 half-track (with a V-12 engine, it was used to tow Tiger tanks) and one of four existing German Borgward Type BIV vehicles (a 10-foot-long remote-controlled transport that was used to drop explosives). A great collection that would be improved by better signage—too many vehicles are unmarked.

7. Mount Ormel Monument/Battlefield Trail (Mémorial de Montormel) ★★★★

Off D16, southeast of Point 6 in Montormel
T: (0)2-33-67-3861
Daily, 9 a.m.-6 p.m., May-September; Wednesday, Saturday, Sunday, 10 a.m.-5 p.m., October-March; Daily, 10 a.m.-5 p.m., April
Adult: €4.50; Student: €3.50; Child (5-12): €3

This powerful stone-wall monument stands 15 feet high and 100 feet long. It's flanked by an armored car, tank and flags of France, the U.S., Canada, Great Britain and Poland. The monument stands where 1,800 1st Polish Armored Division soldiers under Polish hero General Stanislaw Maczek held fast through intense fighting to close the last escape road out of the Falaise gap, leading to the climax of the Normandy campaign. At battle's end, only 114 of the original Polish force were still fit for action. Maczek died in Edinburgh, Scotland, in 1994, at age 102. An orientation table describes the panoramic views of the battlefield. The central feature of the small museum is a large relief map that lights up to show various battle positions. There's little else of note inside, but the location and views are excellent. From the museum, a 5.25-mile trail covers the hillside battle area.

8. Rommel Injury Site ★

Leaving the town of Vimoutiers, turn left onto D979, proceed about 200 yards beyond the Shell gas station to an extremely small bridge (a pair of 10-foot-long green rails supported by three 2-foot-high concrete stanchions on both sides) crossing over a hidden creek. Nearest landmarks are a brick castlelike gatekeeper's house with a heavy iron gate (just beyond bridge, on left side of road), stone highway marker (across from gatekeeper's house), concrete pylon and stone highway marker bearing numbers D979 and 0 sunk into the ground at the bridge itself. For all this, the site is unmarked and easy to miss.

There's nothing really to see here, but the site may be worthwhile for those with an interest in Field Marshal Erwin Rommel, arguably Germany's most gifted commander. Rommel's car was attacked and hit at this spot by a Spitfire (possibly Typhoon) of the RAF 602nd Squadron on July 17, 1944. Thrown from the car, Rommel suffered multiple skull fractures, was hospitalized and thus removed from the Battle of Normandy at a critical juncture. Implicated in a Hitler assassination plot, he committed suicide in October 1944.

9. Tiger Tank ★★★

On D979, 2 km southeast of Vimoutiers. From Vimoutiers head toward L'Aingle. From Point 8, follow D979 back toward (and past) Vimoutiers.

Painted in green camouflage, a well-preserved Tiger Type E tank stands on the side of the highway. At 27 feet long, 10 feet wide and nine feet high with a weight of 56 tons, it was the largest tank produced during World War II. Though it had flaws—rapacious fuel consumption, ponderous turret movement—the Tiger had no tank equal in terms of power. As historian John Keegan wrote: "The cough of the Tiger's engine starting up in the distance was something all Allied soldiers remembered with respect."

10. June '44 Museum (Musée Juin 44) (Zero stars)

Place Fulbert de Beina in L'Aigle
T: (0)2-33-84-1616
Wednesday, Saturday, Sunday, 2-6 p.m., April-October (open Tuesdays 2-6 p.m. in July, August)
Adult: €4; Child: €2

Suckers entering this tourist nightmare must follow a painfully slow-moving route featuring small scenes with "talking" wax figures animated by the recorded voice of an oratorically ungifted British child narrating such episodes as Roosevelt, Churchill and Stalin meeting at Tehran and D-Day landings in Normandy. The wax figures are terrible—Stalin looks like Mark Twain, Churchill would be unrecognizable without the cigar, FDR looks like no one in particular, but appears fit enough to run a marathon. The audio runs in English and French, but speakers of any language should run from this tourist trap.

RELATED SITES BEYOND NORMANDY

Though this chapter is concerned with the eastward extension of the Normandy breakout, the campaign also involved important American and Allied thrusts west (to capture Brittany ports) and south. See Auxiliary Sites chapter, France, under headings of Channel Islands, Ile de Cézembre, Saumur and Submarine Pens/St-Nazaire.

German Cemetery ★★★

On D75, 18 km west of Avranches.

Take D27 to 4 km east of Mont St-Michel, turn south on D107, follow signs to D75 and Deutscher Soldatenfriedhof 1939-45 MONT-D'HUISNES Cimetière Militaire Allemand.

In the shadow of Mont St-Michel, 11,956 Germans are buried in this large field, one of six German military cemeteries in Normandy. (See page 8 for more information on German cemeteries.)

Tiger tank, La Gleize, Belgium, page 63

Arromanches/Gold Beach, Normandy, France, page 19

Jewish Museum, Berlin, Germany, page 84

Normandy, near Omaha Beach, page 4

White Cliffs of Dover, England, page 108

Normandy American Cemetery, Normandy, page 10

Bastogne, Belgium, page 50

Higgins boat, Utah Beach, Normandy, France, page 7

Longues Battery, Normandy, France, page 19

Eagle's Nest, Berchtesgaden, Germany, page 240

Führer's rostrum, Nuremberg, Germany, page 160

Dresden, Germany, page 241

Trinity Cathedral, Ponyri, Russia, page 229

U.S. 1st Division Monument, Omaha
Beach, page 11

Battery Todt, Pas de Calais, page 74

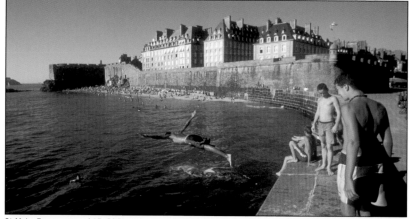

St-Malo, France, pages 145, 236

Gate of Death, Auschwitz-Birkenau, Poland,
page 44

Pontaubault Bridge, Normandy, France, page 142

B-17 Memphis Belle replica, Duxford Imperial War Museum, England, page 168

Hitler schoolbook, Remember Museum, Belgium, page 61

Anzio, Italy, page 216

FDR Memorial, Washington, D.C., page 94

Pillboxes, Sicily, page 245

East Anglia, England, page 170

Dragon Teeth, near Aachen, Germany, pages 62, 213

Allied Forces Memorial, Dunkirk, France, page 72

Luxembourg Palace, Paris, page 123

Dachau Concentration Camp, Munich, Germany, page 152

Capitoline Hill, Rome, page 204

Patton's Grave, Luxembourg, page 64

Spitfire, RAF Museum Hendon, London, page 35

Paratrooper's Vespa (French production) with anti-tank gun, Saumur
Tank Museum, France, page 238

Flour Mill, Volgograd, Russia, page 177

Great Patriotic War Museum, Moscow,
page 134

Diekirch Military Museum, Luxembourg, page 65

Lavenham Airfield Control Tower, East Anglia, England, page 168

Amalfi Coast, Italy, page 117

Other Area Attractions

Mont St-Michel

9 km north of Pontorson
T: (0)2-33-89-8000
Daily, 9 a.m.-7 p.m., May-August
9:30 a.m.-6 p.m., September-April
Closed January 1, May 1, December 25
Adult: €8; Youth (18-25): €5;
Under 18: Free

Dating back more than 1,000 years, Mont St-Michel is the pride of Normandy. About 40 km west of Avranches, the small, steep slope rises from the sea at the end of a narrow spit, its entire area covered with overpowering Gothic architecture visible from miles away. Other than a few monks and caretakers, there are no longer any residents, but its shop-filled streets and staircases are usually crowded with tourists—avoided even in summer by visiting early morning or evening.

St-Malo

It's in Brittany (48 km west of Pontorson), but the beauty of this medieval port city justly places it on many travelers' check-lists. Though buildings within the vast walled old city were damaged by Allied bombing, most have been rebuilt to pre-war specifications. The walled city today exists largely for tourists, but that hardly diminishes its physical majesty and popular beaches.

Getting To/Around Normandy

Dozens of airlines fly nonstop to Paris' Roissy-Charles-de-Gaulle Airport (page 126). Continental (800-231-0856), American (800-433-7300) and Delta (800-241-4141) are among airlines that offer nonstop flights from the United States. See page 12 for train information to Normandy. A vehicle is necessary for touring the Normandy battlefields (see Driving, page xv). The essential road map is Michelin's "Battle of Normandy" (Michelin map Number 102), available in larger U.S. bookstores and on internet book sites. Once in Normandy, a number of Battle of Normandy maps are available at most museums. These have less road detail, but are easier to read. A good choice among several is the "Carte Touristique et Historique: Bataille de Normandie 1944" published by France-based OREP (info@orep-pub.com). Lonely Planet's *Normandy* isn't satisfactory for those interested in World War II, but, with many maps of small towns and insightful cultural notes, it's the best general guide to the area.

Accommodations

Pontorson
Hôtel Montgomery

13 rue Couesnon, Pontorson
T: (0)2-33-60-0009 F: (0)2-33-60-3766
www.hotel-montgomery.com
32 rooms
€93-135 (high season)
€55-90 (low season)

In the primary tourist town supporting Mont St-Michel, 20 km west of Avranches, this three-star Best Western property is the top hotel in the area. On a street with restaurants, grocers and patisseries, the hotel has an upscale restaurant far better than one would expect in a town this size.

Mont St-Michel
Hôtel Mercure

B.P. 8, Route du Mont St-Michel in Le-Mont-St-Michel
T: (0)2-33-60-1418 F: (0)2-33-60-3928
www.mercure.com
100 rooms
€67-82

Two km from Mont St-Michel and 22 km west of Avranches, this good chain hotel is the best in the tourist strip fronting Mont St-Michel. Amenities include a good restaurant, bar and basic rooms. The drawback is lack of anything special with-in immediate walking distance.

15

Munich
GERMANY

Frauenkirche

THE WAR YEARS

With defeat in World War I and impossible reparation demands thrust upon it by the Treaty of Versailles, Germany of the 1920s was a nation of political chaos. A haven for political expression—bohemians, communists, conservatives, even secessionists—the baroque Bavarian capital of Munich became a center of social unrest. Within this milieu, an unknown, Austrian-born German Army corporal named Adolf Hitler discovered an assortment of hidden talents—speaker, agitator, organizer, bully—that would transform him into the lead player in one of the darkest chapters in human history.

Attracted to its polemic stances against war profiteers, Jews, Bolsheviks and other alleged traitors, Hitler became Member Number 55 of the fringe German Workers' Party on January 1, 1920. Shouting down rivals with force, not logic, he quickly became the tiny party's dynamic force. His speeches promising the rise of a greater Germany drew thousands of frustrated locals into beer halls such as the famed Hofbräuhaus. Attracting a cadre of devoted acolytes, Hitler assumed control of the renamed National Socialist German Workers' Party (NSDAP)—from which the abbreviation Nazi would emerge—and created as its symbol the bright red flag with white disk and menacing black swastika in the center.

On November 8, 1923, Hitler and the Nazis made their first bid for power, bursting into a Bavarian government assembly at Munich's Bürgerbräukeller beer hall in what would become known as the Beer Hall Putsch. Hitler leaped atop a table, fired a revolver into the ceiling and declared, "The National Revolution has begun!" Nazi strongmen briefly held the top three government officials hostage, but their coup was thwarted the following day when state police fired upon 3,000 Nazis marching on the Feldherrnhalle (Field Marshals' Hall) monument in Odeonsplatz. Hitler was arrested, but served just nine months in the relaxed confines of Landsberg fortress west of Munich. Referring to his time there as "university paid for by the state," Hitler received daily visitors and dictated his memoirs, *Mein Kampf* (My Struggle). Filled with rambling opinion and repetitive anti-Semitic venom, it would become the bible of the Nazi Party. In the 1920s, however, it remained an obscure screed around which a determined Hitler, once more living an austere life in Munich, dedicated himself to rebuilding the Nazi Party.

In a nation of 66 million, the Nazis of the late 1920s counted just 178,000 dues-paying members. But the Depression that engulfed the world in 1929 raised German unemployment from 1.3 million in 1929 to 6.1 million in 1932, provoked anger against government and presented Hitler an opportunity he wouldn't squander. With unexpected successes in national elections in 1930, the NSDAP seemingly overnight became Germany's second-largest political party. In late 1932, Nazi candidates won a controlling bloc of national government seats. In January 1933, Hitler was installed as Chancellor of Germany.

Though Hitler's government shifted to Berlin, Munich remained an important Third Reich city, designated both the Capital of the Movement and Germany's City of the Arts. A more realistic example of what was to come, however, was provided by the Dachau Concentration Camp, a prison for political dissenters built outside of Munich only weeks after Hitler's 1933 ascendancy to power. Dachau was the Nazis' first concentration camp; and its rows of crude barracks, sadistic SS guards and medical experimentation facilities provided the blueprint for the network of camps to come. Though Dachau was a prison camp, not an extermination center, conditions were brutal. Hunger, disease, forced labor, torture and murder—more than 4,000 Soviet POWs were gunned down on the SS shooting range in 1941—contributed to the daily horror. "The transformation of the theories of National-Socialism into a bloody reality began in the concentration camp at Dachau," according to one German text. By the time the camp was liberated (by U.S. troops, April 29, 1945), more than 206,000 individuals from 34 European nations had been imprisoned there. Of these, 31,951 had died.

Munich again found itself at center stage September 29-30, 1938, when Hitler, Italian dictator Benito Mussolini, British Prime Minister Neville Chamberlain and French Prime Minister Edouard Daladier convened for the Munich Conference. The summit was meant to placate Hitler's demands for territory in western Czechoslovakia's largely German-speaking Sudetenland and forestall another world war. Thoroughly intimidated, the British and French—despite possessing clear military supremacy—buckled to Hitler's demands. Germany was given 11,000 square miles of Czech territory and three million of its people. (Poland and Hungary were also permitted to carve off sections of the dismembered country.) Chamberlain returned to England, waving a copy of the Munich Agreement and proclaiming "peace in our time" and "peace with honor." The agreement produced neither. In Germany, the triumph consecrated Hitler's reputation for black magic, gilding his position inside the Nazi terror state with an unbreakable veneer. In less than a year, total war would be at hand with the German invasion of Poland.

"In scarcely four and a half years this man of lowly origins had catapulted a disarmed, chaotic, nearly bankrupt Germany, the weakest of the big powers in Europe, to a position where she was regarded as the mightiest nation of the Old World, before which all others, Britain even and France, trembled," wrote journalist William Shirer of the "surrender at Munich."

The conference laid the foundations of tragedy for Europe, but the city in which Hitler planned to be buried would suffer fatal retribution. Bombed from the air throughout the war, an estimated 75 percent of Munich's downtown buildings were destroyed, as many as 6,600 residents killed. U.S. troops began the occupation of the city on April 30, 1945, only a week before the end of the war. Their post-war investigations uncovered not a single local who admitted to belonging to the Nazi Party.

SOURCES & OTHER READING

The Rise and Fall of the Third Reich: A History of Nazi Germany, Shirer, William, Simon & Schuster, 1960

Hitler: a Study in Tyranny, Bullock, Alan, Harper, 1952

Explaining Hitler: The Search for the Origins of His Evil, Rosenbaum, Ron, Random House, 1998

Munich: Prologue to Tragedy, Wheeler-Bennett, J.W., Macmillan, 1948

Munich 1923: The Story of Hitler's First Grab for Power, Dornberg, John, Harper & Row, 1982

Dachau Concentration Camp, Comité International de Dachau, 1972

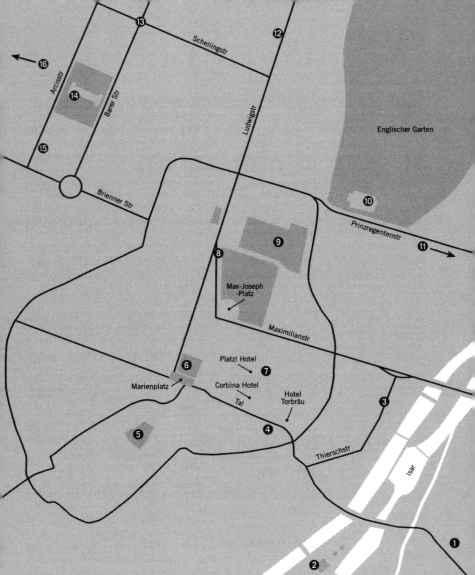

Schellingstr

Arcisstr

Barer Str

Ludwigstr

Englischer Garten

Prinzregentenstr

Brienner Str

Max-Joseph
-Platz

Maximilianstr

Platzl Hotel

Marienplatz

Cortiina Hotel

Tal

Hotel
Torbräu

Thierschstr

Isar

N

0.5 KM

Munich

1. Bürgerbräukeller Plaque
2. German Museum
3. 41 Thierschstrasse
4. 54 Sterneckerstrasse
5. Munich City Museum
6. New City Hall
7. Hofbräuhaus
8. Odeonsplatz/Feldherrnhalle
9. Hofgarten War Monument
10. Haus der Kunst
11. Prinzregentenplatz 16
12. White Rose Museum
13. Schellingstrasse 50-62
14. Wounds of Remembrance Memorial
15. Führerbrau/Munich Agreement Site
16. Dachau Concentration Camp

MUNICH TODAY

Storybook German architecture, 46 museums and a world-renowned Oktoberfest (16 days, finishing the first Sunday in October) that pulls in six million beer drinkers each year make Munich Germany's top destination for foreign visitors. Rebuilt to pre-war specifications, the capital of (formerly independent) Bavaria also attracts Germans. With 11 universities, 84,000 students and nationally low unemployment rates, it's one of Germany's most prosperous cities, generally listed among the country's most desirable places to live.

Anchored by the beautiful Marienplatz, the Old Town (*Alstadt*) is the major area of interest for travelers. The photogenic public square, dominated by the gothic New City Hall (*Neues Rathaus*) and dual towers of the Frauenkirche (Church of Our Lady), has for centuries been Munich's center of politics, commerce and entertainment. A five-minute walk east is the famed Hofbräuhaus—the beer hall where Adolf Hitler made his first important speech is a major attraction in its own right. The rest of the city is divided into small neighborhoods such as Max-Joseph-Platz, for high-end shopping on Maximilianstrasse; Englischer Garten, one of the largest city parks on the continent; and Theresienwiese (Theresa Meadow or "Wies'n") the vast, open space southwest of the city center where Oktoberfest action takes place. With the exception of Dachau, most points of interest are concentrated in the easy-to-walk city center and can be seen in a day.

POINTS OF INTEREST

U/S indicates nearest U-Bahn (subway) or S-Bahn (train) station

1. Bürgerbräukeller Plaque ★

At Rosenheimer Platz, directly behind Hilton Hotel in courtyard between hotel and public library
S: Rosenheimer Platz

A copper plaque (in front of the large, tuba-like sculpture) embedded in the ground marks the site of the destroyed Bürgerbräukeller, the huge beer hall where Hitler began the Beer Hall Putsch of 1923. The plaque also recalls the beer hall as the site of a failed November 1939 assassination attempt on Hitler by Georg Elser.

2. German Museum (Deutsches Museum) ★★★

Museumsinsel 1
S: Isartor; U: Fraunhoferstrasse
T: (0)89-2-1791
Daily 9 a.m.-5 p.m.

Closed January 1, Shrove Tuesday, Good Friday, May 1, November 1, December 24, 25, 31
Adult: €8.50; Student/Child: €3; Family: €15

This sprawling museum has absorbing displays on everything from chronometry to space exploration. The mint-condition World War II German aircraft on display include an Me-109, an Me-163 and a Fieseler F-156 Storch. The aviation annex (Deutsches Museum Flugwerft Schleissheim, Effnerstrasse 18, 089-31-5714) is at the wartime Schleissheim air base. Its collection features modern jets—WWII aircraft are limited to a Bücker Bestmann and an American-built Douglas C-47D.

3. 41 Thierschstrasse ★

S: Isartor

In 1920, Hitler lived in an apartment at 41 Thierschstrasse. The building survived the war.

4. 54 Sterneckerstrasse (Tal 54) ★

S: Isartor

The first German Workers' Party headquarters was on the second floor of the former Sterneckerbrau beer hall that stood at this address. Hitler attended his first party meeting here on September 12, 1919.

5. Munich City Museum/Jewish Museum and Cultural Center (Stadtmuseum/Jüdische Museum München) ★★

St.-Jakobs-Platz 1

U: Marienplatz, Sendlinger Tor

T: (0)89-233-2-2370

Tuesday-Sunday, 10 a.m.-6 p.m.

Closed Monday, select holidays

Adult: €4; Senior, Student/Child (under 15): €2; Family: €6

The museum includes a display on the city as hub of fascist power 1918-45. The German-only Third Reich map ("München im, Dritten Reich") lists 36 former or extant sites pertaining to the Nazis. In November 2006, a large and impressive Jewish Center, featuring a synagogue and museum, opened across the street.

6. New City Hall (Neues Rathaus) ★★★

Marienplatz

U: Marienplatz

Built in 1909, this spectacular neo-Gothic structure in Munich's main square—site of large Nazi rallies—survived the war relatively intact. The U.S. Army administration was based here following the war.

7. Hofbräuhaus ★★★★

Platzl 9

T: (0)89-29-0136

U: Marienplatz

Daily, 9 a.m.-11:30 a.m.

With long tables, arched ceilings, constant din, room for 5,000 guests and more than four centuries of history, this famous beer hall is a major tourist attraction, but it's fun and still a "must" on the Munich tourist circuit. The second-floor hall was the site of Hitler's first major public speech, attended by an angry crowd of 2,000 whom Hitler regaled with anti-Semitic invective and promises of a reborn Germany.

8. Odeonsplatz/Feldherrnhalle ★★★

On Ludwigstrasse

U: Odeonsplatz

At the southern end of Odeonsplatz is the Feldherrnhalle (Field Marshals' Hall) an arched memorial to Bavarian war heroes, where the 1923 Beer Hall Putsch was vanquished by police, who killed 14 Nazis and eventually arrested Hitler. Upon Hitler's rise to power, a memorial to the 14 Nazi martyrs was erected on the east side of the Feldherrnhalle. All who passed it were required to give the Nazi salute. Those who didn't want to salute passed the monument via the Viscardigasse (Shirker's Lane), the marked side street behind the monument.

9. Hofgarten War Monument (Kriegerdenkmal) ★★

Behind the State Chancellery (Neue Staatskanzlei) at Hofgarten

U: Odeonsplatz

This tomb-shaped memorial envelops a large bronze German soldier clutching a rifle in death. The inscription commemorates 99,000 Munich soldiers who died in the war and 6,600 victims of air raids.

10. Haus der Kunst ★★

Prinzregentenstrasse 1

U: Odeonsplatz

T: (0)89-21-1270

Daily, 10 a.m.-8 p.m. (closed at 10 p.m. on Thursdays)

Adult: €8; Student/Senior: €6; under 18: €2.50

Built to house Nazi-sanctioned art, this museum is notable as the Third Reich's "first cultural achievement." Hitler meant its exhibitions to "cleanse" Germany of modern art. The colonnaded structure was put to post-war use as an American officers club. It's now once again an important art museum.

11. Prinzregentenplatz 16 ★★

U: Prinzregentenplatz

In 1929, Hitler moved into a luxurious apartment on the second floor of this modern-day office building. Inside, his 23-year-old niece and probable lover, Geli Raubal, shot herself in September 1931.

12. White Rose Museum (Weisse Rose) ★★

Ludwigstrasse 1 (Ludwig-Maximilians-Universität). Enter main hall in front of fountain, follow short stairs to right, pass inner courtyard to room on left signed Denkstätte Weisse Rose.
U: Universität
T: (0)89-36-5445
Weekdays, 10 a.m.-4 p.m. (closed 3 p.m. on Friday)

This small, college-campus museum recounts the White Rose student organization—led by brother and sister Hans and Sophie Scholl—that distributed leaflets on campus decrying Nazi atrocities. Hans, Sophie and a collaborator were executed in February 1943. Copies of the leaflets are embedded in the walkway outside the hall that houses the collection. The 2005 German film *Sophie Scholl: The Final Days* is a powerful re-telling of the story.

13. Schellingstrasse 50-62 ★★★

Corner of Schellingstrasse and Barer Strasse
U: Universität

The building at Number 50 housed the second Nazi Party headquarters. Hitler frequented still-operating Osteria Italiana at Number 62, but his favorite restaurant was Schelling Salon (089-272-0788, closed Tuesday, Wednesday) at Number 56. Having retained its old-time coffee-shop feel (a rarity in Munich), this is one of the best places in the city to step into the past.

14. Wounds of Remembrance Memorial (Alte Pinakothek) ★★

Arcistrasse, between Theresienstrasse and Gabelsbergerstrasse
U: Königsplatz

At the Pinakothek museum, a statue of a man and horse riddled with bullet holes recalls WWII suffering. The museum's exterior repairs indicate air-raid damage.

15. Führerbrau/Munich Agreement Site ★★★

12 Arcistrasse
U: Königsplatz

Hitler hoped to reconstruct Munich according to the imposing style expressed in the long, three-story Führerbrau (Hitler's Office) fronted by four columns. It's now a music school. Rarely opened, Hitler's large bunker beneath the building remains intact. At the corner, on each side of Brienner Strasse, are foundation stones of Nazi memorials erected to the martyrs of the Beer Hall Putsch. At the corner of Arcistrasse and Brienner Strasse, an interpretive map (in German) shows locations of 53 former Nazi buildings in this significant NSDAP area. Hitler planned to be buried here within a monumental tomb. The 1938 Munich Agreement was signed in the "Brown House" (since destroyed) around the corner at Brienner Strasse 45.

16. Dachau Concentration Camp (KZ-Gedenkstätte Dachau)

Along Alte Römerstrasse, west of Munich center. From Dachau train station, buses 724 and 726 (€1) make the 15-minute trip to the camp stop at KZ-Gedenkstätte. Taxis also available from the station.
S: Dachau
T: (0)81-31-66-9970
Tuesday-Sunday, 9 a.m.-5 p.m.
Brief introduction in English at 12:30 p.m.; Guided tours in English (2.5 hours) at 1:30 p.m.; English audio guide: €2.50

The most important and most visited war-related site in Munich, the extensive grounds of Nazi Germany's first concentration camp are surrounded by concrete walls, barbed wire and ominous watchtowers. The main exhibit includes graphic photos and other materials recounting the appalling conditions of camp life, medical experiments, the concentration camp system and the Holocaust. Other areas include the "bunker" punishment center (site of floggings and pole-hangings), roll-call field, International Memorial, camp road, reconstructed barracks, original barracks foundations, Jewish Memorial, crematorium and gas chamber (disguised with showerheads, it was never used) and SS shooting range. As one might expect, a visit to Dachau, established as a memorial in 1965, is a sobering yet illuminating experience. Average visits last two to three hours.

RELATED SITES BEYOND MUNICH

Golden Goose Restaurant/Hitler Sites (Zur Goldenen Gans Restaurant) ★

Planeggerstrasse 31 in Pasing
T: (0)89-83-7033
Daily, 10 a.m.-1 a.m.

Though no mention is made of the fact today, this very good traditional Bavarian restaurant in the Pasing area, west of the city center, was a Hitler favorite. Other sites of note for Hitler historians are at 34 Schleissheimer Strasse, where the future dictator had his first room in Munich, and Landsberg prison, about 50 km west of Munich near highways 17 and 96, where he was incarcerated in 1924 and wrote *Mein Kampf.*

GETTING TO/AROUND MUNICH

Munich's Franz-Josef Strauss international airport is served by direct flights from around the world. Delta Airlines (800-221-1212) flies direct from Atlanta. Continental Airlines (800-231-0856) flies direct from Newark, New Jersey. From Franz-Josef Strauss airport, train lines S1 and S8 make the 40-minute trip to Munich's Hauptbahnhof (€8.80 each way) every 10 minutes between 3:30 a.m. and 12:30 a.m. Taxi fare from the airport to downtown is about €60. Munich is easily reached by express train from around Germany and Europe. The main station (Hauptbahnhof) is 1 km west of the central Marienplatz. Die Bahn (national rail system) information number for travel throughout Germany is (0)180-599-6633.

Munich's subway and train network (MVV) is excellent and taxis are readily available, but walking is the quickest way around. Mike's Bike Tours (Hochbrückenstrasse, 089-25-54-3988) and Radius Tours and Bikes/Original Munich Walks (Arnulfstrasse 3, 089-55-02-9374) conduct Third Reich, Dachau, Jewish and Munich history walking and bicycle tours. Both also rent bikes.

City maps are available at most hotels. The Munich Tourist Office has branches at the Hauptbahnhof (daily, 089-23-33-0257) and City Hall (*Neues Rathaus*) at Marienplatz (Monday-Saturday, 089-23-32-8242).

ACCOMMODATIONS

Platzl Hotel

Sparkassenstrasse 10
www.platzl.de
T: (0)89-23-7030 F: (0)89-23-70-3800
167 rooms
€99-216

Around the corner from the Hofbräuhaus and a three-minute walk from Marienplatz, this historic property has been updated with individually furnished rooms and a fitness center with sauna, steam room and sun bed. Friendly staff. Above-average breakfast buffet included.

Hotel Torbräu

Tal 41
T: (0)89-24-2340 F: (0)89-24-23-4235
www.torbraeu.de

91 rooms
€144-286

Two blocks from Marienplatz, this four-star hotel has good-size rooms with marble bathrooms and all amenities. La Famiglia Italian restaurant is in the hotel.

Cortiina Hotel

Ledererstrasse 8
T: (0)89-242-2490 F: (0)89-242-24-9100
www.cortiina.com
33 rooms
€156-286

All rooms in this slick boutique hotel have oak paneling, oak floors, crafted furniture, "bathrooms featuring natural Jura stone" and internet connections. Great location a few blocks off Marienplatz.

16

Nuremberg

G E R M A N Y

Altstadt

THE WAR YEARS

From its obscure beginnings as a fringe political group, the Nazi party's astonishing rise to power was attended by a masterful use of propaganda. Designated as one of five privileged "Führer's cities" (alongside Berlin, Hamburg, Linz and Munich), Nuremberg became the site of Nazi Germany's greatest displays of symbolism and mass political inculcation. Directed by Nazi Minister of Propaganda Josef Goebbels and notorious anti-Semite publisher Julius Streicher, all six Nazi party rallies of the Third Reich were staged in the city.

"I see Nuremberg as a city to which we shall yearly make a pilgrimage to give thanks for German victory over the forces of Versailles evil, the spreading cancer of the Jew and Bolshevism," Adolf Hitler predicted in 1938.

Nuremberg's classic Teutonic architecture and history—the city was the traditional center of German imperial diets—were used to lend weight to Third Reich efforts to associate itself with German history. During rally weeks, its population swelled from 420,000 to 1.1 million. Throngs gathered in front of Hitler's Hotel Deutscher Hof headquarters, their chants ringing through the streets: "We want to see our Führer!" Increasingly, Hitler would come to be viewed as a near deity.

Designed to instill patriotism, promote a spirit of war and, above all, imbue Hitler and the party into the fabric of society, the gigantic dimensions and apparent lock-step perfection of the 1933-38 rallies inspired Germany's "almost limitless reservoir of militant manhood ... to the point of fanaticism," according to a *New York Times* report of the day, and froze the marrow of the international community. In fact, the vaunted organization of Nazi events was an illusion. Problems included insufficient sanitation, disorganized marchers and committee dissension, but flaws were successfully concealed from the world press, which breathlessly reported on the proceedings.

Occupying four square miles on the outskirts of the city, the rally grounds and attendant structures were designed by Nazi chief architect Albert Speer, just 28 years old in 1933. Dominated by a stone tribune and an enormous swastika, 160,000 could assemble before Hitler at the Zeppelin Field. The vast Luitpold Arena was the site of seemingly endless parades of menacing Storm Troopers, Hitler Youth and other groups marching with frightening precision. Enduring images were captured in *Triumph of the Will*, the powerful 1934 documentary by official director of Nazi films, Leni Riefenstahl. Among the film's memorable inclusions was the quote: "Our motto shall be, 'If you will not be German, I will bash your skull in.'"

Though sport, music and dance were part of rally festivities, it was the formations of heavy bombers flying over roaring masses and military marches that aroused the greatest enthusiasm. "It is difficult to exaggerate the frenzy of 300,000 German spectators when they saw their soldiers go into action, heard the thunder of the guns, and smelt the powder," wrote American journalist and eyewitness William Shirer in 1933. The climax of the week-long rallies was Hitler's speech. When the Führer ascended his rostrum, 150 concealed searchlights would illuminate a circle around him, part of Speer's unforgettable Cathedral of Light unveiled at the 1936 Olympic Games in Berlin. With undeniable magnetism, Hitler would hold forth for up to two hours in a stadium ringed by 21,000 Nazi flags.

"Tedious tautology was his forte," wrote author Alan Wykes. "He never wrote once anything that could be written six times—a literary habit he caught from his own speech-making."

The rallies were also used to advance ideology. Most infamous were the 1935 Nuremberg Laws that deprived Jews of German citizenship, forbade marriage between Germans and Jews (the so-called Law of Protection of German Blood and Honor) and "legally" set in motion what was to become the Holocaust. With enforcement of these laws, even those who simply associated with Jews became social outcasts.

The Nazi rallies ended in 1938, after which Hitler's government found more lethal ways to exercise its military fascination. The final rally was the most foreboding. "It is difficult to recall the dark and almost unbearable tension that gripped the capitals of Europe as the Nuremberg Party Rally ... approached its climax on September 12, when Hitler was scheduled to make his closing speech and expected to proclaim to the world his final decision for peace or war with Czechoslovakia," wrote Shirer.

From 1942, the city was a target of punishing American and British air raids. Locals hid in shelters at night, continued to work by day and protected the art of their ancient churches in a medieval tunnel system originally built to store beer. By war's end, only 250 of the central town's 3,000 buildings remained standing. About 6,000 residents had been killed. When American troops entered the city on April 20, 1945, Nuremberg was a colossal, smoking ruin.

Partly due to its symbolic position in the Reich (and because no suitable facility remained in Berlin), the Allies chose Nuremberg as the site of their unprecedented, post-war International Military Tribunal, otherwise known as the Nuremberg War Crimes Trial. Presided over by the United States, Soviet Union, Great Britain and France—each country had its own judge and prosecutors—the trial indicted the Reich cabinet, SS, Gestapo, SA (Storm Troopers), Wehrmacht command and other groups as criminal organizations. Twenty-one representatives of the Nazi regime sat in the defendants box, including Speer, Streicher and Luftwaffe Reichsmarschall Hermann Göring. Under scrutiny of a stunned international community, which followed the daily revelations of Nazi horrors, the trial lasted from November 20, 1945 to October 1, 1946. Eleven defendants were sentenced to death, seven to life or long-term imprisonment. Three were acquitted. Speer received a 20-year sentence, which he served in full. On October 16, 1946, those sentenced to death, including Streicher, were hanged in Nuremberg.

SOURCES & OTHER READING

The Rise and Fall of the Third Reich: A History of Nazi Germany, Shirer, William, Simon & Schuster, 1960

The Nuremberg Rallies, Wykes, Alan, Ballantine Books, 1970

The Nuremberg Party Rallies: 1923-1939, Burden, Hamilton, Praeger, 1967

Fascination and Terror Documentation Visitors Center Guide, Nuremberg

Adolf Hitler, Toland, John, Doubleday, 1976

Goebbels, Heiber, Helmut, Hawthorn Books, 1972

Albert Speer: His Battle With Truth, Sereny, Gitta, Macmillian, 1995

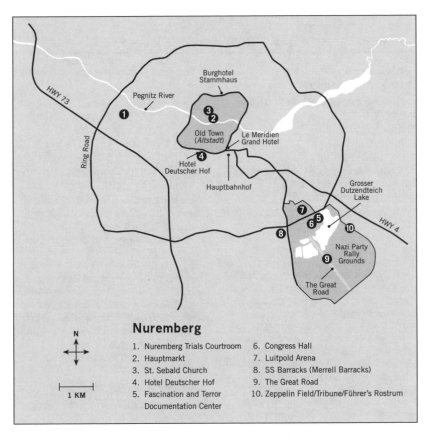

Nuremberg

1. Nuremberg Trials Courtroom
2. Hauptmarkt
3. St. Sebald Church
4. Hotel Deutscher Hof
5. Fascination and Terror Documentation Center
6. Congress Hall
7. Luitpold Arena
8. SS Barracks (Merrell Barracks)
9. The Great Road
10. Zeppelin Field/Tribune/Führer's Rostrum

1 KM

NUREMBERG TODAY

Population: 500,000 • Country Code: 49 • €1 = $1.36/£0.67

"We have 950 years of history; the Nazis were here for only 12 of them." So say Nuremberg city officials and not without understandable exasperation. A quick walk around the pedestrian-friendly Old Town (*Altstadt*) makes the argument more effectively than a thousand brochures—with a number of attractions inevitably, and regrettably, overshadowed by its 20th-century infamy, Nuremberg (also Nürnberg) is one of Germany's treasures.

Following the war, an intense local debate was waged: Rebuild flattened Nuremberg to its pre-war state or construct an entirely new, modern city? The restorationists won out. The subsequent work of reconstruction architects and contractors has been

extraordinary. Using surviving structures as focal points, and salvaging as much original material as possible, Nuremberg's walled Old Town miraculously regained its medieval atmosphere. (Outside the walls, modern, generic suburbs have risen in a vague and uninteresting sprawl.) With the Hauptmarkt at its center, Old Town is a compact maze of narrow streets and alleys, open squares, churches and original half-timbered houses. Old Town is Nuremberg's prime area of interest—not counting the Nazi Party Rally Grounds—for visitors.

One long day is needed to cover all sites in this chapter.

U/T indicates nearest underground or street tram station or stop

1. Nuremberg Trials Courtroom/Palace of Justice ★★★★

Further Strasse 110
U/T: Bärenschanz
T: (0)911-231-8411
Saturday and Sunday only. Compulsory tours begin on the hour 1-4 p.m.
Adult: €2; Student/Child: €1

On November 20, 1945, the International Military Tribunal convened in Courtroom 600 (still its number today) to try Nazi war criminals. American Supreme Court Justice and IMT Chief Prosecutor Robert Jackson opened the trial by telling the court, "The wrongs which we seek to condemn and punish have been so calculated, so malignant and so devastating, that civilization cannot tolerate their being ignored, because it cannot survive their being repeated." One of the more infamous episodes occurred after the trial when, the night before he was to be executed, Luftwaffe Reichsmarschall Hermann Göring cheated the hangman by poisoning himself with cyanide—his American guard likely supplied the poison. In the Palace of Justice, Courtroom 600 is still used for trials. It's open to the public (since 2000) on weekends only. Tours (in English and German) last an hour and include a 15-minute documentary inside the courtroom. The point of a visit really is to stand in the courtroom that was once at the center of the world's attention. Though rearranged to a degree, most of the room remains in recognizable IMT form, including the placement of the defendants dock. The judge's bench—which directly faced the dock during the trial—has been moved to the side.

2. Hauptmarkt ★★

Central town square

Renamed Adolf Hitler Platz during the war, the busy commercial square was devastated by Allied bombing and today bears no evidence of its Nazi-era role as municipal focal point of Hitler fanaticism.

3. St. Sebald Church/Underground Tour ★★

T: (0) 911-214-2500
Daily, 9:30 a.m.-4 p.m., January-March
Daily, 9:30 a.m.-6 p.m., April, May, October-December
Daily, 9:30 a.m.-8 p.m., June-September
Sebalder Platz, one block north of Hauptmarkt

Inside the gorgeous 1525-built Protestant church are a few photos and paintings of a swastika-covered Hauptmarkt during rally days and subsequent aerial destruction of the church. Stored underground during the war, all of the church's stained-glass is original. Nuremberg Cellar tours (0911-22-7066) begin at the monument of artist Albrecht Dürer at Dürer Platz, a block or two north of St. Sebald, just off Agnesgasse. In German only, tours of the 700-year-old beer cellars begin at 11 a.m., 1, 3, and 5 p.m. and last two hours. Minimum five people.

4. Hotel Deutscher Hof ★★

See Accommodations section for hotel details.

Though the management would rather not publicize it, this was Hitler's Nuremberg headquarters hotel throughout the 1930s. During rally weeks, enormous crowds would scream for the Führer to emerge onto his balcony. The walls of his rooms overlooking the street were ripped apart after the war and the entire floor redesigned (as were upper floors used by Nazi officials). Rooms 105 and 106 reportedly occupy the rooms from which Hitler addressed crowds. The old balcony has been removed. Along a narrow street next to the hotel is the Carlton Hotel, formerly the Frankischer Hof, constructed in the 1930s for Nazi officials. A stone emblem on the façade retains its original eagle-and-swastika imprint. German law forbids displays of Nazi symbols, so the emblem will inevitably be removed.

Nazi Party Rally Grounds ★★★★★

About 4 km southeast of Old Town, the following sites are spread around the 4.25-square-mile area used for the Nazi rallies of the 1930s. It's best to begin at the Documentation Center (Point 5). In addition to providing extremely helpful maps of the area, the Center's first-rate "Fascination and Terror" exhibit provides context for sites that might otherwise be unrecognizable.

To reach the Documentation Center and Rally Grounds, take street tram number 9 to the Doku-Zentrum stop. The ride takes 10 to 15 minutes from Old Town. Taxis are also available. Average Documentation Center visits last two hours. A full afternoon is needed to walk the entire area. The Documentation Center keeps opening hours, but the grounds are a public park and always open. The restructured grounds—most of the fields have been split up—are now used for large events. The Rolling Stones played a concert in 2000 using the remnants of the Zeppelin Field Tribune as a backdrop.

5. Fascination and Terror Documentation Center (Faszination und Gewalt Dokumentationszentrum/Reichsparteitagsgelände) ★★★★★

Bayernstrasse 110
U/T: Doku-Zentrum
T: (0)911-231-5666
Daily, 9 a.m.-6 p.m. (open
at 10 a.m. Saturday-Sunday)
Last entry 5 p.m.
Adult: €5; Student/Child: €2.50

Opened only since 2002—an indication of Nuremberg's newfound willingness to examine its past—this state-of-the-art center is one of the most absorbing World War II museums anywhere. Visits begin with a stunning 38-minute documentary (subtitled in English), featuring historical images interspersed with engrossing testimony from rally participants, including octogenarians unabashedly owning up to their enthusiasm for the Nazi hysteria in which they were swept up. One aged soldier returns to the rally grounds to demonstrate the goose step (now outlawed) that once made him "proud as a peacock." English audio guides offer succinct, on-demand descriptions of hundreds of exhibits, allowing visitors to move at their own pace. The Nazi Party is examined in unflinching detail—everything from Albert Speer's plans for the Rally Grounds to the Hitler cult of personality, Holocaust, *Einsatzgruppen* (death squads) and much more. Text, videos, artifacts and enormous photographs are packed into 19 riveting exhibition areas. On the site where the Nazi Party consecrated itself, this is one of the war's most important museums.

6. Congress Hall ★★★

See Point 5

The Documentation Center is located in the north wing of the Congress Hall, a huge indoor arena designed to hold 50,000 people. Construction began in 1935 and though it was never completed, the half-finished structure is the country's largest remaining example of the Monumental Style of Third Reich architecture. The Documentation Center route ends at a large bank of windows with views into the Congress Hall's unfinished brick interior. From the outside, visitors will recognize the granite façade's intentional resemblance to the Colosseum in Rome.

7. Luitpold Arena ★

10-minute walk northwest of Point 5 or at Luitpold street tram stop (just before Doku-Zentrum stop)

The monument to World War I dead—erected in 1929 and later rededicated to include World War II dead—still stands, but the rest of the arena's structures are gone. In front of the monument, the open field where massive military parades and party assemblies frightened the world is now a tree-filled public park, populated by runners, bikers and dog-walkers. A few hundred yards opposite the monument, the small rise indicates the location of the stage that once stood at the head of the field.

8. SS Barracks (Merrell Barracks) ★★

On Franken Strasse near Münchener Strasse, 15- to 20-minute walk from Point 5

On the northwest edge of the rally grounds, the SS Barracks were constructed in the late 1930s and occupied by troops throughout the war. From 1945 to 1952, the U.S. Army used the complex (renamed Merrell Barracks). Today it houses the Federal Office for the Recognition of Foreign Refugees.

9. The Great Road ★★

10-minute walk southwest of Point 5

Laid out in 1939, this 1.25-mile long, 200-foot-wide road was planned as the central axis of the rally grounds, linking its major facilities and lining up with the road to the city center, thus providing a symbolic link between historic Nuremberg and the Nazi Party. Following the war, the U.S. Air Force used it as a runway. It's now a parking area.

10. Zeppelin Field and Tribune/Führer's Rostrum ★★★★★

30-minute walk southeast of Point 5

Though long sections of the original grandstands remain, the great assembly field sits behind fences and parking lots, partitioned into smaller soccer fields and other recreational spaces. At its head, however, stands one of the war's most dramatic relics—the monumental stone tribune that provided the backdrop for the most famous Nazi rally speeches throughout the 1930s. The gargantuan, gilded copper swastika that towered above the tribune was destroyed by the U.S. Army in 1945, but the bulk of the 100-yard-long stage—modeled after the Hellenistic Pergamon Altar in Turkey—rises like a time-warp relic from the totalitarian age. Still dominating the center of the complex is the Führer's rostrum, where Hitler would address the 100,000-plus crowds while obsequious Nazi officials sat behind him. Though the rows of square columns that flanked the stage were demolished in 1967, it's still possible to stand on the rostrum and look out over the reduced field and grandstands. The tribune is always open and used often by skateboarders who favor the long, even planes of the seating area to perform tricks where top Nazis once boasted that their empire would last 1,000 years.

Other Rally Ground Sites ★

The map provided by the Documentation Center shows former locations or planned construction sites of several vanished points of interest. These include the German Stadium (excavated, never built, now beneath the waters of Silbersee Lake), March Field (unfinished, destroyed in 1960s for building development), Camp Zone (now the suburb of Langwasser) and KdF Town recreational area (burned down during World War II). There's little to see of these sites, which require an extra hour or two of walking time.

OTHER AREA ATTRACTIONS

Sausages and Christmas

In Germany, Nuremberg's fame rests less on the Nazi rallies than on its unique, small fried sausages, regarded by many as the best in Germany. Served in bunches of 6, 8, 10 or 12, they resemble American breakfast links but taste much better. Few Germans would think of visiting Nuremberg without at least one meal featuring the stubby sausages (often served with horseradish sauce). The Old Town is also famed for its Christmas Market (*Cristkindlmarkt*), which runs from the last week in November (official start is Friday before Advent) until Christmas. Nuremberg's gingerbread architecture, combined with hundreds of vendors centered in the Hauptmarkt, musical events, lights displays in Gothic cathedrals and other holiday exhibits, make this arguably Germany's best Christmas market. The event draws huge crowds from all over the world. For information, contact Nuremberg Tourist Information (0911-233-6132, www.tourismus.nuernberg.de).

GETTING TO/AROUND NUREMBERG

Nuremberg is a rail hub (another feature that made it attractive to Nazi rally organizers), easily reached from around the country. Die Bahn (national rail system) information number for travel throughout Germany is (0)180-599-6633. Nuremberg Airport is generally accessed via domestic flights. Subway line number 2 runs from the airport to the Hauptbahnhof (main train station) every 10 or 15 minutes. The nearest major airports are in Frankfurt (140 km northwest) and Munich (200 km southeast). The drive or express trains from either city take less than two hours.

Once in Nuremberg, there's no need for a car. It's a hassle in the Old Town and cheap subway, street tram and other public transportation run to most points of interest outside the medieval walls. City maps are available from hotels or the Tourist Information office (0911-233-6132; Monday-Saturday, 9 a.m.-7 p.m), across from the main train station on the southeast edge of the Old Town at 93 Königstrasse. There's also a Tourist Information booth at Hauptmarkt (0911-233-6135), open daily, including Sunday.

Nuremberg Cards (€18) are good for two days of unlimited travel on public transportation, free entry to all museums and various discounts. Those booking at least one night in a Nuremberg hotel can purchase the cards at a discounted rate. Tourist Information offices and hotels can provide details. Or call (0)911-283-4646.

ACCOMMODATIONS

Le Meridien Grand Hotel Nürnberg

Bahnhofstrasse 1-3
T: (0)911-2-3220 F: (0)911-232-2444
www.grand-hotel.de
186 rooms
From €215

Directly across from the main train station at the entry to the Old Town and on the direct street tram line to the Nazi Party Rally Grounds, Nuremberg's top hotel has a prime location. Large, updated rooms are decorated in Art Nouveau style. The Atelier Bar has a creative cocktail menu.

Hotel Deutscher Hof

Frauentorgraben 29
T: (0)911-2-4940 F: (0)911-211-7634
50 rooms
€97-130

Once Hitler's Nuremberg hotel of choice, the Deutscher Hof has been cleansed of all Nazi remnants (see Point 4). It's now a solid business-class hotel with basic rooms and a typical German wine tavern called Bocksbeutelkeller. Located just outside the medieval wall, a five-minute walk from the main train station.

Burghotel Stammhaus

Schildgasse 14
T: (0)911-20-3040 F: (0)911-22-6503
www.burghotel-stamm.de
21 rooms
€40-159

This family-run hotel has gained a following for no-frills, clean, affordable rooms at the north end of the Old Town. A few-minutes walk from Hauptmarkt and other ancient buildings that survived Allied air raids.

17

East Anglia

ENGLAND

Duxford Imperial War Museum

THE WAR YEARS

I n the spring of 1944, nearly half of all American pilots and aircrew in uniform were stationed in the United Kingdom. With half a million men and 9,000 combat-ready aircraft, the U.S. 8th and 9th Army Air Forces occupied more than 120 airfields in the country. This was the "friendly invasion" of the British Isles, and nowhere were its effects more evident than East Anglia, the flatland just north of London—and a short hop across the English Channel to Fortress Europe—that became home to 350,000 U.S. servicemen between 1942 and 1945.

East Anglia was home to several Royal Air Force (RAF) stations during the 1940 Battle of Britain—the land acquisition and programs that built the airfields have been called the biggest construction project ever undertaken in Great Britain. But its legacy was forged by the joint RAF and American bomber campaign over Europe launched from its often foggy, sodden airfields, and the enormous social impact created by the arrival of tens of thousands of Americans. "The peace of the rural countryside was utterly shattered," wrote one historian. Typically housing 3,000 men, bases became known as "Little Americas," replete with softball games, concerts and weekend dances. With an average age of 21 and a one-in-three survival rate in 1943, combat-squadron personnel made their presence felt, riding bicycles through the small towns (generally destined for local pubs), loaded with the kind of money and privilege that made ration-weary locals both resentful and curious. "Overpaid, oversexed and over here" became the epigram to describe Americans in England. East Anglia-based fliers included Paul Tibbets (pilot of the *Enola Gay* mission over Hiroshima), future astronaut Chuck Yeager and actor Jimmy Stewart. Enduring relationships developed between American airmen and local farmers—not to mention 4,000 British war brides—evident in modern sister-city relations between American and East Anglian towns.

Prior to World War II, strategic bombing existed in theory only. By the time the U.S. 8th Air Force arrived in East Anglia—other units flew from here, but the "Mighty Eighth" was the significant force—proponents of various strategies for the annihilation of Germany by air were battling for supremacy. Though Anglo-American cooperation was close, American concepts weren't much advanced by the inexperienced 8th Air Force's lackluster record in 1942 and 1943. Even Winston Churchill complained that "it would be the greatest pity to choke up all our best airfields with more Americans." Yank shortcomings were crystallized on "Black Tuesday," October 14, 1943, when a force of 291 B-17 Flying Fortresses was mauled by Luftwaffe fighters over the German city of Schweinfurt. Sixty B-17s were lost, more than 130 damaged. For all their criticism, the British bomber record was no better. *The Oxford Essential Guide to World War II* called it "feeble," adding, "undeniably, for sheer mindless violence, Britain's Bomber Command took first place." In truth, for sheer mindless violence, first place rather more easily belonged to Germany's helter-skelter V1, V2 and other air attacks on London and other European cities.

With time, tactics improved. Flying "precision raids" (bombing accuracy was at best questionable throughout the war) American B-17s and B-24s attacked Germany by day; RAF Lancasters practiced "area bombing" at night. Targets ranged from railway stations (advocated by British command) to aircraft factories and oil installations (favored by Americans). The acumen of Lieutenant-General Jimmy Doolittle, who assumed command of the 8th Air Force in January 1944, further boosted American success rates.

But the most important development came in late 1943 with the introduction of the newly re-engineered P-51 Mustang, a long-range fighter assigned to defend bomber formations over enemy territory. Extended range enabled the single-prop aircraft to take off from East Anglia and accompany bombers on raids over the "Big B" (as pilots called Berlin) or Romanian oil installations. With Mustang protection against German fighters, bomber losses fell dramatically.

Germany was pulverized from the air—"In the area of the East Anglian bases, it seemed that the sky was never still," wrote historian Roger Freeman—but neither its morale nor industrial production were fully extinguished. In the end, Germany was conquered the old-fashioned way—overrun with ground troops—leaving historians to debate the contribution strategic bombing made to the outcome of the war. For just two examples: Despite determined bombing of its factories, German aircraft output increased from 15,288 in 1942 to 25,094 in 1943 and 39,275 in 1944. Even so, as one Luftwaffe officer revealed after the war: "The American devastation of our airfields, factories and oil depots made it impossible for us to keep going." A Nuremberg nursing student more succinctly noted, "Once the bombs began falling on our cities, we knew we'd lost the war." More significant than statistics, the aerial campaign ushered in a new and vastly more corrupt form of warfare. "When World War II began the principle that civilians should not be killed was generally accepted," wrote historian Mark Arnold-Foster. "When the bombing began this principle was forgotten."

While the airfields of East Anglia roared with activity, a distinctly more subtle war effort was being undertaken just miles away at an obscure hunting lodge called Bletchley Park. Beginning in 1939, behind a screen of near-perfect secrecy, one of the greatest collections of minds—mathematicians, linguists, historians—was assembled in dozens of drab working huts for the singular effort of breaking Axis communications codes. As with the bomber command, the Anglo-American alliance (with crucial assistance from Polish mathematicians) was often contentious. In the end, it was a British triumph—the "Bombe" decoding machine designed by Alan Turing and Gordon Welchman—that in 1940 first broke the formidable German Enigma military code, providing intelligence that shortened the war by perhaps two years. Before the war was over, Bletchley workers produced the world's first programmable electronic computer (Colossus), beginning a revolution that would shape the modern world to perhaps an even greater degree than the atomic bomb collectively developed in equally clandestine circumstances in the New Mexico desert.

SOURCES & OTHER READING

The Mighty Eighth in the Second World War, Smith, Graham, Countryside Books, 2001

The Mighty Eighth, Freeman, Roger A., McDonald & Jones, 1970

The Bomber War: Arthur Harris and the Allied Bomber Offensive 1939-1945, Neillands, Robin, John Murray Publishers, 2001

Winged Victory: The Army Air Forces in World War II, Perret, Geoffrey, Random House, 1993

The Right of the Line: The Royal Air Force in the European War, 1939-1945, Terraine, John, Hodder and Stoughton, 1985

The Hut Six Story: Breaking the Enigma Codes, Welchman, Gordon, McGraw-Hill, 1982

Enigma, Harris, Robert, Ivy Books, 1995

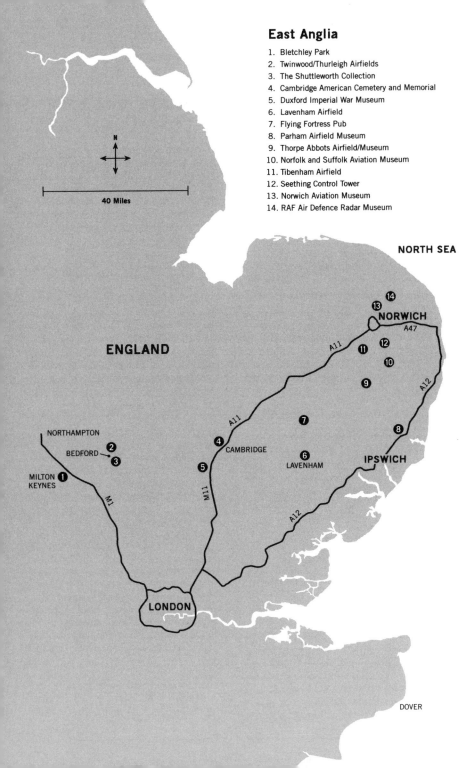

East Anglia

1. Bletchley Park
2. Twinwood/Thurleigh Airfields
3. The Shuttleworth Collection
4. Cambridge American Cemetery and Memorial
5. Duxford Imperial War Museum
6. Lavenham Airfield
7. Flying Fortress Pub
8. Parham Airfield Museum
9. Thorpe Abbots Airfield/Museum
10. Norfolk and Suffolk Aviation Museum
11. Tibenham Airfield
12. Seething Control Tower
13. Norwich Aviation Museum
14. RAF Air Defence Radar Museum

NORTH SEA

N

40 Miles

ENGLAND

NORWICH

A47

A11

NORTHAMPTON

BEDFORD

MILTON KEYNES

A11

CAMBRIDGE

LAVENHAM

IPSWICH

A12

M1

M11

A12

LONDON

DOVER

EAST ANGLIA TODAY

Country Code: 44 • Population: 100,000 (Cambridge); 2,000 (Lavenham); 126,000 (Norwich) • £1 = $2.02/€1.48

Wide, flat tracts of farmland made East Anglia the perfect site for Allied air bases. After the war, most of the area reverted to its agricultural tradition. Like the American Midwest, its rolling fields bloom with stunning colors in fall, then turn bleak, hard and foggy in winter. Picturesque small towns punctuate the rustic scenes along slow, two-lane highways. Game birds, especially emerald-headed pheasant, are a common site for those making their ways through the backcountry.

In the decades after the war, most vestiges of military buildup were torn down or allowed to rot. With exceptions, it's mostly been over the last decade that restoration efforts have been undertaken at many sites. Today, few places offer such a concentra-tion of high-quality World War II exhibits. From the airfields of the countryside to the computers of Bletchley Park, one might argue that no place on earth presents a more complete example of the brawn and, more critically than in any conflict before, the brain necessary to win World War II.

Three cities provide the best hubs for East Anglia visits. The famed university town of Cambridge is almost impossibly atmospheric. Lavenham is widely regarded as Britain's best-preserved Tudor village. With its own medieval center, the "cathedral city" of Norwich was headquarters of the U.S. 2nd Air Division (the headquarters building at Ketteringham Hall is now privately occupied). Three to four days are recommended to cover all sites in this chapter.

POINTS OF INTEREST

1. Bletchley Park ★★★★★

Off Buckingham Road (B4034) in Milton Keynes (about 50 miles north of London), a 350-yard walk from Bletchley railway station. Free car park on weekends at rail station. The train from London's Euston Station takes 40 minutes.
T: (0)190-864-0404
Weekdays, 9:30 a.m.-5 p.m., April-October
Weekdays, 10:30 a.m.-4 p.m., November-March
Weekends, 10:30 a.m.-5 p.m. (closed at 4 p.m. November-March)
Adult: £10; Senior/Student: £8; Child (12-16): £6; Family: £22.50
Guided tour (about 2 hours): additional £2

Just west of the East Anglia border and covering 26 of the original facility's 55 acres, Bletchley Park (aka Station X and exactly halfway between Oxford and Cambridge) was one of the most remarkable arenas of the war. Because there's so much back story and because volunteer guides are so good, tours are highly recommended. Barring that, the £3 souvenir program includes maps of the 22-point trail through the sprawling grounds. Visits begin at the famous mansion—its mishmash of 11 architectural styles provides an appropriate introduction to the place where so many brilliant, eclectic minds gathered to break Nazi codes. Nearby are several original work huts—the window at which Alan Turing sat can be seen. Other highlights: the work area where the first Enigma message was deciphered; a replica of the Turing-Welchman "Bombe" machine; the spot where Colossus, the world's first programmable computer, was built; the Cryptology Trail through rooms of text and equipment, including an amazing complete replica of Colossus. In 2007, a restaurant and bar were opened in an old codebreaking hut, and a superb, life-size statue of Turing—made from half a million pieces of stacked slate—was unveiled. The gorgeous grounds are marked by wide lawns framed with large chestnut and oak trees. Open to the public only since the mid-1990s, this is a historic spot worth a several-hour visit.

2. Twinwood Airfield Glenn Miller Museum and Thurleigh Airfield Museum ★★★

Twinwood:

Off Twinwood Road, Clapham. From A6, turn right on Twinwood Road (just north of Clapham), then right at sign for Twinwood Events LTD and Twinwood Arena, and follow Glenn Miller signs.
The museum is 3 miles north of Bedford Railway Station, served by Thameslink and Midland Mainline trains from London.
T: (0)123-435-0413
Weekends, bank holidays, 10:30 a.m.-4 p.m. May be closed winter weekends (check www.twinwoodevents.com)
for winter schedule.
Adult: £3; Under 17: Free

Thurleigh:

Located across from the Twinwood Airfield, from A6 follow signs to Bedford Technology Park.
T: (0)123-470-8715
Weekends, bank holidays, 10:30 a.m.-4 p.m., March-October
Adult: £3; Under 17: Free

On the foggy night of December 15, 1944, beloved bandleader and American officer Glenn Miller took off from this field as a passenger in a Noorduyn Norseman bound for Paris. His plane was never seen again—despite several bizarre theories, it almost certainly went down in the English Channel. The control tower has been preserved as it was on the night of the fatal flight. Inside, the lovingly assembled museum, opened in 2003, has photos and memorabilia. Although Miller is the musician most associated with World War II, country star Roy Acuff was ranked by GIs in Europe as their favorite performer.

3. The Shuttleworth Collection ★★

At Shuttleworth (Old Warden) Aerodrome, two miles due west of the A1 where it

bypasses Biggleswade, approximately 30 miles from Junction 23 of the M25. Well-signed from road.
The museum is 3 miles west of Biggleswade Station, served by Great Northern Line trains from London's Kings Cross Station.
T: (0) 176-762-7949
Daily, 10 a.m.-5 p.m., April-October (closed at 4 p.m. November-March)
Last entry one hour before closing
Adult: £10; Senior: £9; Under 17: Free

This private collection of more than 40 aircraft and numerous vehicles is largely for World War I enthusiasts. The crowning glory is the pristine 1910 Avro Triplane IV. Immaculate and fully operational World War II–era planes include a Hawker Hurricane and 1931 Tiger Moth.

4. Cambridge American Cemetery and Memorial ★★★★

On A1303 in Madingley, three miles west of Cambridge, 50 miles north of London. Cambridge is reached by train from London's Kings Cross and Liverpool Street Stations.
Daily, 9 a.m.-5 p.m.
Closed December 25, January 1
T: (0)195-421-0350

The only American World War II cemetery in the British Isles, this is also one of the American Battle Monuments Commission's most striking properties. In addition to the 30 manicured acres and sobering rows of gleaming marble crosses and Stars of David—3,811 war dead are buried here—distinctive features are a long reflecting pool and statues representing a soldier, a sailor, an airman and a Coast Guardsman. The 85-foot-long memorial houses a giant map depicting "The Great Air Assault" on Germany. Along a stone wall (472 feet long) are names of 5,126 soldiers missing in action, including Alton G. Miller, better known as band leader Glenn Miller. According to East Anglia military historian Graham Smith, "A visit to Madingley is a most rewarding and humbling experience that cannot be too highly recommended."

5. Duxford Imperial War Museum
★★★★★

Off A505 (at Junction 10 off M11) just south of Cambridge, 50 miles north of London.
See Point 4 for train information.
T: (0)122-383-5000
Daily, 10 a.m.-6 p.m., mid-March-late October (closed at 4 p.m. at other times)
Closed December 24-26
Adult: £14.95; Senior: £11.50; Student: £8.50; Under 16: Free

This is the best air museum in Europe, if not the world. With five hangars jammed with aircraft, plus the enormous American Air Museum in Britain, and a building devoted to land warfare, the museum is beyond massive—which is why a free shuttle transports visitors around the grounds of what was a key World War II airfield. The museum chronicles the history of flight—from the Wright Brothers to present—but World War II stars in most hangars. The entire roll call of aircraft is too long to list, but includes Spitfires, Hurricanes, Lancasters, B-17s, a P-40 Kittyhawk, a Grumman F7F Tigercat, a P-47 Thunderbolt, Corsairs, Me-109s, a Lavochkin Soviet fighter and dozens more. Many planes are in flying condition (see below). The high point is the American Air Museum, opened in 1997, a state-of-the-art palace in a huge glass-fronted hangar. Touch-screen displays, videos and extensive text tell the stories of military aircraft on display from every major U.S. conflict—including a herculean B-52 bomber. WWII aircraft include a P-51 Mustang (with black-and-white checkerboard nose as it appeared when on active duty at Duxford), B-29, Douglas C-47 and others. The Land Warfare Hall includes a good D-Day exhibit. This extraordinary museum requires four hours to a full day.

6. Lavenham Airfield/Lavenham ★★★

Airfield is off A134, 1.5 miles north of Lavenham. From Lavenham Tourist Office, proceed down hill, turn right on High Street, then left at T intersection. Turn right just after the Church of St. Peter and St. Paul onto Bridge Street, follow to end and turn right at T onto A134. After 1.5 miles, turn right at telephone-icon sign into the Glebe. Follow this road left. At the end of the road (past Lavenham Lodge) is the two-story control tower.
T: (0) 128-482-8226
Lavenham is linked by direct buses to trains at Sudbury (Monday-Saturday) and Ipswich (Sunday). Contact Traveline (0870-608-2608; www.traveline.org.uk) or BritRail (0845-748-4950; www.britrail.net) for information. The control tower/airfield is privately owned—visitors must first fill out permission forms at Lavenham Tourist Office on Lady Street (01787-248-207; 10 a.m.-4:45 p.m., open daily in summer, weekends only in winter) in center of town.

The restored control tower was the focal point of a base for 3,000 men of the U.S. 487th Bomb Group. More than 185 missions and 6,000 sorties flew from this field. The Tudor village of Lavenham (see page 170) is the real reason to stop. In the beautiful Church of St. Peter and St. Paul—dating to the 1300s—a U.S. flag flies in the "American Corner," a testament to the impact U.S. troops had here. In front of the

---

Flying Legends at Duxford ★★★★

The World War II enthusiast can get no closer to aviation Valhalla than this annual, two-day air show of piston-engine aircraft (most from WWII). The program brings together an unparalleled selection of classic American and European fighting craft, and usually culminates with a mass fly-by. The show is generally held the first or second weekend of July. Tickets cost about $60. Coupled with access to the Duxford museum, it's as memorable an experience as walking the D-Day beaches in Normandy or tracing the Battle of the Bulge through Belgium. Call the museum or check the website (www.iwm.org.uk) for dates and details.

famed Guildhall in the town square, a bronze plaque commemorates the U.S. 487th Bomb Group. The Swan hotel's low-ceilinged Old Bar (see Accommodations) is a must. It was a favorite pub of airmen—many left their names on the walls.

7. Flying Fortress Pub ★

Mount Road, Great Barton (just east of Bury St. Edmunds)
Traveling east on A14, turn left at Exit 45, proceed about a mile, turn left at "T" and proceed another mile. Pub is on left, down a driveway, easy to miss.
T: (0)128-478-7665

The pub is decorated with photos, aircraft models and reminders of the war—the building was a supply depot and observation post for the adjacent airfield, the wartime home of the U.S. 4th Bomb Group. Today the airfield is privately operated.

8. Parham Airfield Museum ★★

Off A12, 2 miles southeast of Framlingham, just north of Ipswich. Traveling north, turn left off A12 directly opposite Glenham Hall.
T: (0)172-862-1373
Sunday, bank holiday Mondays, 11 a.m.-5 p.m., March-October; Wednesday, 11 a.m.-4 p.m., June-September
Open by appointment

The restored control tower holds two museums: one for the U.S. 390th Bomb Group, and one for the little-known British underground resistance network, organized in preparation for possible German invasion. Exhibits include Allied and German aircraft parts and bomb-making equipment.

9. Thorpe Abbots Airfield/Museum ★★

Common Road, Dickleburgh. Off A143 (26 miles north of Ipswich), turn left (if traveling northeast) onto single-lane road marked with small sign for Thorpe Abbots. Follow this road 2 miles to left turn onto Common Road and proceed about half a mile.
T: (0)37-974-0708
Saturday, Sunday, bank holidays, 10 a.m.-5 p.m. (closed 4:30 p.m. in winter)
Also open Wednesday, 10 a.m.-5 p.m., May-September; closed November-January.

Inside a restored control tower is an excellent small museum memorializing the snakebit "Bloody Hundredths" (U.S. 100th Bomb Group), whose consistent heavy losses on missions earned it a reputation as "the jinx outfit" of the 8th Air Force.

10. Norfolk and Suffolk Aviation Museum ★★★

On B1062 (off A143) in Flixton, a mile west of Bungay, southeast of Norwich
T: (0)198-689-6644
Sunday-Thursday, 10 a.m.-5 p.m., April-October
Tuesday, Wednesday, Sunday, 10 a.m.-4 p.m., November-March
Last entry one hour before closing
Closed December 15-January 15

The presentation here has all the charm of a junk shop. Of the roughly 40 aircraft (most outside), only two are from World War II. The lone Spitfire is badly neglected, surrounded by wounded craft and mysteriously positioned piles of used paperbacks for sale. But the several huts with World War II exhibits—U.S. 446th Bomb Group, Royal Observer Corps, RAF Bomber Command—are loaded with fascinating items, from large weaponry to squadron insignias. From here, the 446th was given the honor of leading the 8th Air Force on its momentous June 6, 1944, D-Day missions. The lack of entry fee likely contributes to its unkempt condition.

11. Tibenham Airfield (Jimmy Stewart airfield) ★

Off Plantation Road, less than a mile south of Tibenham, about 15 miles south of Norwich. From Norwich, take A140 south to B1134 west. After 2.4 miles, turn right on Plantation Road at sign for Tibenham Airfield, proceed 0.9 miles to left turn onto unmarked road (at sign for Norfolk Glider Club). Airfield is on left after 0.6 miles.

Aside from a small monument to the U.S. 445th Bomb Group (H) and some rusting Quonset huts, there's little to see at this still-operational rural airfield. Jimmy Stewart served here as the 703rd Squadron commander. The glider club office has photos and information on the field's history.

12. Seething Control Tower ★★

Toad Lane, Seething (7 miles southeast of Norwich). Traveling north on B1332, turn right onto Church Road at Hedenham's Mermaid Pub. Turn right after 2 miles at sign onto Toad Lane. Tower is on left.
T: (0)150-855-0453
First Sunday of month only,
10 a.m.-5 p.m., May-October

The restored tower—overlooking the privately operated Seething Airfield—pays tribute to the U.S. 448th Bomb Group, which flew B-24 Liberators from here. Displays include models, uniforms, airplane parts and communications equipment.

13. Norwich Aviation Museum ★

Old Norwich Road, Horsham St. Faith, on the north edge of Norwich International Airport. Off A140, just north of Norwich, turn right on Church Street (unmarked) and follow small brown signs for Aviation Museum for 1.1 miles.
T: (0)160-389-3080
Tuesday-Saturday, 10 a.m.-5 p.m., April-October
Sunday, bank holidays, noon-5 p.m., April-October
Wednesday, Saturday, 10 a.m.-4 p.m.,
November-March
Sunday, noon-4 p.m., November-March
Closed December 21-January 5
Adult: £3.50; Senior: £3; Child: £2
Family: £10; Under 5: Free

Adjacent to the museum, Norwich International Airport was used by the RAF's 100 Group and later by elements of the U.S. 8th Air Force. A section of the small museum is dedicated to the 100 Group.

14. RAF Air Defence Radar Museum ★★

RAF Neatishead, near Horning (northeast of Norwich). From A1062 follow signs for RAF Neatishead and Radar Museum.
T: (0)169-263-1485
Second Saturday of each month, Tuesday, Thursday, bank holiday Mondays,
10 a.m.-5 p.m., April-October
Adult: £4; Senior: £3.50; Youth (12-17): £3; Under 12: Free

This museum tracing the history of radar from home defense to space communications is absorbing. The WWII section—when radar was "as much art as science"—includes primitive equipment. The highlight is the imposing Cold War Operations Room, preserved in mid-1980s condition. The 75-minute tours (every half-hour from 10:30 a.m. to 3 p.m.) are excellent.

OTHER AREA ATTRACTIONS

Cambridge and Lavenham

East Anglia is dotted with photogenic towns worthy of standing in as "charming English village" in any Hollywood period production. Two that shouldn't be missed are Cambridge and Lavenham.

Home to world-renowned colleges such as Trinity, King's, Corpus Christi and others, Cambridge is one of England's most stately and striking cities. Stone towers and brick halls stand magnificently above manicured lawns and gardens. Two-hour walking tours (0906-586-2526 for local tourist information) include most sites in the compact city. Of note is **The Eagle Pub** ★★★, where the structure of DNA was announced by James Watson and Francis Crick in 1953 and where, in the Airforce

Bar, the ceiling is covered with names and squadron numbers of RAF and U.S. airmen who frequented the pub during the war.

The most picturesque small town in East Anglia, Lavenham is justly famed as England's best-preserved Tudor village. At the center is the timber-framed Guildhall, built circa 1530. As many of its old structures reflect, Lavenham prospered for centuries as a wool producer. Walking tours take in many sites in the compact, hilly town, including the Priory, Old Grammar School, Great House and more (see Point 6). The Tourist Information Office (01787-24-8207) is located in the town center, on Lady Street, around the corner from the Guildhall. It's open daily in summer, on weekends only from November-March.

GETTING TO/AROUND EAST ANGLIA

Sites in this chapter are located one to three hours from London, by car or rail. See Getting To/Around London (page 36) for flight information.

Many sites are accessible by train (from London or elsewhere) and short taxi or bus ride. For train inquiries, contact BritRail (0845-748-4950; www.britrail.net). Trains can be booked from the United States through RailEurope (800-782-2424).

Especially for those intent on locating old airfields, the best way to get around East Anglia is by car. Auto Europe (888-233-5555 in North America; 00-800-233-55555 from anywhere in the United Kingdom or Europe) is one of many discount car-rental agencies. All major American companies operate in the region, including Avis (800-331-1084) and National (800-227-7368). Most rental agencies in Britain allow pick-up and drop-off at different locations, without a drop fee. If driving in congested London is intimidating, one might take a train to Cambridge or Norwich, and pick up a car there. There's a National Car Rental office at the train station at Bletchley Park, for just one example.

Two maps are essential. The USAAF Airfields Guide and Map, published by the East of England Tourist Board (01473-822-922; www.visiteastofengland.com) lists the names and locations of 126 former airfields (most now vanished) and 11 headquarters. The map sells for £4.95 and is available at gas stations, shops, museums, tourist offices or can be downloaded at no cost from the "Aviation Heritage" section of the website above.

The USAAF Airfields map isn't adequate as a road map. To navigate the region's maze of expressways, farm roads and dirt lanes, one can make few better £4.95 investments than the A-Z East Anglia Road Atlas published by Geographers' A-Z Map Company (020-7440-9500 in London; www.a-zmaps.co.uk). The 60-page, booklet-size atlas lists existing airfields and local roads in detail—it's big enough to read with ease, small enough to consult while driving.

ACCOMMODATIONS

Cambridge
Crowne Plaza
Downing Street
T: (0)870-400-9180 F: (0)122-346-4440
www.cambridge.crowneplaza.com
198 rooms
£190-350

Fifteen minutes from Duxford Imperial War Museum and within easy walking distance of many sites, the Crowne Plaza has an unbeatable location. Rooms come with satellite TV, mini-bar and other amenities.

Lavenham
The Swan
High Street
T: (0)870-400-8116 F: (0)178-724-8286
www.macdonald-hotels.co.uk
49 rooms
£70-180 (high season)

£60-160 (low season)
This extraordinary, thoroughly modernized hotel occupies a building that dates from 1425. Exposed timber beams, open hearth fireplaces, atmospheric public areas and select rooms with four-poster beds create an Old World ambience.

Norwich
Marriott Sprowston Manor Hotel and Country Club
Sprowston Park, Wroxham Road
T: (0)160-341-0871 F: (0)160-342-3911
www.marriott.com
94 rooms
From £80

The huge main building is a converted Victorian mansion. On the grounds is an impeccable 18-hole golf course, spa, fitness room, indoor pool and award-winning Manor Restaurant. A great bargain.

18

Volgograd

(Stalingrad)

RUSSIA

Mamaev Mound

THE WAR YEARS

G ermany's 1941 attempt to capture Moscow having failed, Adolf Hitler looked to change fortunes on the Eastern Front in 1942 by redirecting his still-formidable military toward southern Russia. In the Caucasus Mountains, the Baku oil fields produced 90 percent of the Soviet Union's fuel, most of it transported via the Volga River (and parallel railways) through an industrial heartland anchored by the armaments-factory city of Stalingrad (called Volgograd since 1961). With his massive Army Group South, Hitler believed that by cutting the vital Volga transportation link near Stalingrad and grabbing the oil fields he could deliver a fatal blow to the Soviet war machine.

After taking Kharkov in May and the Black Sea port of Sevastopol in July, the German Army controlled almost half the Soviet Union (in terms of population and resources). Brimming with confidence, Hitler made the fateful decision to split Army Group South into two commands. One group would head toward the Caucasus, the other would smash Russian forces concentrated around Stalingrad.

Led by conservative General Friedrich Paulus, Germany's vaunted 6th Army—conquerors of Poland, Belgium and Paris—began the Battle of Stalingrad on August 23, 1942, with a massive bombardment that killed perhaps 40,000 in a matter of hours. Panicked civilians fled in boats across the Volga, while Luftwaffe dive bombers strafed the crowded river. Demonstrating the recalcitrant cruelty that made him Hitler's dictatorial equal, Soviet leader Josef Stalin issued his famous "Not a step back!" directive to Stalingrad's defenders and civilians. Hitler followed with his own fight-to-the-death order, setting up Stalingrad as the climax of a personal duel between the two despots. "Stalin's determination not to lose the city of his name, and Hitler's equal determination to take it, blinded both sides ... Stalingrad became the Verdun of the Second World War," according to *The Cassell Atlas of the Second World War*.

On the banks of the Volga, Stalingrad was an unorthodox city—25 miles long, just two to three miles wide—ill suited to encirclement. Paulus instead approached from the west along a wide front, quickly capturing 90 percent of the city. Vastly outnumbered, 40,000 to 50,000 Soviet troops clung to a 10-mile-long strip of riverbank that, in places, narrowed to just 500 yards. Beaten by any rational assessment, the Soviets refused to surrender. Savage fighting reduced virtually all of Stalingrad to rubble. By late October, Germans had penetrated every major industrial plant—legendary hand-to-hand fights were waged at the Red October steel foundry, Barrikady ordnance plant and Tractor Works—though they never managed to clear the factory district of Soviet defenders. Soldiers fought over piles of broken brick. Starvation was rampant. Winter descended in November. The only drinking water came from melted snow. "Eighty days and nights of hand-to-hand fighting," wrote a German soldier. "Stalingrad is no longer a town. It is an enormous cloud of burning, blinding smoke."

Belligerent, acerbic and seemingly indestructible, 42-year-old General Vasili Chuikov directed the Soviet defense. His energetic leadership was an important force behind the Soviets' mad resolve, but Red Army soldiers feared their own tyrannical officers as much as the Germans. The Red Army executed 13,500 of its own men at Stalingrad for cowardice or desertion. But its supernatural ability to withstand punishment conferred upon the Russian soldier an aura of invincibility. German soldiers believed they were fighting animals—"Because of his simple and primitive nature, all sorts of hardships bring him but few emotional reactions," wrote one German officer. The Russians regarded their enemy in similarly sub-human terms. "One can bear anything: the plague and hunger and death," reported a Red Army newspaper. "But we cannot live as long as these gray-green slugs are alive."

The Germans correctly perceived the importance of Stalingrad, but they badly underestimated their opponent's strength. "The Russians no longer have any reserves worth mentioning and are not capable of launching a large-scale offensive," reported Chief of the German General Staff Kurt Zeitzler on November 18. He couldn't have been more wrong—or more characteristic of unrealistic German expectations. The following day, Chuikov launched the great Soviet counter-offensive, with 750,000 reservists advancing along three fronts toward Germany's rear flank at the Don River, 55 miles west of Stalingrad in an area defended by Romanian troops. Badly outnumbered, Romanian resistance quickly collapsed. When the Soviet fronts met near Kalach on November 23, 250,000 Germans of the 6th Army, once the largest formation in the entire Wehrmacht, were surrounded.

Air-drop and land efforts to relieve the troops failed disastrously. Trapped within what they called the *kessel* (cauldron), the 6th Army was doomed. Ravaged by disease, frostbite, starvation, suicide and enemy fire, tens of thousands died in the following weeks. The remnants retreated into the city, where Paulus was captured—one of 24 generals taken prisoner at Stalingrad—on January 31, 1943. Paulus refused to sign a surrender document, leaving subordinate officers to handle the details of the most traumatic defeat in the history of German arms. Most of the 91,000 Germans taken prisoner were sent to Siberian POW camps—fewer than 6,000 would return.

A mega-wattage bloodbath charged by nationalism, dread and loathing, Stalingrad left one side broken (250,000 troops and six months of German material production were lost at Stalingrad), the other on the path to superpower status. Hitler lost a measure of personal composure that he would never regain. His army had suffered a shattering defeat, giving the Red Army (despite an estimated 250,000 to one million Soviet casualties) the initiative it would hold for the rest of the war. "After Stalingrad the British and Americans had to reckon with a war that would be won largely by the Soviet Union—a power that would be in a position to dominate post-war Europe," wrote historian Geoffrey Roberts.

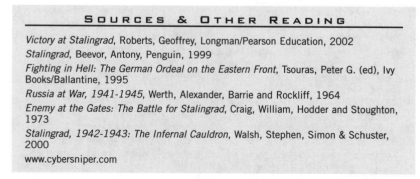

SOURCES & OTHER READING

Victory at Stalingrad, Roberts, Geoffrey, Longman/Pearson Education, 2002

Stalingrad, Beevor, Antony, Penguin, 1999

Fighting in Hell: The German Ordeal on the Eastern Front, Tsouras, Peter G. (ed), Ivy Books/Ballantine, 1995

Russia at War, 1941-1945, Werth, Alexander, Barrie and Rockliff, 1964

Enemy at the Gates: The Battle for Stalingrad, Craig, William, Hodder and Stoughton, 1973

Stalingrad, 1942-1943: The Infernal Cauldron, Walsh, Stephen, Simon & Schuster, 2000

www.cybersniper.com

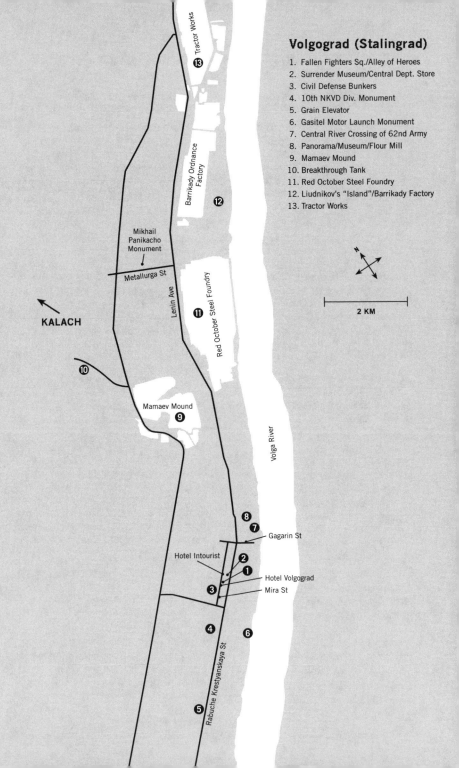

Volgograd (Stalingrad)

1. Fallen Fighters Sq./Alley of Heroes
2. Surrender Museum/Central Dept. Store
3. Civil Defense Bunkers
4. 10th NKVD Div. Monument
5. Grain Elevator
6. Gasitel Motor Launch Monument
7. Central River Crossing of 62nd Army
8. Panorama/Museum/Flour Mill
9. Mamaev Mound
10. Breakthrough Tank
11. Red October Steel Foundry
12. Liudnikov's "Island"/Barrikady Factory
13. Tractor Works

2 KM

KALACH

Tractor Works

Barrikady Ordnance Factory

Mikhail Panikacho Monument

Metallurga St

Lenin Ave

Red October Steel Foundry

Volga River

Mamaev Mound

Gagarin St

Hotel Intourist

Hotel Volgograd

Mira St

Rabuche Krestyanskaya St

VOLGOGRAD TODAY

Population: 1 million • Country Code: 7 • 100 rubles = $3.50/£1.80/€2.70

Veering from nondescript to ugly, this still-important industrial center—petroleum, aluminum, shipping—presents a typical vision of big-city Russia. Lacking color and vibrancy, the city isn't so much depressing as it is discouraging. Few tourists make it to Volgograd and for obvious reason.

Stretching for 70 km along the west bank of the Volga River, the oddly shaped city is now nine times its wartime size and looks nothing like it did in 1942. Flattened by the battle, its post-war layout was completely altered by ambitious Soviet city planners who harbored grand designs for the prestigious "Hero City" named after the Soviet Union's then-ruler. But poor economic times have left the wide Parisian-style boulevards and sterile architecture somewhat in disrepair. Stalingrad's name was changed to Volgograd in 1961 after the Communist Party denounced Stalin.

It's not all bad. There are some good restaurants and hotels. Late spring and early fall can be pleasant. People are friendly, if not outgoing. Still, the primary reason to visit is for the city's unassailable position in 20th-century history. In this, Volgograd doesn't disappoint. Amid the preserved ruins and factories, the city's wartime image is easy to conjure. One or two days are needed to see all points covered in this chapter. The five-hour round-trip to Kalach (recommended only for those with special interest) requires an extra day.

POINTS OF INTEREST

1. Fallen Fighters Square/Alley of Heroes (Alleya Gerouev) ★★

Mira Street, between Hotel Intourist and Hotel Volgograd

A 50-foot obelisk marks a mass grave of Battle of Stalingrad victims. Behind the obelisk and eternal flame, the long Alley of Heroes stretches to the Volga River. In the center of the walkway is a large poplar tree, the only thing to turn green amid the charred city in spring 1943. Bullet scars can be found above the plaque at the base of the tree.

2. Surrender Museum/Central Department Store (Ounivermag) ★★★

Fallen Fighters Square 2, across street to north of Point 1
T: 8442-33-5397
Daily, 9 a.m.-5 p.m., Closed Sunday
Adult: 50 rubles (with Russian guide)

The Central Department Store (rebuilt with the same name and function) served as

final headquarters of German Field Marshal Friedrich Paulus. He was captured here on January 31, 1943. His basement command center became a national memorial in 1947, forever preserved in its wartime state. Its concrete corridors transport the imaginative visitor to the bleak days of 1942-43. The 15-minute documentary (in Russian) is worth seeing if only as proof that Soviet cameramen were as crazy-fearless as their infantry.

3. Civil Defense Bunkers ★

In Comsomol Garden. From Hotel Volgograd, walk across main traffic square. Just past the theater (west side of square) is a diagonal footpath leading to the bunker entries.

A pair of white, 12-foot-tall concrete structures encase the sealed-off entries to extensive subterranean tunnels used to administer the defense of the city. Nearby is a likeness of the Order of Lenin medal.

4. 10th NKVD Division Monument
(Pamiatnik Desiataya Diviziya) ★

Off Rabuche Krestyanskaya Street, at south end of bridge

In a gritty neighborhood overlooking the Volga, this 40-foot tower topped by a sword-wielding NKVD soldier is cracking and unkempt. From the entire NKVD division that fought here (about 12,000 men), only 1,000 survived the battle.

5. Grain Elevator (Elevator) ★★★

Rabuche Krestyanskaya Street, about 2 km south of Point 4

Forming the highest point on the southern side of Stalingrad, more than 25 enormous, side-by-side grain elevators were the focus of furious fighting. In September 1942, 40 marines held the complex, yet it took thousands of German troops several days to seize it. In front of the brick elevators is a 25-foot statue of a Soviet marine carrying an anti-tank rifle.

6. Gasitel Motor Launch Monument
(Pamiatnik Gasitel) ★★

Off Lenin Avenue on bank of Volga River, about 2 km north of Point 5

On the site of a perilous river crossing, a tower and fire-extinguishing ship (sunk in battle and raised from the river bottom) celebrate the men and motley fleet of the Volga flotilla that evacuated citizens across the river on the "Road of Life."

7. Central River Crossing of the 62nd Army
(Centralnaya Pereprave Shesbesat DVA) ★★

At Embankment of the 62nd Army near Gagarin Street

At the central defense position of the famed Soviet 62nd Army are a replica warship and sailors monument. Without this precarious riverbank stronghold, the Volga couldn't have been kept open to Soviet traffic. Although the Wehrmacht continually rained explosives on the site from the hilltop barely 100 yards inland, it never succeeded in taking the position. This is a good place to get open views of the Volga and appreciate the terrifying proximity of front lines during the battle.

8. Panorama of Stalingrad/Museum of the
Defense/Flour Mill (Panorama) ★★★★

Chuikov Embankment 47 (at Muzey Oborony Stalingrada)
T: 8442-34-6723
Daily, 10 a.m.-5 p.m. (closed Monday)
Adult: 50 rubles; Student/Child: 25 rubles

This major museum chronicles the Battle of Stalingrad with modern exhibits ranging from weaponry to photos, maps, relics and more. High points include a large model of the ruins of Stalingrad and rifle belonging to sniper Vasili Zaitsev (see Point 11). Personal effects of leading Soviet figures are displayed in the Hall of Glory. General G.A. Glazkov died with 168 bullet wounds in his body—his bullet-ridden death jacket offers stunning testimony to the violence of the battle. Up a circular staircase (no elevator) to the height of seven stories, the 360-degree Panorama covers a canvas measuring 400 feet around and 50 feet high. The awesome artistic rendering re-creates the Soviet capture of Mamaev Mound on January 26, 1943.

Along Embankment Chuikov (the road leading to the Panorama and Museum) are a succession of memorials, including a roadside tank turret (one of 17 such turrets scattered along the riverfront indicating the line of German advance) and large statue of General Vasili Chuikov.

9. Mamaev Mound (Mamaev Kurgan)
★★★★★

Entry on Lenin Avenue (at Mamaev Kurgan tram stop)

Symbols of Soviet glory don't come any more glorious, or Soviet, than this. Standing 236 feet high with a 36-foot sword raised above her head (from heel to head the Statue of Liberty is 111 feet high), the mammoth Mother Russia statue atop Mamaev Mound is famed throughout the country. For four months, the hill was the scene of inhuman battle, its peak and slopes changing hands frequently. The historic walk uphill (from Lenin Avenue) is flanked by large allegorical sculptures and relief carvings depicting battle scenes.

Audio loops of battle sounds and martial music dramatize the walk. Moving uphill, beyond the Square of Heroes, an enormous wall depicting smiling soldiers is dedicated to victory in battle. Inside the Golden Hall Memorial to the Fallen are an honor guard, an eternal flame, gold-mosaic walls, mournful music and the names of 7,200 Soviet soldiers representing 600,000 Russian troops killed at Stalingrad. Beneath Mother Russia at least 35,000 bodies are buried in a common grave.

10. Breakthrough Tank ★

On unnamed road linking Mamaev Mound with Rostov Highway, 2 km west of Point 9

On a roadside pedestal sits the first tank of the counter-offensive to break through the German lines at Stalingrad, at roughly this spot, January 26, 1943.

11. Red October Steel Foundry (Krasny Oktiabr) ★★

Off Lenin Avenue, 6 km north of city center

This key battle point—held under constant duress by indefatigable Siberian troops—still functions as a (rebuilt) steel factory. It's not open to the public, but is of interest for several reasons, not the least being famed Russian sharpshooter Vasili Zaitsev. Stalingrad spawned endless legends of heroism, none more famous than the supposed sniper duel around the Red October foundry between Zaitsev and a German rival alternately identified as master sniper Heinz Thorvald and a "Major Koenig" from Berlin. Dramatized in the book and 2001 film *Enemy at the Gates*, the duel probably never took place—story discrepancies and lack of records suggest it was simply a brilliant invention of Soviet propaganda. In his mid-20s during the war, Zaitsev was a real sniper, an extraordinary camouflage expert said to have killed 200 Germans. If nothing else, the legend he either earned or had conferred upon him at this factory (some versions place the action at the Tractor Works, Point 13) epitomizes the many tense sniper battles amid the ruins of the city that have come to characterize much of the fighting in Stalingrad.

About a half-km in front of the factory, along Metallurga Street, a dramatic, outsized sculpture of Mikhail Panikacho depicts the young partisan engulfed in flames. He burned to death after destroying a German tank with Molotov cocktails.

12. Liudnikov's "Island" and Barrikady Factory (Ostrov Liudnikova) ★★

Off Lenin Avenue in Nizhny neighborhood. From Lenin Avenue, take road toward river paralleling southern side of Barrikady Factory, then turn left (north) on road paralleling river. The ruins are next to the SC Rotor soccer team's practice field.

On a narrow patch of riverbank stands the burned-out brick wreck of the building used as headquarters by Colonel-General Ivan Liudnikov and the 138th Infantry Division. Occupied on October 16, 1942, the position was surrounded by Germans and completely cut off on November 11. Despite thousands of Soviet deaths, it was never overrun. Nearby mounds (bordered by concrete) signify common graves of the 138th. Closed to the public, the immense and still-functioning Barrikady factory was a major battle area.

13. Tractor Works (Traktorny Zavod) ★★

Off Lenin Avenue, 16 km north of city center

Probably the most famous of Stalingrad's factory battlefields—it provided the setting for part of the sniper duel in the film *Enemy at the Gates*—was contested in sustained room-to-room fighting, yet never completely captured by the Germans. In front is a statue of factory founder Felix Dzerzhinsky, infamous butcher of the Soviet Revolution—responsible for the deaths of perhaps millions of anti-Soviet Russians—who also founded the intelligence organization that would become the KGB. There's a small factory museum inside with a minor section devoted to World War II. The only reason to see the museum is to get inside the factory (otherwise closed) for a look around the rebuilt premises. Museum visits must be prearranged—contact Three Whales travel agency (page 137).

RELATED SITES BEYOND VOLGOGRAD

Meeting of the Fronts Monument at Kalach/Don River ★★

About 90 km west of Stalingrad, off highway from Stalingrad to Rostov, turn left at sign for village of Piatimorsk (a few kilometers before Kalach). Proceed through village. Pass Lenin statue (2.2 km from highway turnoff), veer left after another 0.5 km, right after 0.2 km and straight to monument at river bank.

This 70-foot-tall sculpture depicts four intrepid soldiers—tankist, pilot, infantryman, trumpeter—at the spot where the Russian encirclement of the German 6th Army was completed on January 23, 1943. The event spelled doom for Germany, but didn't come without cost to Russia.

According to the United Press, the steppe was "strewn with ... gun carriages, wrecked tanks, guns, (dead horses) and no end of corpses. Kalach was a shambles." Minus the carnage, the steppe is little changed. Up the highway about 16 km (beyond Kalach, toward Rostov), the road crosses the scenic Don River. Atop the rise across the bridge is a small memorial to Soviet pilots in the battle. There are great views of the battlefield from heights used by Soviet scouts. It's a long haul from Stalingrad through ramshackle rural settlements, but the drive provides a glimpse of the trackless and undeveloped landscape that so vexed the Wehrmacht on its exhausting push through Russia.

GETTING TO/AROUND VOLGOGRAD

For Russia visa and travel information, see Getting To/Around Moscow (page 136).

Volgograd is reached from Moscow via a 90-minute direct flight offered by Aeroflot (8442-36-2948 in Volgograd, 095-753-5555 in Moscow; 212-245-1100 in New York) or Volga Air (8442-36-3063 or 8442-33-5966). From the airport, mini-buses (7 rubles) leave every half-hour for the 20- to 30-minute drive to the city center. Taxis also available for about $20-$25 to town.

Trains for Volgograd depart from Moscow's Paletsky Station. The 1,000-km journey can take up to 24 hours.

Volgograd's city center is walkable. A street trolley (3 or 4 rubles, depending on destination) runs along the 25-km-long main thoroughfare of Lenin Avenue, with a stop at Mamaev Mound on the route. Taxis are plentiful—some have meters, some require negotiation.

Of countries covered in this book, Russia presents the biggest challenge to the independent traveler seeking World War II sites. A guide service makes sense in Russia. See page 137 for information on Moscow-based Three Whales travel agency.

ACCOMMODATIONS

Hotel Intourist

Mira St. 14
T: 8442-33-7713 F: 8442-36-1648
98 rooms
$155-317

Volgograd's top hotel is just across from the Alley of Heroes and within walking distance of good restaurants. It has its own upscale European/Russian restaurant, with elegant lobby and public areas to match. Air-conditioned.

Hotel Volgograd

Mira St. 12
T: 8442-40-8030 F: 8442-40-8033
www.hotelvolgograd.ru
173 rooms
$110-160

The rooms here are spacious and air-conditioned, with decent bathrooms. The restaurant isn't bad, but it's best for the good breakfast buffet (included in the price of most rooms).

19

Norway

Kristiansand

THE WAR YEARS

Even as 71 warships were advancing on five Norwegian towns in the early morning hours of April 9, 1940, it wasn't clear to Norway who the enemy was. By the time the Norwegians realized Germany—not Britain—had unleashed its army, navy and air force in history's first combined land-sea-air operation, the occupation had begun. Incredulous and unorganized, the Norwegian military put up brave but scattered resistance. Before noon, Germany had occupied Norway—and Denmark—in one precise, overwhelming operation.

For Germany, Scandinavia's importance was clear: access to 1,200 miles of western coastline from which an attack on Britain might be launched (or an attack from Britain repelled) and control of the iron-ore railway that ran from the mines of northern Sweden to the port of Narvik. These points had not gone unnoticed by Winston Churchill, Britain's First Lord of the Admiralty, who believed that by cutting off Germany from the raw materials crucial for artillery production the war would be over within months. To stop shipments from Narvik to Germany, Britain had been mining the Norwegian coast—Churchill even had his own April invasion plan ready. Bitter after losing the race to secure the country, Churchill later railed about a Norwegian policy he'd felt compelled to violate: "The strict observance of neutrality by Norway has been a contributory cause to the sufferings to which she is now exposed and to the limits of the aid which we can give her."

Outnumbered and outmaneuvered by invasion forces, Norway's military gave up on all areas except Trondheim. Though British support troops landed near the crucial port on April 14, the operation was plagued by what historian François Kersaudy called baffling deficiencies: "None of the plans drawn up since April 9 seemed to mention the thickness of the snow ... the troops had no snowshoes, no skis either—though in fact the soldiers would have had little use for such implements, since most had never seen a mountain in their lives." Unable to crack Germany's hold on southern and central Norway, the Allies evacuated on May 2. Eight days later, Winston Churchill replaced Neville Chamberlain as British prime minister.

In the north, the battle continued. Although Germany suffered considerable losses at Narvik in ferocious naval clashes April 10-13 (the first major Anglo-German military exchanges of the war), they continued to hold the city. By April 24, 25,000 Allied troops had landed nearby for a final assault. On May 27, British, Polish and French troops captured the town after a fierce land battle. But with Germany overrunning the Netherlands, Belgium and Luxembourg, and an attack on Great Britain imminent, the Allies could no longer afford to fight in Norway. By June 8, they'd be gone—though not before sabotaging Narvik's port and railway. For the Norwegians, they left 3,000 rifles and some ammunition.

Norway's political situation was just as unsettled. On the evening of invasion day, Norwegian anti-Communist leader Vidkun Quisling made a radio announcement explaining why Germany had "offered its assistance" to the government. That the government's highest-ranking members, including King Håkon VII, had already fled Oslo wasn't mentioned by Quisling, who had secretly met Hitler before the war to offer assistance in fighting Soviet encroachment in Scandinavia. For his help, Quisling was named prime minister upon occupation (his name later entered into the English language as a synonym for traitor). But the fugitive king's refusal to accede to German demands and remotely "appoint" Quisling ensured the fascist's traitorous reputation among the Norwegian people, forcing Hitler to demote him a week later in favor of Josef Terboven, one of his loyal German henchmen. Quisling would nevertheless play an important role in Norway's wartime Administrative Council.

Norwegians enjoyed the dubious distinction of being regarded by the Nazis as kindred Aryan brethren—as a result, their wartime domestic life was mild compared to that of other German-occupied countries. Still, the vast majority of Norwegians refused to cooperate with occupation directives. As the war dragged on and Germany ruthlessly plundered the country's resources, standards of living declined. Food rationing became severe. A full third of national income went to pay occupation costs.

The king's passionate rejection of the occupation added fuel to the Norwegians' contempt for Nazification. From exile in London, he would throughout the war help direct one of the bravest resistance movements of World War II. Underground intelligence groups, clandestine newspapers and raids by Norwegian resistance fighters and British commandos pestered Germany throughout the war. Among the most famous acts of resistance were operations at the Norsk Hydro plant at Rjukan. A pair of daring special operations raids in February 1943 and subsequent U.S. air bombardment knocked out the plant's production of heavy water, a hydrogen byproduct and critical ingredient in Germany's nascent atomic-bomb program.

After Finland made peace with the Soviets in August 1944, the Red Army began a push along the Finnish border into northern Norway, trailing 200,000 retreating German troops. On October 25, the Soviets captured Kirkenes, making it the first Norwegian town to be liberated. During their retreat, the Germans applied a scorched-earth policy to all of northern Finland and Norway that terrorized villagers and burned entire towns. Immediately after Germany surrendered in Norway on May 7, 1945, Terboven committed suicide. Quisling was executed within months. Welcomed by throngs of adoring countrymen, King Håkon VII returned to Oslo on June 7.

Although occupation of Norway ensured access to iron ore and increased Hitler's military prestige, most historians conclude the invasion and occupation were disastrous for Germany. The Narvik battles alone cut Germany's naval fleet in half, and Hitler's gross over-fortification of the country—400,000 troops and 350 coastal batteries—forced him to divert supplies from more important operations, including an attack on Great Britain, which Norway's seizure was intended to facilitate.

SOURCES & OTHER READING

Hitler's Arctic War: The German Campaign in Norway, Finland and the U.S.S.R. 1940-1945, Mann and Jörgensen, Thomas Dunne Books, 2002

Norway 1940, Kersaudy, Francois, Bison Books, 1987

Assault in Norway: Sabotaging the Nazi Nuclear Program, Gallagher, Thomas, The Lyons Press, 1975

Report From #24, Sonsteby, Gunnar, Barricade Books, 1965

War and Innocence: A Young Girl's Life in Occupied Norway (1940-1945), Helmersen, Hanna Åsvik, Hara Publishing Group, 1999

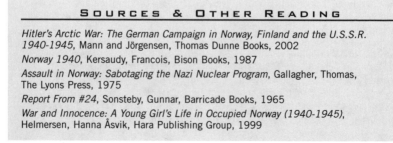

N

250 KM

HAMMERFEST

ALTA

KIRKENES

TROMSØ

HARSTAD

RUSSIA

Lofoten Islands

NARVIK
⓭-⓮

NORWEGIAN SEA

SVOLVÆR

BODØ
ROGNAN

⓫-⓬
TRONDHEIM

SWEDEN

FINLAND

GULF OF BOTHNIA

NORWAY

❽-❿
BERGEN

❺-❻

❶-❹

RJUKAN

OSLO

❼
KRISTIANSAND

NORTH SEA

Norway

1. Norwegian Resistance Museum
2. Armed Forces Museum
3. City Hall Resistance Mural/Oslo City Hall
4. Oscarsborg Fortress
5. Industrial Workers Museum at Vemork
6. *Ammonia* Ferry
7. Kannonmuseum
8. Theta Museum
9. Mt. Fløyen Resistance Monuments
10. Bergen Maritime Museum
11. Army and Resistance Museum
12. Falstad Museum and Memorial
13. Norway Red Cross War Memorial Museum
14. Peace Cemetery and Chapel

NORWAY TODAY

Population: 4.5 million • Country Code: 47 • 1 krone = $0.17/£0.85/€0.125

Though Norway's cities and villages are clean, charming and full of impossibly friendly people, tourists come here for its wildly diverse terrain. The dramatic western fjords, between Bergen and Trondheim, anchor Norway's tourism industry, drawing visitors by the boatload. There are islands and sandy beaches in the south. The country's gorgeous (and overlooked) alpine interior offers fine skiing and hiking, most notably in Telemark county. Above the Arctic Circle, densely forested inlets in the south give way to expanses of stark, rocky shore in the far north.

Because they weren't obliterated by German bombs, cities and towns in southern Norway have predictable markers of Old Europe—large cathedrals, busy town squares, charming main streets. In the far north, oddly juxtaposed amid tracts of

undeveloped, primitive landscape, Narvik, Kirkenes and Hammerfest, targets of some of the war's most destructive attacks, have been rebuilt into thoroughly modern towns. The ravages of World War II fostered a renewed pride among Norwegians in the natural beauty of their country. Today Norway is arguably the "greenest" nation in the world, with stringent anti-pollution laws and general appreciation for environmental protection (though Norway does allow commercial whaling, a policy that draws the ire of other European nations but speaks to an independence this non-E.U. country cherishes).

A visit to the widely scattered sites below takes a minimum of 10 days. Add a tour of the western fjords and at least two weeks are required to adequately cover this majestic country.

POINTS OF INTEREST

Oslo

1. Norwegian Resistance Museum (Norges Hjemmefrontmuseum) ★★★★

Bygning, 21. Akershus Fortress complex, central Oslo waterfront
T: 23-09-3138
Daily, 10 a.m.-4 p.m., June-August (open 11 a.m. Sundays)
Daily, 10 a.m.-4 p.m., September-May (open 11 a.m. Sundays)
Adult: 30kr; Child: 15kr

An excellent introduction to wartime Norway, this dark, labyrinthine museum is located on the grounds of Oslo's 14th-century, coastal-defense Akershus Fortress, used by Germans to torture Norwegian war prisoners. Among dozens of moving, well-organized displays are push-button sound clips of Hitler and Churchill, and Quisling's April 9, 1940, grating speech proclaiming

himself leader. Effective dioramas provide geographical perspective on the obliteration of coastal villages and battles of Narvik. Outside is a small courtyard where 42 Norwegians were executed during the war. An unassuming statue of U.S. President Franklin Roosevelt stands 100 yards west of the museum, near the water.

2. Armed Forces Museum (Forsvarmuseet) ★

Akershus Fortress complex, central Oslo waterfront
T: 23-09-3570
Weekdays, 10 a.m.-5 p.m., weekends, 11 a.m.-5 p.m., June-August
Weekdays, 11 a.m.-5 p.m., weekends, 11 a.m.-4 p.m., September-April (closed Mondays)
Closed Easter, December 24-26, 31, January 1

Battlefield dioramas, dozens of weapons

and department-store mannequins in authentic uniforms—exhibits here are mostly disappointing, but perhaps the dismal state of a museum dedicated to the military history of a historically neutral country shouldn't come as a surprise.

3. City Hall Resistance Mural/Oslo City Hall (Radhuset i Oslo) ★★

Town center, west of Akershus Fortress, at Radhusgata and Roald Amundsen's Gate
T: 23-46-1600
Daily, 9 a.m.-5 p.m., May-August
(closed 4 p.m. September-April)

Immense murals depicting Norwegian achievement ornament the large, light-filled lobby of Oslo's modernistic city hall. The dramatic east-wall mural "War and Occupation" honors the resistance.

4. Oscarsborg Fortress ★★

In Drøbak, 25 km south of Oslo. Boat tours depart from the Drøbak tourist office at Havnegata 4.
T: 64-90-4161
Weekdays, 12:30 p.m. and 4:15 p.m.; weekends, noon and 2:30 p.m., June-August
Adult: 50kr; Child: 25kr

The most important Norwegian victory of the war came on April 9, 1940, with the unlikely sinking of the German heavy cruiser *Blücher* in Oslofjord—achieved with a cannon built in 1893 and fired from this fort. About 1,000 German sailors were killed when the ship sank—many jumped overboard only to be burned alive by flaming oil. The strike allowed King Håkon VII to escape Oslo and mobilize the country's defense from London. The boat tour to and from the small island from which the shots came (a museum is housed within the fortress) takes 2.5 hours.

Rjukan

5. Industrial Workers Museum at Vemork (Norsk Industriarbeidermuseum) ★★★★

3660 Rjukan, Vemork; 7 km north of Rjukan
T: 35-09-9000
Daily, 10 a.m.-4 p.m., May-September

(closed at 6 p.m. mid-June-mid-August)
Weekends only, 11 a.m.-4 p.m., October
Closed November-April, May 17, December 24-26, December 31
Adult: 65kr; Senior/Student: 55kr; Child (up to 15): 35kr

Set against a steep, forested hillside, the former Norsk Hydro plant can be accessed only by narrow road—and over an even narrower suspension bridge spanning the V-shaped valley—that terminates in front of the plant's stark but stylized façade. Though the museum is dedicated to Norway's industrial workers, its main draw is an exhibit on the plant's role in Germany's atomic-bomb program. In 1940, this was the world's largest hydro-gen factory, targeted for seizure by Germany well before the invasion because of the heavy-water byproduct produced here (crucial for making an atomic bomb). Allied attempts to dismantle the program included commando raids by British and Norwegian saboteurs who, after descend-ing the steep hill above the plant under cover of darkness, placed explosive charges on the main container of heavy water and destroyed it. They then made a daring (and, considering the number of German troops stationed at the plant, improbable) escape up the opposite hill-side into the relative safety of the moun-tains. The small but excellent exhibit on heavy water and the raids—which inspired the 1965 Kirk Douglas film *The Heroes of Telemark*—has effective displays, film clips and a short propaganda-style film, *If Hitler Had the Bomb.*

6. *Ammonia* Ferry ★★★

In Mael on Highway 40, 3 km east of Rjukan
At press time the *Ammonia* was closed due to lack of funding. To check on its status, call the Rjukan tourist office (located at Torget 2) at 35-09-1290.

On the night of February 20, 1944, Allied-backed saboteurs exploded the ferry *Hydro* as it carried stores of heavy water the Germans were attempting to evacuate. The explosion killed four German soldiers and 14 Norwegian civilians—all the heavy water was sunk. The Mael ferry stop is home to the *Ammonia*, the sister ship of the *Hydro* and a near replica.

Kristiansand

7. Kannonmuseum ★★★

In Møvig, 7 km west of Kristiansand. Take Highway 456, then Highway 457. Or, far easier, take Bus 01 from Kristiansand's main bus terminal.
T: 38-08-5090
Daily, 11 a.m.-6 p.m., mid-June-mid-August
Monday-Wednesday, 11 a.m.-3 p.m., Thursday-Sunday, 11 a.m.-5 p.m., May-mid-June, mid-August-September
50kr

This immense German coastal gun required a crew of 55 men—10 alone were needed to load the 1,700-pound shell, which could reach a target more than 32 miles away. The immaculately preserved and fully accessible gun battery comprises a rail track and cranes used for lifting the massive shell into the cannon. The bunker museum contains the dozens of pieces of equipment required to fire a single round. Near the gun, ruins of a casemate offer impressive views of the Kristiansand area.

Bergen

8. Theta Museum (Thetamuseum) ★★★

Enhjørningsgården, in the Bryggen. The museum is hidden on the third floor of the building with the unicorn in front, above a restaurant. Call the tourist office (55-55-2000) for specific directions.
T: 55-31-5393
Tuesday, Saturday, Sunday, 2 p.m.-4 p.m., mid-May-mid-September
Adult: 20kr; Child: 5kr

The smallest museum in Norway occupies the former headquarters of the underground resistance group "Theta," which for two years worked to transmit intelligence to England from a storeroom along the waterfront. Theta was discovered when a German soldier fell through the ceiling while searching the building. Lucky for the soldier he didn't come through the ingen-

iously booby-trapped door that would trip an explosion if opened. The museum is an exact re-creation of the original room, with period equipment and furnishings—and a replica of the door device.

9. Mt. Fløyen Resistance Monuments ★

Mt. Fløyen is accessed by the Fløibanen Cable Car, Vetrlidsalmenningen 21
Sunrise-midnight in summer
(to 11 p.m. rest of the year)
Adult: 50kr; Child: 25kr

Mt. Fløyen offers spectacular views of the entire city. At the summit is a monument to Norwegian athletes who died in World War II. Another war memorial is on the Route 5 road down the hill.

10. Bergen Maritime Museum (Bergens Sjøfartmuseum) ★★

15 Håkon Sheteligs Plass, near town center
T: 55-54-9600
Daily, 11 a.m.-3 p.m., June-August
Sunday-Friday, 11 a.m.-2 p.m., September-May
Adult: 30kr; Student/Child: Free

The museum offers detailed models and compelling video displays on the Shetland Bus (a route used for transporting supplies and personnel from Bergen to Britain's Shetland Islands), German attacks on Arctic Ocean supply convoys and documentary footage of the liberation.

Trondheim

11. Army and Resistance Museum (Rustkammeret med Hjemmefrontmuseet) ★★

West wing of Archbishop's Palace, at Prinsens Gate and Bispegata
T: 73-99-5280
Weekdays, 9 a.m.-3 p.m., weekends, 11 a.m.-4 p.m., June-August
Weekends only, 11 a.m.-4 p.m., September-October, March-May
Closed November-February

The second floor of the museum in the 12th-century Archbishop's Palace is dedicated to the resistance and includes information on the many attempts to sink the *Tirpitz*, a battleship the Germans went to almost laughable lengths to hide in a fjord. There's also an exhibit on Nazi sympathizers.

12. Falstad Museum and Memorial ★★

In Levanger, on Highway E6, 50 km northeast of Trondheim
T: 74-02-8040
Tuesday-Sunday, noon-4 p.m., May-August
Adult: 35kr; Student/Child: 25kr

Norway's largest World War II prison camp, Falstad held 5,000 prisoners between 1941 and 1945, including 50 Trondheim Jews later transported to Auschwitz. (About 700 Norwegian Jews died in Nazi concentration camps during the war.) After the liberation, the camp held Norwegian Nazis. The museum is located in the Falstad Building's basement and torture chamber. At least 220 POWs, mostly of Russian and Yugoslavian descent, were executed in the spruce forest near Falstad—their names are listed on a cenotaph there.

Narvik

13. Norway Red Cross War Memorial Museum (Nordland Røde Kors Krigsminnermuseum) ★★★★

Daily, 11 a.m.-5 p.m., March-June
Daily, 10 a.m.-2 p.m., June-mid-August
Daily, 10 a.m.-4 p.m., mid-August-September
By appointment rest of year, or try ringing the bell during off-season.
T: 76-94-4426
Adult: 40kr; Child: 10kr

Visits begin with an excellent film (crude yet effective computer animation) recounting battles for Narvik. The large museum overflows with photographs so compelling that you have to remind yourself to also take in the impressive collection of uniforms, propaganda posters and weaponry. Photos document the extensive destruction of Narvik and mass evacuation of the area. A major museum expansion was completed in 2004.

14. Peace Cemetery and Chapel ★★★

From Point 13, follow Kongensgate 3.5 km from the museum, over the railroad where the road turns into highway E6. About 450 yards past the railroad, look for cemetery on right.

In this picturesque cemetery overlooking the town and fjord, French soldiers are buried 10 yards to the right of the front gate; the Polish and British section is 50 yards in and 10 yards to the right. Fifty yards to the left of the gate is a large Norwegian section marked by dozens of rustic, stylized crosses.

Sites Above the Arctic Circle

From dozens of local war museums to remains of German-built coastal fortifications, remote northern Norway—where the bulk of combat occurred—offers the most fascinating collection of sites in the country. Highlights are listed geographically, roughly from south to north. For a comprehensive survey of World War II sites above the Arctic Circle, visit www.arcticwar.com, an excellent website maintained by World War II enthusiast Lars Gyllenhål. "Holiday Guides" on Nordland, Troms and Finnmark, available from the Norwegian Tourist Board (212-885-9700 in New York), are also helpful.

Nordland county

In **Rognan ★★★**, the Saltdal Museum or Blood Road Museum (T: 75-69-0060); Monday-Friday, 10 a.m.-3:30 p.m.; Saturday 1-4 p.m.; Sunday: 1-6 p.m.; Adult: 30kr) is dedicated to Russian, Polish and Serbian POWs who helped build a section of the Arctic Highway, now known as the Blood Road, from Saltnes to Saksenvik. There are war cemeteries in Botn and memorials in Stamnes, Sundby, Røkland and Storjord. In **Bodø ★★**, the Norwegian Aviation Museum (T: 75-50-7850) has two large exhibition halls, one dedicated to about 20 military aircraft.

The handful of World War II airplanes include a Gloster Gladiator II, Supermarine Spitfire, Junkers JU-88 and North American T-6 Harvard. In **Svolvær ★★★** in the Lofoten Islands, the excellent War Memorial Museum (T: 91-73-0328) has an extensive collection of uniforms and an exhibit on a British commando raid on Lofoten. In **Rombaksbotn ★★★**, the wreck of German destroyer *Georg Thiele* lies partly out of the water. In **Bjørnfjell ★★**, German commander Eduard Dietl's home and headquarters during the battles at Narvik remain in excellent condition. In **Bjerkvik ★** stands a monument to civilians accidentally killed by British fighter pilots.

Troms county

In **Harstad ★★★★**, the magnificent Adolf Gun (77-01-8989) on the coast is one of the largest cannons in the world. In **Senja ★★**, four guns remain at Skrolsvik Fortress. Nearby is a coastal-defense museum. In **Tromsø ★★**, the port from which King Håkon VII sailed to London on the day before the 1940 German invasion, the Military Museum (T: 77-62-8540 or 77-62-8836) is based around six restored German cannons.

Finnmark county

In **Alta ★★★**, the Alta Museum (T: 78-45-6330) offers information on the *Tirpitz*, which the Germans hid in Altafjord, as well as bunkers and artillery emplacements on the Arctic Highway. There's a Soviet cemetery at Tommernes. In **Hammerfest ★★**, the Museum of Post-War Reconstruction (T: 78-42-2630) is dedicated to the thousands of Norwegians displaced by German bombing in the north. **Kirkenes ★★★** has German bunkers in and around the town, which saw some of the most destructive bombing of World War II. Near the town center are monuments honoring Kirkenes' war mothers and Soviet liberators. The Frontier Museum has a World War II exhibit. In **Bjørnevatn ★★**, tunnels once used to house displaced Kirkenes civilians are accessible to the public.

RELATED SITES BEYOND NORWAY

See Auxiliary Sites, Finland (page 235).

OTHER AREA ATTRACTIONS

Fjords

Norway's foremost attraction, the glacier-carved western fjords, provide some of the most breathtaking views in Europe. The most popular are the narrow Hardangerfjord, the sheer, towering and relatively diminutive Geirangerfjord and the 120-mile-long and stereotypically majestic Sognefjord, Norway's longest and deepest. The tourist office in Bergen (55-55-2000), a good starting point for fjord excursions, offers a number of tours, including the popular "Norway in a Nutshell," which whisks visitors in and around the fjords during a seven-hour tour (about 580kr) that includes a breathtaking ride on the Flåmsbana, one of the steepest railways in the world.

GETTING TO/AROUND NORWAY

Scandinavian Airlines (800-221-2350 in U.S.) and its subsidiaries Bråthens (81-52-0000) and Widerøe (81-00-1200) offer a wide range of flights to and throughout Norway. Kato Airlines (76-98-1385) offers flights from Bodø to Narvik. Though Kato's prop plane has an exemplary safety record, turbulence associated with entering Vestjorden and Ofotfjorden can make the trip loud and disconcerting.

The very terrain that makes Norway so scenic forces travelers to consider all manner of transportation during a tour of the country. It's best to start in Oslo and drive (though car rental is very expensive, see Driving, page xv) or bus to Rjukan. From here it's possible to drive to Kristiansand via Kongsberg, then drive or train (about 400kr) to Stavanger. Between Stavanger and Bergen, travelers are forced to contend with the western fjords. Flaggruten (55-23-8780) offers a four-hour coastal boat ride from Stavanger to Bergen (600kr). The popular Bergen-based Hurtigrute coastal cruise (81-03-0000) calls on Trondheim before terminating in Kirkenes in the far north. The round trip takes 11 days and costs between 10,000kr and 25,000kr. Airfare from Bergen to Trondheim is about 2,400kr.

Accommodations

Oslo

Thon Hotel Europa

St. Olavs Gate 31
www.thonhotels.no/europa
T: 23-25-6300 F: 23-25-6363
167 rooms
From 790kr

Inexpensive rooms within walking distance of the Resistance Museum, the king's palace and town center. Completely refurbished in 1995. Good restaurant and bar.

Rjukan

Park Hotel

Sam Eydes Gate 67
www.parkhotell-rjukan.no
T: 35-08-2188 F: 35-08-2189
39 rooms
645-995kr

Across the street from the bus station, this is the best choice within the town limits. Friendly staff, enjoyable restaurant and bar.

Kristiansand

Hotel Clarion Ernst

Rådhusgaten 2
www.ernst.no
T: 38-12-8600 F: 38-02-0307
135 rooms
645-995kr

The Ernst was used as the Germans' Kristiansand headquarters during the war. Rooms here vary in size. There's a free internet station near the front desk.

Bergen

Thon Hotel Rosenkrantz

Rosenkrantzgate 7
www.thonhotels.no/rosenkrantz
T: 55-30-1400 F: 55-31-1476
129 rooms
From 1295kr

This property is within easy walking distance of all major attractions. Spacious rooms, good breakfast buffet, cozy bar and (sometimes) lively nightclub.

Trondheim

Britannia Hotel

Dronningensgt. 5
www.britannia.no
T: 73-80-0800 F: 73-80-0801
247 rooms
From 1650kr

Trondheim's first great luxury hotel is now a solid, business-class property in the center of town. Rooms are comfortable and up to date. The breakfast buffet is included with the price of most rooms.

Narvik

Radisson SAS

Kongensgate 64
www.radissonsas.com
T: 76-97-7000 F: 76-97-7007
165 rooms
From 1,000kr

The former Grand Hotel was the only building in the city center to survive German bombing. Rooms are small but modern.

20

Netherlands

Operation Market-Garden

John Frost Bridge, Arnhem

THE WAR YEARS

I t began as a dream, besotted by wild ambition. In September 1944, the Allied rout in Normandy complete, Germany's army was retreating faster than the Allies could chase it. With a final push, it seemed, five years of war in Europe could be over by Christmas.

The architect of the dream, and the bold plan that sprang from it—Operation Market-Garden (OMG)—was Great Britain's most successful and controversial general, Field Marshal Bernard Montgomery. Sensing German collapse, the 56-year-old "Monty" looked at the Allied forces in recently liberated Belgium and saw the instrument of Germany's ultimate demise. To the north, in the occupied Netherlands—on May 10, 1940, Germany had invaded and easily overrun its neighbor—Montgomery believed a concentrated blow against the Wehrmacht could open a path across the Rhine river into Germany. All the Allies needed was control of 60 miles of road (linked by 20 bridges) to conclude the war and, not incidentally, win indisputable acclaim for Montgomery.

With Germany's defeat *fait accompli*, this was a time when reputations would be sealed, legends made. But Montgomery's "single thrust" strategy contradicted Supreme Allied Commander Dwight Eisenhower's "broad front" strategy against Germany. Eisenhower questioned Montgomery's case for a "rapier-like thrust." Rival American generals Omar Bradley and George Patton, who considered Montgomery inept, privately joked about Monty's "butter-knife thrust."

Ultimately, Eisenhower approved Montgomery's daring plan to drop airborne troops far behind enemy lines to secure bridges and clear the way for British forces already in Belgium to advance into Germany. The plan would involve the largest use of airborne troops in history—20,000 paratroopers (Americans, British and Poles) dropping into occupied territory at three zones—the U.S. 82nd Airborne near Grave and Groesbeek, U.S. 101st Airborne near Eindhoven and Veghel, 1st British Airborne and 1st Polish Parachute Brigade near Arnhem. Like links in a chain, each bridge was as important as the next. Nevertheless, failure at the farthest bridge at Arnhem would lend itself to the idea that the campaign had reached "a bridge too far," a phrase uttered by a British officer and popularized by Cornelius Ryan in his book (and subsequent film) of the same name.

OMG began on September 17, 1944, with the arrival of a massive "skytrain" over the Netherlands. As Allied paratroopers descended against a bright blue sky, locals, believing liberation was at hand, launched into raucous celebrations. Soldiers were met with beer and kisses. The Germans were caught flat-footed. Americans captured bridges at Eindhoven, Veghel, Grave and other points. Soon, though, events began to turn against the Allies.

Historians debate reasons for the failure of OMG—poor intelligence, bad weather (after the first day), insufficient troop strength, inoperable radios, lack of supplies and simple bad luck. Overriding all, however, was the masterful response of the still vigorous German military. At Arnhem, German troops were commanded by the ruthless Field Marshal Walther Model—"Can't that be done faster?" was a pet phrase. After the shock of the Allied landings, Model formed a quick appreciation of the unfolding scenario. (In this he was later aided by full OMG plans recovered from a downed glider.) Employing an SS panzer corps at Arnhem, he directed a remarkable if piecemeal defense. At Son, a handful of German trainees blew the bridge, causing major delays. North of Eindhoven, terrible fighting along the road earned it the nickname "Hell's Highway." At Nijmegen, American troops took the bridge only after a costly frontal assault in frail canvas rowboats.

The worst fight took place at Arnhem, where about 600 British soldiers under the unflappable Lieutenant-Colonel John Frost (portrayed by Anthony Hopkins in the film *A Bridge Too Far*) captured and held the north end of the bridge. In a series of violent assaults, both British and Germans attempted to capture the opposite ends. One eyewitness described the scene as "screeching shells, fire-spouting tanks, strafing planes, sleepless nights, foodless days." Due to poor weather and nonexistent communications, less than 10 percent of the supplies meant for the lightly equipped British paratroopers reached them. Still, Frost contemptuously refused a German surrender offer. For 88 continuous hours his men fought without relief, until finally, on September 21, their epic stand was exhausted. Arnhem was left obliterated.

"There was no formal surrender," wrote historian Stephen Badsey. "In small groups the British either ran out of ammunition or were overwhelmed." Some fought on with knives.

Of the 9,000 men dropped in the Arnhem zone, 1,500 were killed, 6,500 others—most wounded, including Frost—were taken prisoner. With Arnhem gone, the operation couldn't succeed. OMG ended on September 26 with an Allied withdrawal—16,805 men had been killed or wounded. German casualties are estimated at 2,000 killed, 6,000 wounded.

OMG, especially Arnhem, has since become a point of obsession among a core of enthusiasts, primarily British, who find in its details one of the century's great What Ifs. "If it had been won," posits OMG veteran John Waddy in his *A Tour of the Arnhem Battlefields*, "the Allied armies in 1944 might have broken into the heartland of Germany, reached Berlin before Soviet forces ... preventing the nations of Eastern Europe falling under Soviet domination." In fact, OMG was overly ambitious from the start and, as Badsey has pointed out, its timetable "only made sense if the German troops were not in fact going to fight." A foolish supposition at this stage of the war.

As for the Netherlands, much of the country would endure another miserable winter under Nazi rule, its citizens and Resistance members suffering vicious reprisals for their support of OMG. Arnhem was at last liberated by British troops of the 1st Canadian Army on April 14, 1945.

 SOURCES & OTHER READING

Arnhem 1944: Operation Market Garden, Badsey, Stephen, Osprey Publishing, 1993

Arnhem 1944: The Airborne Battle, 17-26 September, Middlebrook, Martin, Viking, 1994

The Devil's Birthday: The Bridges at Arnhem, 1944, Powell, Geoffrey, Buchan & Enright, 1984

Monty: The Lonely Leader, 1944-1945, Horne, Alistair, HarperCollins, 1994

A Bridge Too Far, Ryan, Cornelius, Hamish Hamilton, 1974

Major and Mrs Holt's Battlefield Guide to Operation Market-Garden, Holt and Holt, Leo Cooper, 2001

A Tour of the Arnhem Battlefields, Waddy, John, Leo Cooper, 1999

Netherlands (Operation Market-Garden)

1. Leopoldsburg/Sherman Tank
2. Sherman Tank
3. German War Cemetery
4. Polish Cemetery
5. Joe's Bridge
6. Liberation Monument/Commonwealth Cemetery
7. Dommel Bridge
8. 101st Airborne Division Monument/Eindhoven
9. Son Bridge
10. Airborne Soldiers Memorial
11. Wings of Liberation Museum
12. Joe Mann Memorial
13. Airborne "Kangaroo" Memorial/Taylor Headquarters
14. Grave Bridge/Monument
15. National War and Resistance Museum
16. National Liberation Museum 1944-1945
17. Nijmegen Bridge/Hunnerpark
18. River Waal Crossing Monument
19. Arnhem Oosterbeek War Cemetery
20. 21st Parachute Company Marker/Café Schnoonoord
21. Airborne Museum "Hartenstein"
22. Tafelberg House/Hotel
23. Eusebius Church
24. John Frost Bridge/Airborneplein
25. Arnhem War Museum 40-45

NETHERLANDS TODAY

Population: 16 million (Country); 135,000 (Arnhem); 147,000 (Nijmegen); (198,000) Eindhoven • Country Code: 31 • €1 = $1.36/£0.67

American World War II soldiers with experience across Europe often regarded the Dutch as the most friendly and open of all the people they encountered—the same generalization might be made today. The Netherlands is a country in which locals happily step forward to assist bewildered travelers or simply strike up conversations. English is widely spoken. In short, this is one of the most hassle-free countries to visit on the continent.

With a maritime climate, the Netherlands rarely experiences harsh temperatures. Winters are mild and though summers are warm, it can be rainy and gray, even in August. It makes sense that a country this crowded—it's Europe's most densely populated—and level would attract cyclists in throngs. Even so, the ubiquity of bicycles—more bikes than people, by one estimate—and degree to which cycling penetrates everyday life is immediately and impressively apparent.

The country's principal cities—Amsterdam, Rotterdam, the Hague—are located west and north of the OMG area, each less than two hours by car or train. Most points of interest in this chapter are located in the southern provinces of Noord Brabant and Gelderland, areas steeped in a martial history that began when Romans sacked Nijmegen in 70 A.D. Both provinces are typified by broad expanses of agricultural land blighted by islands of heavy industry.

The OMG corridor can be driven in an afternoon. Two to three days are recommended to cover all points of interest.

POINTS OF INTEREST

Listed are the high points of more than 250 OMG sites throughout the countryside. For those with a more intense interest, *Major and Mrs Holt's Battlefield Guide to Operation Market-Garden* is an indispensable guide (with a thorough map). John Waddy's *A Tour of the Arnhem Battlefields* expertly covers the Arnhem area.

1. Leopoldsburg/Sherman Tank ★★

Corner of Stationsstraat and Nicolay Laan, Leopoldsburg, Belgium

A U.S. Sherman tank sits in front of the small station. Kitty-corner is the site of the Cinema Splendid where British Lieutenant-General Brain Horrocks gave a long-winded briefing to rouse his troops. In town are signs to a Commonwealth war cemetery and, in the vicinity of a Belgian Army base, several tanks, guns, memorials and a military museum (011-34-4804, open weekdays, 1-5 p.m.) with a small OMG section.

2. Sherman Tank ★★

In Hechtel, Belgium, at intersection of N73 (called Peerderbaan here) and N175, 8 km east of Point 1

The well-preserved tank bears names of civilians and British soldiers killed during the fight for the town.

3. German War Cemetery ★★★★

In Lommel, Belgium, on N746 (near N715), 13 km from Point 2
Monday-Friday, 8 a.m.-4 p.m., Saturday-Sunday, 11 a.m.-4 p.m. (gates often remain open into the evening)

The 39,102 war graves make it the largest German World War II cemetery outside of Germany. Many of those buried here are teenagers. The majority were killed during the 1940 invasion of Belgium and battles of the Bulge, Aachen, Hürtgen Forest and Remagen. See page 8 for more on German cemeteries.

4. Polish Cemetery ★★

In Lommel, Belgium, on N175, 8 km from Point 3

This small plot contains 256 graves and a large stone monument topped by a cross.

5. Joe's Bridge ★★

On N175/715 (in Belgium), 2 km north of Point 4

On September 10, 1944, a week before OMG officially began, this bridge was seized by Irish Guards led by Lieutenant-Colonel J.O.E. Vandeleur. From here, OMG ground forces commenced the drive north. Though the site is significant, the post-war trestle-span in place today is unremarkable.

6. Liberation Monument/Commonwealth Cemetery ★★

In Valkenswaard area, on N69, 9 km north of Point 5

In front of a cafe, a five-foot-tall mosaic monument notes the "very spot the British liberators set foot on Dutch soil for the first time." Up the road a few hundred yards, the small Valkenswaard Common-wealth War Graves Commission cemetery contains 222 British soldiers.

7. Dommel Bridge ★

On N69, 3 km north of Point 6

Though unmarked, this low brick bridge over a thin stream is significant as the first bridge captured (by Irish Guards) fol-lowing the September 17 airborne drops.

8. 101st Airborne Division Monument/Eindhoven ★

On Airbornelaan at N265 exit, Eindhoven, about 5.5 km from Point 7

A wooden signboard bearing the 101st Division's famed "Screaming Eagle" insignia adorns a small roadside park, not-ing Eindhoven as the first Dutch city liber-ated, by the U.S. 506th Parachute Infantry Division (later made famous by the *Band of Brothers* book and film) and other members of the 101st Airborne. Though the capture of Eindhoven was a major American goal, there's little to see in this business and industrial city. In the center of town, the Eindhoven Liberation Monument depicts

soldiers of both occupation and liberation. From the Eindhoven train station, walk south down Demer (McDonald's on corner), turn right on Kerkstraat (at the church), then walk one block and turn left on Wal. The monument is on the left, about 150 yards down the road.

9. Son Bridge ★★

On N265, in Son, 4 km from Point 8

Son was captured by Allied troops, but not before its critical bridge was destroyed by the Germans on September 18. In an impressive feat of engineering and build-ing, a British Bailey Bridge was assembled overnight. Ground forces began crossing the 100-foot-long bridge on September 19.

10. Airborne Soldiers Memorial ★★

On Europlaan, in Son, about 1 km from Point 9. From Point 9, continue north on N265 to the traffic light in the center of Son. At the light, turn left toward Best, then right onto Europlaan. Proceed about 200 yards. Park at tennis courts on left.

This life-size figure on a pedestal depicts an intrepid soldier dragging a parachute and drawing a weapon. The village was the 101st Airborne Division Command Post during the first three days of OMG.

11. Wings of Liberation Museum ★★★★

Sonseweg 39 (along Boslaan road). 3.5 km from Point 10, off A2, in Best. From Eindhoven take A2 north, then exit 28 (Best) and follow signs to Best-centrum. After about 1.5 km, veer right at the round-about and follow signs to Son en Breugel.
T: (0)4-99-32-9722
Daily, 10 a.m.-5 p.m.
Closed December 25, 31
Adult: €6; Child (6 to 14): €3.50

One of Europe's best World War II museums, this collection encompasses eight buildings and 16 hectares. The draw is the amount of heavy equipment—air-craft, tanks, trucks, motorcycles, artillery pieces. Fascinating items include: a Russian Katyusha rocket-launcher truck, T-34 tank, mint-condition German search-light, all manner of American wartime vehicles (Ford, GMC, Dodge). The centerpiece is a pair of C-47 Dakota transport aircraft of the type that dropped airborne soldiers into OMG battle zones.

12. Joe Mann Memorial ★

Off Boslaan Road, in Son. About 150 yards (toward Best) from Point 11, turn down small road for Joe Mann Paviljoen.

A 20-foot-high memorial is named for American Medal of Honor recipient Joe Mann, who, after having been shot four times, flung his body over a German grenade, saving the lives of many around him. The monument is in the shape of a pelican, selflessly protecting her young.

13. Airborne "Kangaroo" Memorial/Taylor Headquarters ★★

At corner of Hoogstraat and Kolonel Johnsonstraat, in downtown Veghel, 19 km from Point 12

The 101st Airborne's primary role in the liberation of Veghel is recalled in the shape of a kangaroo, symbolic of troops leaping across the Netherlands' rivers and canals. Behind the monument, at 8 Hoogstraat, the two-story mansion was used as a command post by American General Maxwell Taylor. To follow the OMG advance from Veghel, take N265 (then N324) through Uden and Grave to Nijmegen.

14. Grave Bridge/Monument ★★

Off N324, in Grave, 25 km from Point 13

The Grave Bridge was captured with relative ease by elements of the U.S. 82nd Airborne on September 17. Two days later, British ground forces crossed the bridge. Today, along an access road on the southern end of the bridge is a silver monument in the shape of a parachute. With nine spans painted white, red and green (symbolizing local regions), the 650-yard-long bridge is one of OMG's more impressive. To follow the OMG route, continue to Point 17 on the main road connecting Grave, Nederasselt, Wijchen and Nijmegen.

15. National War and Resistance Museum (National Oorlogs-en-Verzetsmuseum) ★★★★

Museumpark 1, Overloon
Off A73, in Overloon, 36 km from Point 14

T: (0)4-78-64-1250
Daily, 10 a.m.-6 p.m., July-August
Daily, 10 a.m.-5 p.m., September-June
Last entry 30 minutes before closing
Closed December 24, 25, 31, January 1
Adult: €9.50; Senior: €8.50; Child (5-18): €6.50

This 35-acre park has exhibits covering the details of Dutch life in 1940-45—the occupation, resistance and campaign for liberation. Through film, text (including English) and life-size dioramas, the museum covers everything from civilian wartime privations to nearly 100 large pieces. Included are tanks (panzer, T-34, Sherman), aircraft (Spitfire, B-25) and a Bailey Bridge. A major museum.

16. National Liberation Museum 1944-45 (Nationaal Bevrijdingsmuseum 1944-45) ★★★

From the giant windmill in Groesbeek, turn onto Pennenstraat, proceed through town about 2.5 km, veer left at sign for "Golfbaan Het," then right at sign for "Wyler 3." Museum is about 200 yards down this road. About 30 km from Point 15.
Wylerbaan 4, Groesbeek
T: (0)24-397-4404
Monday-Saturday, 10 a.m.-5 p.m.
Sunday, noon-5 p.m.
Closed December 25, January 1
Adult: €8; Senior: €7; Child (7-15): €4

The unique feature of this midsize museum is its roof, built to resemble a parachute. Models, film and artifacts pertain to the occupation, liberation and post-war reconstruction.

17. Nijmegen Bridge/Hunnerpark ★★★

On N325 (near intersection with N326) at east end of Nijmegen

After prolonged fighting, the bridge at Nijmegen was taken in a magnificent direct assault (led by Robert Redford in *A Bridge Too Far*) by rowboat across the River Waal. Small monuments are scattered throughout the city, the more interesting found near the famed bridge (on N325 heading to Arnhem). Starting at the east end of Hunnerpark (intersection of St. Jorisstraat and General James Gavin

Straat), the center of the large interchange features a sculpture of Jan Van Hoof, Nijmigen's most venerated Resistance fighter. Next to the statue is a maple tree, a tribute to Canadian troops who played an important role in the city's liberation. Walking north into the park, about 100 yards from the statue, a plaque marks an OMG time capsule, to be opened in 2044. Continue north, through the brick arch, following the sign for "Belvedere." About 250 yards from the time capsule is a castle tower, which has a good view of the large bridge across the river and houses the upscale Restaurant Belvedere (024-322-6861). Stairs lead to a rusting German anti-tank gun and bridge

stanchion, upon which a plaque commemorates the British Grenadier Guards.

18. River Waal Crossing Monument ★★

From Point 17, follow N325 across the bridge toward Arnhem. Once across, take the "Lent-West" exit. Follow the exit road toward the river and, after about a km, turn right on Oosterhoutsedjik (the small road paralleling the river). Follow this road for 2 km. Location is about 5 km from Point 17.

Two stone memorials mark the point where, on September 20, 1944, American paratroopers of the 82nd Airborne Division and British Armored Guards crossed the river in their heroic attack on the bridge.

Oosterbeek

Excepting Point 19, the following sites are best reached on foot after parking at or near the Oosterbeek train station/VVV on Utrechtseweg. Parking also available at Point 21.

19. Arnhem Oosterbeek War Cemetery ★★

On Utrechtseweg, walk west toward town. After about 200 yards, a sign points to the Arnhem Oosterbeek War Cemetery, "250 meters" away. (The actual walking distance is just less than 1 km.)

In a secluded, wooded area are the graves of 1,754 mostly British soldiers. Most died near Arnhem. Maps and text describe the liberation of the Netherlands.

20. 21st Parachute Company Marker and Café Schnoonoord ★★

Intersection of Utrechtseweg and Stationsweg

A triangular marker in front of a large white house recalls the British paratroopers who fought here, almost to the last man. Kitty-corner is the cafe—with evocative battle paintings and photos inside—where a bloody medical station was located.

21. Airborne Museum "Hartenstein" ★★★

232 Utrechtseweg
From Point 20, continue west on Utrechtseweg about 300 yards.

T: (0)26-333-7710
Monday-Saturday, 10 a.m.-5 p.m., Sunday and holidays, noon-5 p.m. (open at 11 a.m. on weekdays, November-March)
Last entry 4:30 p.m.
Closed December 25, January 1
Adult: €5.50; Veteran/Senior: €4.50; Child (5-16): €3.50

In a house that served as headquarters of the British 1st Airborne Division, the museum depicts events at Arnhem with artifacts, film and very good displays.

22. Tafelberg House/Hotel ★

Return to crossroad at Point 19 and walk about 400 yards south along Pietersbergseweg.

This dilapidated house was the headquarters of Field Marshal Walther Model, who abandoned it as soon as news of the Allied landings reached him. The building served as an Allied medical station and changed hands several times during the battle.

From Oosterbeek, drive east on Utrechtseweg toward Arnhem (about five km away), following signs toward Centrum. This is the road British forces used to advance on Arnhem. The VVV in Arnhem (Willemsplein 8, 0-900-202-4075) has free walking maps of the city.

23. Eusebius Church ★★★

Kerkplein 1 (Arnhem center)
T: (0)26-443-5068
Tuesday-Saturday, 10 a.m.-5 p.m., April-October
Tuesday-Saturday, 11 a.m.-4 p.m.,
Sunday, noon-4 p.m., November-March
Closed Mondays
€2.50 for elevator

The rebuilt church tower has a 220-foot-high observation gallery reached by elevator. Interpretive signage and orientation tables point out Oosterbeek, Nijmegen and, just below the tower, the John Frost Bridge. Bullet holes can be seen along the four-story brick building next to the church—called Devil's House, it somehow survived the battle.

24. John Frost Bridge/Airborneplein ★★★★★

From Point 23 (front of church), walk along Turfstraat/Walburgstraat, staying in front of large St. Walburg's Church. After Walburgstraat jogs into Nijmegseweg, follow signs to Airborneplein. About 350 yards from Point 23

In the middle of the large traffic roundabout at the bridge across the Rhine is a large, gray stone simply marked "17 September 1944," the official opening date of OMG. From this stone, walk about 50 yards along Nijmegseweg toward the bridge. The original bridge was demolished in October 1944. This replica was rebuilt

in 1950. At the north end of the bridge, a bronze plaque reads: "This is the bridge for which John D. Frost fought leading his soldiers persistent and brave in an advance where freedom was sought a bridge too far ..." Frost's headquarters were located almost directly behind this plaque, about two blocks away. From the plaque, walk down the steps, turn right on the street below and walk about 100 yards. On the left side is a small park with a well-preserved 25-pound field gun, its barrel about eight-feet long. Walk back toward the bridge. After less than 50 yards a staircase leads to street level. At the top of the stairs, in a small vestibule, a plaque recalls the gallantry of the British troops. The bridge is one of the most evocative sites of the war, arguably the most crucial point of OMG and surely its most remembered.

25. Arnhem War Museum 40-45 ★★

Off A12, about 10 km from Point 24
Kemperbergerweg 780, Arnhem
T: (0)26-442-0958
Daily, 10 a.m.-5 p.m.
Closed Monday, December 25, January 1
Adult: €3.50; Child: €2.50
From Arnhem center, take Apeldoorn road north, following signs to Openlucht Museum-Burgers Zoo. After lights at Burgers Zoo entrance, take second road on right, toward Schaarsbergen.

Dealing with all of World War II, not just OMG, this museum includes weapons, uniforms and an assortment of vehicles.

RELATED SITES BEYOND OMG

See Netherlands American Cemetery and Memorial, page 213.

OTHER AREA ATTRACTIONS

Kröller-Müller Museum

Within De Hoge Veluwe National Park, a few kilometers north of Arnhem. From A1, A50 or A12, follow signs for Park Hoge Veluwe.
Houtkampweg 6, Otterlo
T: (0)318-59-1241
Tuesday-Sunday, 10 a.m.-5 p.m.
Closed Monday and January 1

Adult: €14; Child (6-12): €7
Car: €7

The world's greatest collection of Van Gogh paintings—and an impressive collection of art by other masters—makes this one of Europe's finest art museums. It's located within the woody boundaries of the country's largest national park (a haven for bicyclists).

Getting To/Around the Netherlands

The Netherlands capital of Amsterdam's Schiphol Airport is served daily by airlines flying nonstop from North American and countless international cities. It's the hub of Dutch carrier KLM and its American partner Northwest Airlines (800-225-2525). The OMG area is also a two- to three-hour drive from Brussels, Belgium.

The Netherlands has an extensive rail system operated by Netherlands Railways (0-900-9292), but a car is needed to tour the battle sites effectively (see Driving, page xv). Widely available in larger U.S. bookstores and online services, Michelin's Benelux map (covering the Netherlands, Belgium and Luxembourg) is a good all-purpose road map. Available in local tourist offices, the more-detailed *Zuid Nederland* (South Netherlands) map, published by the VVV (national tourist office) and ANWB (the national tourist organization for drivers, bicyclists and walkers), covers all locations in this chapter.

VVV tourist offices are generally found near central train stations (triangular VVV signs mark their locations) and are extremely helpful for local maps and information. VVV offices pertinent to this chapter can be found just east of the train station in Arnhem (Willemsplein 8, 0-900-202-4075), in front of the train station in Oosterbeek (Raadhuisplein 1, 026-333-3172), a few blocks east of the train station in Nijmegen (Keizer Karelplein 2, 0-900-112-2344) and in front of the train station in Eindhoven (Stationsplein 1, 040-246-3005). The Netherlands National Tourist Office in New York (212-370-7367) is also helpful.

Bike paths are everywhere and rentals are available in most decent-size cities. For general biking information call the ANWB in Amsterdam (020-673-0844) or the train-station bicycle-rental shops in Arnhem (026-442-1782), Nijmegen (080-322-9618) or Eindhoven (VVV at 040-246-3005). A unique way to see OMG sites is by joining the "Airborne Fietstoertocht" OMG bicycle tour, which in the past has operated in August. It involves separate routes of 15, 25, 50 and 93 miles. Information is available at (0)26-381-9311.

Accommodations

Arnhem—NH Rijnhotel

Onderlangs 10
T: (0)26-443-4642 F: (0)26-445-4847
www.nh-hotels.com
68 rooms
€131-145

Located at the banks of the Rhine river, this four-star hotel is within walking distance of Arnhem's center.

Arnhem—Best Western Hotel Haarhuis

Stationsplein 1
T: (0)26-442-7441 F: (0)26-442-7449
www.hotelhaarhuis.nl
84 rooms
€103-205

Opposite the main train station, this hotel is within walking distance of OMG sites.

Nijmegen—Hotel Belvoir

Graadt van Roggenstraat 101
T: (0)24-323-2344 F: (0)24-323-9960
www.belvoir.nl
75 rooms
From €125

On the river Waal, the hotel is not far from the Nijmegen-Arnhem bridge, and within a few minutes of the old city center.

Eindhoven—Mandarin Park Plaza

Geldropseweg 17
T: (0)40-212-5055 F: (0)40-212-1555
www.parkplazaww.com
102 rooms
From €145

This hotel in the heart of Eindhoven is adjacent to the business district and shops.

21

UN POPOLO D POETI D ARTISTI DI EROI
DI SANTI DI PENSATORI DI SCIENZIATI
DI NAVIGATORI DI TRASMIGRATORI

Rome

ITALY

Square Colosseum, E.U.R.

THE WAR YEARS

U nder the fascist government of Benito Mussolini, Rome entered the 1940s
with great optimism. As an Axis partner, Italy viewed itself as a world power. The
capital city was to be showcased in a 1942 World Exposition. But Mussolini's
alliance with Adolf Hitler was little strengthened by his decision to join the war
against France in 1940 and the United States in 1941. The dictator's ambitions
outstripped the country's meager industrial resources, and with war, Rome's fortunes tumbled. Rationing was so severe by 1941 that gasoline was no longer available
to citizens. Food consumption eventually fell to less than 1,000 calories per day. Driven
by black marketeers, Rome devolved into a "city of spies, double agents, informers, tor-
turers, fugitives, hunted Jews, and hungry people," according to historian Robert Katz.

Allied forces invaded Sicily on July 10, 1943. A week later, 700 Allied planes bombed
Rome for the first time. On July 25, Italian King Victor Emmanuel III—Mussolini's willing puppet since his 1920s rise to power—summoned the dictator to Quirinale Palace.
"At this moment, you are the most hated man in Italy," the diminutive king told his old
benefactor. Mussolini was arrested, imprisoned at the Hotel Campo mountain resort,
rescued by German commandos and installed as Hitler-backed leader of an impotent
republic in northern Italy. (In April 1945, he was captured by partisans, shot and hung
upside down from the roof of a Milan gas station.)

In Rome, new government head Pietro Badoglio assessed Italy's grim situation and made
a fast deal with the Allies. On September 8, he and U.S. General Dwight Eisenhower
announced to an astonished world that Italy had surrendered without a fight. In reality,
no one had control of the country. Following the surrender announcement, German
troops rushed to the capital. Declaring Rome an open city, they proceeded to turn it
into a staging area for their fight against the Allies in the south and a theater of evil
for Hitler, who treated Italy's "betrayal" of Germany with a particularly ruthless hand.

"Badoglio's and the king's scheme to switch sides and thus avoid disaster had back-
fired," wrote *New York Times* correspondent C.L. Sulzberger. "Italy had by now become
a battleground in which the Italians themselves figured only as doleful victims."

Badoglio and the royal family cravenly fled the city, but underground resistance
increased—often with tragically unintended results. On March 23, 1944, along narrow
Via Rasella, partisans set off massive dynamite charges that killed 33 German soldiers.
Hitler called for revenge that would "make the world tremble." On his order, 335
Romans—10 for every one German life lost—were gathered from city jails, taken to
Ardeatine Caves south of the city and executed. Victims were forced to kneel on the
growing pile of corpses, some still writhing in half-life, before being shot by wildly
drunken Germans.

The Ardeatine massacre was overseen by SS commander Lieutenant-Colonel Herbert
Kappler, the most feared man in Rome during the nine months of Nazi occupation.
Soon after his arrival, the now-emblematic roundups of Jews began, culminating in mass
deportations. Roughly 8,000 Italian Jews (20 percent of Italy's Semitic population) died
in the Holocaust.

After Mussolini, wartime Rome's most important figure was Pope Pius XII, recently judged as a negligent or even willing conspirator with the Nazi agenda. Pius' record is too complex for the space available here. What's clear is the complicated political situation he found himself in with a war declared by Mussolini—the man who had granted the Vatican city-state status in 1929—and his German ally. To save the buildings and art of the Vatican and Rome, Pius feverishly worked diplomatic channels with the Germans, whose troops throughout the war surrounded Vatican City, but never violated its sovereignty. Rome largely escaped wartime destruction, but Pius' silence in the face of Nazi atrocities—of which he was certainly aware—has tainted his legacy.

"The Pope should have lifted his voice simply because it was the morally right thing to do, whatever the consequences," wrote Katz. "That appears to be the judgment of history."

Downtrodden Rome was liberated on June 4, 1944, when U.S.-Canadian forces led by U.S. 5th Army Lieutenant-General Mark Clark broke from positions near Anzio in the south and entered the capital. Rather than fight, the Wehrmacht vacated the city in an astonishing, chaotic retreat. Unopposed, Allied soldiers were met with hugs, kisses and wine from a "jubilant-crazy populace," according to one veteran. The nonstop liberation party was among the greatest events in Rome's history.

It was also attended by immediate controversy. Widely despised for his vainglorious, pompous manner, the tall, hawk-nosed Clark had in taking Rome allegedly disobeyed orders of Allied commander General Sir Harold Alexander. From Anzio, Clark was to have cut off the German retreat south of Rome and destroyed its army. But the Eternal City was too great a prize to resist. Clark later defended his actions, but his march on Rome is regarded among the most personally motivated acts of the Allied war effort.

"It had come down to this," wrote Katz. "The choice between a plan to end the war in all of Italy by destroying the Germany Army and a plan for Mark Clark to win the race for Rome and claim the trophy for America."

On June 5, 1944, Clark ascended the massive stairs overlooking Piazza Venezia and delivered a victory address that omitted mention of Alexander or the British 8th Army for their parts in the grueling Italian campaign. Whatever his motives, Clark's glory—or ignominy—would be short lived. The following day, June 6, 1944, the world's attention would turn irrevocably to the Allied D-Day invasion of Normandy. Dropped from the front pages, Rome would be left in the shadows of world events to repair its ancient, battered soul.

SOURCES & OTHER READING

The Battle for Rome, Katz, Robert, Simon & Schuster, 2003
Rome '44: The Battle for the Eternal City, Trevelyan, Raleigh, Seker & Warburg, 1981
Mussolini, Bosworth, R.J.B., Oxford University Press, 2002
Hitler's Pope: The Secret History of Pius XII, Cornwell, John, Viking, 1999
Calculated Risk, Clark, Mark, Harper, 1950

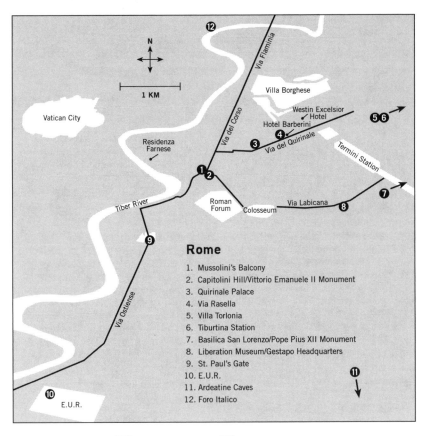

Rome

1. Mussolini's Balcony
2. Capitolini Hill/Vittorio Emanuele II Monument
3. Quirinale Palace
4. Via Rasella
5. Villa Torlonia
6. Tiburtina Station
7. Basilica San Lorenzo/Pope Pius XII Monument
8. Liberation Museum/Gestapo Headquarters
9. St. Paul's Gate
10. E.U.R.
11. Ardeatine Caves
12. Foro Italico

ROME TODAY

Population: 5.5 million • Country Code: 39 • €1 = $1.36/£0.67

Throughout the war, Romans worried that their city would be burned like London or flattened like Normandy. Through diplomacy, strategy and luck, Rome was spared major destruction. Its 2,700-year repository of Western architecture and culture thus preserved, Rome swiftly regained its title as Europe's most exhilarating capital.

It's also one of its most frustrating. With wide piazzas, monumental fountains, even oversized doorways, little in this sprawling metropolis is built to mortal scale. Cars, motorcycles, bikes and pedestrians battle for space here as nowhere else. Noise and crowds can be overwhelming. According to local humor, "Everything in Rome is designed to make life a little more difficult." For all this, Romans are almost unfailingly friendly and energetic.

Italians have been criticized for not scrutinizing or cleansing the national psyche of Mussolini's regime. For decades, the subject was taboo. A new, somewhat strange consciousness is emerging. Twisting nostalgia and conservative politics, the topic is now fair game in many areas—Mussolini's likeness is found on trading cards and bottles of wine—though on a deeper level, the fascist era can still make for an awkward topic of conversation.

Two to three days are needed to cover sites in this chapter.

POINTS OF INTEREST

M indicates nearest Metro station

1. Mussolini's Balcony ★★★

Palazzo di Venezia
Via del Plebiscito, 18
M: Colosseo
T: (0)6-673-2810
Tuesday-Sunday, 8:30 a.m.-7:30 p.m.
(last entry 6:30 p.m.)
Closed Mondays, January 1, December 25
Adult: €4; Student: €4; Under 18: Free

On the palace façade overlooking the piazza is the small balcony from which Benito Mussolini declared war on France in 1940, on the United States in 1941, and made numerous speeches to cheering throngs below. The palace itself was Il Duce's headquarters. Today, it houses the Museo Nationale del Palazzo di Venezia art museum. One of the exhibit areas occupies Mussolini's expansive personal office, but the balcony isn't accessible.

2. Capitoline Hill/Vittorio Emanuele II Monument ★★★

Piazza Venezia
M: Colosseo
9:30 a.m.-4:30 p.m. (gates usually remain open later in summer)

About 100 yards from Point 1, grand marble steps lead to the awesome monument featuring the 40-foot-high by 30-foot-wide statue of Vittorio Emanuele II on horseback. On June 5, 1944, U.S. General Mark Clark climbed to the top of these steps to deliver a self-serving speech (he neglected to credit British soldiers or mention Roman citizenry) announcing the liberation of Rome. For this he was savaged in the press. Said one American newsman at the scene: "On this historic occasion, I feel like vomiting." Few views in Rome are as good as those from atop these steps. Part way up, the Tomb of the Unknown Soldier from the First World War remains under 24-hour military guard.

3. Quirinale Palace (Palazzo del Quirinale) ★★

Piazza del Quirinale, at Via del Quirinale, 10-minute walk from Point 1

M: Barberini
T: (0)6-4-6991
Interior open Sundays only, 8:30-11 a.m.
No access on certain Sundays
Adult: €5

In a corner study, Mussolini was lured to a meeting with King Victor Emmanuel III and placed under arrest on July 25, 1943, completing his overthrow by the Grand Fascist Council. Nothing inside the palace today notes the event.

4. Via Rasella ★

M: Barberini

On this short, narrow street, partisan forces exploded 40 pounds of dynamite during a March 23, 1944, fascist rally. Thirty-three German soldiers were killed, prompting an enraged Hitler to order reprisal killings of 10 Romans for every German lost, leading to the Ardeatine Caves slaughter (Point 11). Completely restored, the historic street is now lined with hotels, shops and businesses.

5. Villa Torlonia (Mussolini's Residence) ★

Via Nomentana, 66
M: Policlinico
T: (0) 6-820-59127
Daily, 9 a.m.-7 p.m., April-September
(closed at 5:30 p.m. in March, October;
closed at 4:30 p.m. November-February)
Adult: €6.50; Senior/Student: €3M

The Torlonia family—members of the "black aristocracy" that supported Mussolini—gave the dictator this manor estate for use as a private residence. Visible from the street behind a faux Egyptian obelisk, the neoclassical mansion has recently been restored.

6. Tiburtina Station ★

M: Tiburtina

On October 16, 1943, more than 1,000 Jews were deported from this station to concentration camps in the East. Just 15 survived the experience. Near the clock in front of the main train (not subway) platforms, a large stone plaque (in Italian) commemorates the deportation and honors the victims. Smaller, similar plaques are mounted nearby.

7. Basilica San Lorenzo/Pope Pius XII Monument ★★

Piazzalle de Verano, 3. At intersection of Via Tiburtina and Viale Regina Elena.
M: Policlinico
T: (0) 6-49-1511
Daily, 7:30 a.m.-12:30 p.m.,
3:30-6:30 p.m.
Closed Catholic holidays

Dating to the fourth century, this grand church is located in the San Lorenzo district, near Citta Universitaria. An important railway center for German troops bound for the front, the area suffered Rome's heaviest Allied bombing. After the church was hit, Pope Pius XII made one of his few wartime appearances outside the Vatican, coming here to condemn the Allies and help restore the church. Today, a large statue of Pope Pius XII, with arms outstretched, stands outside the church. Inside the cloister (one of the oldest in Rome, it's accessible behind the main altar), a chunk of a bomb that hit the church is displayed. Destroyed by Allied bombs, the bell tower in front has been completely rebuilt. Adjacent is a cemetery (Cimitero del Verano) with memorials to victims of Nazi violence.

8. Liberation Museum/Gestapo Headquarters (Il Museo Storico della Liberazione di Roma) ★★★

Via Tasso, 145
M: Manzoni
T: (0)6-700-3866
Tuesday, Thursday, Friday, 10 a.m.-12:30 p.m., 4-7 p.m.
Wednesday, 10:30 a.m.-12:30 p.m.
Saturday, Sunday, 9:30 a.m.-12:30 p.m.

The headquarters of SS commander Herbert Kappler—among that dark organization's most sinister members—was also used as a prison and torture chamber. Today, solitary-confinement and torture cells house displays—mostly photos and text, all in Italian—relating to Nazi-Fascist oppression. Particularly evocative are two narrow cells left empty, their walls encased in glass to preserve words of despair and defiance carved by prisoners. The small museum begins on the second floor. Printed English guide available.

9. St. Paul's Gate (Porta San Palo) ★★

Piazalle Ostiense (opposite the large pyramid)
M: Piramide

At the ancient gate where Romans "for 17 centuries defended against the barbarians," Italian partisans clashed for the first time with Nazi soldiers on September 10, 1943. Across the street from the brick twin-towered gate is a memorial to victims of Nazi slaughter—human forms made of metal with hands bound by chains. Also on the piazalle, a plaque commemorates the victims of war. Another notes this as the area through which American and Canadian Special Forces led the liberation drive into Rome on June 4, 1944—they actually entered via the Appian Way gate, about a mile southeast of here.

10. E.U.R. ★★★

M: E.U.R. Palasport

In 1938, Mussolini ordered construction of a new Rome based on mammoth, rationalist architecture. The new buildings would meld classic Italian style with the fascist ideology of strength, power and function and serve as the center point of a 1942 World Exposition (canceled due to the war). The result is the E.U.R. (Esposizione Universale), an area south of the city center filled with large buildings of austere limestone and rigid angles that invoke the demagoguery and architecture of the Roman Empire. The most well-known is the "Square Colosseum" (Palazzo della Civilita del Lavoro) on Quadrato della Concordia, at the end of Viale della Civilita. Its arched windows and classic-style statuary are obvious nods to ancient Roman glory. Corporate and government offices moved into the area after the war. The many surrounding 1960s and '70s structures are a distraction, but the E.U.R. remains both oddity and marvel, a unique legacy of a bygone era.

11. Ardeatine Caves (Fosse Ardeatine) ★★★

Via Ardeatine, 174
No Metro. Bus No. 218 (originates at Piazza Porto San Giovani, makes many stops through Rome) stops at Largo Martiri Fosse Ardeatine.
T: (0)6-513-6742
Daily, 8:15 a.m.-5:45 p.m. (8:45 a.m.-5:15 p.m. on holidays)
Closed January 1, Easter Sunday, May 1, August 15, December 25

The caves where 335 Romans were slaughtered on March 24, 1944, following the Via Rasella partisan bombing and Hitler's order for reprisal executions, are now a national shrine. Bullet holes are visible in the tunnels. A large crypt built into the rock is lined with 335 stone "caskets." A sculpture of three bound figures represents human suffering. A museum recalls the horrific event with photos, text (in Italian), underground newspapers and Nazi weaponry. This eerie, emotional site is considered Rome's most important reminder of the war's tragic consequences.

12. Foro Italico ★

Viale del Foro Italico
M: Flaminio

The once-prominent fascist monuments and reminders at this 1930s-built sports complex have faded, deteriorated or been removed. Just across the Ponte Duca D'Aosta bridge over the Tiber River stands the exception: a marble monolith inscribed with Mussolini's name.

RELATED SITES BEYOND ROME

See Auxiliary Sites, Italy (page 244).

OTHER AREA ATTRACTIONS

Vatican City

M: Ottaviano, Cipro

Choosing a single "must" Rome attraction is impossible. There's simply too much to see. In addition to being of interest to World War II enthusiasts, however, the Vatican is a revelation even to those without interest in matters of the Catholic spirit. Beneath its imposing dome, St. Peter's Basilica houses what's considered the world's greatest collection of Renaissance art. With its ceiling painted by Michelangelo, the 10,000-square-foot Sistine Chapel lives up to its gilded reputation. The 18 rooms of the Vatican Picture Gallery (Pinacoteca) are filled with masterpieces. This is but a meager sampling of the 108-acre city-state, inside which Pope Pius XII spent most of World War II. The Vatican Tourist Information Office (06-6-988-1662; Monday-Saturday, 8:30 a.m.-7 p.m.) is next to the entry to St. Peter's Basilica. Entry fee required for some exhibits.

GETTING TO/AROUND ROME

Dozens of airlines fly nonstop to Rome's Leonardo da Vinci International Airport from many North American and international cities. Alitalia (800-223-5730 in the United States; 06-6-563 in Rome) is Italy's national carrier.

From the da Vinci Airport, express and local trains run to Rome's main Termini Station. Signs in the airport (not easy to find in every terminal) mark the way to "Stazione" and "Railroad Station." Express trains depart the airport every hour from 7:30 a.m. to 11:37 p.m. Cost is €11, one way. Tickets are purchased from machines or counters. The express trip to Termini takes 30 minutes. In hours when the train isn't operating, buses run the same route about once an hour until 3:45 a.m. Taxis from the airport to central Rome take about an hour and cost €60-75.

Driving in Rome is reserved for locals and those who have simply run out of challenges in life. The Metro and bus lines are good. So are taxis, though they're pricey (€8-12 is a typical fare within the city) and notoriously hard to get during rush hours. Visitors should plan on much walking. All medium and major hotels have complimentary street maps.

With free detailed maps and creative publications—everything from guides of movies filmed in Rome to the history of the Colosseum—the main tourist information office (Azienda di Promozione Turistica di Roma; 06-3-600-4399) is an invaluable resource for visitors. The main office is located at Via Parigi, 11, near the Republica and Termini Metro stations. It's open daily, 9 a.m.-7 p.m. A branch office is located in Terminal B of Leonardo da Vinci International Airport.

For knowledge of ancient and World War II history, as well as Rome's Byzantine network of roads and transportation system, it's difficult to imagine a better local guide than accredited and unflappable Carlo Begliuti (06-7030-1774; info@roma7.it). He speaks perfect English.

ACCOMMODATIONS

Residenza Farnese

Via del Mascherone, 59 (off Piazza Farnesse)
M: Colosseo
T: (0)6-6-821-0980 F: (0)6-6-821-0980
www.residenzafarneseroma.it
29 rooms
From €250

Near the old Jewish Ghetto in the heart of Rome—the "real Rome," according to many locals—this upscale boutique hotel occupies a building from the 1400s. Rooms are individually furnished, with rich wood mirrors, tables and furniture. Some have internet capability. The draw, however, is the neighborhood, one of the best in the city for walking and eating. Just minutes away, Piazza Navona has been featured in numerous films. The nearest Metro station (Colosseo) is a 15-minute walk.

Hotel Barberini

Via Rasella, 3
M: Barberini
T: (0)6-481-4993 F: (0)6-481-5211
www.hotelbarberini.com
31 rooms
€235-430

There are countless four-star hotels in Rome. For World War II enthusiasts, this one's location at the top of Via Rasella (see Point 4 and The War Years) is of interest. It's also within walking distance of famed Trevi Fountain. Rooms are soundproofed (a nice touch in noisy Rome) and spacious, with individual decor and marble bathrooms. The staff is first-rate.

Westin Excelsior Rome

Via Vittorio Veneto, 125
M: Barberini
T: (0)6-4-7081 F: (0)6-482-6205
www.starwood.com
316 rooms
€325-700

This Starwood hotel is one of Rome's most lavish. Crystal chandeliers, ostentatious furnishings and appropriately toadying service put it at or near the top of any local hotel list. Superb restaurants and bar. The hotel also features what is reportedly the largest suite in Europe, the Villa La Cupola.

22

Remagen/Eifel Region

GERMANY

Ludendorff Bridge

THE WAR YEARS

By September 1944, the German military was in full retreat across western Europe, with Allied forces in pursuit along a broad, coordinated front. Having raced past their lines of supply, the Allied advance stalled in September, allowing Nazi command time to reorganize its forces near the German border.

Nevertheless, on September 11, 1944—96 days after the D-Day landings—the first Allied penetration into Germany occurred near Stolzembourg, Luxembourg, when six American soldiers and a French translation officer waded across the Our River. Staff Sergeant Warner Holzinger became the first American to enter Germany, leading his patrol for two hours through a series of abandoned stations of the Siegfried Line (or Westwall). Constructed in the late 1930s, the line of 22,000 interlocking positions—from single-gun pillboxes to underground strongholds for 80 men—guarded Germany from the North Sea to the Swiss border "like the scaly concrete spine of some ugly primeval monster," according to historian Charles Whiting. "It was a tremendous fortification line, the likes of which the world had not seen since the building of the Great Wall of China."

Within 72 hours of Holzinger's feat, Allied forces were attacking across the remote Eifel region through which Germany had poured invasion forces into western Europe in 1940. German resistance stiffened at the Hürtgen Forest, a 50-square-mile triangle bounded by the German towns of Aachen, Düren and Monschau. On October 21, after weeks of terrifying combat—GIs called Hürtgen the "Death Factory"—Aachen became the first German city captured by the Allies. Still, the inch-by-inch Hürtgen battle raged for three months, costing 58,000 American lives (the approximate U.S. death toll for the entire Vietnam War) and ending in failure when Germany launched its December counteroffensive, eventually known as the Battle of the Bulge. The first concerted Allied ground attack on the German homeland had failed. The Siegfried Line had held.

With the "Bulge" successfully dealt with, Allied forces renewed attacks on the Eifel frontier in February 1945, chasing the spent Wehrmacht beyond the Siegfried Line to the banks of the river Rhine, the traditional protective moat of the German heartland. As village after village fell to the Allied rush across the country, German troops blew Rhine bridges behind them as they retreated across the river. With no illusions of an easy crossing of the Rhine, Allied command planned for British General Bernard Montgomery to lead a massive and difficult river crossing in the north. But the central-front U.S. 1st Army—commanded by U.S. General Courtney Hodges, a brilliant tactician who'd nevertheless flunked his West Point exams and entered the Army as a private—snatched the spotlight when a U.S. 9th Armored Division patrol made a startling discovery upon entering the small town of Remagen on March 7. Packed with retreating soldiers and civilians, the town's 1,069-foot-long, arched bridge crossing the Rhine was, unaccountably, still standing.

Unimportant during most of the war, Remagen's Ludendorff Bridge had been left with thin defenses and disorganized command. Though 600 kilograms of military-grade explosives had been ordered for its demolition, only 300 kilograms of inferior, commercial-grade explosives had been delivered. In full view of Americans charging through the town, a German attempt to destroy the bridge failed with a dramatic but ineffective explosion. With German engineers scurrying to reset charges, an American company led by Second Lieutenant Karl Timmermann—son of an American World War I deserter and born just 60 miles from Remagen—took on the suicide mission, charging through a hail of machine-gun and mortar fire to capture the bridge intact. A 34-year-old Holland, Ohio, butcher, Sergeant Alex Drabik, was the first to reach the east bank, and within 24 hours, 8,000 Americans and supporting tanks had crossed the bridge. Within a week, seven full armies rushed over the river on 62 temporary spans quickly built by American engineers. A road to the German heartland had unexpectedly opened. Dwight Eisenhower later called the surprise capture of the bridge "one of my happiest moments of the war." Upon hearing the news, both houses of the U.S. Congress interrupted proceedings for a loud, sustained cheer.

When he heard the news, "Hitler's anguished rage knew no bounds," according to historian Ken Hechler. The Nazi dictator swiftly executed four officer scapegoats, replaced Western Front commander in chief Field Marshal Gerd von Rundstedt with Field Marshal Albrecht Kesselring and ordered the bridge destroyed. Germany deployed 20,000 men, numerous bombers, V2 rockets, even commando swimmers (all captured) against the bridge. Though never directly hit, continuous vibration stress brought the bridge down with a terrible howl of yawning steel on March 17. The collapse killed 27 Americans, but with dozens of new bridges built around the fulcrum of Remagen, the German heartland pierced and the hopes of its soldiers gutted, irreversible military and psychological damage had been done. "Remagen killed us," German generals confided after the war.

Ever on the lookout for opportunities of grand symbolism, Winston Churchill toured the conquered Siegfried Line in late March, adding an unorthodox exclamation point on the Nazi defeat when his entourage stopped at a row of "dragon's teeth" concrete tank obstacles. "There, while they all waited agog for what the Great Man would do, he fumbled with his fly, cigar between his lips," reported Whiting. "'Gentlemen, I'd like to ask you to join me. Let us all urinate on the great West Wall of Germany. ... [to the photographers] This is one of those operations connected with this great war which must not be reproduced graphically.' Duly the great and good followed the Prime Minister's example."

Eisenhower put a more urbane spin on the significance of Remagen. "The final defeat of the enemy, which we had long calculated would be accomplished in the spring and summer campaigning of 1945, was suddenly now just around the corner," he wrote after the war.

SOURCES & OTHER READING

The Bridge at Remagen: The Amazing Story of March 7, 1945—The Day the Rhine River Was Crossed, Hechler, Ken, Ballantine Books, 1957

Remagen in March 1945: Key Factors of Events Leading Up to the End of World War II, Brüne and Weiler, Warlich Druck und Verlagsgesellschaft, 1995

Rhineland: The Battle to End the War, Whitaker and Whitaker, St. Martin's Press, 1989

A Traveller's Guide to the Battle for the German Frontier, Whiting, Charles, Interlink Books, 2000

"After the Battle" Number 16 ("Crossing the Rhine"), Battle of Britain Prints/After the Battle, 1977

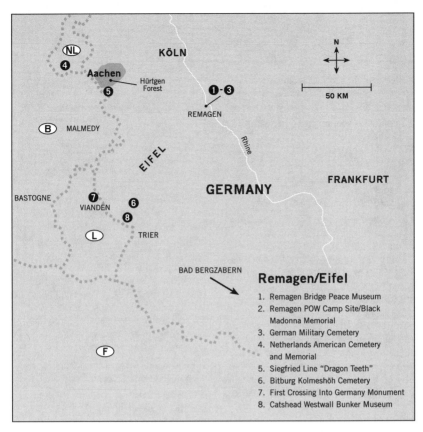

Remagen/Eifel

1. Remagen Bridge Peace Museum
2. Remagen POW Camp Site/Black Madonna Memorial
3. German Military Cemetery
4. Netherlands American Cemetery and Memorial
5. Siegfried Line "Dragon Teeth"
6. Bitburg Kolmeshöh Cemetery
7. First Crossing Into Germany Monument
8. Catshead Westwall Bunker Museum

REMAGEN/EIFEL TODAY

Population: 17,000 (Remagen) • Country Code: 49 • €1 = $1.36/£0.67

Remagen is a pleasant river town with an ancient pedigree. A small ruin of the Roman fort that controlled the area between the first and fourth centuries is the focus of the town's second most interesting museum—the humble Das Römische (Via Principalis, 0264-2-2010). Generic, modern commercial zones dominate Remagen's outskirts, but despite extensive wartime air-raid damage, its pedestrian-only core retains a traditional German feel. It takes barely an afternoon to see Remagen and the bridge.

Ask residents of the Eifel where the region officially begins and they'll likely point to the next town. This is a bit of regional humor—because the neglected rural area has traditionally been economically depressed, few Germans jump to be associated with it. The rolling green agricultural and timber region runs roughly from the borders of Luxembourg and Belgium east to the Rhine, and from Köln in the north to Trier in the south. It's a land of small towns and church steeples. Driving its narrow, two-lane highways, the visitor gains an appreciation of the difficulty its low "mountains," plunging valleys and gentle but irregular topography presented to the advance of a modern army dependent on tanks, trucks and other vehicles.

By car, it's possible to visit all Eifel attractions (including Remagen) in a single long day, but it's easier to do in two.

1. Remagen Bridge Peace Museum (Friedensmuseum Brücke Von Remagen)
★★★★★

Rheinpromenade, about 1 km southeast of city center
T: (0)2642-2-1863
Daily, 10 a.m.-5 p.m. (closed at 6 p.m., May-August), March 7-late November
Closed all other months
Adult: €3.50; Student/Child: €1 Family: €7

Following its wartime collapse, the famed Ludendorff Bridge was destroyed and never rebuilt. What remains are twin sets of support towers—two on each side of the river. Built in 1918, the 75-foot-high towers of black basalt blocks resemble a medieval fortress and are among the best original war relics in Germany. The Rhine is wide here—the original bridge spanned the length of more than three football fields across the river. Towers on the Remagen side—from which the Americans approached—house a small but interesting museum examining German and American battle perspectives through photos and exhibits on each of five interior landings accessed via spiral staircase. Relics include uniforms, mortar shells, field equipment and a 1,000-kilogram German bomb (a dud) discovered by the Allies at the base of the bridge. There's a display of photos of Remagen destruction by famed combat photographer Hilmar Pabel. Pabel was photographing production of 1968's *The Bridge at Remagen* in Prague—logistical problems prevented filming in Remagen—when the Prague Spring Uprising broke out. His smuggled-out photos, on display here, were among the first to reach the West. (Somewhat dated, the well-known film's story bears little relation to historical fact, though its treatment of broader points of the battle is accurate.) Small pieces of the original bridge encased in Plexiglas are sold at the museum for €30. Proceeds help maintain the museum. There's no English signage, but a free, one-page English guide is available.

On the opposite bank, the bridge towers and rail tunnel occupied by German soldiers and civilians during the battle are permanently sealed off. The sheer, 600-foot rock massif towering above the east bank is known as Erpeler Ley (the town of Erpel sits opposite Remagen). From these heights Germans pounded advancing Americans with anti-aircraft guns. The position was eventually taken by Americans who scaled the cliffs. A famous photo of an American soldier looking down on the bridge was taken after the battle from atop Erpeler Ley—a Peace Cross now stands atop the cliff. From here the visitor gets panoramic views of the bridge, battlefield, town and route of American approach. It's reached via ferry from Kripp (2 km southeast of Remagen) to Linz, then back along the riverside road to Erpel and Erpeler-Ley Strasse to the top of the hill.

2. Remagen POW Camp Site/Black Madonna Memorial (Katelle Schwarze Madonna) ★★

On Goethestrasse, just beyond Remagen town boundary, 1 km roughly east of Point 1

Remagen is also infamous in Germany as the site of POW camps where German soldiers suffered tremendous hardships at the hands of American captors, with no shelter through the cold, rainy spring and little food or medical treatment. The inhumane treatment was brought to light by Canadian author James Bacque's 1989 sensationalist *Other Losses*. Though the book was a bestseller in Germany, partly due to its highly publicized claims blaming Dwight Eisenhower for deliberately starving to death at least 800,000 German POWs, Bacque's wildly inflated statistics and conspiracy claims were roundly dismissed as fantasy, "worse than worthless," by scholars. Still, mass suffering at sites such as this one undeniably occurred. About 1,200 German POWs are believed to have died at this spot, now marked by a 25-foot-high wooden memorial with six angled arches topped by a crown of thorns.

3. German Military Cemetery (Kriegsgräberstätte) ★★

Just off Route 266 (at sign for Kriegsgräberstätte) in village of Bad Bodendorf, 5 km southwest of Remagen

Identified by a stone tower with a green copper roof, this plot is typical of German military cemeteries. Granite crosses stand in poignant clumps over a field with gravestones embedded in the ground. For more on German cemeteries, see page 8.

4. Netherlands American Cemetery and Memorial ★★★★

On N278 at west end of small Magraten (Netherlands), 10 km east of Maastricht or 22 km west of German border at Aachen
Daily, 9 a.m.-5 p.m.
Closed December 25, January 1
T: 703-696-6897 (Arlington, Virginia)

Interred at this large, impeccably maintained cemetery are the remains of 8,301 American servicemen who died in the region. Graves are marked by brilliant white marble crosses and Stars of David, arranged in parallel arcs sweeping across a broad, green lawn. At the head of the cemetery are names and home states of 1,723 missing soldiers inscribed within the large and sobering Court of Honor. The chapel tower rises 101 feet, its walls recalling the names of important area battles—Arnhem, Cologne, Ruhr, others. Massive engraved maps record Normandy D-Day landings, Operation Market-Garden and the drive into Germany. The cemetery provides a stunning, visceral and strangely picturesque reminder of the war's enormous toll on American lives.

5. Siegfried Line "Dragon Teeth" ★★

At intersection of Schmidhof Strasse and Monschauer Strasse, in village of Schmidhof (Germany), 9 km south of Aachen along alternate road between Aachen and Monshau (not 258)

Remnants of the Siegfried Line (Westwall) are visible at many points along Germany's western border. This is one of the easiest places to find a long line of "dragon teeth" concrete tank obstacles. A large field of the three-foot-high, pyramid-like obstacles sits behind a fence at the intersection described above.

6. Bitburg Kolmeshöh Cemetery (Ehrenfriedhof Kolmeshöh) ★★

On Zur Kolmeshöh, off B51, about 1.5 km southwest of city center. Entering city center from B51, turn right on Karenweg, right on Triererstrasse, right at roundabout onto Franz-Mecker-Strasse and follow this road to cemetery. The Tourist Information office (on Glockenhausen in city center) has maps of town and cemetery.

During the U.S. Army's 1945 drive into Germany, Bitburg was devastated by American bombardment. General George Patton found the town in such dire shape that he ordered troops to share rations with the townspeople. Completely rebuilt, Bitburg is now one of the more interesting towns in the region. On May 5, 1985, its small German military cemetery (about 2,000 World War I and II dead are buried here) became the focal point of a political firestorm when U.S. President Ronald Reagan laid a wreath at the base of its memorial tower. The gesture was meant to suggest American-German reconciliation, but the existence of 49 SS troops among the buried (unknown to Reagan when he initially agreed to the meeting with German Chancellor Helmut Kohl) gave the event a quite different meaning. "It is out of the question for the leader of the Western world to lay a wreath in a war cemetery where Nazi storm troopers are buried," wrote *The Washington Post* in an editorial that typified reaction prior to the visit. Nevertheless, Reagan refused to cancel the visit—the controversial episode dogs his reputation to this day. The cemetery remains—small, peaceful, dominated by the infamous stone memorial tower.

7. First Crossing Into Germany Monument ★

Stolzembourg, Luxembourg, on N10, 30 km west of Bitburg

At the southern end of tiny Stolzembourg, along the main highway, U.S. and Luxembourg flags fly over a small stone plaque commemorating the first breach of German territory by six Americans and one French lieutenant. This is the lone monument to the event. From this spot, on September 11, 1944, the reconnaissance team waded across the river to Germany, reconnoitered about 80 abandoned pillboxes along the Siegfried Line and, two hours later, returned to Luxembourg. According to signage, "The information was radioed to the headquarters of the U.S. 1st Army, which flashed that night the news to the world that it had crossed the German border."

8. Catshead Westwall Bunker Museum (Panzerwerk Katzenkopf Westwallmuseum) ★★★

Freiwillie Feuerwehr, Irrel
Off E29/257, 16 km south of Bitburg. In small Irrel, follow signs to Westwallmuseum.
T: (0)65-2-5492

Sunday, holidays, 2-5 p.m., April-September
Other times and months by appointment
Open some summer Saturdays.
Adult: €2; Child (up to 16): €1

There's not much left of Hitler's enormous Siegfried Line, but this extensive bunker illustrates just how lethal and elaborate the network was. Inside is a decent collection of weapons, photos and relics, but the point is the bunker itself, one of the largest of the estimated 22,000 (some estimates say 14,000) Siegfried Line structures. The "Catshead" was built for 80 men and defended by topside machine guns and flamethrowers. It plunges four floors below ground and in wartime was subdivided into more than 50 rooms. With dense concrete walls, the bottom-floor galleries total 450 feet in length. Temperature inside is a constant 45 degrees, making sweatshirts indispensable, even in summer.

RELATED SITES BEYOND REMAGEN/EIFEL

Westwallmuseum ★★

Kurfürstenstrasse (off B427, 7 minutes north of train station) in small Bad Bergzabern, about 200 km southeast of Remagen, near Karlsruhe (just north of Stuttgart)
T: (0)639-8367
Every Sunday, 10 a.m.-4 p.m., July-October

First Sunday of month, 10 a.m.-4 p.m., March-June, and during certain holidays. Open Easter Sunday and by appointment
Adult: €2

Two large concrete bunkers—Siegfried Line leftovers—have been converted into a small museum with photos, text, various armaments, original equipment and access to the imposing R.B. 516 artillery bunkers.

OTHER AREA ATTRACTIONS

Köln and Aachen

An hour north of Remagen, historic Köln (aka Cologne, population 1 million) is anchored by the leviathan Kölner Dom cathedral. Gaudy and enormous, the French Gothic church—built between 1248 and 1880—survived the war intact and must be seen to be appreciated. Most of Köln was badly damaged by Allied bombing, but rapid restoration re-established the city among Germany's top tourist draws.

Straddling three borders—Germany, Netherlands, Belgium—Aachen (popula-

tion 250,000) was the first Germany city captured by the Western Allies (October 1944). Rebuilding efforts have erased virtually all traces of the horrendous struggle that took place here—most of the modern city is unremarkable. The highlight is the rebuilt Old Town (Grabenring) and octagonal Aachen Cathedral, built by Charlemagne (first sovereign of the Christian empire of the West) and consecrated as his court chapel in 805. Tours include Charlemagne's throne and tomb (he died in Aachen in 814).

The closest major airport to Remagen is Frankfurt Airport, about two hours away by car. With direct flights from all over the world, it's the continent's busiest airport. Among others, American Airlines (800-433-7300) flies directly from the United States. An hour from Remagen by car, the Köln/Bonn airport is serviced by numerous airlines with inter-Europe connections.

Remagen is also reached by frequent train service from around the country. Die Bahn (national rail system) information number for travel throughout Germany is (0)180-599-6633. Once in Remagen, it's easiest to get around on foot. Attractions are concentrated in a scenic, pedestrian-only zone, a two-minute walk from the train station. The Ludendorff Bridge is just less than a km down the riverside promenade. Taxis are usually available at the train station. The Remagen Tourist Information office (Kirchstrasse 6; 02642-2-0187) is located in the center of town and has good local maps.

Beyond Remagen, sites are accessible via train and taxi, but because they're spread out and sometimes far from train stations, it's best to visit the Eifel by car (see Driving, page xv). In addition to numerous Germany road maps, Michelin's "Benelux" map (Belgium, Netherlands, Luxembourg) includes western Germany spillover that includes all locations in this chapter, with the exception of the Westwallmuseum at Bad Bergzabern.

Accommodations

Remagen
Pinger Hotel
Geschwister-Scholl-Strasse 1
T: (0)26-42-9-3840 F: (0)26-42-9-9384-690
www.pingerhotels.de
39 rooms
€76-119

Remagen's top hotel is located directly across from the train station. It's convenient but a bit noisy in early mornings. Still, the English-fluent staff is friendly, the small bar lively and restaurant good. "Comfort class" rooms are larger and have updated bathrooms. The hotel is a five-minute walk from the Rhine.

Vianden, Luxembourg
Hotel Victor Hugo
1 rue Victor Hugo
T: 352-83-4160 F: 352-84-9122
www.hotel-victor-hugo.lu
20 rooms
€53-110

Those looking for a quaint village stopover will enjoy Vianden, 32 km west of Bitburg (Point 6) and 6 km south of Stolzembourg (Point 7) in Luxembourg. Along the river and at the base of the clifftop Vianden castle, the family-run hotel has simple but updated rooms.

Aachen
VCH-Hotel am Marschiertor
Wallstrasse 1-7
T: (0)241-3-1941 F: (0)241-3-1944
www.vch.de
50 rooms
€82-100

A standard-to-good European hotel with modern rooms. Convenient location next to Aachen's Old Town gate and a couple hundred yards from the train station.

Köln
TOP CityLine Hotel Königshof
Richartzstrasse 14-16
T: (0)221-257-8771 F: (0)221-257-8762
www.top-hotels.de
82 rooms
From €110

The Königshof is a solid, tourist-class hotel (basic, clean rooms) in the Köln city center near museums, theaters, shopping and the famed Dom cathedral.

Anzio

ITALY

THE WAR YEARS

ostly amphibious assaults in World War II are generally associated with U.S. Marines landings in the Pacific—Guadalcanal, Tarawa, Peleliu. The Allied assault at Anzio, Italy, however, belongs on any short list of the war's most brutal seaborne invasions. Unique in the European War, Operation Shingle "was the only amphibious operation in that theater where the Army was unable promptly to exploit a successful landing," wrote U.S. Navy historian Samuel Eliot Morison. "In the entire war there is none to compare with it; even the Okinawa campaign in the Pacific was shorter."

With its Italian offensive stalled at Cassino in January 1944, the Allies sought to out-flank German positions with what British Prime Minister Winston Churchill called a "wildcat hurled onto the beach" at Anzio, a deep-harbor resort town 40 miles behind enemy lines, 30 miles south of Rome. Unloaded from 250 ships, troops from six nations—but almost entirely American and British—hit the beaches on January 22, 1944. British troops landed just north of Anzio, Americans a few miles south of sister-city Nettuno and U.S. and Canadian Special Forces at Anzio's main harbor. With less than 1,000 area Axis defenders, the landings were nearly unopposed—only 13 invaders were killed, 100 wounded. Within a week, 70,000 troops and 18,000 vehicles had been put ashore.

Under the conservative command of U.S. Major-General John Lucas, however, Churchill's wildcat quickly transformed into a "stranded whale." Lucas rested his troops rather than push quickly for Rome. "Lucas on discovering that there were no Germans in his path behaved as though there were," wrote historian Peter Calvocoressi.

Lucas' hesitation gave German Field Marshal Albrecht Kesselring time to react to the surprise invasion. The highly able commander quickly brought six divisions to the area, setting the stage for counterattacks and a protracted battle fought in World War I fashion—between static lines of foxholes, trenches, marshes, waddies (irrigation ditches that inhibited tank movement) and reinforced positions. Within a few days, the Allied perimeter was 7 miles deep and 16 miles wide, but Lucas continued to play it safe. Though supporting naval gunfire and air superiority was maintained throughout the campaign, Lucas' inability to exploit his advantages remains controversial. "Why didn't the enemy, in a quick, daring dash to the Alban Hills ... cut the supply road to the south flank of the (German) Tenth Army?" posited a German general after the war. "He felt himself not strong enough and thereby missed his great chance."

Allied frustration boiled all the way to Churchill, so that by January 30, a massive offensive from Anzio was ordered. Believing he was witnessing the great Allied invasion of Europe, Adolf Hitler ordered his men to fight with "fanatical will" and "holy hatred." The Allies gained some ground, but at terrible cost. In just one action, near the Casino di Anzio, 761 U.S. Rangers were killed and many taken prisoner. German artillery rained incessantly on the congested beachhead, town and inland positions. German midget submarines created havoc in a harbor choked with supply vessels. Anzio suffered near-total destruction. Allied troops were exhausted, bloodied and demoralized.

In February, operational commanders General Sir Harold Alexander and General Mark Clark visited front lines in obvious ill temper. "My head will probably fall in a basket, but I have done my best," said Lucas. He was right ... about his head. On February 22, Lucas was replaced by Major-General Lucian Truscott, an officer in the Patton mold who had distinguished himself in Sicily by exhorting troops to engage the enemy and "carve your name in his face!" Despite the shake-up, there was no immediate change in battle disposition. More terrible yet inconclusive battles were waged at inland sites such as Aprilia, Cisterna di Latina, the "Factory" and Campo di Carne.

Cold, drenching rains and biting winter winds made life a trial for the 90,000 American and 35,500 British troops pinned down around Anzio. Vehicles constantly bogged down in mud and had to be pushed out by men sunk to their knees in slime. The plain behind the beach was pockmarked with bomb craters. By April, 135,000 organized German troops stood between Anzio and Rome.

May brought warmer temperatures and a renewed Allied offensive across Italy. At Cassino, spent German troops broke and retreated north. On May 23, Truscott's pent-up forces finally tore loose from Anzio. Two days later, near the village of Borgo Grappa, south of Latina, Allies heading north from Cassino linked with those driving out of Anzio. It was a glorious but costly charge—the Allies suffered 4,000 combat casualties in less than a week—that culminated with Mark Clark's controversial capture of Rome (see Rome chapter). Thus, the 125-day Anzio ordeal concluded more or less simultaneously with the liberation of Rome.

German casualty estimates at Anzio were 5,500 killed, 17,500 wounded, 4,500 taken prisoner or missing. The Allies suffered 4,926 killed, 18,229 wounded, about 6,800 taken prisoner or missing. Historical consensus regards Operation Shingle among the war's most abysmal Allied failures. Churchill, stubborn proponent of the Italian fiasco, admitted that "the story of Anzio was a story of high opportunity and shattered hopes." General Dwight Eisenhower tried a more positive spin: "We instinctively resent military campaigns in which there is great suffering with little result. But let us admit that the Italian campaign ... was fought *because it had to be fought*."

Anzio wasn't without gain. Though later than hoped, Rome was conquered before any other Axis capital. Furthermore, at least eight German divisions had been engaged in battle when they might otherwise have been sent to the Eastern Front or to defend the June 1944 D-Day beaches. After the war, German commanders testified that the Italian campaign contributed greatly to subsequent Allied victories in France.

Sources & Other Reading

Sicily-Salerno-Anzio, January 1943-June 1944 (History of the United States Naval Operations in World War II, vol. IX), Morison, Samuel Eliot, Little, Brown and Company, 1954

The Sideshow War: The Italian Campaign, 1943-1945, Botjer, George F., Texas A&M University Press, 1996

Anzio 1944: An Unexpected Fury, Verney, Peter, Batsford, 1978

The Battle of Anzio: The Dramatic Story of One of the Major Engagements of World War II, Fehrenbach, T. R., Monarch Books, 1962

Calculated Risk, Clark, Mark, Harper, 1950

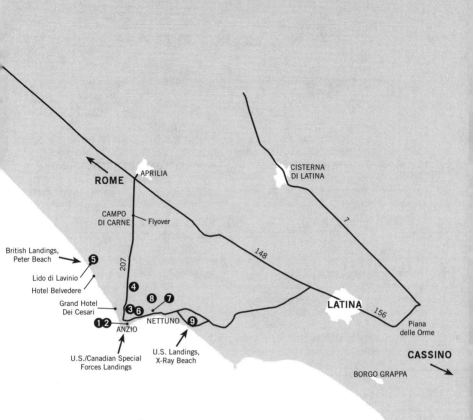

ROME

APRILIA

CISTERNA
DI LATINA

CAMPO
DI CARNE   Flyover

207

148

7

British Landings,
Peter Beach   **5**

Lido di Lavinio

Hotel Belvedere

4

Grand Hotel
Dei Cesari   **3** **6**

8 **7**

1 **2**

NETTUNO   **9**

LATINA   156

Piana
delle Orme

ANZIO

U.S./Canadian Special
Forces Landings

U.S. Landings,
X-Ray Beach

CASSINO

BORGO GRAPPA

10 KM

Anzio-Nettuno

1. Town Square/Harbor
2. Anzio Beachhead Museum
3. Anzio War Cemetery
4. Beach Head War Cemetery
5. Lavinio/Peter Beach
6. Casino di Anzio
7. Nettuno Museum of the Allied Landing
8. Sicily-Rome American Cemetery and Memorial
9. U.S. 3rd Division Landing Monument

ANZIO TODAY

Population: 80,000 (area) • Country Code: 39 • €1 = $1.36/£0.67

Dating to the first millennium B.C., Anzio became a summer retreat for Catholic cardinals in the 1700s. By the early 20th century it was a fashionable seaside resort for wealthy Romans, with numerous majestic buildings of the "Liberty" style dotting the coastline. World War II turned most of Anzio and neighboring Nettuno into smoking rubble. Urban sprawl has since blurred the division between the sister cities, now frequently referred to as a single unit, Anzio-Nettuno.

Following the war, both towns were rebuilt around their few surviving buildings, some of which are visible at the Anzio harbor and old casino (Point 6). Anzio is pleasant, though not particularly special. Its fishing fleet provides a big part of the local character and bigger percentage of local menu items. In summer, tourists congregate around the central Piazza Pia—just behind the main harbor—and beaches north of town. The beaches are somewhat narrow and pebbly in spots—not bad, not breathtaking, either. Most are privately held and accessed via the hotels that crowd the road leading north of town.

Nettuno is the larger of the cities, with a busier center, more shops, restaurants and nightlife. It also has one of the more interesting legacies of Italy's American experience—one of the finer baseball stadiums in Europe (the size of a good collegiate field in the States) and an amateur team that's won 17 Italian and four European baseball championships.

Area war sites can be toured in a single day. Add a half-day for Piana delle Orme.

POINTS OF INTEREST

1. Town Square/Harbor (Piazza Pia/Porto Commerciale) ★★★

Just off the square, at the harbor where U.S. and Canadian Special Forces landed, a 30-foot black-marble monolith is dedicated to Allied soldiers. Behind the monolith, on Via Mimma Pollastrini, a plaque in Italian (attached to the Telecom Italia office) commemorates the U.S. and Canadian Special Forces, and includes the group's distinctive arrowhead logo. Around the corner is the Piazza Pia and Anzio tourist office. The town church includes an original bell taken by an American soldier as loot after the battle. The bell—just nine inches tall and five inches in diameter—wound up in a U.S. museum and was finally returned to Anzio in 1999.

Expanded considerably since the war, Anzio's main harbor—once flooded with troops, equipment and transport ships arriving from North Africa—retains a few pre-war buildings. At Via Porto Innocenziano 13 (the street running out toward the sea), a plaque honors the U.S. 488th Port Battalion. On the side of the reddish-orange castle nearby, a plaque recalls the January 29, 1944, capsizing of the British cruiser H.M.S. *Spartan*, sunk by German air bombardment. A few blocks west of the harbor, along Riviera Mallozzi, stands a large copper sculpture of a girl surrounded by birds of peace—this is the monument to Angelita, a young girl orphaned on the invasion beach, taken care of by British soldiers, but soon killed in a bomb blast. Many dispute the story as legend—the Germans had evacuated Anzio civilians long before the invasion—but fact or myth, Angelita has become a popular symbol of Anzio.

2. Anzio Beachhead Museum (Museo Della Sbarco Di Anzio) ★★

On Via degli Elci (off Viale Mencacci)
T: (0)6-984-5147
Tuesday, Thursday, Saturday, Sunday,
10 a.m.-12:30 p.m., 5-7 p.m. July-August
(Open 4-6 p.m. September-June)

Housed in a 17th-century villa, this small museum is packed with items donated by veterans from all combatant armies. Included are photos, uniforms, full field kitchen, small weaponry, U.S. Navy searchlight and original Ernie Pyle dispatch—he describes the embattled Anzio beach as "tiny and shell-raked." Sergeant Kazuo Masuda, killed in action with the legendary Japanese-American 100th/442nd Regimental Combat Team, is honored.

3. Anzio War Cemetery ★★

Via Nettunense (near Santa Teresa Basilica)

The smaller of Anzio's two British cemeteries holds the graves of 1,056 soldiers solely from the British Isles. Of note is the grave of Able Seaman B.F. Waters (five from the right in the first row), father of Pink Floyd bassist Roger Waters. The cemetery overlooks the sea and Santa Teresa Basilica bell tower, rebuilt with money from the United States.

4. Beach Head War Cemetery ★★

Via Nettunense (just north of point 3)

As at the Anzio War Cemetery, this one includes a small plaque and map describing "The War in Italy." Buried here are 2,312 soldiers of the Commonwealth—Canada, Australia, New Zealand, India, South Africa, others—amid pine trees and flowered trellises.

5. Lavinio/Peter Beach ★★

About 9 km north of Anzio along Via Ardeatina

The principal British force landed at the then almost completely undeveloped area of Lavinio, code-named (and sometimes still called) Peter Beach. Along Lungomare Enea, in front of Lavinio's main square (about 30 yards from the beach), is a monument to the 6th Battalion of the Gordon Highlanders and public access to Peter Beach. Now lined with hotels and villas, the flat, narrow beach is almost unrecognizable, according to many returning vets. South along the coast a little more than a km is Torre Caldara, the Middle Ages tower that marked the southern end of Peter Beach, and survived the battle. Inland from the tower is Tor Caldara Wilderness Reserve, the only area that retains its 1940s appearance.

6. Casino di Anzio ★★

Along the Riviera Zanardelli—the road used by U.S. Rangers to advance from Anzio to Nettuno—is the town's original and spectacular casino, with a massive rotunda and six marble statues in front exemplifying its "Liberty" style design. On the building is a plaque commemorating the Rangers, 300 of whom died during particularly vicious fighting at this spot.

7. Nettuno Museum of the Allied Landing (Museo Dello Scarbo Alleato) ★★

Via Gramsci 5, Nettuno, 2 km from Point 6
T: (0)6-980-3620
Monday, Wednesday, Friday, 8 a.m.-2 p.m.
Tuesday, Thursday, 8 a.m.-2 p.m., 3-6 p.m.

In a Middle Ages fortress on the sea, this good museum has a number of rooms crammed with relics—uniforms, weaponry, and so on. Of note are a number of moving then-and-now photos of young soldiers next to photos of their aged selves. Among many excellent black-and-white enlargements is an interesting GI barber shop: Available cuts listed on a hand-lettered sign include the Shrapnel Trim (40 cents) and Stuka Singe (51 cents). Just up the street, the seaside villas at Via Gramsci 33-45 housed combat journalists, including GI cartoonist Bill Mauldin.

8. Sicily-Rome American Cemetery and Memorial ★★★★

Viale Giacomo Matteotti, Nettuno, about 3 km east of Anzio. The cemetery is signed from Nettuno's main roads, including a sign on Via Gramsci, 0.2 km east of point 7. T: 703-696-6897 (Arlington, Virginia) Daily, 9 a.m.-5 p.m. (closed 4 p.m. in winter) Closed December 25, January 1

On 77 acres of former vineyard where heavy fighting raged (and a field hospital later stood), one of two U.S. military cemeteries in Italy (the other is in Florence) contains 7,860 marble crosses and Stars of David, arranged in arcs sweeping across a broad, green lawn. Those buried here died throughout the Italian campaign, including Sicily. The impressive memorial—thick columns flanked by 80-foot-high flagpoles—is constructed of Roman travertine stone. Carved on one wall is an enormous campaign map, with lengthy inscriptions describing the Allied conquest of Italy. This is Anzio's primary war-related attraction, a place that, given the sheer number of gravestones and scale of combat they represent, provokes somber reflection and a sense of awe.

9. U.S. 3rd Division Landing Monument/X-Ray Beach ★

On Via Latina, 5.1 km east of Point 7

U.S. forces landed at code-named X-Ray Beach, a long, sandy stretch east of Nettuno. On the left side of the main road heading toward Latina is a low stone block marking the landing point of the U.S. 3rd Division and subsequent "four months (of) great sacrifice of human life." The beach is fenced off—it's now a restricted NATO site used for ordnance testing. Permission to access the historic beach can be obtained by calling (06-98-57-6225) or writing to: Centro Militaire Collaudi ed Esperienze per L'Armamento, Ufficio Tecnico Territoriale Armamenti, Terrestri, Piazzale Delgi Eroi, 00048 Nettuno, Italy.

RELATED SITES BEYOND ANZIO

Flyover/Campo di Carne ★

Along SS207 between Anzio and Aprilia, at Campo di Carne train station, about 12 km north of Anzio

The heaviest fighting at Anzio actually occurred inland, far from the town and beaches. Students of the battle will recognize the "Flyover" (the reference is simply to a highway overpass) as a spot of bitter, prolonged battle. Driving here from Peter Beach, one gets a good sense of the flat, exposed terrain across which Allied forces had to advance against determined, professional resistance. Rebuilt to resemble the wartime Flyover, the modern overpass stands between a factory and the old Campo di Carne rail station. From the top of the overpass, visitors get instructive battlefield views of the Alban Hills to the north (toward Rome), from which German guns pummeled this position for months. It's impressive to get a straight-line visual of how far the heavy guns of World War II could accurately fire. During the battle, the area was riddled with foxholes and denuded of vegetation.

Piana delle Orme (Plain of Traces) ★★★★★

Via Migliara 43.5, Borgo Faiti, Latina. From SS148 follow signs to Borgo Faiti, then the museum. About one road hour northeast of Anzio.
T: (0)773-25-8708
Daily, 9 a.m.-7 p.m.
€10

In the middle of an agricultural field, this huge exhibition center documents the history of area farming culture. Five of its 14 enormous halls, however, are devoted to World War II's North African and Italian campaigns. The immense collection and innovative presentations make it one of the best private war museums in the world. Hundreds of pristine, operational vehicles—trucks, jeeps, self-propelled guns, motorcycles, half-tracks and tanks, including the one used in the filming of *The English Patient* and *Life Is*

Beautiful—are too numerous to list here. Other highlights include endless uniforms, life-size battle dioramas (with audio effects loops), a Curtiss P-40 fighter plane dredged from the sea near Anzio, battle footage and much more. The five massive buildings are devoted to Vehicles, El Alamein, Sicily and Messina, Anzio and Cassino. Without argument, this is the best war museum in Italy, among the best in Europe. Allow three to four hours for the World War II section.

Getting To/Around Anzio

About 50 km from Rome (page 206 for airline information), Anzio-Nettuno is reached by taking SS148 (off the G.R.A. ring road in Rome) south to SS207 southwest to Anzio. (See Driving, page xv, for car rental information). Direct buses between Anzio and Rome's Termini Station depart hourly (in both directions) between 4:58 a.m. and 9:56 p.m. The trip takes about an hour. Call (0)6-984-5090 for bus information.

In Anzio, Riviera Zanardelli (used by U.S. Rangers to advance on Nettuno) links with Via Antonio Gramsci for the 3 km drive to Nettuno. Lavinio and Lido di Lavinio, 6.5 km north of Anzio, are reached along Via Ardeatina. Taxis in Anzio-Nettuno are scarce. Hotels can arrange drop-offs and pickups. Both towns are easily covered on foot.

The Anzio tourist information office (06-984-5147) is located in the central square at Piazza Pia 19. Among other valuable information, it has free city maps of Anzio and Nettuno.

Accommodations

Grand Hotel Dei Cesari

Via Mantova 3, Anzio
T: (0)6-98-7901 F: (0)6-98-0835
www.hoteldeicesari.com
108 rooms
€85-120

A five-minute drive north of Anzio's central square, the Grand is the best hotel in town. It sits across the road from the shore and has its own private beach (decent, not great). In an annex building, some rooms overlook the beach. Amenities include a good outdoor pool, fitness center and large restaurant.

Hotel Belvedere

Passeggiata delle Sirene 28,
Lido di Lavinio
T: (0)6-982-2554 F: (0)6-982-0379
30 rooms
€90 (€35 in off season)

In Lavinio, about four miles north of Anzio along Peter Beach, this small, pretty resort has a wide beach (one of the better in the area), huge pool and great ocean views from its terrace bar. Rooms are clean and roomy. A few hundred yards down the beach, its sister hotel (Hotel la Playa) is just as nice.

24

Kursk

RUSSIA

T-34

THE WAR YEARS

The Battle of Kursk is typically remembered as the largest tank battle in history—a titanic clash of metallic monsters in a test as much about science and steel as about blood and blade. More than a practical contest of armies and industry, however, the battle is also regarded as both breaking point and allegory for the epic scale of the war in Russia.

Comparisons of the size and significance of battles fought by the Anglo-American alliance in the West and Soviet Army in the East often lead to pointless dissension. Without either "second" front to contend with, the Nazi war machine quite possibly would have won control of all Europe and certainly killed many more thousands than it eventually did. In terms of sheer proportion, however, any statistical comparison leads to the inescapable conclusion that World War II was won on the Eastern Front by the Soviet Union. The USSR is believed to have lost 27 million lives in its Great Patriotic War. By comparison, the official American death toll was about 405,000; Great Britain lost 270,000 military personnel and 60,000 civilians. Even more telling, of the estimated 13 million German casualties in the war, more than 10 million were sustained on the Eastern Front. Kursk was the theater's decisive set-piece engagement.

Following the winter 1942-43 Soviet victory at Stalingrad, the Russian battlefront stabilized along a more or less rational line running from Leningrad in the north to the Black Sea in the south. The exception was a Soviet salient around the agricultural center of Kursk, about 500 miles south of Moscow. There, a pocket of Soviet troops created a bubble—150 miles from top to bottom—protruding 100 miles west into German-held territory. Sensing opportunity, the German command devised a plan (Operation Citadel) to attack the northern and southern shoulders of the Russian bubble in a classic pincers movement. When the pincers met, presumably near Kursk, Red Army forces would be surrounded and annihilated.

Employing 700,000 troops, 2,400 tanks and armored vehicles, and 1,800 aircraft, the Germans launched Citadel on July 5, 1943. Facing the onslaught were 1.3 million Soviet soldiers, 3,400 tanks and armored vehicles, and 2,100 aircraft. From the outset, Germany ran into harsh defense—half a million mines protected Russian positions—but they made progress, advancing ten miles to the town of Ponyri in the north and 30 miles to Prokhorovka in the south. In places, the gap between German forces was narrowed to barely 50 miles.

Germany's early success was illusory. Red Army commander General Georgi Zhukov well knew that the enveloping tactic was a Wehrmacht favorite. Accurate intelligence and keen sense of enemy tendencies persuaded him to pull back the bulk of his forces during the initial phase of the attack. "At virtually every point the Germans had done what Zhukov had expected them to do and had wanted them to do," wrote historian Mark Arnold-Forster. "He could defeat the Germans more certainly and more decisively if he could allow them to use up fuel and ammunition and generally exhaust themselves before he was obliged to commit his own fresh troops and machines."

This Zhukov did with an enormous counter-offensive on July 12. With the German offensive stalled by an insane defense at Ponyri (the town was nearly wiped from the map), the telling confrontation would come on the southern shoulder. There, in a vast, open field outside Prokhorovka, 800 Soviet tanks and vehicles, along with tens of thousands of infantrymen, descended on 450 German tanks and vehicles (and infantry) in history's single biggest tank engagement. More than size it was utter fury, appalling even by the standards of the Eastern Front, that distinguished the battle. The entire field—2.5 miles wide and 6 miles long—became a chaotic front line. Organized command was impossible. Tanks crashed into tanks, rolled over men, burst into flames. Artillery fire, mortars and machine guns rattled without pause. The sustained, mechanized roar of armored battle seemed to belong to a nightmare vision of a soulless industrialized future. "Hell on Earth" was the description most frequently used by veterans from both sides after the battle.

The hero of Kursk was the Soviet T-34 tank, more reliable, easier to repair and tougher to stop than German panzers, Tigers or huge new Ferdinand tanks. Vital support was provided by much-feared Katyusha "Little Katie" rocket-launchers, a scorching weapon that with terrifying screams fired 16 small rockets one after another from the back of a flatbed truck, incinerating entire acres of land within minutes. For all this the battle wasn't a rout. Russia lost far more men and vehicles—a four-to-one ratio by one count—but with a seemingly inexhaustible supply of men managed to hold its lines. With few reserves, the Germans were forced into a withdrawal that until the end of the war they would never succeed in reversing. A second phase of the Soviet counter-offensive—generally considered part of the overall Kursk campaign—pushed the Germans farther west. Throughout August, Zhukov's armies liberated Russian cities such as Belgrade, Orel and Kharkov.

With the triumph at Kursk, the Red Army for the first time was considered a deadly offensive threat with the power to play makeweight in future European affairs. Savoring a newfound sense of leverage, Soviet leader Josef Stalin finally agreed to a first-ever summit with U.S. President Franklin Roosevelt and British Prime Minister Winston Churchill, at Tehran in September 1943. More significant than Kursk's effects on politicians was its effect on the enemy. "The Prokhorovka tank battle was the swan song of the Panzers as attack spearheads," wrote historian Geoffrey Jukes. "Most German soldiers remained disciplined and skillful to the end, but after Kursk they fought in fear of the consequences of defeat rather than in expectation of victory."

SOURCES & OTHER READING

The Battle of Kursk, Glantz and House, University Press of Kansas, 1999

The Second World War (5): The Eastern Front 1941-1945, Jukes, Geoffrey, Osprey Publishing, 2002

Zhukov, Chaney, Otto Preston, University of Oklahoma Press, 1996 (updated from 1971)

The Memoirs of Marshal Zhukov, Zhukov, G.K., Jonathan Cape, 1971

Russia at War, 1941-1945, Werth, Alexander, Barrie & Rockcliff, 1964

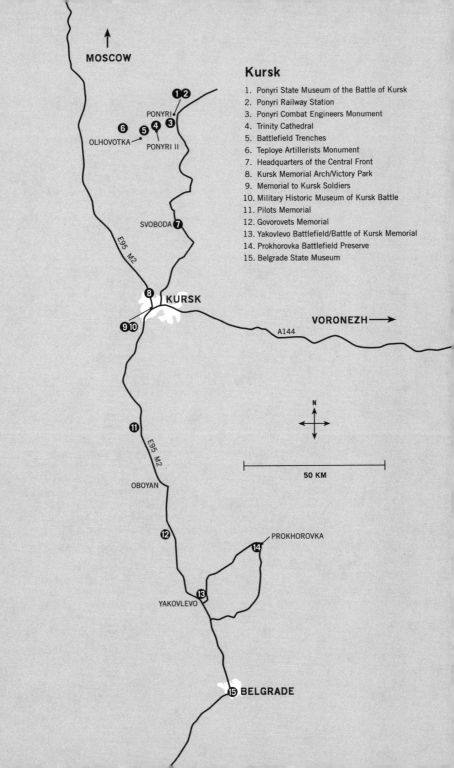

Kursk

1. Ponyri State Museum of the Battle of Kursk
2. Ponyri Railway Station
3. Ponyri Combat Engineers Monument
4. Trinity Cathedral
5. Battlefield Trenches
6. Teploye Artillerists Monument
7. Headquarters of the Central Front
8. Kursk Memorial Arch/Victory Park
9. Memorial to Kursk Soldiers
10. Military Historic Museum of Kursk Battle
11. Pilots Memorial
12. Govorovets Memorial
13. Yakovlevo Battlefield/Battle of Kursk Memorial
14. Prokhorovka Battlefield Preserve
15. Belgrade State Museum

KURSK TODAY

Population: 500,000 (Kursk); 13,600 (Ponyri); 20,000 (Prokhorovka)
Country Code: 7 • 100 rubles = $3.50/£1.80/€2.70

The important thing to understand about Kursk is that the Battle of Kursk took place as far as 100 km north and/or south of the city, not in the city itself—the capture of Kursk was among the unrealized goals of the German attack, hence the name. Roughly equidistant between the northern and southern shoulders of the battle, however, Kursk is centrally located for battlefield tours. The battle arch and park (Point 8) are pleasant on sunny days, but this is largely a sprawling city built on agriculture and transportation, with little to recommend it to casual tourists. There are a few surviving manor houses—gorgeous remnants of aristocratic days that survived Bolshevik destruction—the pearl being the classicist Marjino house.

The surrounding steppe can be attractive in spring and summer, covered with a colorful carpet of grass and flowers. This brightens up the impoverished villages to a considerable degree, which in winter are gray, wet and bleak. Driving the length of the Kursk battlefield, the traveler gains a visceral appreciation of the immensity of the territory and epic difficulty of any military operation designed to conquer and hold it. Kursk edged onto the list of "25 Essential" by virtue of its historic significance, not tourist appeal. It's a place where only those with a serious interest in either the battle or the rigors of Russia's rural countryside should venture. Two full days (lots of slow driving) are needed to see the entire battlefield.

POINTS OF INTEREST

Northern Shoulder

Battle monuments are spread throughout the countryside, particularly around Ponyri. Located on unmarked, country roads, most are hard to locate without a local guide (see Three Whales travel agency, page 137). Villages and agricultural landscapes look much as they did in 1943, providing an unvarnished look at a Russian countryside few travelers bother to explore.

1. Ponyri State Museum of the Battle of Kursk ★★

(Muzey Kurskoy Bitvey)
12 Lenin St., Ponyri (80 km north of Kursk)
T: (0)71-352-1660
Daily, 10 a.m.-5 p.m.
Closed Monday, last Friday of every month
5 rubles

The small town of Ponyri suffered the worst fighting of the northern shoulder—

the front line cut through the town—before the German advance was halted here. On the central square, this three-room museum recounts the battle with small relics recovered from local fields, photos and text (no English signage). A 30-foot-long diorama depicts the battle—an impressive piece for a small museum.

2. Ponyri Railway Station ★★

(Ponyri Zheleznodorozhnye Vokzal)
Square of Victory, Ponyri. About 400 yards from Point 1.

Vicious hand-to-hand combat demolished the wartime train station. On the same foundation, this station was built after the war as a national memorial. The interior is decorated with battle scenes and portraits of important wartime figures, such as Marshal Konstantin Rokossovsky. In the Square of Victory outside the terminal, a black pedestal marks a common military grave containing 2,000 corpses.

3. Ponyri Combat Engineers Monument ★

In suburb of Mayasky, just south of Ponyri

A 40-foot tower featuring oversized combat engineers carrying land mines stands in a field where more than 300 tanks clashed. The monument was erected in November 1943, then rebuilt in the 1960s. A large common grave is on the site.

4. Trinity Cathedral ★★

In Ponyri II, 10 km southwest of Ponyri

Miraculously surviving the battle (bullet scars are visible on the façade), the church is now a monument to ancient Orthodox architecture as well as the Great Patriotic War. The cemetery behind the church was the location of a Soviet artillery position.

5. Battlefield Trenches ★★

On Ponyri II-Olhovotka Road, about 2 km west of Point 4

Along the road is a white monument depicting a tank with the dates 1945 and 1975. To the left of the monument, a path leads into the woods along the edge of a hotly contested battlefield. After less than 100 yards, bomb craters, defense ditches and trenches become apparent off both sides of the path. The path and battle evidence continues for at least a km into the woods. As recently as 2002, a man found a World War II shell in a nearby field, took it home and was killed when it exploded.

6. Teploye Artillerists Monument ★

About 1.5 km east of village of Teploye, about 15 km southwest of Ponyri

The artillery cannon at the base of this obelisk was used in the battle—some of the crew that manned it are buried here. Tablets inscribed with names of the dead mark a common grave. About 1.5 km farther west along the same road is a monument to the 140th NKVD Division from Siberia. It's surrounded by pine trees imported from Siberia.

7. Headquarters of the Central Front ★★

(Komandnye Punkt Zentralnogo Fronta) 38 Soviet St., Svoboda. About 40 km south of Ponyri
T: (0)251-3-1356
Daily, 9 a.m.-5 p.m.
Closed Monday, holidays
10 rubles

General Konstantin Rokossovsky commanded the Soviet Central Front at Kursk. After the war, with Rokossovsky's assistance, his headquarters bunker was rebuilt following the original scheme. Consisting of a hallway, two rooms and replica furnishings, the subterranean log-reinforced bunker is small but evocative.

Kursk City Sites

8. Kursk Memorial Arch/Victory Park ★★

Karl Marx Street, at northern boundary of Kursk

At the northern entrance of Kursk, this marble arch commemorates victory in the Battle of Kursk. Along a wide pedestrian boulevard are a statue of General Zhukov, a ceremonial tribune, an eternal flame, a small cathedral and a line of artillery cannons flanked by a T-34 tank and Katyusha

rocket launcher. About 3 km south, a Soviet military cemetery is identified by the years 1941 and 1945 on the front wall.

9. Memorial to Kursk Soldiers ★

Red Square, Kursk

Kursk's central square has the *de rigueur* Lenin statue, as well as a wall bearing the names of local soldiers who died throughout the war. No matter the size, virtually all Russian towns have such a memorial.

10. Military Historic Museum of Kursk Battle ★★

(Muzey Kurskoy Bitvey)
12 Sonina St.
T: (0)71-256-6298
Wednesday-Sunday, 9 a.m.-4 p.m.
Closed Monday, Tuesday
30 rubles

Housed within the Russian Federation

Army Officers Club, this museum has a collection of photos and small relics. Highlights include a Cossack cavalryman's sword (notches indicate lives taken), a Tiger tank shell carved with symbols and slogans by an artistic German soldier and an enormous campaign wall map. Weaponry includes PPS machine guns, Mauser rifles and various mortars. No English signage.

Southern Shoulder

Mostly located along main roads, Points 11-15 are easier to find than those in the northern shoulder. Still, a local guide is helpful.

11. Pilots Memorial ★

Along Route M2 (aka Moscow-Simpferopol Road), 2 km from the town of Paniky, about 40 km south of Kursk

On the right side of the road (traveling south from Kursk) this three-pillared memorial with a pilot's face is located on farmland that once served as a fighter airfield. About 20 km south along the same road (Route M2), in Oboyan, a post-war MiG jet on a roadside pedestal stands as a memorial to World War II pilots.

12. Govorovets Memorial ★

Along Route M2 (Moscow-Simpferopol Road), at fork in road about 15 km south of Oboyan. From this fork, veer left onto E105 toward Belgrade to continue viewing sites.

In a single, 35-minute battle, pilot Alexander Govorovets was credited with downing nine German planes, ramming the ninth with his own battered machine. His bust stands here on a pedestal. About 1.5 km back up M2 (north toward Oboyan) is the (unmarked) farthest point of German advance in the southern shoulder.

13. Yakovlevo Battlefield/Battle of Kursk Memorial ★★★★

(Memorial Kurskoy Bitvoy)
On E105 at northern edge of Yakovlevo, about 25 km south of Point 12, 100 km south of Kursk

Museum open daily, 9 a.m.-5 p.m.
Closed Monday
15 rubles

On what was known as the Voronezh Front, 400 tanks met in battle on July 6 and 7, in the opening phases of the German offensive. Two panzer corps penetrated the first line of Soviet defenses, setting the stage for the Prokhorovka battle (Point 14) less than a week later. Today the site is dominated by a 100-foot-long wall with tank crew faces carved in relief. The open field behind the wall was the main battle area. Also on the site are a 50-foot memorial tower, a T-34 tank, an eternal flame, a small chapel and a rebuilt trench system visitors can walk through. Beneath the wall is a museum—weaponry, photos, vintage Soviet posters, 20-minute Russian documentary.

14. Prokhorovka Battlefield Preserve ★★★★

(Muzey Zapovednik Prokhorovskaya Bitva)
On southern outskirts of Prokhorovka (just before entering town from highway). From Point 13, proceed south along main road toward Belgrade. Turn left at sign (in Cyrillic) for "Prokhorovka 28." A Katyusha rocket-launcher truck is at the turnoff. Proceed almost 28 km to site.

On July 12, 1943, 450 German tanks confronted 800 Soviet tanks and armored vehicles in a hellish melee—the single largest tank battle in history. On the field today is a golden bell tower and six Soviet tanks and armored vehicles. Preserved as a national historic battlefield, visits here are about simply being at the location of this momentous event. It's possible to walk around the field (often muddy) and find chunks of metal from the battle. Up the road, Prokhorovka's main Chapel of the Apostles Peter and Paul honors Battle of Kursk victims. The names of 15,000 soldiers are inscribed inside. Across the street is a large statue of soldiers standing on the ruins of a German eagle.

15. Belgrade State Museum/Diorama of the Kursk Battle ★★★

(Belgorod Muzey Diarama)
2 Popov St., Belgrade (about 30 km south of turnoff from main road to Point 14)
T: (0)72-232-9689

Daily, 10 a.m.-1 p.m.; 2-5:30 p.m.
Closed Monday, last day of month, January 1
30 rubles

This is the best and largest museum dedicated to the Kursk battle. Professional exhibits are set amid chunks of twisted metal representing the fury of the battle. Though there's no English signage, photos, maps, weaponry and various displays tell the story well. The highlight is an absorbing panorama—the canvas is 220 feet long, 50 feet high—depicting the battle from start to finish (moving right to left, with climax in the center). Outside are a number of tanks, vehicles and copy of a Soviet La-5 fighter plane, important at Kursk.

GETTING TO/AROUND KURSK

Kursk is best reached by train from Moscow's Kursk Railway Station. (See page 136 for Moscow flight information). The trip takes about nine hours; overnight trains available. Information on the national Russian rail system is available at (0)95-266-9333 (in Moscow). Russian trains can be booked from the United States through RailEurope (800-782-2424). It's possible to fly from Moscow to Kursk (Aeroflot 095-753-

5555 in Moscow), but the train is more practical.

Kursk is spread out, but there are plenty of taxis and mini-buses. A vehicle is necessary for anyone wishing to tour the battlefields. Road signs are a. entirely in Cyrillic or b. nonexistent. Driving isn't impossible in Russia, but a local guide is worth considering more here than at any other location in this book. See Three Whales travel agency (page 137).

ACCOMMODATIONS

Kursk
Solovyenaya Rozha Hotel
142a Engelsa St.
T: (0)71-232-5532 F: (0)71-232-6600
50 Rooms
$120

This is Kursk's only tourist-quality hotel. Rooms are large and well kept. The drawback is lack of anything of interest within immediate walking distance.

Kursk Hotel
24 Lenin St.
T: (0)71-22-6980 F: (0)71-22-9711
200 rooms
$30
This hotel has two selling points—price

and location on Kursk's main square. At least half the floors have been updated in recent years. Ask for an updated room.

Belgrade
Belgrade Hotel
Central Square
T: (0)72-232-2512 F: (0)72-232-9764
www.belhotel@bel.ru
100 rooms
$65

If your focus is on the southern shoulder, consider basing out of Belgrade instead of Kursk. A short walk to the Belgrade State Museum and Diorama (Point 15), this is the city's top hotel. The lobby is bright and rooms are a good size.

25

Auxiliary Sites

Pillboxes near Gela, Sicily

AUXILIARY SITES

The war in Europe consumed such an immense area that, given the space limitations of this guide, providing full treatment for all locations involved is impossible. The 25th "site" is therefore left to the reader's interest. A paucity of relics has landed some locations on the following list. Red tape, development and politics have left others less satisfying or more problematic to visit. In all cases, however, each site in this chapter is worth a visit or at least a brief detour for those who happen to be in the region, or have a relative or loved one who was.

AMSTERDAM (NETHERLANDS)

Anne Frank House (Anne Frank Huis)

263 Prinsengracht (Museum entrance at 267 Prinsengracht)
T: (0)20-556-7105
Daily, 9 a.m.-7 p.m. (closed at 9 p.m., March 15-September 14)
Open limited hours: January 1, May 4, December 20, December 25, December 31
Closed Yom Kippur
Adult €7.50; Student (10-17): €3.50; Last admission 30 minutes before closing.

In 1942-44, schoolgirl Anne Frank, a German-born Jew, hid from Nazi persecution (along with her parents, sister and four others) in the "Secret Annex" hidden upstairs rooms in her father's office building in the center of Amsterdam. While in hiding, she kept a diary. Frank eventually died of typhus in Bergen-Belsen concentration camp barely a month before her 16th birthday, but her diary—generally known as *The Diary of Anne Frank*—is one of the world's most widely read accounts of Nazi oppression.

The preserved building where the Franks hid stands among the war's most evocative and most visited museums. Visitors pass through the original, movable bookcase that concealed the annex and climb a series of narrow, steep stairs (not handicap accessible) to the small rooms where the family lived in constant fear of discovery. Anne's empty room is preserved with original wallpaper and pictures of movie stars she pasted to the wall. Film, photo and text exhibits are powerful. Crowds are heaviest on all weekends and in summer between 10 a.m.-2 p.m., when lines can take up to an hour. The museum advises evening visits. Allow one hour for the extremely emotional house and museum experience.

AUSTRIA

On March 12, 1938, German troops marched into independent Austria and absorbed the country's largely German-speaking population into the Third Reich. The "Aunschluss" or annexation occurred when German soldiers crossed the Saalach River into Austria from the small town of Freilassing, Germany, about 6 km from Salzburg, an theatrically immortalized in *The Sound of Music*. Travelers can visit the site of the **Aunschluss Crossing** in Freilassing near the restaurant Gasthaus Zollhäus at 11 Zollhäuslstrasse. About 40 yards from the restaurant, to the right of the police station, a footpath leads 75 yards to the Saalach River. Austria lies across the river. The bridge used by Germans was destroyed, but its original concrete foundation remains on the river bank. There's very little to see—the location is listed for those with a special interest. The Freilassing train station is located just behind Zollhäuslstrasse, a 15-minute walk from the site.

Adolf Hitler's birthplace can be seen at 15 Salzburger Vorstadt in the small, pretty town of Branau, Austria, across the Inn River border from the German town of Simbach, about 150 km east of Munich. The only indication of the three-story building's place in history—even the address numbers are missing, though it's easily found next to 17 Salzburger Vorstadt—is a stone in front of the building brought to the site from Mauthausen concentration camp. The stone's German inscription roughly translates: "For peace, freedom and democracy, never again fascism, the warning of millions of people." Hitler was born inside and lived in the house from 1889-1892. A small shop now occupies the ground floor. To find the house, follow signs for Zentrum (center) and park on Stadtplatz (city square) near the city tower. The house is in the pedestrian-only zone, about 100 yards from the tower.

BALKANS

Germany's swift envelopment of Hungary, Romania, Bulgaria and the fragment countries of former Yugoslavia is beyond the scope of this book—though well deserving of one that isn't focused on guiding travelers to the essential World War II sites. The Balkans suffered enormously during the war, one that they were largely muscled into entering and then losing, before tailspinning through much of the last century. Independent travelers are encouraged to visit these fascinating countries, just not for their overall meager preservation of World War II history.

A few important sites spread over a huge area include **Hungary's Museum of Military History** in Budapest, **Bulgaria's National Museum of History** in Sofia and **Serbia's Military Museum** in Belgrade, all of which include World War II coverage among other historical exhibits. The **Museum of Yugoslav Aviation** at Belgrade airport houses a collection of WWII aircraft, including some rare Italian fighters. **Croatia's Modern History Museum** in Dubrovnik has a substantial collection of WWII documents and memorabilia. About 60 miles south of Zagreb in the clearly cursed town of **Jasenovac**, Croatia's largest (and one of the war's most notorious) concentration camps run by the barbaric Ustasha puppet regime is now a sad, decrepit museum of sorts. A more uplifting experience awaits visitors of the **Franja Partisan Hospital** in northwest Slovenia. In a canyon near the town of Cerkno, this famous medical complex survived two German attacks.

BELARUS

The greatest of the monolithic Soviet monuments to the Great Patriotic War is the colossal **Brest Fortress** (a few km southwest of the city center, Tuesday-Sunday, 9:30 a.m.-6 p.m.) in Brest, near the Polish border. Two regiments at this key fortress held out for a month during the early weeks of the Nazi invasion. The whole huge complex is now an eye-popping monument and museum, from its enormous Soviet star-shaped entry to the "Valor Rock" in the shape of a soldier's head. The museum inside recalls the heroic defense. For anyone finding themselves on the Belarussian frontier, it's a must. The capital of Minsk is home to the extensive, 28-room **Museum of the Great Patriotic War** (Praspekt Francyska Skaryny, 277-5611, Tuesday-Sunday, 10 a.m.-5 p.m.). It presents a particularly graphic and gruesome history of Nazi oppression. On the corner of Vulitsas Zaslavskaja and Melnikatje are bronze figures on a staircase of death, the primary feature of the **Jewish Ghetto Memorial**, on the site of a pit where on March 2, 1942, 5,000 Jews were executed, then buried.

CANADA

Canadian War Museum
General Motors Court
1 Vimy Place
Ottawa, Ontario

T: 819-776-8600 or 800-555-5621
Daily, 9 a.m.-6 p.m. (Thursdays open until 9 p.m.)
From October 9-April 30. Closed 5 p.m. Tuesday-Sunday, and closed on Mondays
Select holiday closures
Adult: $10 (all prices Canadian); Senior/Student: $8; Child: $6; Family: $25

This museum chronicles the history of all Canadian armed forces, but Gallery 3 is devoted to World War II. Canadian troops served with distinction across Europe, most famously in helping spearhead D-Day landings in Normandy. The museum's Vimy House (221 Champagne Ave., North Ottawa) is a large auxiliary location 12 minutes by car from the main museum. It houses tanks, artillery and large military equipment. Contact main museum for limited opening hours.

ENGLAND/CHANNEL ISLANDS

See France, below.

FINLAND

Finland's wild eastern border stretching from the lakelands of Karelia to sub-Arctic Lapland remains about as off-the-radar now as it was when a handful of diehard Finnish divisions and mobile ski units endured freezing conditions and overwhelming odds against an avalanche of Soviet invaders in the 100-day Winter War (1939-40) and later, with temporary German aid, the Continuation War. By 1945, nearly 100,000 Finnish soldiers had been killed, huge tracts of Lapland were scorched by fleeing Nazis and a major chunk of the war zone was ceded to Stalin. Amazingly, Finland made it through World War II with its independence intact. Some austere pride in this feat can be found at **Helsinki's Military Museum** located at Maurinkatu 1 (358-9-1812-6381; Tuesday-Thursday, noon-6 p.m.; Friday, Saturday, 11 a.m.-4 p.m.). The former **home of General C.G.E. Mannerheim** at Kalliolinnantie 14 (358-0963-5443; Friday-Sunday, 11 a.m.-4 p.m.) is now a small museum paying tribute to the career of Finland's most illustrious war hero. These days, Karelia mainly attracts hikers, cross-country skiers and rustic-village hoppers, though some historic battlegrounds, including **Ilomantsi**, **Kuhmo** and **Suomussalmi**, are marked with modest monuments and memorials. Many other famous sites are now over the post-war border on Russian soil, requiring separate visas.

FRANCE

Channel Islands

Only limited space and relative strategic unimportance prevent the Channel Islands from having a dedicated chapter in this book. For World War II enthusiasts, however, few places offer as much to see as these sunny vacation isles. Although the islands belong to Great Britain, their position 20 miles off the northwest coast of France makes them easier and faster to access (via daily car-and-passenger ferry service) from St-Malo, France. Daily scheduled air and sea transport from Great Britain to the principle islands of Jersey and Guernsey is available. Rental cars—essential here—are available on the islands.

The small group of undefended Channel Islands was the only British territory occupied by Germany during the war. The occupation—harsh for most of the 60,000 non-evacuated locals, mild for some—began in late June and early July 1940. An extensive German garrison remained until war's end. The islands were overvalued by Hitler, first as steppingstone to an invasion of Britain, then as a vital piece of his Atlantic Wall fortifications. Because the Germans built extensive defenses bypassed by the war, the islands have been left "covered with an evocative tapestry of strange wartime buildings ... tunnels and earthworks," according to the *Channel Islands: Jersey, Guernsey, Alderney, Sark* guide, by George Forty. Other war sites publications and maps are available on the islands, or by contacting the Channel Islands Occupation Society (CIOS, Binebeca, Petites Capelles, St. Sampson, Guernsey GY2 4GR, England or Chris Le Tissier at cletissier@supanet.com). The Guernsey Tourist Board (01481-72-6611, enquiries@tourism.guernsey.net) and Jersey Tourist Board (01534-50-0700, info@jersey.com) also provide information on travel and lodging.

For war sites, it's difficult to pick between Guernsey and Jersey. **Guernsey** has at least a dozen major points of interest, starting with the German Occupation Museum (at Les Houards in Forest Parish, 01481-23-8205, daily, 10 a.m.-5 p.m., April-October, Tuesday-Sunday, 10 a.m.-1 p.m., winter). La Vallette Underground Military Museum (01481-72-2300) is housed in a German tunnel system. The restored Naval Signals Headquarters includes three concrete bunkers. A large coastal-defense casemate includes its original heavy gun. The colossal Naval Observation and Range-Finding Tower at Pleinmont headland sits atop a cliff overlooking the sea. The Underground Hospital features the largest tunnel network in the islands. There's much more to see.

Jersey has at least eight major sites and four museums: The Channel Islands Military Museum (behind Jersey Woollen Mills, Five Mile Road in St. Ouen, 01534-72-3136, daily, 10 a.m.-5 p.m., April 14-October 31) is a good place to begin. Other museums include St. Peter's Bunker Museum (in St. Peter's Village), La Hougue Bie Museum (near St. Saviour) and the Island Fortress Occupation Museum (9 Esplanade in St. Helier). The Underground Command Bunker at Noirmonte Point, St. Brelade, drops 40 feet below ground. Along Five Mile Road between La Pulente and Le Braye are a large coastal-defense gun and anti-tank casemates. The casemate at Millbrook, opposite La Rue de Galet, contains a rare Czech anti-tank gun. As with Guernsey, there's too much to list in total here.

Once described as the Atlantic Wall's "concrete battleship," **Alderney** has plenty of left-over concrete fortifications, but nothing as dramatic as on Jersey and Guernsey. Tiny **Sark** has a small occupation museum and various ruins.

Ile de Cézembre/St-Malo

A scenic, 30-minute boat ride from St-Malo, the small island of Ile de Cézembre (about a half-mile by quarter-mile) is a little-publicized World War II treasure (almost all visitors come for the small beach, not the relics). During the 1944 Battle of Normandy it became a major pocket of resistance, submitting only after a terrible month-long siege. It's now a well-preserved battlefield, crammed with the debris of German fortifications. From rusted barbed wire to gun emplacements and concrete bunkers, there are 40 or more structure ruins or items in a compact area. The high point is a small railway gun on its original mount on the eastern side of the island. A few bunkers are accessible—flashlight helpful. The island can be walked in an hour. About 240 miles west of Paris, St-Malo is one of the region's most scenic cities. Two companies operate day trips to the island from small kiosk offices at St-Malo's main port just in front of the west wall of the Old City at Porte de Dinan. Etoile des Iles (02-99-40-4872, www.etoile-marine.com) departs at noon, returns at 6 p.m. Corsaire Company (02-23-18-1515) leaves from the same location at 12:40 p.m., returns at 6:20 p.m. Cost is about €10. Hours and days of operation fluctuate with season—call ahead. Boat reservations are often necessary a day or two ahead in summer. There are no roads, vehicles or overnight accommodations on the small island. A decent beach restaurant serves food, drinks and alcohol. In St.-Malo itself, the **39/45 Memorial** (in Fort de la Cité, 02-99-40-7185) has displays, relics, photos and uniforms, but the real draw is its location inside a large, three-level German anti-aircraft bunker.

Lyon

The country's third-largest city (behind Paris and Marseilles) suffers unjust neglect from travelers. A national reputation for brilliant cuisine, wide boulevards (rarely clogged with tourists) and awesome Renaissance architecture—untouched by air raids, it's the second-largest urban area on UNESCO's list of World Heritage Sites—make Lyon the great secret of France. The hidden passageways (***traboules***) of the Renaissance district were used extensively by the French Resistance. Open to the public about 8 a.m.-7 p.m., the *traboule* that connects 54 Rue St-Jean and 27 Rue du Boeuf (accessed from either side) offers an opportunity to walk in the clandestine footsteps of the Resistance. Largely through photos and text (English audio guide available), the **Center of the Resistance and Deportation** (14 Ave. Berthelot, 04-78-72-2311, Wednesday-Sunday, 9 a.m.-5 p.m., subway stop Perrache) chronicles thousands of details of the French Resistance, including a display with a ration card for France's beloved dogs.

Maginot Line

Fort Fermont (Fermont Ligne Maginot)

Longuyon, France, on D174, south of Luxembourg City
T: (0)3-82-39-3534
Times and days vary with season—call ahead
Closed October-March
Adult: €5; Child (7-12): €3
All tours in French. Printed English guide available for €3.

Anticipating static lines of defense similar to those of World War I, France spent the 1930s constructing the Maginot Line, a network of defensive structures anchored by 52 forts on the northeast border of France and Germany between Sedan and the Rhine river. In World War I terms it was something of a super-trench, but Germany's air-and-tank driven blitzkrieg rendered the Maginot Line an anachronism almost as soon as it was completed. The structures of the line are nevertheless fascinating, staggering in their complexity and, for anyone getting as near as southern Belgium or Luxembourg City, well worth a side trip.

Built between 1931 and 1935 by 2,000 laborers, the 25-hectare Fort Fermont is one of the most accessible Maginot Line structures. Dropping 100 feet below ground, it includes endless tunnels and concrete walls almost six feet thick. In June 1940, German forces spent a futile day attacking the fort (they suffered 80 casualties to the fort's one), bypassed it, then occupied it through the war following France's capitulation. The real attraction is the fort's sheer size. Over the compulsory two-and-a-half-hour guided tour, one sees operational, retractable gun turrets that revolve 360 degrees, huge 75 mm guns and countless wartime pieces, including a haunting 1930s surgical theater. The tour includes a 1 km ride through the tunnels on the original and very noisy narrow-gauge railway used to transport men, shells and other supplies through the gargantuan fort. Tours involve a fair amount of walking and stair climbing. The unremitting concrete environment, constant 53-degree temperature (those without sweatshirts will suffer) and lack of English signage can make visits tedious for kids or those entering without prior enthusiasm. For others, this is a superb experience.

Almost due south of Luxembourg City and even larger than Fermont is **Fort du Hackenberg** (61 bis, Grand'rue, Veckring, 03-82-82-3008). The most powerful fort of the Maginot Line, it included 19 blockhouses and 18 pieces of artillery for a 1,034-man crew. The tour is similar to Fermont's, though larger in every way. Two km west of town of Bitche, **Le Simserhof** (03-87-96-3940) was called the "invincible fort of the Maginot Line." Excellent tours of this large complex—100 feet below ground—include film, photos and relics. **Maginot Line** attractions are too numerous to include here, but any of the three major installations listed above can provide information on sister sites.

Natzweiler-Struthof

Fifty-five km southwest of Strasbourg and five km from Rothau, the Natzweiler-Struthof Museum-Memorial (off D130, 03-88-76-7899) on the site of the former concentration camp is the most potent Holocaust memorial in France. Enclosed with barbed wire and eight watchtowers, the grounds include a museum, a prison, an autopsy room, a crematorium and a stunning 130-foot-tall geometric monument looming above a cemetery where 1,120 victims of Nazi oppression are buried.

Oradour-sur-Glane (Village Martyr D'Oradour-sur-Glane)

On Road D3 and D4, 21 km northwest of Limoges
T: (0)555-43-0430
Hours vary by month
Adult: €6; Child (8-17): €4; Family: €18

On June 10, 1944, 200 soldiers of the Waffen SS "Der Führer Unit" entered the village of Oradour, forced all residents into the town square and other locations and embarked on a spree of murder, torture and destruction that spared no living soul. Victims of the point-blank shootings included invalids, children and the elderly. In all, 642 were murdered. The town was subsequently looted and razed to the ground. The slaughter appears to have been Nazi retribution for area resistance efforts. Left as it was on that fateful day, the "martyr's village" is now a national shrine, famous throughout France. Visits begin at the modern Center of Remembrance, a powerful museum that includes a 12-minute film (in English) on the massacre. Behind the center, visitors walk slowly and silently through the extensive rubble of the village. A few burned-out automobiles remain in the street. Inside houses are many items—rusted sewing machines, work equipment, kitchen utensils, and so on. Bullet holes can be found in many walls. The museum and village take two to three hours to see. Few sites leave as lasting an impression.

Saumur

Tank Museum (Musée des Blindes)

1043 Route de Fontevraud (Saumur is between Nantes and Tours, off D952)
T: (0)2-41-83-6999
Daily, 9:30 a.m.-6:30 p.m., summer
10 a.m.-5 p.m., all other months
Adult: €5.50; Child (7-13): €3

This world-class collection of tanks and armored vehicles (more than 850 total, 200 on display at any given time) is astounding both for sheer size and variety. Nearly all vehicles are operational, from World War I prototypes to modern tanks. The extensive World War II display includes a German Tiger II or "King" Tiger and 25 other German tanks and vehicles. The France and Allied Rooms each have about 25 tanks, including the workhorse American Sherman and Soviet T-34. There's good English signage, but the €6 guide is recommended. Two or three hours are needed to see this superb museum.

Submarine Pens/St-Nazaire

The Battle of the Atlantic—in which German submarines (U-boats) traveling in wolf packs prowled the seas in search of Allied ships to attack—was one of the most bitterly contested and crucial struggles of the war. To protect and repair U-boats, Germany built colossal "pens" with reinforced concrete walls as thick as 20 feet along the coast at Brest, Lorient, St-Nazaire, La Pallice (near La Rochelle) and Bordeaux.

The best and easiest pens to visit are at St-Nazaire, along Boulevard de la Légion d'Honneur, near the intersection of Rue de Général de Gaulle. The local tourist office (0820-01-4015) is located inside the pens, some of which are used for commercial purposes (shops, museum, cafe). This fantastically outsized and ominous gray structure (in appearance, pretty much like the other pens, all of which still exist) is perhaps the finest standing remnant of the fearsome U-boat operation in the Atlantic. The gloomy structure—a 16-foot-thick concrete slab covers the roof—was the target of 50 Allied bombing raids, none of which hurt the building, which housed 14 side-by-side pens, 62 workshops, 150 offices, dormitories for submarine crews and two power stations. The buildings are wide open (even at night) and can be wandered freely. The roof—accessed (limited hours) by stairs or elevator (behind the tourist office)—has a good display of photos and text (English included) that tell the story of the base. Across the harbor channel, on the side of a concrete blockhouse (a former covered lock that allowed subs to enter pens in all tides), a yellow staircase leads to the roof and "Terrasse Panoramique," from which one gets an open, raised view of the pens. It's the prime place for pictures. The terrace is open 10 a.m.-5:45 p.m.

Toulon/Southern France

Perhaps the most scenic area in which a World War II Europe campaign was fought, the French Riviera was the site of Operation Anvil (later Dragoon), the Allied invasion of Southern France that began with amphibious landings on August 15, 1944. The armies got ashore with few casualties, fought hard battles to take Toulon and Marseilles, then routed the quickly retreating Germans up the valley of the Rhône in one of the most decisive Allied victories of the war. Amid the sunbathers and yacht set of famed beach communities such as St-Tropez are a number of sites related to the campaign. Looking down on Toulon and the Côte d'Azur, the **Provence Landing Memorial/Museum** (atop Mont Faron at Toulon, 04-94-88-0809) is one of the more fantastically sited museums in Europe. Outside are a U.S. Sherman tank painted with the Lorraine Cross (symbol of the French Resistance) and an orientation map pointing out major operations and landing points around Toulon. Inside are uniforms, weaponry and various relics. It's a good museum, but the payoff for the windy drive up the mountain is the view. Fifty-seven km east, along D559 in Le Rayol Canadel-sur-Mer, a 25-foot-high stone **Allied Landing Monument** along the road (just before entering the town from the west) marks the point above the surf where Allied commandos landed on August 14, 1944. About 15 km east along D559 in Cavalaire-sur-Mer is the **U.S. 3rd Infantry Monument**, recalling the men who made an amphibious assault in the vicinity. The primary point of interest in Southern France is the **Rhône American Cemetery and Memorial** (daily, 9 a.m.-5 p.m., closed December 25, January 1) off N562 in the inland city of Draguignan (consult www.abmc.gov for directions). The 861 Americans who died in Operation Anvil/Dragoon are buried in the 12-acre cemetery, which sits astride the route marched by the U.S. 7th Army. Olive trees, gardens, reflecting pools and an oval wall of limestone surround perfectly aligned rows of marble crosses and Stars of David marking graves. In front of the main chapel, a large bronze relief map plots the Allied path to liberate Southern France. Fifteen km southeast of the cemetery on N7 in Le Muy, the **Liberation Museum** (from city center follow signs to Musée de la Liberacion, 04-94-45-1279, open mid-April-August) is a small, private collection that primarily recalls Allied airborne troops. It's a decent side trip only for those going to the cemetery.

Berchtesgaden/Obersalzberg (Eagle's Nest)

In the southeast corner of Germany, 25 km south of Salzburg, Austria, one of the more celebrated buildings of the Third Reich was Adolf Hitler's "Eagle's Nest." Perched atop 6,017-foot Kehlstein mountain amid the dramatic, rugged peaks of the Bavarian Alps (just above Obersalzberg, a small settlement adjacent to the more famous resort town of Berchtesgaden), the retreat (there were no bedrooms inside, no one spent the night there) and its four-mile winding access road were architectural marvels. From the Eagle's Nest's wide terrace, Hitler and his guests enjoyed some of the most spectacular alpine views in the world. Hitler visited the building—completed in 1938, then and now called Kehlsteinhaus by the Germans—just 13 times, but it was so well known that by 1945 American and French soldiers were racing to claim it as a prestigious prize, an event re-created in the HBO series *Band of Brothers*. Obersalzberg and the Eagle's Nest were captured on May 4, 1945—both sides claim to have gotten to the famed retreat first. The Eagle's Nest's private road is accessible only by bus service (086-52-9448-20) from the Obersalzberg Documentation Center. It's open from roughly mid-May through October (depending on snow pack), via road then 406-foot elevator through the center of the mountain to the house. A hiking trail to the building begins at the sign for "Fussweg zum Kehlstein" (footpath to Kehlstein) off Route 319, just beyond the Documentation Center. The Eagle's Nest has been turned into a restaurant, but visitors can get a visceral sense of the past in the dining hall (formerly the conference room, with large fireplace, exposed wood beams, three-foot-thick foundation walls, picture windows) and open terrace where famous footage of Hitler entertaining guests was shot. There's a bookshop inside and some interpretive signage (in German) on the background of the house, but the Hitler association is otherwise subdued.

Opened in 1999 at the bottom of Kehlstein mountain, the excellent **Obersalzberg Documentation Center** (Salzbergstrasse 41, 086-5294-7960, daily, 9 a.m.-5 p.m., April-October, Tuesday-Sunday, 10 a.m.-3 p.m., November-March, last entry one hour before close, closed January 1, November 1, December 24, 25, 31) has more than 900 photos, documents, videos and other exhibits chronicling atrocities of the Third Reich. The centerpiece is a large section of the 3,000-yard-long tunnel system that connected Nazi buildings throughout Obersalzberg. All signage is in German, but a free English audio guide is available. At the Documentation Center, visitors can get a copy of "Die Bunkeranlagen am Obersalzberg," a four-page brochure that shows the location of area points of interest. These include concrete foundation and retaining wall remains of the once-massive **Berghof** house where Hitler lived from 1927 well into the 1930s and where he was on D-Day when Allied troops landed in Normandy (a 10-minute trail to the site in the woods begins at the Documentation Center), **Hermann Göring's and Martin Bormann's houses and private bunkers** and Golf and Ski Obersalzberg resort (the former **Skytop Lodge** operated by the U.S. Army until the 1990s). Occupying the wartime police headquarters, the 15-room **Hotel Zum Turken** (086-52-2428, €49-98) offers access to its own piece of the extensive tunnel and bunker system (€2.60 entry) even for those not staying at the hotel. A large luxury hotel is being built about 200 yards away. Those with a vehicle should pay the €4 per car toll (plus €1.50 per passenger, not counting driver) to drive the 20 km Rossfeld Road (enter at tollbooth, just beyond the Documentation Center), which in places climbs at a 13-percent grade to amazing vistas (on clear days).

Most area visitors stay in the atmospheric Berchtesgaden, which can be reached by train. Named for former Bavarian royalty whose name was lost to history when the family was defeated by the Hapsburgs, the well-run Hotel Wittelsbach (Maximilianstrasse 16, 086-529-6380, €70) is centrally located. The combination of staggering mountain beauty and historic remains makes Berchtesgaden/Obersalzberg worth at least a two-day visit.

Bergen-Belsen Concentration Camp

Beyond broken foundations, there's little left of the original structures at Bergen-Belsen (Gedenkstatte Bergen-Belsen, 49-5051-6011, daily, 9 a.m.-6 p.m.), but a visit to one of the most notorious Nazi concentration camps—where at least 50,000 died, including Anne Frank—is nevertheless a powerful experience. The Documentation Center includes a 25-minute documentary, graphic photos and other items. Outside, large cement markers denote sites of mass graves along with Jewish, Soviet and German monuments. The camp is located 25 km north of Celle, about seven km from the town of Bergen. When approaching Bergen-Belsen, follow signs to Gedenkstätte.

Dresden

About 180 km south of Berlin, Dresden gained notoriety for being, on the night of February 13, 1945, the target of one of the war's most controversial Allied bomber attacks. Having been captured during the Battle of the Bulge, author Kurt Vonnegut wrote the book (and later film) *Slaughterhouse Five* based on his experiences in Dresden, where he was a prisoner of war held in a meat locker under a slaughterhouse during the destruction of the town. Dresden was a dreary shadow of its former self during the East Germany era, but post-Soviet reconstruction has been so thorough that Dresden ranks again among Germany's most beautiful cities. At the heart of the reconstruction is the mighty **Frauenkirche** (Church of Our Lady). During the inferno of February 15, 1945, this symbol of Dresden was reduced to simply another pile in a sea of rubble. In 1993, the rubble was cleared, sorted and tagged for use in a monumental reconstruction. About 8,400 façade pieces (and 87,000 masonry stones) were recovered (a third of the original mass) and fitted together with new pieces like a giant jigsaw puzzle. What for decades seemed impossible—complete restoration of Frauenkirche—reopened in 2005. The **Dresden Military History Museum** (Olbrichtplatz 3, Tuesday-Sunday, 9 a.m.-5 p.m.) includes a number of World War II relics, including field guns and armored vehicles. On the Frauenkirche square, the Hilton Dresden (An der Frauenkirche 5, 03-581-6420, from €170) has one of the best locations in town.

Frankfurt

A plaque marks **Anne Frank's birthplace** house at 24 Ganghoferstrasse. The family also lived at 307 Marbachweg.

Kiel

Just north of Kiel, in the small town of Laboe, the **U995 Submarine Technical Museum** (located below Marine-Ehrenmal naval memorial, 04343-4-2700, open daily) has a Type VIIC U-boat commissioned in 1943. Among the most important class of U-boat, about 700 Type VIIs were constructed between 1936 and 1945. A walk through the exceedingly cramped quarters of this rare and well-preserved relic imparts a sense of the claustrophobia evoked in the 1981 Battle of the Atlantic film *Das Boot*.

Munster

On the site of the original armor school founded by Colonel Heinz Guderian (architect of Germany's early Panzer Corps victories in western Europe), the **Deutsches Panzermuseum Munster** tank museum (Hans-Krüger Strasse 33, Munster; 49-05-192-2552, various hours, closed January-February) displays 200 armored vehicles. The collection includes about 40 tanks from World War II, including a huge Tiger II, as well as German firearms and battle tunics belonging to Guderian and Erwin Rommel. There's no English signage here, but as the largest military vehicle museum in Germany, it's worth a side trip for those with an interest. Note that the museum is in small Munster (north of Hannover), not the larger, more well-known city of Münster.

Torgau/Leckwitz (American-Russian Armies Meeting Point)

On April 25, 1944, patrols from the American and Russian armies linked up for the first time over the Elbe River, about 70 miles south of Berlin. The most famous, and widely regarded as the first of these historic meetings, occurred at **Torgau**, where soldiers from the United States and USSR crawled across the girders of a demolished bridge to join hands above the river. Banquets, drinking, dancing and endless embraces marked the ensuing party with American and Soviet soldiers discovering they had more in common than did their wary governments. The Soviet Union, then in control of East Germany, erected a pair of monuments to mark the occasion. The first is a 40-foot stone tower topped with rifles and carved Soviet and American flags. Imposing, austere, somewhat sterile, it's a fascinating anachronism of Soviet propagandist design. A smaller relief carving depicts Soviet soldiers being warmly welcomed by locals—a bit of disingenuousness, as civilians had long since been evacuated from the battlefield and, at any rate, were mostly terrified at the prospect of falling under Kremlin control. The monuments and original bridge foundations in Torgau are on the river bank, just beneath **Hartenfels Castle** (Schloss Hartenfels) on Schlosstrasse, about 200 yards north of the modern bridge crossing the Elbe (carrying routes 87 and 182). Inside the castle is a museum with a small exhibit on the linkup. Torgau's municipal cemetery contains the body of American GI Joe Polowsky, a member of the linkup patrol who spent his life campaigning for friendship between the United States and Soviet Union. Torgau is a pretty city with an impressive castle and several hotels, but it's usually seen as a day trip out of Berlin or Dresden.

Alas, as with so much of history, veracity and popular mythology are often at odds. Such appears to be the case regarding the U.S.-USSR linkup. On the morning of April 25 there were in fact several U.S. patrols in the Torgau area flagrantly defying 5 km perimeter orders in the hope of finding the Soviets. According to the meticulous and highly respected British journal *After the Battle,* a U.S. patrol led by 21-year-old Lieutenant Albert Kotzebue beat the Torgau party by at least 45 minutes when, in the speck of a farming settlement called **Leckwitz**, the group encountered a lone Russian horseman at 11:30 a.m. As described by combat historian Captain William J. Fox (quoted in *After the Battle*) the meeting was hardly a love-fest: "The Russian was a cavalryman. He was extremely reticent. He was quiet, reserved, aloof, suspicious, not enthusiastic. The first meeting of the two armies certainly was not one of wild joy, but rather of cautious fencing." The Russian directed the Americans toward the Russian command (and a more joyous welcome) at Strehla, then rode off. The Soviet soldier was later identified as Aitkalia Alibekov, a recruit from Kazakhstan with distinctly Mongol features and a rugged bearing. Today, driving through the often colorless, open farmland of former East Germany, it's interesting to speculate on the thoughts of a solitary Central Asian horseman riding amid a corpse-littered German battleground toward his appointment (underpublicized as it is) with history. The precise spot of the Kotzebue-Alibekov encounter is located by following Route 182 south from Torgau to Strehla (about 20 km). On the edge of Strehla, turn right (west) on the farm road at the sign for Sahlassan, 2 km away. At Sahlassan, turn left (south) on another farm road at the sign for Leckwitz, 2 km away. Upon entering tiny Leckwitz, make the first possible left on Lindhofstrasse. About 50 yards down the road on the right are a pair of stone buildings (one bearing the number 10). The small lane separating the buildings leads to an inner courtyard where Kotzebue and Alibekov met. No sign or monument marks the historic albeit almost-forgotten event.

Wallendorf

Just across a small bridge between Luxembourg and Germany, at small Wallendorf, Germany (just north of Echternach, Luxembourg), are a number of excellent remains of **Siegfried Line** (Westwall) bunkers. At Wallendorf, crossing the small bridge from Luxembourg, one comes to a T intersection. Directly in front of the intersection is a German C-werk bunker, with accompanying interpretive signage in English and German. Access is blocked, though enterprising types might climb in through the open firing port and terraced bullet deflectors. From here, veer right and proceed a few hundred yards to left turn at the church (and sign for "Körperich 6 km"), veering right at the Haus Wallstein hotel and sign for Sportplatz. Proceed uphill a few hundred yards (passing a small German war cemetery with 326 burials) to another bunker directly in front of the point where the road splits in three directions. This B-werk bunker was built in 1938. Designed for a squad of 10 to 12, its concrete walls are almost five feet thick. According to signage, Hitler stood on top of this bunker during an inspection tour in 1938, and gazed into Luxembourg across the river. It's easy to do the same today. Access to the interior is blocked. Return downhill to Wallendorf veering left at first fork, then right (uphill) at the sign for Brunnennstrasse. Proceed on this small road 150 yards, veering left at first fork and proceeding another few hundred yards to an interpretive sign. Down a small path is the most interesting of the three bunkers, a large structure that can be entered (it's often filled with ankle-deep water). A flashlight is necessary here. There are several separated chambers inside—a diagram in front shows the layout. The bunker was shelled by Americans in September 1944.

GREECE

Greece's World War II trail is less discernible these days than those crowds at the Acropolis, commuters to Santorini and ouzo-intoxicated barhoppers in Athens. That said, some faded signs of the war's severe impact on Greece are scattered over land and sea, and best combined with this alluring country's more obvious attractions. Following Italy's inept attempts to invade Greece via Albania in late 1940, Germany swept in through Yugoslavia the following spring, taking Athens in a matter of weeks. The Wehrmacht's resistance-scarred occupation of Greece brought four years of famine, wiped-out villages and terrifying acts of barbarism to the country, only to be followed by a civil war that claimed even more lives. The **War Museum of Athens** (Vassilissis Sophias Avenue and Rizari 2, 210-72-9-0543) chronicles Greece's role in World War II (and other conflicts) through photos, weapons and letters. Scattered attractions on smaller Greek islands—for instance, a small memorial and **British cemetery** on Leros, a **Royal Navy warship wreck** off of Donoussa—aren't alone worth the trip. World War II all but wiped out Greece's Jewish population, centered in the northeastern port city of Thessaloniki (Salonika). In 1986, the city dedicated a square to the memory of 55,000 Greek Holocaust victims. A **Holocaust Memorial** has also been erected at the city's Jewish Cemetery.

Crete

Following the Greek Islands tourist trail to its largest and southernmost idyll is worthwhile for all the obvious reasons—Mediterranean beaches, gorgeous backcountry, quaint villages and layer upon layer of superb archaeological sites. Crete's World War II attractions, on the other hand, won't rank as high for most visitors. In May 1941, Crete was overtaken within about a week by a landmark invasion of German airborne troops, followed by a swift and only semi-successful evacuation of outmanned British and Commonwealth troops. Initial Luftwaffe paratroop drops took place along the north coast, just west of Heraklion, just east of Retimo and on either side of Maleme.

Harassed by small pockets of resistance, the Wehrmacht occupied the island until late in the war. Today, Crete's most popular attractions are Iraklio's outstanding Archaeological Museum (second in Greece only to the one in Athens) and the tomb of local hero and *Zorba* writer Nikos Kazantzakis. The nearby **Museum of the Battle of Crete and National Resistance** (Doukos Beaufort and I. Chatzidaki; 30-2810-221227) houses a decent collection of World War II photos, weapons, uniforms and letters. A portion of the **Historical Museum of Crete** (Lyssimachou Kalokairinou Street; 30-2810-28-8708) is devoted to the war years and Crete-born wartime Prime Minister Emmanouil Tsouderos. About 1,500 soldiers are buried at a well-maintained **British and Commonwealth Cemetery** at Souda, a few miles east of Hania along the north coast. More than 4,000 are buried at the **German Cemetery** on a hill behind the airfield at Maleme, where a number of young paratroopers died. On the island's quieter south side is **Moni Preveli**, a famous monastery that sheltered many Allied soldiers during the evacuation and was later plundered by German invaders.

ITALY

Florence

Covering 70 acres of wooded hills, the **Florence American Cemetery and Memorial** (daily, 9 a.m.-5 p.m., closed December 25, January 1) contains graves of 4,402 American soldiers, most of whom died in fighting in northern Italy. Huge marble operation maps record the progress of U.S. forces in the region. The unforgettable American Battle Monuments Commission cemetery is located on the west side of Via Cassia, about 12 km south of Florence (consult www.abmc.gov for directions).

Milan

In April 1945, Italian dictator Benito Mussolini, his mistress Claretta Petacci and fellow fascists were shot and strung upside down from the girders of a gas station in Milan's **Piazzale Loreto**, where the Germans had displayed bodies of executed partisans in 1944. An immense crowd gathered to shout insults at, spit on, kick and shoot more bullets into the bodies. The Banca Popolare was later built at the site. The Milan red line subway stops at Loreto.

Pietrasanta

In a small park in Pietrasanta (just east of A12, between Pisa and La Spezia) stands the **Sadao Munemori Monument**, a handsome bronze statue of Medal of Honor recipient Private Sadao Munemori, a member of the Japanese-American 100th Infantry Battalion. Later combined with the 442nd Regimental Combat Team, the 100th/442nd "Go for Broke" group of soldiers became the most decorated unit of its size in the history of the U.S. Army. In 1999, a large, granite monument etched with the names of more than 16,000 World War II Japanese-American veterans was unveiled in Los Angeles, California's, Little Tokyo. There are otherwise few material reminders of this storied group who fought for the United States—with particular valor in Italy—even while many of their relatives were imprisoned in stateside relocation camps.

Sicily

On July 10, 1943, the joint American, British and Canadian invasion of Sicily (Operation Husky) saw the greatest invasion fleet ever assembled to that date. An armada of 3,200 ships deployed 150,000 troops onto the beaches within three days (300,000 more would follow). The bulk of Sicily's 350,000 defenders were Italians who wanted mostly to surrender. Its 60,000 Germans fought tenaciously, particularly against British troops on the eastern side of the island. The campaign lasted 38 days—far longer than Allied planners expected—and allowed most of the German force to escape to the Italian mainland. Nevertheless, it kicked off the invasion of Italy and Allied offensive on Fortress Europe.

Gorgeous though the island is—in places it will remind some of scenery in *Catch-22*, though the Mediterranean airfield shots in that movie were filmed largely near Guaymas, Mexico—its visible wartime reminders are few. One of the better tourist towns on the island, **Taormina** (its ancient Greek theater overlooking the azure Mediterranean and Mt. Etna is stunning) was the site of Luftwaffe headquarters at present-day, four-star San Domenico Palace Hotel (0942-61-3111, www.thi.it). The hotel and neighboring church were heavily bombed, and the town was eventually taken by British forces. On display in the center of Taormina's superb public garden is a two-man Italian "Pig" submarine, a 15-foot-long torpedo guided by external divers. Trees in the park bear small plaques dedicated to World War I and II soldiers.

The British initially landed on the coast between Syracuse and Noto, and east and west of Pachino. There are several **British Commonwealth cemeteries** on the eastern side of the island. Europe's only exclusively Canadian Second World War cemetery is the **Agira Canadian War Cemetery** in the center of Sicily (71 km from Catania), where 490 Canadians are buried. Other sites related to British and Canadian operations reported but not visited during research for this guide include **pillboxes** along the coast highway (SS114) between Messina and Scalletta, pillboxes around Catania and a monument at the **Primosole Bridge** south of Catania.

On the southern coast, U.S. forces landed on beaches just east and west of Scoglitti (south of Vittoria), just east of Gela and east and west of Licata. No markers or monuments at these beaches recall the landings. **Scoglitti** landing beaches are accessed just north of the town near a small road sign for Capo Zafaglione, and a few km south of the village, along the coast road, just past the Club Med. There are several access points via agricultural or residential roads. The beach near **Gela** is dominated by a sprawling and hideous oil refinery. The most accessible and scenic American landing beach is 12 km north of **Licata** along SS115. From SS115, follow signs toward the beach for "Tor di Gaffe." The tower was the landmark for the northernmost point of invasion Beach Red. Looming above the beach is "Telegraph Hill," from whose heights Germans raked the shore with fire. The hill is now covered with upscale homes and, like the beach, betrays no immediate evidence of its violent past. The best maps of all landing beaches are found in Volume IX of Samuel Eliot Morison's *History of the United States Naval Operations in World War II* (see Bibliography).

Intact pillboxes rise ominously from fields around Sicily. An accessible site is 8 km north of Gela on SS117 (at the intersection with SS190) where three **pillboxes** (behind a fence) and the **Battle of Gela monument** in the shape of a pyramid sit along the road. Just across the highway are more pillboxes. Better is the stretch of SS115 between Gela and Vittoria, where numerous **pillboxes** can be seen from the road (traveling toward Vittoria, the direction from which they're most easily seen) at about 7.5 km and then 13 km from the huge oil refinery on the outskirts of Gela. About 14 km east of Licata on SS115, more than 15 **pillboxes** can be seen on both sides of the road. It should be noted that the entire American-landings area of Sicily is now overwhelmed by agricultural greenhouses, heavy industry and lackluster, impoverished towns with few amenities (even the best hotels are lousy) and little else to recommend them to tourists.

One of the most notorious and publicized episodes of the war was U.S. General George Patton's berating of one and slapping of another hospitalized American soldier, whom the general accused of cowardice. The event took place at a field hospital near **Nicosia**.

LUXEMBOURG

See Belgium/Luxembourg chapter, page 56.

MALTA

A linchpin in the battle for the Mediterranean during World War II (and countless other wars over the centuries), the 124-square-mile Republic of Malta (population 400,000) is better known for its prehistoric temples, medieval walled cities, beach resorts and never-ending saint's-day celebrations than its marginal supply of World War II–related offerings. Surviving one of the most ferocious aerial bombing campaigns of the war, Malta was ravaged by Italian and German air raids for nearly seven straight months, with just a single 24-hour reprieve, between January 1 and July 24, 1942. Over three years, the Axis conducted 3,340 air raids on Malta. Mass destruction, near-starvation, months of living underground and a typhoid epidemic were a few of the hardships Malta's population faced. The struggle and defense of the Maltese Islands are commemorated at the very popular **National War Museum** (at Fort St. Elmo in Valletta, 356-2122-2430), where haunting photographic panels, weaponry and an illuminated scroll presented to the "People and Defenders of Malta" by U.S. President Franklin Roosevelt (who visited in 1943) are exhibited. A highlight is "Faith," a restored British Gloster Gladiator fighter plane, a handful of which provided the island's primary defense in the early days of the air battle. Important **airfields** on this island of runways included Hal Far, Luqa, Safo, Marsa Race Course and Ta'Qali, where the small **Malta Aviation Museum** (Hut 161 Crafts Village; 356-41-6095) has a Spitfire, Vampire T11 and Fiat G91R. Several popular wreck dives off the coast include the British Destroyer **HMS *Maori*** and the hospital barge ***Carolita***.

NORTH AFRICA

Travelers itching to check off El Alamein, swim at Erwin Rommel's favorite beach or pay respects at Carthage might still want to pack a few other reasons to make these commutes—be it haggling in Marrakesh, marveling at the Egyptian pyramids, boarding a Saharan camel or sending a postcard from the coast of Tunisia. Strewn over thousands of hot, sandy miles from western Egypt to Morocco, sites from the fierce seesaw of tank and air battles in North Africa remain as challengingly situated as ever. Many, like Kasserine (near the Battle of Kasserine Pass), a dull industry town in central Tunisia once swarming with panzers, have virtually erased all memory of the war. Libya is open only to Americans traveling with pre-arranged visas. Algeria is similarly far off the map.

An easy 60-mile day-trip can be made from Alexandria (along a condo-packed coast road) or three-hour drive from Cairo to the small Egyptian town of **El Alamein**. The most famous showdown site between General Bernard Montgomery's victorious 8th Army and Rommel's Afrika Korps during the Western Desert campaign is otherwise not a very thrilling place for most travelers. The **Medinat el-Alamein War Museum** contains photos, uniforms, maps, tanks and artillery, plus a brief Italian-produced documentary. Among the exhibits are a wartime Chevrolet truck discovered in a sand dune in the 1990s—it worked perfectly upon recovery. More than 7,000 tombstones of British, Australian, New Zealand, French, Greek, South African, East and West African, Malaysian and East Indian soldiers line the **Commonwealth War Cemetery** on the east end of town. Four miles west of El Alamein are German and Italian **war memorials**. Farther west along the coast in Marsa Matruh, various "Desert Fox" memorabilia is housed at the **Rommel Museum**, right next door to **Rommel Beach** where the German Field Marshal reportedly enjoyed daily swims. Visiting the **El Alamein battlefield** is difficult without an arranged group. Still, as reported by British author Richard Holmes in *Battlefields of the Second World War*, the desert contains "abundant signs of defensive positions, like occasional bulldozed scrapes for tanks, some concrete emplacements ... and sanguars (circular infantry breastworks)." The battlefield remains littered with German and British mines, which still explode and kill unsuspecting wanderers. The best place for relics is near the southern edge of the battlefield at the dramatic Qattara Depression. Again Holmes: "All around lies the jetsam of war," including rusty ammunition boxes, jerry cans, live ammunition, shell fragments, barbed wire, empty bottles, and so on.

More tanks, cannons, planes and WWII cemeteries as well as Rommel's underground headquarters are on display across the border in **Tobruk, Libya**. On 27 acres, the **North Africa American Cemetery and Memorial** (daily, 9 a.m.-5 p.m., closed December 25, January 1) in **Carthage, Tunisia**, contains graves of U.S. soldiers and a remembrance wall listing nearly 3,724 more names. Author Rick Atkinson opened his celebrated 2002 book *An Army at Dawn* with a description of the cemetery: "There are no obelisks, no tombs, no ostentatious monuments, just 2,841 bone-white marble markers, two feet high and arrayed in ranks as straight as gun shots." In **Casablanca, Morocco,** President Franklin Roosevelt and British Prime Minister Winston Churchill met in January 1943 at the **Anfa Hotel** (aka Hotel d'Anfa) in the affluent suburb of Anfa. With sweeping views of the Atlantic, the hotel stood as a derelict shell for years after the war before being enlarged and converted to a condominium complex. Roosevelt actually watched the newly released *Casablanca* starring Humphrey Bogart before departing for the summit. His trip and the November 1942 launch of Operation Torch—which landed American troops on the coast north and south of Casablanca—just north of Mehdia, just north of Fedala and just south of Safi—gave the film an unexpected publicity boost. Though it was filmed entirely in Hollywood, fans of the movie can visit touristy **Rick's Bar** in the Hyatt Regency Casablanca (in city center on Place des Nations Unies, 212-2243-1234), where waiters dress in trench coats and fedoras. Maps of American and Allied landings and campaigns in Africa (including the capture of Casablanca, November 8-11, 1942) can be found in Atkinson's *An Army at Dawn*, an essential history for anyone (particularly Americans) traveling in North Africa.

POLAND

See map on page 41.

Treblinka Concentration Camp

The second-largest Nazi concentration camp (after Auschwitz-Birkenau), Treblinka stands off Route 677 (just west of main Route 63), about 100 km northeast of Warsaw, 8 km south of Malkinia. About 800,000 died at the camp—actually two camps, Treblinka I and Treblinka II, separated by 2 km. Foundations of prisoner barracks can be found at Treblinka I, but little else remains of the camps. The **Museum of Struggle and Martyrdom** is more of a memorial at the site of each camp. The most moving display is a "cemetery" of 17,000 granite stones in an enormous field at Treblinka II. Because public transportation to this remote area is a long and complicated hassle, few tourists make it to the site—the quietude makes a visit here an all the more disarming and sobering experience.

Walbrzych/Project RIESE

Near Walbrzych, southwest of Wróclaw
T: (0)74-842-2200 (Walbrzych Tourist Information office)

For World War II travelers, the most exciting "new" war site is undoubtedly the massive underground complex known as Project RIESE (Giant). In 1943-45, more than 200,000 cubic meters of concrete tunnels were cut into a 75-square-mile area of the Sowie Mountains in the southwestern corner of the country around the polluted mining town of Walbrzych. Certainly the enormity renders all other known Nazi construction puny by comparison. Adding to the intrigue, no one seems to know exactly what the Nazis were up to with RIESE. The extravagant complex was designed as a gargantuan underground armaments factory, but it was also likely slated as a military headquarters, perhaps the future center of all German military activity. Speculation also raises the possibility that the complex was being designed and used as the new center of Germany's atomic weapons and energy program. The region is rich in uranium and still-existing RIESE construction can be interpreted as a primitive reactor with cooling tanks.

Opened only since the mid-1990s, the RIESE facilities are rarely visited, little publicized and only now being studied and appreciated. Only 97,000 cubic meters of the tunnels have been found. Many are blocked. What's hidden inside is anybody's guess. For visitors, two tunnels are accessible—the size of these is generally described as "mind-blowing." Opened in 1995, the **Ostra tunnel system**, known locally as "Kompleks Rzeczka," is located in Walim at Muzeum Sztolni Walimskich (ul. 3-go Maja 26, Walim; 48-74-845-7300; daily, 9 a.m.-6 p.m. in summer, 9 a.m.-5 p.m. in winter). Compulsory guided tours are available in Polish and German. Opened in 1996, the **Osowka tunnel system**, known locally as "Kompleks Osowka," is about 3 km southeast of Gluszyca. Information can be obtained from Podziemne Miasto Gluszyca-Kompleks Osowka (ul. Dolna 2, Gluszyca, 48-74-845-6332; daily, 10 a.m.-6 p.m. in summer, 10 a.m.-4 p.m. in winter). Compulsory guided tours are available in Polish and German. Above ground, remnants of affiliated barracks, bunkers and other structures are scattered about the countryside. The tunnel that was to have served as Hitler's residence is located directly beneath the courtyard at **Ksiaz Castle** in Walbrzych (ul. Piastow Slaskich 1, 48-74-843-2840). Built by at least 28,000 slave laborers, the RIESE complex was connected to nearby **Gross-Rosen concentration camp** (near the town of Rogoznica, off Highway 374 between Legnica and Swidnica), which has a preserved main gate, several buildings, crematorium and museum. Oregon-based Alpventures (888-991-6718, www.alpventures.com) operates excellent tours to the RIESE and Gross-Rosen area.

Warsaw/Jewish Ghetto

With 80 to 90 percent of its structures destroyed and at least 700,000 (more than half the city's population) killed during five nightmare years of Nazi occupation from September 1940 to January 1945, no city suffered as much as Warsaw during the Second World War. Completely rebuilt, it's now a modern city (population 1.7 million). Restoration of the 17th- and 18th-century appearance of the Old Town (Stare Miasto), center of tourist activity, was so remarkable that the area has been deemed a UNESCO World Heritage site. The former **Jewish Ghetto**—mercilessly razed by Nazis in the Ghetto and Warsaw Uprisings—stood northwest of the city center in today's Mirów and Muranów areas. It's now a commercial and residential district, pretty much like any other part of the city. Points of interest include Warsaw's only surviving synagogue, **Nozyk Synagogue** (ul. Twarda 6, Sunday-Friday, 9 a.m.-5 p.m.). Marked by 16 engraved black stones, the 20-minute **Memorial Route to the Struggle and Martyrdom of the Jews 1940-43** is worthwhile. Markers and stone monuments include the Memorial to the Warsaw Ghetto Uprising (on the spot where the armed confrontation began) and the Umschlagplatz Wall Monument, on the spot where 300,000 Jews were deported to the Treblinka death camp. Farther southwest, the **Jewish Historical Institute** (ul. Tlomackie 3/5, 827-9221, open Monday, Wednesday, Friday) has a permanent exhibit on the Ghetto. Monuments and a small museum at **Pawiak Prison** (ul. Dzielna 24/26) recount its infamous use as a Nazi prison and torture center. The **Polish Army Museum** (Al Jerozolimslie 3, 629-5271,

Wednesday-Sunday, 10 a.m.-4 p.m.) has an impressive collection of World War II weaponry, including tanks and heavy armor.

In Old Town, the 60-room **Historical Museum of Warsaw** (Rynek Starego Miasta 42, 635-1625, closed Monday) shows a dramatic documentary recalling the immense suffering of the city. A few blocks southwest at the **Polish Army Field Cathedral** (ul. Dluga 13/15), carvings and plaques commemorate Polish soldiers who died during the war. Across the street is the **Monument to the Warsaw Uprising**.

Wolf's Lair (Wolfsschanze or Wilczy Szaniec)

Near tiny Gierloz, 8 km east of Ketrzyn, a few km off Route 592
T: 752-4429
Daily, 8 a.m.-dusk
About $2
Freelance guides, about $20 per 90-minute tour

Astonishingly well-concealed in the forests of the Great Masurian Lake District of north-eastern Poland (the former East Prussia), the 1.2-square-mile complex of 80 concrete bunkers known as the Wolf's Lair—even the name reeked with the puerile military fantasies of the Nazi crowd—was Adolf Hitler's command headquarters and primary resi-dence for nearly half the war. From June 26, 1941, to November 20, 1944, Hitler left this command post for only brief periods. With concrete walls as thick as 25 feet, an airstrip, a network of tunnels, a surrounding field of barbed wire and more than 50,000 mines, the nearly impregnable Wolf's Lair was the site of the July 20, 1944, Colonel Claus von Stauffenberg bomb-assassination attempt that nearly killed Hitler. With the advance of the Red Army, the complex was blown up by retreating German troops. Today, visitors can walk a marked loop trail—a fast walk takes 30 minutes, but most visitors will want a minimum of two hours—amid the enormous, double-reinforced concrete ruins, all of them above ground, many in good, recognizable condition. The entrance is marked by a parking lot (small fee) with several shops and inexpensive English-speaking freelance guides at the ready. Area maps and English pamphlets are available, but a map at the entrance shows locations of most points of interest. Hitler's "Führer Bunker" has concrete walls standing up to 60 feet high and much of the roof caved in. Blown off the rooftop by German demolition, its largely intact concrete A/A bunker rests on its side in the reservoir about 40 feet away. Other sites include the loca-tion of the von Stauffenberg debacle and private bunkers belonging to Luftwaffe Reichsmarschall Hermann Göring (the roof is unofficially accessible via ring ladder) and Secretary to the Führer Martin Bormann and General Alfred Jodl's headquarters building. Though smaller than other structures, the latter is one of the more intact ruins, with walls and a roof rising from the forest in dramatic fashion. As it was during the war, the summer mosquito problem can be terrible. Repellent is advised. In nearby **Mauerwald** are headquar-ters of Foreign Minister Joachim von Ribbentrop and Reichsführer-SS Heinrich Himmler's bunker at Boyen Fortress. In addition to its historic importance, this remote site is worth the drive if only for the breathtaking, unspoiled scenery of the lake region. Oregon-based Alpventures (888-991-6718, www.alpventures.com or www.wolfslairtours.com) operates tours to the site. Alpventures also operates excellent "Ruins of the Third Reich" tours throughout Germany and its wartime frontiers, as well as other war-related sites.

PRAGUE (CZECH REPUBLIC)

Though less significant in terms of war strategy, Prague (population 1.2 million) competes with any city in this book for sheer tourist appeal. A contender for title of world's most-beautiful city, Prague—with Czechoslovakia—fell under Nazi control in March 1939. The

Red Army liberated the city in May 1945. Prague today is dynamic, one of Europe's top tourist destinations. Though it's a fantastic city, the surfeit of Gaps, KFCs and high-priced Western shops inhabiting so many of the noble Hapsburg Empire–era manses is somewhat depressing—so much so that a kind of Communist-era nostalgia has settled in with a certain crowd. Nowhere is this more evident than at the small **Museum of Communism** (Na Prikope 10, Prague 1, 24-212-966, daily, 9 a.m.-7 p.m., closed holidays), pointedly located upstairs from a McDonalds. There's a small section on Hitler's annexation of the country (called the protectorate of Bohemia and Moravia by the Nazis), but mostly this is an engrossing and critical look at Cold War-era Soviet iniquities. Of the 92,000 Jews in Czechoslovakia at the start of the war, about 80,000 were deported to concentration camps. Fewer than 10,000 of these would return. A stark monument to this tragedy—one of the most moving in Europe—is within Pinkas Synagogue, part of **The Jewish Museum Prague** complex (Panska 7, Prague 1, 224-819-456, daily except Saturday and Jewish holidays, 9 a.m.-6 p.m., summer, 9 a.m.-4:30 p.m., winter). On its pristine white walls are inscribed, all by hand, the names of 80,000 victims of Nazi oppression. The synagogue and museum is located in the heart of the old Jewish Ghetto. Almost as moving is the small museum and crypt at the **Cathedral of Saints Cyril and Methodius** (corner of Reslova and Na Zderaze streets, Prague 1, Tuesday-Sunday, 10 a.m.-4 p.m., closed holidays). In December 1941, seven Czech paratroopers, trained in England, dropped into their native land to carry out the assassination of SS Obergrüppenführer Reinhard Heydrich, the Nazi ruler of Prague and Czechoslovakia and among the most ruthless figures of the Third Reich. The assassination was successful, but the subsequent search for the killers led to the basement crypt of this church where most of the paratroopers were killed by Nazis (or committed suicide). Bullet holes and battle scars inside remain plainly evident. In this cold stone crypt, one can readily imagine the terror of a Nazi manhunt at its chilling climax. A small museum upstairs recounts (in English) the mission to kill Heydrich. On the church wall facing Reslova Street is a relief carving of a paratrooper and clergy above original bullet holes. Heydrich, incidentally, had earlier ignored local legend that said anyone other than the king wearing the Czech crown jewels would be stricken dead. Locked away at **Hradcany Castle** (Prague 1, 224-37-3368, castle entry 9 a.m.-4 p.m.), the jewels were brought out for Heydrich's indulgence. Weeks later, the Czech commandos fulfilled the legend's curse. Heydrich's sons, who also donned the jewels, were subsequently killed, one in an accident, the other in battle. The former **Gestapo Headquarters** building (it houses the current Czech Trade Office) is at Politickych venzno 20, Prague 1. Interrogations and tortures were routine inside this grim building. Outside, a statue commemorates 120 students executed in 1939 for "anti-Nazi plotting." The small **Army Shop and Antik** (Kremencova 7, Prague 1, 224-930-952, 11:30 a.m.-5 p.m.) deals in small regalia and relics (pistols, grenades, medals, and so forth) from World War II Germany and post-war Soviet and U.S. militaries. Prices range from $10 to $500.

About 10 km west of Prague, the village of **Lidice** was razed by Nazis (its name even removed from maps) in June 1942 as part of Hitler-ordered reprisals for the killing of Heydrich. All 173 men over age 16 were executed. Women and children were deported to concentration camps. Lidice was rebuilt after the war with a memorial and museum. About 70 km northwest of Prague, the entire town of Terezin was transformed into a camp and way station for those being transported to Auschwitz, Treblinka and other camps—the so-called "waiting room to hell." The **Terezin Memorial** (420-416-78-2225) stands where approximately 30,000 prisoners were liberated by Soviet troops on May 12, 1945. The town and fortress is a national memorial. English guides are available. There's much to see—including a fortress and museum—tours can last up to four hours.

RUSSIA

St. Petersburg (Leningrad)

Built along the Baltic Sea and Neva River, St. Petersburg (Leningrad during the war) is Russia's most charming city. It was also the site of one of the most vicious sieges in the annals of human history. From September 8, 1941, to January 27, 1944, German troops surrounded and blockaded the city, a "900-day" (almost) ordeal that produced episodes of unimaginable cruelty and pain. People devoured pets, rats and insects, then bread enriched with sawdust before resorting to cannibalism, often of their own relatives. About 800,000 civilians died, mostly from cold and starvation. Amid unimaginable conditions— the Germans lobbed more than 150,000 bombs at the city—and the constant aura of death, the city held out. A few buildings still bear the scars of the ordeal. The **Museum of the Defense of Leningrad** or Blockade Museum (Solyanoy per 9, 275-7208, Thursday-Tuesday, 10 a.m.-4 p.m.) has photos, military displays and personal items from survivors. The enormous **Artillery Museum** (Alexandrovsky Park 7, 232-0296) has an impressive World War II exposition that includes a Katyusha mobile rocket launcher. The large **Central Naval Museum** (Birzhevaya Square 4, 328-2501) deals with centuries of Russian maritime history. The World War II exposition is devoted in large part to the role of the Soviet Baltic Fleet in the defense and supply of Leningrad during the siege. The monument to the **Heroic Defenders of Leningrad** at Moskovsky Praspekt (10 a.m.-6 p.m., closed Wednesday) is an enormous 164-foot obelisk surrounded by bronze figures representing aspects of the siege. This is a breathtaking monument. Breathtaking and depressing is **Piskaryovskoe Cemetery** (off Praspekt Nepokoryonnykh, about 20 minutes from the city center, 247-5716, daily, 10 a.m.-6 p.m.) where more than half a million victims are buried in 186 mass graves. Earthen mounds with red stars (military) or hammer and sickle (civilian), serve as poignant grave markers. About 90 minutes east of the city, scenic Lake Ladoga became Leningrad's frozen "Road of Life" in winter, its only line of supply (consistently attacked by the Germans) for trucks bringing in meager supplies and evacuating the wounded. The multiple-hall **Road of Life Museum** recounts the episode.

SICILY

See Italy.

UNITED STATES

The National World War II Museum

945 Magazine St. (Entrance on Andrew Higgins Drive)
New Orleans, Louisiana
T: 504-527-6012
Daily, 9 a.m.-5 p.m.
Closed Thanksgiving, Christmas Eve, Christmas Day, Mardi Gras, and all Mondays

This museum—founded by historian Stephen Ambrose and opened in 2000—is a large and stunning facility that commemorates action across both Atlantic and Pacific theaters. The 16,000-square-foot gallery is divided into four state-of-the-art exhibits that mix oral histories from veterans worldwide, relics, documents, photos and archival film. Visitors wind through displays chronicling the weeks and days leading up to the D-Days of World War II, climaxing with the Allied landings on the beaches of Normandy. A number of excellent U.S. museums deal with the war—this is the best. Allow 2-3 hours.

BIBLIOGRAPHY

In addition to works cited in each chapter, the following books were consulted frequently during the preparation of this text.

Arnold-Forster, Mark. *The World at War.* London: Thames Mandarin, 1973.

Astor, Gerald. *The Greatest War: Americans in Combat 1941-1945.* Novato, Calif.: Presidio, 1999.

Badsey, Stephen, ed. *Atlas of World War II Battle Plans: Before and After.* Sandhurst, England: Helicon Publishing, 2000.

Brinkley, Douglas, ed. *World War II: The Documents, Speeches, Diaries and Newspaper Reporting That Defined World War II. Vols. 1-2.* New York: The New York Times Company and Agincourt Press, 2003.

Calvocoressi, Peter and Guy Wint. *Total War: Causes and Courses of the Second World War.* London: Allen Lane the Penguin Press, 1972.

Churchill, Sir Winston. *The Second World War. Vols. 1-6.* London: Cassell, 1948-54.

Cressman, Robert J. *Official Chronology of the U.S. Navy in World War II.* Annapolis: Naval Institute Press, 2000.

Davidson, Edward and Dale Manning. *Chronology of World War Two.* London: Cassell, 1999.

Dear, I.C.B. and M.R.D. Foot, eds. *The Oxford Companion to World War II.* Oxford: Oxford University Press, 1995.

Denfeld, Duane. *World War II Museums and Relics of Europe.* Manhattan, Kan.: MA/AH Publishing-Sunflower University Press, 1980.

Eisenhower, Dwight D. *Crusade in Europe.* Garden City, N.Y.: Doubleday, 1948.

Evans, Martin Marix. *Vital Guide Battles of World War II.* Shrewsbury, England: Airlife, 2002.

Glantz, David and Jonathan House. *When Titans Clashed: How the Red Army Stopped Hitler.* Lawrence, Kan.: University Press of Kansas, 1995.

Holmes, Richard. *Battlefields of the Second World War.* London: BBC Worldwide Limited, 2001.

Keegan, John. *The Second World War.* New York: Viking, 1989.

Keegan, John, ed. *Who's Who in World War II.* London: Weidenfeld & Nicolson, 1978.

Leckie, Robert. *Delivered From Evil: The Saga of World War II.* New York: Harper & Row, 1987.

Liddell Hart, B.H. *History of the Second World War.* London: Cassell, 1970.

Morison, Samuel Eliot. *History of United States Naval Operations in World War II.* Vols. 1-15. Boston: Little, Brown, 1947-62.

O'Neill, William L. *The Oxford Essential Guide to World War II.* New York: Oxford University Press, 2002.

Parker, Robert Alexander Clarke. *Struggle for Survival: The History of the Second World War.* New York: Oxford University Press, 1989.

Shirer, William L. *The Rise and Fall of the Third Reich: A History of Nazi Germany.* New York: Simon & Schuster, 1960.

Snyder, Louis L. *The War: A Concise History 1939-1945.* New York: Julian Messner, 1960.

Speer, Albert. *Inside the Third Reich: Memoirs.* New York: Macmillan, 1970.

Sulzberger, C.L. *World War II.* New York: American Heritage, 1966.

Terrance, Marc. *Concentration Camps: A Traveler's Guide to World War II Sites.* Self-published, 2000.

Wheal, Elizabeth-Anne and Stephen Pope. *The Macmillan Dictionary of the Second World War.* London: Macmillan, 1997.

Wright, Gordon. *The Ordeal of Total War, 1939-1945.* New York: Harper & Row, 1968.

Young, Peter, ed. *The Cassell Atlas of the Second World War.* London: Cassell, 1973.

INDEX

Q

Quisling, Vidkun 181, 182, 184

R

Raubal, Geli 151
Reagan, Ronald 213
Remagen 95, 194
Remagen/Eifel Region 208-215
Rjukan, Norway 182, 185, 189
Rome 111, 112, 117, 200-207, 217-219, 221-223
Rommel, Erwin 11, 16, 23, 91, 144, 241, 246, 247
Roosevelt, Franklin 22, 31, 32, 91, 92, 94-97, 144, 184, 226, 246, 247
Russia 34, 52, 79, 80, 85, 91, 128-137, 172-179, 224-231, 251
  St. Petersburg (Leningrad) 251

S

Schindler, Oskar 44, 45
Seelow Heights 87
Sevareid, Eric 105
Shirer, William 148, 155, 156
Sicily 95, 98, 111, 112, 201, 218, 221-223, 244, 245, 251
Siegfried Line 62, 209, 210, 213, 214, 243
Speer, Albert 79, 155, 156
Stalin, Josef 79, 85, 129-134, 137, 144, 173, 176, 226
Stalingrad: See Volgograd
Stonehenge 108
Submarine Pens 144, 238, 239

T

Tehran 130, 144, 226
Tiger Tank 59, 63, 107, 135, 141, 143, 144, 226, 230, 238, 241

U

United States museum 251

V

Versailles 124, 127, 147, 155
Volgograd (Stalingrad) 52, 137, 172-179
Von Rundstedt, Karl Gerd 57, 63, 210
Von Stauffenberg, Claus 84, 249
Vonnegut, Kurt 241

W

Wannsee 80, 82, 87, 88
Washington, D.C. 90-99
Waters, Roger 221
World War II movies
  A Bridge Too Far 191, 192, 196
  Band of Brothers 5, 7, 8, 47, 48, 52, 58, 195, 240
  Battle of San Pietro 116
  Casablanca 247
  Catch-22 245
  Das Boot 241
  Enemy at the Gates 178
  Life is Beautiful 223
  Saving Private Ryan 5, 10
  Schindler's List 44, 45
  Slaughterhouse Five 241
  Sophie Scholl: The Final Days 152
  The Bridge at Remagen 210, 212
  The English Patient 223
  The Heroes of Telemark 185
  The Longest Day 2, 4, 5, 23
  The Sound of Music 233
  The Winds of War 37
  Triumph of the Will 155
  Windtalkers 98

Y

Yalta 79, 130

Z

Zaitsev, Vasili 177, 178
Zhukov, Georgi 80, 129, 130, 132, 225, 226, 229

Chuck Thompson is the author of *The 25 Best World War II Sites: Pacific Theater* and the travel memoir *Smile When You're Lying*. He is the former editor in chief of *Travelocity* magazine and features editor of *Maxim* magazine, and his writing and photography have appeared in *The Atlantic Monthly, Esquire, National Geographic Adventure, Playboy, Reader's Digest, The Los Angeles Times,* and many other publications and on television, including MTV. Originally from Juneau, Alaska, Chuck has traveled extensively throughout Europe and the Pacific.